LATIN AMERICA

THE POLITICS

OF IMMOBILITY

ROBERT F. ADIE

The University of Winnipeg

GUY E. POITRAS

Trinity University, San Antonio

Prentice-Hall, Inc., Englewood Cliffs, New Jersey

Library of Congress Cataloging in Publication Data

ADIE, ROBERT, F.
   Latin America: the politics of immobility.

   Includes bibliographies.
   1. Pressure groups—Latin America. 2. Latin
America—Politics—1948–   I. Poitras, Guy E.,
joint author.   II. Title.
JL964.P7A35   320.9′8′003   73-7729
ISBN 0-13-524272-X

© 1974 by Prentice-Hall, Inc., Englewood Cliffs, New Jersey

Printed in the United States of Amercia

10   9   8   7   6   5   4   3   2   1

PRENTICE-HALL INTERNATIONAL, INC., *London*
PRENTICE-HALL OF AUSTRALIA, PTY. LTD., *Sydney*
PRENTICE-HALL OF CANADA, LTD., *Toronto*
PRENTICE-HALL OF INDIA PRIVATE LTD., *New Delhi*
PRENTICE-HALL OF JAPAN, INC., *Tokyo*

*To Archibald, Linda, Adam,
Jack, Lynn, Dede, and Jan*

CONTENTS

PREFACE

At first glance, Latin American politics appears to be such a broad and complex subject that the beginning student becomes understandably perplexed at the prospect of attempting to learn something general as well as specific about the topic. Can one learn something about Latin America as a unit without obtaining only a superficial acquaintance with the area? Can one learn something about the individual countries of Latin America and still have a unified perspective of the entire region? These questions plague the beginning students of Latin American politics as well as those who assume the task of writing text-books for these students.

One alternative for studying Latin American politics at the introductory level is the country-by-country approach, from which one learns something specific about each country of the area. For example, the student might learn that Mexico has undergone a revolutionary process which few other Latin American countries have experienced. However, if the student relies solely on this approach, he is in danger of losing sight of profound political and social forces which affect not only Mexican politics but those of other Latin American countries as well.

Another alternative is to treat Latin America as an entity. The advantage of this approach is that it attempts to make generalizations about politics in Latin America as a whole. However, it sacrifices specifics for this high level of generality. One learns a little about all the features of Latin America—race, geography, economics, culture, resources, constitution, courts, legislatures, executives, the Church, the military, political parties, and so forth. In short, this approach offers only a very superficial acquaintance with the topic.

An alternative to these two approaches is the single book concerned with one particular country or with one particular topic. The advantage of this approach for an introductory student is that he achieves greater in-depth understanding of a country or of a topic. However, such books are not textbooks in the sense that few courses at the introductory level are specific enough to allow their use. Beginning students should be encouraged to pursue a more in-depth understanding of Latin American politics, but they also need an appreciation of basic perspectives on the topic.

Another alternative, and one which we have adopted here, is to generalize about a small number of basic topics in Latin American politics from a certain perspective—that Latin American politics will not change very rapidly because political groups, individually and together, block effective government. This approach has some convincing advantages: it enables the student to evaluate a few topics in some detail; it uses a common theme which spans the entire area rather than concentrating upon one country or dissipating effort on too many topics; and it is easily adapted to other readings as a supplement to other approaches. We hope that this approach to Latin American politics will spare the reader extreme generality as well as extreme triviality.

The authors wish to acknowledge the people who helped us in various ways in writing this book. Professor David E. Schmitt of Northeastern University generously made suggestions on an earlier version of the first chapter. Linda Adie provided pithy critiques of our efforts to write a readable book for undergraduates. Not to be forgotten is the staff of the Latin American Collection of the University of Texas at Austin whose patient cooperation greatly helped us do the research for this broad and complex topic. Despite the help and encouragement of these individuals and institutions, any lapse in perspective or in factual information is our and not their responsibility.

CHAPTER 1

AN INTRODUCTION TO LATIN AMERICAN POLITICS

Latin America reflects an extremely wide variety of images and poses a number of difficult questions for the person attempting to understand its politics. It can be viewed as a perplexing area of the world in which the old and the new are juxtaposed. It seems also to embody a way of life that is both tranquil and turbulent. Some are attracted to its economic potential and its extremely diverse natural resources. Others view the area as a cultural and historical unit which, as a product of Hispanic influence and colonization, is distinct from any other area of the world. Still others, foreigners in general and North Americans in particular, tend to view Latin America as some sort of "problem" to be solved. They ask, for example, "Why do Latin Americans nationalize foreign investments when these investments aid their countries?" Or, "Why do Latin Americans seem to resent everything North Americans are and everything they do?"

Perhaps the concern most common among persons turning their attention for the first time to Latin America is not its politics but rather its physical attributes, which by any standard are impressive. The land mass, which spans the lower northern and the southern hemispheres from the northwestern tip of Mexico to the Tierra del Fuego in the far south, includes nearly every geographical and climatic condition to be found in the world. National variety is also a physical attribute of the region. For example, Brazil, with a land mass of 3,286,473 square miles, is the world's fourth largest country. On the other hand, nine of the Latin American countries in the Central American and the Caribbean areas are considerably smaller

1

than many of Brazil's states. In short, whether one examines the area as a whole or by individual countries, diversity is an important feature of Latin American geography.

The people who inhabit this region of the world are racially and culturally quite mixed. Miscegenation between indigenous populations and people of Spanish and Portuguese descent has blurred racial lines far more thoroughly than in North America. The largest racial category in Latin America, except for such countries as Argentina, Chile and Costa Rica, is "mixed-blood." *Mestizos* of Spanish and Indian parentage, *mulatos* of Spanish (or Portuguese) and Negro parentage, and *zambos* of Negro and Indian parentage testify to the fact that most Latin Americans are neither Indian nor Negro nor "Latin." Culturally, Latin Americans today are the product of Hispanic and Indian traditions, the blending of which has resulted in a number of subtly different cultures that cannot meaningfully be described as either Hispanic or Indian. Brazil and the Caribbean area also have cultural affinities to Black Africa. Chile is more closely tied to Western Europe, and Argentina and Peru are tied to Eastern and Western Europe.

An understanding of Latin American politics cannot be completely divorced from the area's economic status. Although there are some important differences between a country such as Brazil which is industrializing and a country such as Haiti which has a traditional, one-crop economy, Latin American countries in general have economies which are less "developed" than the West's more industrialized, more productive, and more technological economies. Latin American economies are still largely agricultural and to varying degrees are just beginning the arduous process of development (which will be discussed in more detail later). In their present state, the economies of Latin America are "peripheral" to the international economy and the world markets which are dominated by the more developed countries. That is, these economies basically supply raw materials and goods to more developed ones, whether it be in the form of fruit from Central America, petroleum from Venezuela, or coffee from Colombia. However, Latin Americans, as evidenced by recent manifestations of economic nationalism, have become more intolerant of foreign dominance of their economies. Today, the economic dilemma for Latin Americans is how to pursue a relatively independent course of national development without driving out capital or becoming even more subordinate to foreign (American) economic interests. In sum, the economic problems of Latin America are immense, but the Latin Americans themselves have only partial control over achieving a solution.

Politically, Latin America often appears enigmatical. Why do many refer to political changes in Latin America when actually very little important political change apparently occurs? Why are many governments so unstable? Why is violence, of one form or another, so prevalent in Latin

American politics? What are the peculiarities of "revolution" in Latin America? Will other Latin American countries adopt the Cuban model in an attempt to overcome their problems of underdevelopment?

In the last decade or so, Latin American politics has received a growing amount of scholarly and popular attention in the attempt to answer these questions and many others of a similar nature. Before 1959, North Americans, as well as other foreigners, generally maintained a bemused, if not befuddled, perspective on Latin American politics (or what the mass media related to them about those politics). The most that many North Americans knew about Latin American political events was that the standard way to remove an administration was to encircle the national palace with army tanks—to many Americans the volatility of Latin American politics was only matched by its comic-opera overtones. However, after 1959 and the advent to power of Fidel Castro in Cuba, Latin American politics, rightly or wrongly, assumed a grimmer hue to most North Americans. The intrusion of a Communist government into the Western hemisphere was perceived by many to be a serious breach with the past and a dangerous precedent for the future. Latin American governments, it was thought, would be extremely susceptible to the tactics of well-organized guerrilla units encouraged by the Communist Bloc through Cuba. A wave of social and probably Communist-inspired revolutions was gloomily predicted for the entire region. Shortly, the Alliance for Progress was conceived as a means of preventing this catastrophe.

Such premature judgments ignored some fundamental considerations about continuity and change in Latin American politics. Certain features of the various Latin American political systems have proved to be quite effective in resisting not only Communist-inspired change, but change promoted by the Alliance for Progress. More specifically, these judgments tended to ignore the basic factors involved in "development."

THE CONCEPT OF DEVELOPMENT

We have used the word "development" several times in this introductory discussion, and it seems appropriate at this point to devote some effort to examining what the term means and how it relates to Latin America. The following discussion is intended to provide an initial familiarity with the concept rather than an exhaustive examination of its multiple and subtle complexities.

If one thinks about the concept of "development" for a brief time, it becomes apparent that the term implies a progression from one level to another. If man, for example, is a highly "developed" form of mammal, it seems logical to expect that there are other mammals in the animal kingdom that are less "developed" or that have not reached the same level of evolutionary progress. The term therefore implies a ranking of certain phenomena according to specified criteria.

"Development" implies more than merely different levels or stages. It also implies growth or mobility from one level to a higher level. For example, the evolution of man testifies to the growth of certain faculties which enable *homo sapiens* to accomplish many more things than can be achieved by other members of the primate order. That is, today's man is not the same creature he was many centuries ago. Therefore, development is important for the study of man's activities because it suggests change; not just change of any sort, but change in which man's activities evolve to a higher, more complex, level. "Development" in this sense may not always be a "good" thing. Is the quality of life of many beleaguered New Yorkers "better" than that of those who live in less complex settings in Latin America?

"Development" is also a continuous phenomenon. That is, an economic system, for example, is neither "developed" nor "undeveloped," but rather is at some intermediate point between these two ideal types or poles of the continuum. Ultimately, therefore, the making of distinctions between various levels or stages of development is an arbitrary exercise. For example, when does a "developing" economic system become a "developed" one? When it has $1,001.00 per capita annual income instead of only $1,000.00? Even if one has specific standards of "development" in mind, the answer to such questions must be based eventually upon an arbitrary judgment.

The concept of "development" in social science theory has been applied in different forms to many areas of human activity. The three principal areas of activity with which we are here concerned are economic, social, and political development. We want to examine what development means in an economic, social, and political sense so that some understanding of Latin America may be gained.

ECONOMIC DEVELOPMENT

Discussion of economic development can begin by noting that large economic discrepancies clearly exist between and even within countries. The most obvious difference lies between the United States, Western Europe, Japan, and the Soviet Union on the one hand, and the rest of the world on the other. Paraguay, for instance, cannot match the United States in the production and consumption of such goods as televisions, automobiles, packaged food, "fashionable" clothes, or such services as communications, transportation, schools, and so forth. There are other less visible differences as well. Economically developed countries such as the Soviet Union and Japan have a tremendous capacity to invest savings in economic activities and to apply modern technology to highly complex problems. In comparison, such Latin American countries as Haiti, Bolivia, or even Brazil fall far behind. In less developed countries—Latin American, African, and Asian—the public and the private sectors of the economy are unable to save enough investment capital to propel their economies toward an advanced stage of high consumption and production or to establish large industrial bases of development. The discrepancies between the very highly developed countries and the not very highly developed countries are of major importance in international, as well as domestic, political and economic relations, and they continue to grow.

Most leaders of Latin America recognize the necessity of economic development for the progress of their countries. However, the problem of development is further complicated by the fact that the experience of the West (the United States and Europe) cannot be replicated exactly in other parts of the world. Indeed, some countries such as Haiti, Nicaragua, Honduras, and others in Latin America have little hope of ever pursuing economic development in the sense in which the West has. The problem, basically, is that the so-called "developing" world faces different conditions and circumstances than did the West when it was undergoing economic development decades ago. For one thing, the "developing" areas of the contemporary world have in many ways a much more difficult task to accomplish within a much shorter period of time. The West, and especially Great Britain and the United States, used capitalism to achieve its development gradually, over a period of one hundred years or more, but this may be inappropriate for other countries. Moreover, the magnitude of the problems facing the first developing countries seemed to be less than those of the countries undergoing the traumatic process today. There were at that time no super-powers, no population problems, and no technological innovations which upset normal patterns of behavior, as is the case in the mid-twentieth century. There is general agreement among most leaders of the contemporary "developing" world that their problems are more urgent and less amenable to solution and portend more disastrous consequences than did the problems of those countries that first underwent the Industrial Revolution.

To differentiate between these two paths of development, Richard Adams has made a distinction between what he terms "primary development" and "secondary development."[1] According to Adams, primary development involves technological inventions and discoveries and produces social and economic structures to meet the consequences. This was the experience of the United States and Western Europe during the Industrial Revolution. On the other hand, secondary development involves the dis-

---

[1] Richard N. Adams, *The Second Sowing: Power and Secondary Development in Latin America* (San Francisco: Chandler, 1967).

covery of social innovations to handle newly introduced, but already elaborated, technical and economic structures. It is this second, and in some ways more difficult, path which the "developing" countries of Latin America today are attempting to follow.

The problem of economic development in Latin America is much broader than the term "economic" might indicate. Viewed from Adams' perspective, development is a complex process involving social, cultural, and political, as well as economic, innovations. In a very real sense, it becomes somewhat tenuous to argue that the economic progress of Latin America is independent of other aspects of human activity. If industrialization, technology, higher incomes and savings, urbanization, higher production and consumption, and other elements of economic development are to be achieved in Latin America, important transformations in primarily non-economic spheres must also take place. For example, how can a country like Ecuador even hope to become more economically developed if its government does not make a satisfactory effort to educate a literate and trained work force? Without a trained and educated work force, a country is severely handicapped in the process of economic development. But education and training of a work force does not have simply economic implications. Most educational programs, including those of Latin American countries, also involve the learning of diverse attitudes, ideas, and notions. These ideas not only affect the individual's concept of himself in the world but in the long run have some important, if not always anticipated, effects on the society as a whole. An educational program that reaches masses of individuals may be able to reverse the traditional attitude that an individual has no control over events and things around him. If individuals in sufficiently large numbers reverse their perspective, they begin to expect and even to insist on actively improving their lot in life. Such a turn of events would not only have a profound effect upon the economic system of an underdeveloped country; it would also have important effects upon that country's political and social systems as well.

Economic development in Latin America also requires other non-economic innovations. Large industrial firms, commercial enterprises, and other modern forms of economic endeavor require a social organization of manpower that is not often found in countries toward the lower end of the "development" continuum. As Banfield has pointed out, people must be willing and able to trust each other sufficiently to pool their resources and to cooperate toward the realization of some goal. If, on the other hand, individuals are suspicious of everyone outside their own immediate kinship group or clan, modern forms of economic and social organization cannot operate.[2] This transformation of traditional cultural values regarding

[2] Edward Banfield, *The Moral Basis of a Backward Society* (New York: Free Press, 1958).

interpersonal relations is one of many important non-economic changes which are necessary for economic progress to take place in the "developing" countries of Latin America.

This elementary examination of economic development can be simply summarized. Economic development is a process rather than an outcome, and involves a complex mixture of economic and non-economic requisites. Economic development involves high levels of production, consumption, income, industrialization, use of technology, capital, savings, and investment. It also requires such non-economic features as an educated work force and modern attitudes toward the world and toward man's place in the world. It would be highly optimistic to believe that all Latin American countries will be able to succeed in this often perilous and disruptive process within the immediate or even distant future. However, the view of most Latin Americans is that the present situation should and must be changed. A brief glance at the economic situation can demonstrate the reasons for this uneasiness.

Per capita annual income is very low throughout Latin America, ranging from $835.00 in Venezuela to $63.00 in Haiti, and averages only $346.00 for the entire region. The typical diet is inadequate, as are such things as housing and transportation. The mean percent of literacy for the region is only 63, and only 21 percent of the population between the ages of 13 and 18 are attending school. Medically, Latin America also falls behind the more developed countries, averaging only 5.2 doctors per 10,000 persons, and 3.1 hospital beds per 10,000 persons.[3] The region as a whole can be classified as only 45 percent urban, with Uruguay (73 percent), Argentina (72 percent), and Chile (68 percent) leading the rest.[4] Economic growth as measured by annual increase in per capita gross domestic product (GDP) has not matched the goal of 2.5 percent set by the Alliance for Progress. In fact, some Latin American countries, such as Haiti, Uruguay, the Dominican Republic, and Colombia, have actually suffered declines in per capita GDP. Success in eliminating or at least alleviating these and other problems is by no means inevitable; but the alternative, not making an effort to solve these problems through economic development, is becoming less politically acceptable in most Latin American countries.

SOCIAL DEVELOPMENT

Just as countries can develop economically, so can they develop socially. However, it is easier to prove that economic development has

[3] Ernest A. Duff and John F. McCamant, "Measuring Social and Political Requirements for System Stability in Latin America," in *American Political Science Review,* Vol. 62, No. 4, December, 1968.

[4] Ibid.

occurred than it is to show that social development has occurred. Simply put, it is harder to describe what social development actually is.

One of the things that is pretty obvious, however, is that social development is generally a question of democratic values. That is, social development to some extent involves the greater opportunity of all people from any social class to make something of their lives. Logically, then, a country such as Haiti has not developed very much socially because it has a very rigid class structure in which a few rich people run the lives of many very poor people. Most people in such a situation do not have a relatively equal chance to improve their lot. In other words, social development partially means equality of opportunity.

Implied in this, of course, is the notion that individuals are valued for what they achieve and not for what they are or who their parents were. In traditional societies, an individual's success in life was determined by his status at birth rather than by what he did later. To let a person go as far as he can on his individual merits rather than limiting him by tradition requires that the social structure be relatively open, that he be permitted to move upward from one social class to another. An open society requires and thrives on individual achievement. Also, social development suggests a sense of social justice and fair play. One is not to be discriminated against because he looks like an Indian, has no rich relatives, or knows little of the cultural affectations of the upper classes. It is at this point that the conflict between economic and social development may become acute.

Governments in Latin America may have to choose economic development over social development in which, for a time at least, the rich may get richer and the poor poorer. A more just and equitable division of the wealth would hamper the accumulation of wealth needed to promote economic growth. Very rare are the governmental leaders in Latin America or anywhere else for that matter who clearly choose to help the poor and powerless and to slight the rich and powerful.

THE POLITICAL SYSTEM AND ITS DEVELOPMENT

Before confronting the concept of political development, it might be appropriate to review some basic terms of political science that are especially relevant to that concept. The first such term is "political system," which is to political science what the term "economy" is to economics. Despite disagreement over how the term should be defined, the political system concept does serve as language for discussing the nature of government and politics. Obviously, the term "government" is too restrictive by itself: it focuses on the formal political institutions of a society and ignores such factors as political parties, interest groups, voting behavior, and other elements which must be considered if one is to gain any real understanding of politics. The concept of the political system attempts to provide such an understanding. Many views of the political system exist, but none seems to be completely adequate. Without becoming deeply enmeshed in controversies concerning the concept, we can briefly present one version of it that emphasizes the role of the political system in using legitimate physical coercion over societies.[5] In other words, the right to punish for defying legitimate authority is a common aspect of the political system. The political system generally exercises this role for the entire society, and its position in society allows it to allocate benefits, services, and privileges within the society as a whole. The term political system also involves an "interdependence of parts." When one of these parts changes, one might expect other parts to do likewise. For an extreme example, the Cuban Revolution eliminated large private landowners, and with this important group gone, the Cuban political system was considerably transformed. Other groups, especially farm workers, were affected in ways that were not previously conceivable. Today, for instance, such things as housing and education are much more readily available to rural labor. Also, a political system has a boundary that sets it off from its environment. This boundary is rarely fixed and generally it varies over time. For example, as popular participation in government is promoted through the extension of the right to vote, individuals who were not in the political system previously are now included. Simply put, the political system is an interrelated system of parts which has the use of legitimate coercion to make binding decisions on the entire society. As such, it can maintain the status quo or transform it through its unique political role in society.

Two further points deserve special mention at this time because they have a direct bearing on the discussion of political development and its application to the main concerns of this book. The first is the idea that demands are placed on the system and the second concerns the idea of system capabilities in meeting these demands.

The demands on political systems are several. First, people might demand that their government allocate goods and services in a certain way. For example, some individuals might demand that more roads be constructed by the government so that they can take their produce to market areas, while others might demand that the money that could be used for constructing roads be used instead for expanding primary level education. Second, demands might involve the regulation of behavior. For example, domestic investors in some Latin American country might demand that the

[5] The following discussion of the political systems owes much to David Easton, "An Approach to the Analysis of Political Systems," in *World Politics,* April 1957; and Gabriel Almond and G. Bingham Powell, *Comparative Politics: A Developmental Approach* (Boston: Little, Brown, 1966), pp. 25–26. Another form of input, that of supports, will not be considered in detail at this time.

government take more restrictive measures to limit foreign investment and privileges. There are also demands on the political system to expand the number of people who can participate in political affairs. Demands for participation involve the right to vote, the right to hold office, the right to organize political parties, and other activities. This kind of demand is a very important one in Latin America because it implies a dimension of political change and suggests who will control the rate of change. For example, the military regime in Brazil which came to power in 1964 has pursued a policy of restricting the political participation of certain groups, such as organized urban labor, who want more rapid change than some military officers are willing to allow. Another demand is one for communication and information. Many people want to be informed of the government's intentions regarding policy, or they may want a reaffirmation of past political values. In demanding such communication and information, people obtain a better understanding of what to expect from the political system, and therefore their lives become a little more predictable, if not more comfortable, under any particular regime. All of these demands should receive some study if we are to understand how political systems, in Latin America or elsewhere, operate and undergo change.

The capabilities of a political system involve how well it performs in its setting.[6] It is important to realize that political systems differ significantly in their capabilities. Totalitarian systems such as the Soviet Union's have a highly developed "regulative" capability, or control over individual and group behavior. Some systems emphasize the "extractive" capability which involves drawing resources from the environment. For example, such Latin American countries as Chile, Ecuador, and Brazil are more effective than others such as Paraguay, El Salvador, and Guatemala in collecting taxes and other revenue from their environments. Still others are more effective in recruiting competent public servants and other human resources. For that matter, a not unimportant factor in determining extractive capability is the system's effectiveness in obtaining funds from international aid programs. The "distributive" capability refers to the political system allocating and dispensing benefits to individuals and groups. Again, countries differ in this capability, if for no other reason than that countries differ in their capability to extract resources for allocation and distribution. Cuba, for example, today allocates benefits somewhat differently than does, say, Nicaragua, which remains under the control of the traditional oligarchy. "Symbolic" capability involves effectively dispensing symbols from the political system to the society. For example, a Latin American government which is contemplating the seizure of a foreign enterprise will probably use various nationalistic symbols to gain legitimacy for the anticipated action.

6 Almond and Powell, *Comparative Politics,* p. 27.

Finally, the "responsive" capability refers to the relationship between what those outside the political system demand and what the political system actually gives them. Some political systems are more responsive to certain groups than to others. For example, in a country such as Argentina which has been undergoing military intervention and rule intermittently since World War II, the political system is more responsive to military officers than is the system of Costa Rica where civilians are in firm control of a small and largely apolitical National Guard. By examining these various capabilities of political systems, we can better assess the problem of political change. If a political system lacks certain capabilities, then it cannot effectively promote change in the general society even if political leaders wish to do so.

POLITICAL DEVELOPMENT

Like economic systems, political systems can also change and develop, although our understanding of political change and development is more imperfect than our understanding of economic change and development. However, at least one thing seems certain: political development involves political change, but political change does not necessarily involve political development.

What is political development? There are many different definitions of political development currently in the literature of political science: the concept has been equated with multidimensional social change, the politics of industrial societies, stability and order, the operation of the nation-state, and democracy. Perhaps more than the other ideas, political development seen as "democracy" involves an implicit bias for the political systems of Great Britain and the United States. Using this concept of development, Latin America can become politically developed if it becomes like these Anglo-American systems. We believe that political development viewed as democracy is neither a helpful nor objective way to compare very different political systems.[7]

Given the previous discussion on political systems, two definitions of political development deserve special comment. Gabriel Almond and G. Bingham Powell argue that political development means an increase in the effective and efficient performance of the political system. In other words, political development involves an increase in the capabilities of the political system.[8] Political organizations, institutions, and attitudes change

[7] Lucian W. Pye, *Aspects of Political Development* (Boston: Little, Brown, 1966), Chapter 2. For a democratic notion of political development applied to Latin America, see Martin C. Needler, *Political Development in Latin America: Instability, Violence and Evolutionary Change* (New York: Random House, 1968).

[8] Almond and Powell, previously cited, p. 105.

in such a way that the political system increases its capabilities to handle new demands. However, there is at least one problem here that remains unsolved: How does the political system handle conflicting demands of mutually antagonistic groups as in Latin America? How can governments be made more effective if groups cannot agree on what is to be done?[9] Related to this view is the idea that political development is the ability of a political system to sustain continuously new types of political demands and organizations.[10] Or perhaps political development should be defined as the ability to sustain certain social goals (rather than political demands) and institutions (rather than informal organizations). These three very similar definitions should be kept in mind as we refer to political development throughout the course of this book.

Despite all these notions of political development, none explains how change comes about in the developmental process. How do institutions and behavior change? What is developmental change? How do we get from one level of development to another? Do we need to view developmental change in terms of levels? Finally, how do we induce developmental change? No completely convincing or plausible answers to these questions are available. Although they are certainly important questions, this book is more concerned with other problems which will be discussed later in this chapter.

We stated earlier that political change is not the same as political development, a point well argued by Samuel Huntington.[11] In making this argument, Huntington attacks the implicit assumption that political development follows an inevitable path of uninterrupted political evolution. To the contrary, Huntington argues that countries attempting to develop politically may also find themselves in a state of political decay. In other words, there are ups and downs in the process, and change may be the harbinger of decay as well as of development. As Huntington sees it, political decay occurs when a political system is generally incapable of meeting new and changing demands from its environment. That is, if demands outrun the capability of the political system to meet them, political decay is the result. On the other hand, political development occurs if the political system is able to institutionalize political organizations and procedures. Only then can the political system perform well enough to meet such demands.

9 See I. L. Horowitz, "The Norm of Illegitimacy: The Political Sociology of Latin America" in I. L. Horowitz, Josuede Castro, and John Gerassi (eds.), *Latin American Radicalism* (New York: Vintage, 1969).

10 See S. N. Eisenstadt "Bureaucracy and Political Development," in Joseph LaPalombara (ed.), *Bureaucracy and Political Development* (Princeton, N.J.: Princeton University Press, 1963), Chapter 4.

11 Samuel Huntington, *Political Order in Changing Societies* (New Haven: Yale University Press, 1968), Chapter 1.

Although some have quarreled with Huntington's notion of political development as being too conservative and emphasizing stability over change, it does seem that Huntington clearly has a valid point in arguing that change may mean retarded development as well as increased development.

Latin America is an excellent example of the lack of political development. In agreeing with Huntington, one observer took a special look at Latin America and found that many of the Latin American countries have progressed in terms of the socio-economic indicators often mentioned, but political development has not taken place.[12] Moreover, it has been noted that the region's growing urbanization is not necessarily related to developmental attitudes of people; urban dwellers have not become political agitators working for radical changes, and neither education nor primary group relations has broken down traditional attitudes in urban areas of Latin America. Obviously, Latin American politics present a better example of no significant change or, at worst, decay than it does of development. It is with this immobility, or lack of important political changes, that this book is basically concerned.

SOCIAL STRUCTURE

The argument that political change in Latin America is often slow and almost imperceptible may seem to be a strange point of view to someone who imagines that Latin America is bordering on violent upheaval and political instability. Is it possible that Latin America is both politically stagnant and politically volatile? This suggests a more detailed examination of the politics of this region, with special attention devoted to the problems of change and development.

Since the political systems of all Latin American countries are closely intertwined with their social, economic, and cultural systems, one cannot understand Latin American politics without examining the environment in which political behavior occurs. Obviously, we are using the term environment here to refer to human, nonpolitical activity rather than to natural or physical features in which political systems operate.

One environmental influence on politics in Latin America is social structure. When we refer to social structure here, the term implies the relationship between social classes. A social structure may have two, three, four, or more social classes because people have different levels of income, prestige, and other values. Despite the variations of social structure among the Latin American countries, it is an important factor which determines

[12] Alfred Stepan, "Political Development Theory: The Latin American Experience," in *Journal of International Affairs*, Vol. 20, No. 2, 1966.

the nature of political institutions in the area. According to Lambert, some Latin American countries such as Argentina and Uruguay have a relatively developed and homogeneous social structure; others like Haiti have an archaic social structure.[13] Most, however, have developed unevenly with a dual social structure like that found in Brazil, Mexico, Colombia and Venezuela. The dual social structure involves a combination of the archaic and the developed. Since there are basically two different societies in many Latin American countries, governmental institutions are unable to effectively and legitimately perform modern functions. Instead, governmental centralization of power in Latin America is more apparent than real because the dual social structure is a primary obstacle to developing effective political institutions at the national level.

Lambert also argues that the nature of a dualistic social structure has specific effects on some of the democratic political institutions of Latin America. In societies that have the old and new juxtaposed, such as in Latin American societies, the old but powerful rural elites have more power in the national legislature than their numbers would suggest. Consequently, the adoption of democratic forms from such countries as the United States has had unintended effects in Latin America, in that democratic processes have become the bastion of the traditional power holders who still manage to have some influence at the national level. Another specific consequence of social structure affecting politics is the dominance of the president over other branches of the national government. The president in many countries has broad legislative and quasi-judicial powers which permit him to overrule the other branches. Most Latin American countries, for example, have constitutional provisions granting power to the president to call a state of siege. During the emergency conditions of a state of siege, the president may suspend civil liberties for a period of time. Except in a few countries such as Costa Rica and Chile, where the national legislature does have some powers to counteract the president, unchallenged presidential dominance is the rule rather than the exception. This prevents the social structure from completely immobilizing governmental action at the national level. Since legislatures are often controlled by localistic and traditional power groups, these institutions cannot be relied upon for effective action to overcome the problems of development that most of these countries face.

There has been some controversy concerning the effect of changing social structures in Latin America upon the political process. For example, John J. Johnson has argued that the emergence of the middle sectors (which are not classes in a strict sense) is linked to economic development and is a primary force for promoting change, greater economic benefits for all,

---

[13] Jacques Lambert, *Latin America: Social Structures and Political Institutions* (Berkeley: University of California Press, 1967).

and expanded political participation.[14] More recent analyses have cast some doubt on this judgment. One social scientist, for example, argues that the so-called middle sector does not really exist. Culturally, there are really only two sectors, an upper sector and a lower sector.[15] What Johnson terms the middle sector is really a part of the upper sector which values prestige symbols and the manipulation of power. The lower sector values wealth as a goal and work as the means to attain it. The problem of the lower sector is survival. The middle-income groups do not identify with the lower sector who are extremely poor, apathetic, and without much political influence. The middle-income groups have no class ideology or consciousness. For example, the Brazilian military coup of 1964 was supported by these groups in order to decelerate political and economic changes which threatened their position by providing the lower classes with too many benefits and too much power. It does seem plausible that these middle-income groups are different from their counterparts in the more developed countries of the West. They are not necessarily progressive; they identify with those who do not want rapid change, and they fear the unpredictability of change, which might bring a loss of newly found position and wealth.

THE ECONOMIC SYSTEM

The economies of Latin American countries have also had some important effects on the political processes of the area. To the extent that economics determines social structure, we have already discussed its effects on politics. But economics also has an effect of its own on the political process. For example, a traditional economy based upon subsistence or plantation agriculture will not be able to provide many resources to the government. This, in turn, will limit the government's capabilities for promoting development. Moreover, extensive foreign investment and control over major economic ventures has the effect of removing some economic policy-making from the national governments. Of course, these governments do receive tax support from foreign enterprises but many Latin Americans continue to regard nationalization of foreign enterprises as a necessary step toward independent economic development.

While economic systems and those who control them often present serious obstacles to the capabilities of political systems, it seems to be the task of governments in Latin America to transform and develop these economies. Unlike those of the West, governments of Latin America have a very heavy burden for actively promoting economic development, which

[14] John J. Johnson, *Political Change in Latin America: The Emergence of the Middle Sectors* (Stanford, Calif.: Stanford University Press, 1958).

[15] Richard N. Adams, *The Second Sowing*, Chapter 3.

is certainly no easy task. Latin American national governments are faced with strong obstacles at the sub-national and international levels that thwart the evolution of a national, independent, and modern economy. For example, at the sub-national level, large landowners resist economic integration into the national system for fear of losing their socio-economic position.

At the international level, Latin American economies are tied to foreign markets. Despite some recent changes, Latin America still functions as a peripheral area of the international economy, supplying raw materials and basic products to the advanced countries. Thus, it is very difficult for the national governments to overcome foreign economic control of their countries, although some like Peru, Bolivia, and Chile are in different ways trying to do so. Change of any systemic importance will not come about unless the economic systems of Latin America and the governments' role in the economy undergo considerable revision.

The setting of Latin American politics is also molded by the foreign policies of the United States. Approximately at the time of Castro's rise to power in Cuba, the United States government concluded that the best way to avoid Communist revolution in Latin America was to promote peaceful change and reform coupled with economic development aid. In setting up the Alliance for Progress, American foreign policy-makers assumed that they could work through existing political and economic institutions in Latin America. They of course hoped that Latin Americans themselves would make the necessary reforms in their institutions to assimilate the aid and to make progress within the system. This condition has not in fact materialized. The Alliance for Progress and the Latin American countries are both responsible for the fact that the region has not been able to meet the goal of an increase in annual per capita income of 2.5 percent. The failure of the Alliance for Progress has led American foreign policy makers to a reassessment of the problem, if not an important commitment, to find a new solution. The Latin Americans do not particularly want relatively small amounts of aid from the United States. What they do appear to want are favorable terms of trade for their goods in the world market so that they can finance their own economic development. In other words, Latins want what the United States economic interests will be reluctant or unable to give.

Overall, then, the impact of the United States, intentionally or not, has been to impede the economic, social, and political development of Latin America. Historically, the United States has rarely taken a consistent stand on promoting socio-economic change. All the way back to the Monroe Doctrine, which was announced unilaterally by the United States in 1823, the United States warned against changes in power relations in which "foreign" (non-American) nations might actively intervene. Somewhat hypocritically, the United States reserved the right to do exactly the same thing on its own behalf. Vacillating between benign neglect and spasmodic panic, the United States, for most of the nineteenth century and much of the twentieth, regarded Latin America as its unofficial colony and took an active interest in the region only if it perceived a direct threat to its own security or economic interests. Despite the advent of a more friendly but still condescending policy during the Hoover and Roosevelt years, United States policy to Latin America has changed remarkably little. As the dominant power over twenty or so far weaker ones, the United States began its economic aid to Latin America to stave off economic disaster and more Cubas but did not give enough help to end the region's economic dependency on the giant to the north.[16] More rhetoric about an equal partnership with Latin America has not yet led the United States policy-makers to fashion a policy which frees Latin America from the web of trade, finance, and economic aid that strengthens rather than weakens the bonds of dependency that prevent Latin America from pursuing an independent and effective course of development.

Although it would be inaccurate as well as unfair to blame the United States for all the troubles that Latin America faces today, the United States has done very little to help the region overcome its own problems. Perhaps because Latin America is not all that important to the United States, policy-makers in Washington have spectacularly failed to promote democracy in Latin America, to foster stable governments, to promote economic development that jeopardizes American interests and holdings in the region, or to gain the trust and respect of the progressive elements of Latin America. The long-run results of such policies may leave the United States without allies or supporters in the southern hemisphere.

American policies toward Latin America have been thoroughly discredited but the apathy of the United States toward the region has not generated any coherent substitutes. Aid has been attacked as being a way to help the rich and prop up a flagging system; the Nixon administration has de-emphasized it. America's holding on to large multinational corporations has spurred intense anti-American feelings, especially in Chile and Peru; the Nixon administration seeks a low profile but does not retract its demand for compensation for nationalized properties. The threats of guerrilla activity and other security issues wane; but the United States continues its aid and trade in military hardware to governments who use them against their political opponents. It is hard to imagine that this tactic of avoiding confrontations is a new beginning in which the United States seeks to overturn the network of relations that keeps Latin America down or denies important powers within the United States their demands for protection in

[16] Jerome Levinson and Juan de Onis, *The Alliance That Lost Its Way* (Chicago: Quadrangle, 1970).

Latin America. The Nixon administration has given no specific indications that it intends to change things fundamentally in United States-Latin American relations. However, it has tried to soften its image. Since 1969, official policy from Washington has appeared to be less directive and paternalistic. Unfortunately, many Latin Americans also see this new image as one of indifference, especially in light of the failure of the United States government to grant special trade preferences as was promised. In conclusion, the United States has learned to adapt to all changes, rather than to resist, in the hope that losses can be minimized and that nothing substantial will be done to jeopardize its hold on Latin America. It is fairly safe to predict that the United States government will not easily abandon a relationship with Latin America that has greatly benefited its interests at the expense of promoting independent economic development in the region.

INFORMAL POLITICAL STRUCTURES

In addition to examining the effect of non-political factors on Latin American political systems, we should also discuss, of course, the various aspects of the systems themselves. For the sake of convenience, we will divide our discussion of political systems in Latin America into two categories: the formal institutions of government, and the informal political structures which link government to the general society. This discussion is based upon the earlier examination of the political system which obviously includes far more than formal institutions of government but does not extend to all non-political activities of the general society.

It is immediately clear that the structural links between the societies and the political systems of Latin American countries are different from those of the so-called countries in North America and Western Europe. For one thing, interest groups in the more developed countries are more readily discernible and more obviously perform the function of articulating their interests to the political systems. In Latin America, interest groups either do not exist in the same way they do in the developed countries, or do not perform this function as regularly or as consistently. If an "interest group" is viewed as a group of individuals who organize to articulate their demands on the political system, then it becomes apparent that Latin American countries have fewer of these groups than do the more developed countries, and that they do not play such an important role in Latin America as they do, for instance, in the United States. Moreover, Latin American political systems do not contain political parties of the type and of the scope found in more developed countries. Many of the parties in Latin America are personalistic and temporary bands of followers of a leader whose party is not based upon large masses of the electorate but upon narrow social groups. For example, there is a long list of "political parties" that bear the name of their leader and that disappear with the political misfortune of the leader. As such, they do not aggregate various demands of numerous and diverse groups to present policy alternatives to the electorate. Except for the Institutional Revolutionary Party of Mexico (the PRI), this picture still dominates much of Latin America and therefore differs from the picture in developed countries. Latin American parties perform the function of representing narrow groups but do not combine them, do not recruit individuals into the political process, and do not provide support for government policies. Political parties in Latin America generally seem to be a consequence of initial steps toward development rather than an independent and influential force in affecting governmental policy toward development.

Given these and other differences between interest groups and political parties of Latin America and those of the more developed countries, it seems logical to resist the temptation to think about these informal political structures in exactly the same way that we think about them in more developed contexts. One critique of studies which fail to resist this temptation is particularly worth citing. Charles Anderson has argued that the application of the "group process" technique (with its Western assumptions) to Latin America has not resulted in accurate analyses of the political systems of Latin America. Instead, the importance of interest groups is exaggerated, or superficial similarities between Latin America and the developed countries emerge.[17]

In short, very few interest groups exist in Latin America, if we use the usual Western definitions of such groups. Let us, therefore, examine how groups place demands on the political systems of Latin America without making the usual assumptions about interest groups made in other contexts.

What we will call simply a "group" and what Anderson calls a "power contender" covers a broad range of individuals who organize to seek the implementation of their demands by government, to use the capabilities of the political system to produce certain policies regarding development and, in other ways, to use the legitimate power of government to affect society in general. In other words, these groups run governments as well as influence them. Although most of these groups are not interest groups in any proper (Western) sense, they do encompass a wide variety of important sectors of the Latin American societies. The military is certainly one such group with a particularly unique position due to its near-monopoly of force. Other

---

[17] Charles W. Anderson, *Politics and Economic Change in Latin America* (New York: Van Nostrand Reinhold, 1967), p. 89. Anderson is especially critical of George I. Blanksten for his analysis of "Political Groups in Latin America," in *American Political Science Review*, Vol. 53, March 1969.

groups have primarily economic identities, such as: peasants, businessmen, and labor. Each of these groups has different resources for making demands upon the political systems of Latin America. Workers and peasants have numbers; businessmen have relative affluence. Even the Roman Catholic clergy make demands on the systems of Latin America although their influence varies considerably throughout the area. None of these groups are unified. In fact, some of them are noted for their division rather than for their unity. For example, the military in Argentina and Brazil, which has intervened directly and indirectly in national politics in recent years, is divided politically according to branch of service, rank within the service, and other criteria. Other groups should be regarded more as socio-economic categories rather than as organized, associational groups which have a commonly perceived goal. For some purposes, the peasants would certainly be classified as a category. Many of these groups express demands upon the political systems of the region simply as a result of the activity of small elites who claim, sometimes not very convincingly, that they represent the huge mass of individuals who have little or no conception of a national government which might respond to their demands. In other words, the term "group" is broad and amorphous. Any concrete meaning it may have in this book must be noted from the context in which the term is found.

One of the main problems of Latin American politics is that groups of all kinds fail to agree on the basic rules of the political game and do not share the same resources for influencing, and/or making demands upon, their political systems.[18] This major problem is often the underlying reason for the apparent instability of governments and the recurring violence of Latin American politics. For example, let us assume that the military opposes the growth and increasing power of urban labor as was the case in Brazil just prior to the 1964 coup. Since the military will not regard any arrangement as legitimate that permits the importance of labor and its potential threat to the military position to increase, the military officers unite temporarily to demonstrate their resource of physical coercion. By demonstrating such a resource, or actually exercising it in the form of the coup, the military is able to realize its demands for restricting the political power of its rival, urban labor. Furthermore, groups must demonstrate their political resources if their leaders wish to be taken seriously by other groups. Urban labor, with large numbers, could call a general strike. Other demonstrations of political resources may be more extreme. Urban terrorism in recent years, for example, has become increasingly more frequent in Venezuela, Guatemala, and Brazil. Much of the political violence in Latin America that makes headlines in the North American news media

---

[18] The following discussion closely follows that of Anderson, *Politics and Economic Change in Latin America,* pp. 93–94.

is merely the exercise of some demonstrated resource and does not necessarily indicate a basic instability of the entire political system. Once the demonstrated power of some group is recognized by the other groups, the group is admitted to the political process of manipulation and negotiation. Such a group has the opportunity, if not necessarily the capacity, to demand and receive governmental favors.

Despite the fact that the apparent political instability and violence of Latin American countries testifies to meager consensus on the basic rules of the game, there appears to be one essential rule that helps to account for the immobility of the political process. Primarily, this rule involves the implicit stipulation that a group will be admitted to the political process if it does not jeopardize the position of other groups in the system. For example, students in Latin America are reknowned for their radical rhetoric. But, unless a social revolution of major proportions occurs, students must recognize the political position of the traditional oligarchy, such as the church, the military, and the large landowners. The rule of admitting new groups and not eliminating old groups from the political process in Latin America suggests that political change can only occur within very narrow limits. These limits often become the source of much frustration for members of the new groups which favor accelerated change and development.

FORMAL STRUCTURES

Finally, a general discussion of Latin American politics must include an examination, however brief, of the formal institutions of government which are the target of demands and upon which fall the burdens of meeting these demands. As with the informal political groups briefly examined above, the formal political institutions of most Latin American countries bear a superficial resemblance to those in the developed Western countries which were their source of inspiration. This superficial or formalistic resemblance to other political systems is easily seen.

Latin American constitutions present a haunting familiarity in tone and style to the written constitutions of the Western democracies. They are usually characterized by detailed legalism, an affinity to French and American constitutionalism, extensive discourse on the rights of man and, finally, an irrelevance for the actual operation of Latin American political systems. The content of written Latin American constitutions, much of which was grafted on from other contexts, diverges widely from the realities of Latin American politics. If a student of Latin American politics wanted to gain some sophisticated appreciation of what happens politically and why, he would perhaps be well advised not to read initially the national constitutions of the area because he would probably gain some highly misleading impressions.

The gap between constitutional norms and political realities is an example of a general condition which Fred W. Riggs calls "formalism." "Formalism," a widespread characteristic of most "developing" countries, exists when forms diverge from reality.[19] Latin American constitutions are highly formalistic in this sense. They are not very accurate descriptions of what is; instead they are statements of what ought to be. As such, many Latin American constitutions are designed to provide some legitimacy to whoever happens to be in power at any particular time. In other words, Latin American constitutions do not describe accurately the basic rules of the political game in the political system. They are simply symbolic instrumentalities of those in power.[20]

The separation of powers is one of the norms embodied in many Latin American constitutions. The concept of separation of powers, of course, evolved from the constitutional history of the West. Grafted onto the Latin American political scene, this concept, like the constitutions of Latin America, becomes a formalistic misrepresentation of reality. The separation of powers doctrine is violated in Latin America principally by the unchallenged dominance of the president over the legislature and the courts. This dominant position has been attributed to several factors, not the least of which is the fact that politics is a route for obtaining wealth and power in a relatively closed society, and the presidency is a position which promotes this goal. Consequently, political instability revolves around the presidency, but this, in turn, is rarely an indication of fundamental revolution in the entire society. Non-electoral means of recruiting aspiring elites have become a standard procedure.[21]

Implicitly, presidential dominance also means legislative and judicial weakness. Most presidents in Latin America can issue decree-laws or take other quasi-legislative steps to run the government without substantial help from the legislatures. As a matter of political reality, the Latin American chief executive has considerably more fiscal and budgetary power than does his North American counterpart. For example, the president in many Latin American countries may carry out fiscal policy without legislative approval simply by continuing past practice. Even with legislative cooperation, the Latin American executive has considerable control over expenditures and revenue. In many countries and on many issues, then, the Latin

[19] Fred W. Riggs, *Administration in Developing Countries: The Theory of Prismatic Society* (Boston: Houghton Mifflin, 1964).

[20] R. A. Gomez, *Government and Politics in Latin America*, rev. ed. (New York: Random House, 1964), pp. 24–34.

[21] For further discussion of Latin American Constitutions, see J. Floyd Mecham, "Latin American Constitutions: Nominal or Real?" in *Journal of Politics*, Vol. 21, No. 2, May 1959.

American legislature is a rubber stamp for executive action. It is simply not an independent and relatively equal rival to the president.

The judicial branch in Latin America is also a weak member of the formal triumvirate of the separation of powers doctrine. Unlike its counterpart in the United States and in some systems of Western Europe, the judiciary in Latin America generally does not have the power of judicial review. Consequently, the judiciary is unable to invalidate legislative or especially executive action as "unconstitutional." Instead of using its position to limit the other branches of government, the judiciary tends to expend more effort to protect individuals in their relations with government. Many Latin American countries have special courts concerned with such functional areas as administration, labor, and elections. The degree of autonomy for these specialized courts and for the entire judicial system varies from country to country, but it is obvious that the judiciary can be dominated by the executive through appointments or through the executive's unchallenged power to ignore court rulings. The judiciary presents no serious threat to executive dominance.[22]

A formal institution of government in Latin America that has not received much attention is the bureaucracy. Perhaps the major reason that so little is known about the national bureaucracies of these countries is that students of Latin American politics have focused on the visible and powerful chief executive. It has not really occurred to many scholars that bureaucracy has some important policy-making prerogatives of its own. However, the growth of bureaucracy in Latin America has been impressive in the recent years. Bureaucracy has been assigned important tasks in promoting agrarian reform and production, of establishing welfare systems, of operating national educational systems, and of serving as public entrepreneurs for economic development. The complexity of these tasks makes it virtually impossible for the chief executive himself to maintain day-to-day vigilance over their execution. For example, the Mexican presidency has been instrumental in establishing numerous ministries and more than four hundred semi-independent agencies, some of which deal directly with development, and over which the president has a declining amount of real control. As a result, in Mexico, as well as in some of the other Latin American countries that have established large national bureaucracies, the chief executive has relinquished some of his policy-making powers.[23] In short, although he has better control over some areas of bureaucratic policy-making than others, his control over the bureaucracy should by no means be taken for granted.

[22] For more on the judiciary, see Helen L. Clagett, *The Administration of Justice in Latin America* (New York: Oceana Publications, 1952).

[23] L. Vincent Padgett, *The Mexican Political System* (Boston: Houghton Mifflin, 1966), p. 161.

It seems clear that the bureaucracy in Latin America is not merely an administrative instrument of the president but is also a political institution that has some capability for making demands on the system and for making decisions concerning which demands should be recognized and processed. Bureaucrats are at the nexus of the political system. Without a strong party system, the bureaucracy may be the only plausible political institution for making and aggregating demands. As an institution with much potential political power, the bureaucracy has considerable opportunity to decide the crucial political issues of who gets what and when.

Before concluding this introductory discussion of Latin American politics, it should be noted that the bureaucracy, like the other formal political institutions, reflects the political and social systems within which it operates. Those North American advisors who hope that Latin American public administration can be modeled along the traditional mechanistic principles of economy and efficiency have often failed to take note of this fact of life. Bureaucracy in Latin Amercia cannot be efficient if other groups in the political process, such as political parties and interest groups, are either nonexistent or inadequate as articulators of demands. The bureaucracy cannot be very efficient administratively if much of its task is to determine the specific goals of development it should pursue. Nor can bureaucracy be very efficient if public servants are recruited on the basis of family, friendships, and other traditional criteria which are also important in developing societies. These and other factors permeate the operation of Latin American bureaucracy. Consequently, we cannot study bureaucracy as somehow remote from the incessant play of social, political, and economic factors peculiar to the environment in which the bureaucracy must survive and, hopefully, serve.

It has not been our purpose in this brief discussion of the elements and actors of Latin American politics to provide the reader with a comprehensive introduction to the Latin American political process. Entire books are devoted to such tasks. It has, however, been our purpose to describe selected aspects of Latin American politics which are particularly relevant to the remaining discussion of this book.

AN APPROACH TO POLITICAL CHANGE IN LATIN AMERICA

The study of Latin American politics offers many opportunities of inquiry, and the beginning student could concentrate his time and effort on any number of particular topics. What we propose is to concentrate upon a particular topic which has already received brief attention in this chapter. Although the topic is specific, its central importance to an understanding of Latin American politics magnifies its interest for the student of the area.

Specifically, we argue that much can be understood about problems of change, and especially the role of Latin American political systems in the process of change, by focusing on those groups which make demands on the political systems of Latin America, and assessing the extent to which the political systems respond to these demands. This approach involves an appreciation of the place of Latin American political systems within the larger social and economic context. The student therefore comes to assess the complex process of change and development from a perspective that does not divorce politics from economics or sociology from politics. We are concerned, then, with (1) describing what these groups want in terms of socio-economic changes (2) discussing the demands such groups make on the political system for realization of these wants and (3) analyzing how the political system responds to these demands.

The reader will recognize that this approach is founded on our earlier discussion of the political system. However, we are not attempting to examine each political system of Latin America in its entirety. Instead, we are focusing upon certain parts of the system in order to better understand why changes do or do not occur. Specifically, we are concerned with analyzing the relationship of various political groups to the political system and how this relationship promotes or retards change.

Earlier, we rejected the notion that the concept of "interest groups" is very relevant for the study of Latin American politics. However, we intend to use the term "group" to indicate a broader range of phenomena. When we use the term "group," we are not refering to interest group in a strict sense. Instead, the term "group" refers to any power contender in Latin American politics who attempts to make demands on the political system. As such, groups in Latin America are a diverse and complicated topic of inquiry. We have, therefore, limited our concern to the following groups: Bureaucrats, Businessmen, Catholic Clergy, Labor (Urban), Military Officers, Peasants and Landowners, and Students. These groups represent most if not all of the principal groups or power contenders who make demands on the political systems of Latin America. However, they are considerably different from each other in some ways. For example, each of these groups has its own degree of organization. The peasants, except for a few peasant leaders who may not themselves be peasants, are not highly organized. Consequently, they have not been able to use their numbers effectively to make demands upon most of the political systems of the area. On the other hand, groups such as the military officers and bureaucrats have common identities based upon organization. Moreover, unlike the peasants, they may be considered not only within the political system, but sometimes can be considered a governmental elite.

These groups also differ in their degree of unity. In fact, it might be more accurate to speak of military groups, student groups, and labor groups rather than to give the impression that each of these groups is unified in purpose and tactics. The military, for example, has evolved over the years to the extent that in many Latin American countries the military officers form several groups with different political attitudes and different social backgrounds. The military in some countries therefore reflects, to some extent, the general divisions of the larger society. In some cases, the sense of unity may be so low among some groups that it would be more accurate simply to regard such groups as socio-economic categories. This is probably the case for labor and for peasants.

The term "group," then, embodies a wide array of very different actors in society. They may range from militant student organizations to apathetic peasants. The common feature of all these groups, however, is that they, or leaders claiming to represent them, attempt to make demands on the political system for certain benefits. They either want to promote change through government action as a way to increase their socio-economic well-being, or they want to prevent it in order to protect what they have. What stance they take depends on the issue and their relative position within the political system.

As we examine what these groups want, what they demand, and what they get from the political systems of Latin America, a general theme will develop emphasizing the relative immobility of governmental action to promote socio-economic changes in the general society. If demands from groups are unclear, ambiguous, or infrequent, the government may have little information about what policies to formulate. Without the cooperation of important groups such as landowners, the military, and other members of the traditional oligarchy, the government cannot realistically hope to implement such change-oriented policies as agrarian reform. Furthermore, Latin American politics are dominated to some extent by a deadlock among diverse groups. As Anderson has noted, political groups are admitted to the political process if they recognize the right of the other groups in the process to maintain their influential positions. Consequently, groups are added to the political process, but they are rarely if ever eliminated from it. Therefore, the immobility of governmental action in many Latin American countries in promoting important changes is partially attributable to the fact that groups which have very different stakes in society are all represented in the system. This means that unanimity or near-unanimity among these groups is required if any important changes in governmental policy are to be formulated and implemented. Since rarely can this condition be met, the politics of immobility becomes a way of life.

We mentioned earlier that political change does not necessarily imply political development. The term change, however, requires more elaboration in our study of the politics of immobility in Latin America. We stated that political development involves significant changes in the capabilities of the political system to meet new demands. Political decay on the other hand, involves a relative decrease in the capabilities of the political system to meet new demands. Political immobility implies no significant change toward development or decay. New demands are not being articulated; therefore capabilities are not being increased. Or, if demands are articulated, disagreement over which demands should be met leads to an unresponsive political system which does not increase its capabilities.

We can discuss the magnitude as well as the direction of political change in Latin America. One of the most common, but least consequential, kinds of change in Latin American politics has been, and continues to be in some political systems, the change of governmental personnel. Latin American political leaders are often recruited into high government positions through means which are not recognized as legitimate in such countries as Great Britain and the United States. Armed force, rather than an electoral majority, may be the primary factor favoring one power-holder over another. Similarly, this process of recruiting government elites can remove someone from power just as quickly as he came to power. Despite their apparent political importance, such personnel changes, at least until recently, did not tend toward much change in government policy and tended even less toward changing the basic foundations of society. A new governmental elite would simply rule in its own behalf just as its predecessor had. Once it had achieved power, the new elite had no intention of rearranging a system which permitted it to occupy such official positions of political power.

Another kind of change involves a shift in policy. A change in policy is obviously going to have more impact on the entire political system and society than merely a change of personnel. Will policy continue to favor the landowners against the peasants? Will agrarian reform bills actually be adopted as policy by a government? Will the agrarian policy be implemented as well as adopted? These are the kinds of questions which a change in policy raises.

Another kind of change involves a social revolution or transformation. This kind of change is extremely rare in Latin America, and by almost any standard, Latin America has experienced only three social revolutions. In 1910, a long and tortuous process began which eventually eliminated the traditional oligarchy of landowners, the military, and the church as the principal groups contending for power in Mexico. In 1952, Bolivia experienced a somewhat similar convulsion, but in the last decade the revolutionary process has slowed and perhaps has even terminated. On January 1, 1959, Fidel Castro came to power in Cuba with the first Communist-oriented regime in Latin America since the unsuccessful Guatemalan experience of 1951–1954. In many ways, it is much too early to make any conclusive judgments about the success or future course of the Cuban Revolution. However, it is interesting to note that only one decade after

Castro assumed power, some of the principal groups contending for power in pre-Castro Cuba have been eliminated. The large landowners and foreign entrepreneurs are the primary examples of those groups which were eliminated from the Cuban political process.

Of these three kinds of political change, the approach outlined here is principally concerned with changes in policy. That is, the primary interest here is with changes in policy that are the product of demands upon the system, as well as with implementation of policies for those who make the demands. In other words, we hope to explore the realistic role of government in promoting policies which foment significant changes in Latin America. Personnel changes by themselves are not of great enough magnitude to be considered; social revolution is a possibility but a remote one that should not be unrealistically exaggerated.

As revealed in later chapters, trying to use policy to promote gradual change is more often than not frustrating and more often than not a failure. But as Albert Hirschman lucidly argued a decade ago, there is no real alternative.[24] The reformer who uses policies to bring gradual socio-economic change to Latin America must fight against odds that most people would see as completely hopeless. Mainly, the reformers face the fact that, in Latin America, any reform is going to be opposed by someone powerful. The hope of the reformer is to use a combination of astute devices such as decentralized violence, provoked crisis, and changing alliances of friends. To "contrive reform" in this way requires an abundance of good luck and a flexible strategy which divides and isolates the conservative opposition in favor of a coalition of very different groups who happen to see an advantage to sticking together on a particular problem. The roads to reform are few, precipitous, and harrowing. But they are available and sometimes, quite unexpectedly, provide the opportunity to balance off the tendency to immobility in Latin American politics.

These and other related problems are the concern of the following chapters. Each chapter is devoted to a particular group. First, the group's setting is described, then, what each group wants in terms of change, what it demands of the political system to realize these desires, and, finally, what it actually receives from the political system.

FURTHER READING

ADAMS, RICHARD N., *The Second Sowing: Power and Secondary Development in Latin America*. San Francisco: Chandler, 1967.

ALBA, VICTOR, *Alliance Without Allies: The Mythology of Progress in Latin America*. New York: Praeger, 1965.

[24] Albert O. Hirschman, *Journeys toward Progress: Studies of Economic Policy-making in Latin America* (Garden City, N.Y.: Doubleday, 1963), Chapter 5.

ALMOND, GABRIEL and POWELL, G. BINGHAM, *Comparative Politics: A Developmental Approach*. Boston: Little, Brown, 1966.

ANDERSON, CHARLES W. et al., *Issues of Political Development*. Englewood Cliffs, N.J.: Prentice-Hall, 1967.

ANDERSON, CHARLES W., *Politics and Economic Change in Latin America*. New York: Van Nostrand Reinhold, 1967.

AZEVEDO, THALES DE, *Social Change in Brazil*. Latin American Monograph Series. Gainesville: University of Florida Press, 1963.

BACHMURA, FRANK T. (ed.), *Human Resources in Latin America: An Interdisciplinary Focus*. Bloomington, Ind.: Bureau of Business Research, Graduate School of Business, Indiana University, 1968.

BARRINGER, HERBERT R. et al. (eds.), *Social Change in Developing Areas*. Cambridge, Mass.: Schenkman Publishing Co., 1965.

BLASIER, COLE (ed.), *Constructive Change in Latin America*. Pittsburgh, Pa.: University of Pittsburgh Press, 1968.

BLOUGH, ROY (ed.), *Economic Development Issues: Latin America*. New York: Committee for Economic Development, 1967.

BOORSTEIN, EDWARD, *The Economic Transformation of Cuba*. New York: Monthly Review Press, 1968.

BURNETT, BEN G. and KENNETH F. JOHNSON (eds.), *Political Forces in Latin America: Dimensions of the Quest for Stability*. Belmont, Calif.: Wadsworth, 1970.

BUSEY, JAMES L., *Latin America*. New York: Random House, 1964.

CLAGETT, HELEN L., *The Administration of Justice in Latin America*. New York: Oceana Publications, 1952.

DE OLIVEIRA CAMPOS, ROBERTO, *Reflections on Latin American Development*. Austin: University of Texas Press, 1967.

DEUTSCHMAN, PAUL J. et al., *Communication and Social Change in Latin America: Introducing New Technology*. New York: Praeger, 1968.

DIX, ROBERT H., *Colombia: The Political Dimensions of Change*. New Haven: Yale University Press, 1967.

FAGEN, RICHARD R., *The Transformation of Political Culture in Cuba*. Stanford, Calif.: Stanford University Press, 1969.

FAGEN, RICHARD R. and WAYNE A. CORNELIUS, JR., *Political Power in Latin America*. Englewood Cliffs, N.J.: Prentice-Hall, 1970.

FILLOL, ROBERTO, *Social Factors in Economic Development: The Argentine Case*. Cambridge: M.I.T. Press, 1961.

FINKLE, JASON L. and RICHARD W. GABLE (eds.), *Political Development and Social Change*. New York: John Wiley, 1966.

GOMEZ, R. A., *Government and Politics in Latin America,* rev. ed. New York: Random House, 1964.

GORDON, WENDELL C., *The Political Economy of Latin America*. New York: Columbia University Press, 1965.

HIRSCHMAN, ALBERT O., *Journeys Toward Progress*. Garden City, N.Y.: Doubleday, 1963.

HOROWITZ, IRVING LOUIS, *Revolution in Brazil: Politics and Society in a Developing Nation*. New York: Dutton, 1964.

HOROWITZ, IRVING LOUIS, JOSUE DE CASTRO, and JOHN GERASSI (eds.), *Latin American Radicalism*. New York: Vintage, 1969.

HUNTINGTON, SAMUEL, *Political Order in Changing Societies*. New Haven: Yale University Press, 1968.

JAFFE, A. J., *People, Jobs and Economic Development*. New York: Free Press, 1959.

JAGUARIBE, HELIO, *Economic and Political Development: A Theoretical Approach and a Brazilian Case Study*. Cambridge: Harvard University Press, 1968.

JOHNSON, JOHN J. (ed.), *Continuity and Change in Latin America*. Stanford, Calif.: Stanford University Press, 1964.

——————, *Political Change in Latin America*. Stanford, Calif.: Stanford University Press, 1964.

KILTY, DANIEL R., *Planning for Development in Peru*. New York: Praeger, 1967.

LAMBERT, JACQUES, *Latin America: Social Structures and Political Institutions*. Berkeley: University of California Press, 1967.

LEVINSON, JEROME and JUAN DE ONIS, *The Alliance That Lost Its Way*. Chicago: Quadrangle, 1970.

LEVY, FRED D., JR., *Economic Planning in Venezuela*. New York: Praeger, 1968.

LIPSET, SEYMOUR MARTIN and ALDO SOLARI (eds.), *Elites in Latin America*. New York: Oxford University Press, 1967.

MANDER, JOHN, *The Unrevolutionary Society: The Power of Latin American Conservatism in a Changing World*. New York: Knopf, 1969.

MARTZ, JOHN D. (ed.), *The Dynamics of Change in Latin American Politics*. Englewood Cliffs, N.J.: Prentice-Hall, 1965.

MECHAM, J. LLOYD, "Latin American Constitutions: Nominal or Real?" in *Journal of Politics*, Vol 21, No. 2, May 1959.

MONTGOMERY, JOHN D. and WILLIAM J. SIFFIN (eds.), *Approaches to Development: Politics, Administration and Change*. New York: McGraw-Hill, 1966.

NEEDLER, MARTIN C., *Politcial Development in Latin America: Instability, Violence, and Evolutionary Change*. New York: Random House, 1968.

—————— (ed.), *Political Systems of Latin America*. New York: Van Nostrand Reinhold, 1964.

PADGETT, L. VINCENT, *The Mexican Political System*. Boston: Houghton Mifflin, 1966.

PETRAS, JAMES and MAURICE ZEITLIN (eds.), *Latin America: Reform or Revolution?* Greenwich, Conn.: Fawcett Publications, 1968.

POPANEK, GUSTAV F. (ed.), *Development Policy: Theory and Practice.* Cambridge: Harvard University Press, 1968.

PYE, LUCIAN W., *Aspects of Political Development.* Boston: Little, Brown, 1966.

RAYNOLDS, DAVID R., *Rapid Development in Small Economies: The Example of El Salvador.* New York: Praeger, 1967.

RIGGS, FRED W., *Administration in Developing Countries: A Theory of Prismatic Society.* Boston: Houghton Mifflin, 1964.

SMITH, T. LYNN, *Colombia: Social Structure and the Process of Development.* Gainesville: University of Florida Press, 1967.

STEPAN, ALFRED, "Political Development Theory: The Latin American Experience," in *Journal of International Affairs,* Vol. 20, No. 2, 1966.

URQUIDI, VICTOR L., *The Challenge of Development in Latin America.* New York: Praeger, 1964.

VELIZ, CLAUDIO (ed.), *Obstacles to Change in Latin America.* New York: Oxford University Press, 1965.

——————, *The Politics of Conformity in Latin America.* New York: Oxford University Press, 1967.

VERNON, RAYMOND, *The Dilemma of Mexico's Development.* Cambridge: Harvard University Press, 1965.

WELSH, WILLIAM A., *Political Leadership in Latin America.* Columbus, Ohio: Charles E. Merrill, forthcoming.

WIARDA, HOWARD J., *Dictatorship and Development: The Methods of Control in Trujillo's Dominican Republic.* Gainesville: University of Florida Press, 1968.

CHAPTER 2

PEASANTS

AND

LARGE LANDOWNERS

THE CONTEXT: THE LAND TENURE PATTERN,
THE HACIENDA, THE VILLAGE

It may appear odd that two such disparate socio-economic types as peasants and large landowners are considered here in conjunction. Obviously, their aspirations and their political activities in pursuit of those aspirations are not identical. However, one cannot discuss rural Latin America without discussing relationships between the large landowner and the peasant, nor is it possible to discuss the situation of one except vis-a-vis the situation of the other. This should become abundantly clear throughout the course of this chapter.

Perhaps more than in any other socio-economic sector of Latin America as a whole, or of any single country within the area, the agricultural or rural sector is marked by extremes of wealth and poverty. That is, while the situation does vary from country to country, and even from region to region within a single country, the rural population can easily be described as a very small group of "haves" and a huge mass of "have nots." Relatively few of the rural populace fall between these two extremes—certainly not enough to allow one to speak meaningfully of a "rural middle class."

This great discrepancy in socioeconomic equality in rural Latin America is attributable to the prevailing system of land tenure, whereby most of the land, and certainly most of the good agricultural land, is owned in the form of large estates by a handful of individuals, families, or corporations. A recent study[1] has found that in Latin America as a whole there are 105,000 agricultural and stock-breeding holdings of more than 1,000 hectares each. (The hectare is the basic square unit of land measurement in Latin America, and is equivalent to two and one-half acres.) These holdings represent 1.4 percent of all holdings and comprise 470,000,000 hectares, or 65 percent of the total land included in the agricultural and stock-breeding rolls of Latin America. In other words, each of these holdings has an average size of approximately 4,500 hectares—equivalent to an average of 17 square miles. At the other extreme, there are 5,445,000 holdings, comprising 72 percent of the total number of holdings, with less than 20 hectares each. These holdings occupy 27 million hectares, or 3.7 percent of the total land area included on the rolls, and have an average size of less than 5 hectares.

Examining the land tenure structure from another perspective, the United Nations in 1960 estimated that Latin America had a total population of 199,000,000. Of these, 54 percent, or 107,500,000, were classified as "rural." Out of this total rural population it has been estimated that some 30,000,000 comprise the economically active agricultural population, and only 100,000 of these own 65 percent of the total agricultural land in Latin America.[2] Disregarding a very small intermediate land-holding category, the balance of the rural population, comprising approximately 28,000,000 active men (and, if their families are included, a total population of 80,000,000) is made up of small-holders with barely sufficient land to earn a minimum subsistence on their properties, and of agricultural laborers who own no land at all.

Brazil's vast Northeast, approximately 1,500,000 square kilometers in area and composed of nine states, offers a typical example of the extremes in the land tenure structure. As a whole, it has an annual income level of one hundred dollars per inhabitant. In one of the richest states, Pernambuco, a handful of sugar families possess 50 percent of the state's wealth. In the state of Paraiba, approximately 62 percent of all farms have less than 10 hectares each and account for only 6.26 percent of the total land area, while 0.37 percent of all farms possess approximately 25 percent of the total land area.[3]

[1] See Jacques Chonchol, "Land Tenure and Development in Latin America," in Claudio Veliz (ed.), *Obstacles to Change in Latin America* (New York: Oxford University Press, 1965).

[2] Ibid.

[3] Beldon Paulson, "Problems and Prospects for Community Development in Northeast Brazil," in *The Community in Latin America* (Lawrence, Kan.: Center of Latin American Studies, University of Kansas, 1964), Occasional Publications Number 3.

Even in a country such as Mexico, which officially boasts to the rest of the world of its sixty-year-old "agrarian revolution," the land tenure structure, although mitigated, tends to be one of extremes. Hundreds of volumes have been written about this "agrarian" revolution, but despite this verbiage, and despite all regimes' constant reiteration of dedication to land equality, there are well over one million landless peasants in Mexico.[4] There are also, according to one prominent Mexican economist, some 500 private estates ranging in area from 50,000 to 150,000 hectares.[5] Put another way, in 1961, after 50 years of agrarian revolution, less than one percent of all farms possessed 50 percent of all agricultural lands in Mexico.

Cuba is the only country in Latin America which has really made drastic changes in its land tenure structure. Before the Castro revolution, land ownership in Cuba was about as concentrated as anywhere in Latin America. In May of 1959 the 28 largest sugar-cane producers owned 1,400,000 hectares and rented 617,000 hectares, controlling 20 percent of the land in farms and about one-fifth of Cuban territory. The livestock census of 1952 showed that 2 percent of the approximately 90,000 holdings raising cattle had 42.4 percent of the total cattle stock, while farms having under 50 head of cattle comprised 84.7 percent of all holdings but owned less than one-fourth of the total number of cattle.[6] As early as 1961, however, "people's" farms, cane cooperatives, and small farmers possessed approximately 60 percent of the farmland in Cuba. In 1963 a land reform law was passed which increased the state-owned sector to 70 percent of all lands, including all properties over 67 hectares.[7] In short, for better or worse, the Castro regime has transformed the Cuban land tenure structure. Actually, Cuba today is the only country in Latin America that thinks of "progress" or "development" in agricultural terms rather than urban-industrial terms.

The rural population of Latin America can be classified, then, as large land-holders and very-small-holders plus those who hold no land at all. The large land-holder is generically described as a *latifundista* (from *latifundio*, or large estate), but here the more specific term *hacendado* will

[4] Frank Brandenburg, *The Making of Modern Mexico* (Englewood Cliffs, N.J.: Prentice-Hall, 1964), pp. 253–54.

[5] Edmundo Flores, "Balance de la reforma agraria mexicana," in *Visión*, 9 de Mayo de 1969. See also Edmundo Flores, *Tratado de economía agrícola* (Mexico, D.F.: Fondo de Cultura Económica, 1961).

[6] Dudley Seers (ed.), *Cuba: The Economic and Social Revolution* (Chapel Hill, N.C.: University of North Carolina Press, 1964). See chapter 2, "Agriculture—Pre-Revolutionary Background."

[7] Ibid., see chapter 3, "Agriculture—Post-Revolutionary Development," See also Edward Boorstein, *The Economic Transformation of Cuba* (New York: Monthly Review Press, 1968).

be used (the owner of a *hacienda,* which will shortly be described). The balance of the rural population, disregarding the small number of medium-sized land-holders, constitutes the peasantry.

There is no commonly accepted definition of the term "peasant." It appears to vary according to the orientation of the person using the term, in that an anthropologist will define it one way, an economist another, and a social critic still another. One definition, for example, says that a peasant is an agricultural producer in effective control of land who carries on agriculture as a means of livelihood, not as a business for profit.[8] Or, "peasant" has been defined as a quality that a certain group or individual may possess to a greater or lesser extent.[9]

There probably can be no "real" definition of the term—in the sense of being commonly accepted—and for purposes here "peasant" is defined operationally as including all the rural small-holders, Indian and *mestizo* alike, as well as all the *hacienda* resident workers and seasonal employees, whether or not these own or farm an individual plot of land. This broad definition is made necessary by the overlap created by small-holders eking out their subsistence through work on *haciendas,* and by the general inability to determine primary, secondary, and tertiary economic activities pursued by the low-income rural populace.

The *hacienda* (in Brazil, *fazenda*) took its present form in the 17th and 18th centuries under Spanish colonial rule. It is very often referred to as a "feudal" system, but as Richard Adams has correctly pointed out, this is a misnomer, because the owners did not form societies at war with one another. Rather, they formed part of a national and international elite whose position in society depended upon the relative isolation of their enterprises.[10]

It is the *hacienda* that dominates the social, economic, and political life of all rural Latin America. Given this great importance, it is, in one way, rather surprising that so little has been written about it. It has been suggested that Latin American intellectuals apparently fail to see it because it is so ubiquitous, and also because they themselves are largely the products of it.[11] On the other hand, it is not the type of institution that easily lends

[8] See Charles Wagley, "The Peasant," in John J. Johnson (ed.), *Continuity and Change in Latin America* (Stanford, Calif.: Stanford University Press, 1967).

[9] See the introductory chapter by Henry A. Landsberger in Henry A. Landsberger (ed.), *Latin American Peasant Movements* (Ithaca, N.Y.: Cornell University Press, 1969).

[10] Richard N. Adams, *The Second Sowing: Power and Secondary Development in Latin America* (San Francisco: Chandler, 1967), p. 97.

[11] See Frank Tannenbaum, "The Hacienda," in John D. Martz (ed.), *The Dynamics of Change in Latin American Politics* (Englewood Cliffs, N.J.: Prentice-Hall, 1965).

itself to investigation by social scientists, whether these be Latin American or foreign. Social scientists can easily enough descend on a peasant village and, with sufficient regard for local feelings and customs, they can eventually win some degree of social acceptance. However, a social scientist could visit a *hacienda* only on the sufferance of the owner and his top administrators, a situation unlikely to occur often given the elitist nature of *hacendado* society. For that matter, the *hacienda* itself can continue to survive only through its isolation and discouragement of all outside influences.

As Frank Tannenbaum has noted in one of the few objective studies of the *hacienda*,[12] it is not just an agricultural property owned by an individual, but is also a society managed under private auspices, a society controlling the lives of those attached to it from the cradle to the grave. That is, it is more than an economic enterprise, it is a way of life. The people permanently attached to it are as often as not born on its lands, and know very little about the rest of the country, much less of the world. The *hacienda* is generally inherited, so there is no investment in it and no "normal" profit motive in its operation. Its basic aim is to achieve economic self-sufficiency with enough extra production to assure the owner of a life of luxury.

While the aim of self-sufficiency is important, one can perhaps more meaningfully regard the *hacienda* as a system of power ensuring economic gain for the holder of that power.[13] This power is virtually absolute, and the *hacendado*'s decisions are orders to be obeyed. The success of the entire system depends on a surplus of labor, which detracts from any potential ability of the peasants to defy those orders. Furthermore, the *hacienda* worker is maintained at a subsistence level by a wide variety of devices institutionalized through time. As one study has rather bitterly noted, these measures show greater ingenuity in depriving the peasant of material gain than do any measures to put the *hacienda*'s physical resources to more productive use.[14]

The peasants who work on the *hacienda* can conveniently be divided into two types—those who live on the *hacienda* all year and perhaps all their lives, and those who are hired seasonally. The seasonal workers should

---

[12] Ibid.

[13] The "system of power" concept has been suggested by Ernest Feder in an excellent article on the socioeconomic structure of the *hacienda*, "Societal Opposition to Peasant Movements and its Effects on Farm People in Latin America," in Landsberger (ed.), *Latin American Peasant Movements*. For another excellent article in a similar vein see Solon L. Barraclough and Arthur L. Domike, "Agrarian Structure in Seven Latin American Countries," in *Land Economics*, Vol. 42, No. 4, November 1960.

[14] Landsberger, *Latin American Peasant Movements*.

be further divided into those who have no land and who therefore must depend ultimately on the *hacienda* for their continued existence, and those who have some land but who add to their income through work for the *hacienda*.

Although the relationship between the resident peasant and the *hacendado* varies from country to country, some common patterns do exist. One such pattern is for the peasant, in return for a small plot of ground which he tills for himself in accordance with any rules set by the *hacendado* (the type of crop and so forth), to work a certain number of days per week or per year for the *hacendado* on the latter's own crops. The number of days that the peasant works for the *hacendado* varies, but for Latin America as a whole it can be estimated as somewhere between 100 and 200 days per year.[15] That is, in return for the use of a very small plot of land whose production he ultimately controls and which will allow the peasant bare subsistence, the *hacendado* gains so many days of work per week or per year from the peasant. There may be a small wage involved. If there is, it is seldom paid in cash, but rather in kind—and it will probably be in tokens or scrip redeemable at the *hacienda*'s store. Another common pattern is essentially a share-cropping arrangement. The actual arrangement will depend in each case on agreement between peasant and *hacendado,* but in any case the *hacendado* will ultimately determine what is to be produced, how much is to be produced, and what land will be used for its production. The *hacendado* may supply such things as seeds, or the peasant may be required to buy these himself—probably from the *hacienda*'s store. Whichever of these two basic patterns is followed, the members of the peasant's family will generally also be required to put in a certain amount of days working for the *hacendado*. This may be field work necessitated by the inability of the peasant to live up to the terms of a particular arrangement, or the women may be required to serve a certain number of days as maids in the "big house," or in the *hacendado*'s town house, or for members of his family. Children may be required to help with other aspects of farm life, such as stock-tending or weeding garden patches.

Whether the *hacienda* depends on occasional labor from surrounding villages, on resident workers, or on tenants, perhaps the best means for keeping the peasants submissive is job uncertainty. This in turn depends on a large labor surplus. If the surplus does not already exist, or if it begins to be insufficient for exploitation to continue, land can be under-utilized to maintain the imbalance. In fact, there is a tradition of under-utilization of *hacienda* lands throughout Latin America, and Feder states that the large estates in the seven Latin American countries examined in his study have

---

[15] Three days per week is a frequent pattern. See John P. Powelson, *Latin America: Today's Economic and Social Revolution* (New York: McGraw-Hill, 1964), p. 39.

consistently the lowest proportion of land in intensive use. He suggests that the under-utilization of land can be estimated roughly in terms of the number of additional workers who could find employment on *haciendas* if the latter's lands were efficiently utilized. On the basis of only six countries —Argentina, Brazil, Chile, Colombia, Ecuador, and Guatemala—he finds there is a deficit of approximately 34,500,000 potentially employable workers, rather than the huge surplus that actually exists under the present use of the land. Furthermore, whereas earlier it was actually necessary to force a peasant community onto marginal lands so that its members would be available for seasonal labor, this is today unnecessary due to the sheer increased size of the rural labor force which makes seasonal labor readily available.[16]

Another ubiquitous device for maintaining peasants at a subsistence and therefore subservient level is the practice of debt bondage, handled largely through the "company store." A study of Peruvian coastal *haciendas,* for example, describes the practice locally known as *engancho* (from the verb "to hook") whereby recruiters drive trucks to Indian mountain villages, woo the Indians with promises of a good life for only little work, and return with the trucks loaded with recruits. Immediately upon arrival the Indians are encouraged to buy on credit at the *hacienda*'s store, and, once they are in debt, the *enganchados* (the "hooked ones") cannot leave the *hacienda* until the debt is paid. Needless to say, perhaps, further encouragement to buy will ensure that the debt is never fully paid. Often the peasants are encouraged—and there are cases reported where they are required—to spend much of their meager earnings on alcohol, starting a vicious cycle from which they can never escape. Actually, so widespread is the system of debt bondage, and so necessary is it to the *hacienda's* operation, that, legally or otherwise, the peasant's sons are trapped into it through their inheritance of their father's debt.

A private police force to ensure compliance with the *hacendado*'s wishes is not uncommon. For example, the use of strong-arm men (*capangas*) is widespread on the northeastern sugar plantations of Brazil, where force ranges from intimidation through terrorization to outright murder to set an example. And since the *hacendado* is the dominant force in his area, he can pretty well count, if and when necessary, on the full cooperation of the local police and local military in enforcing his regulations.

Many other means exist to control the peasant. He is usually not allowed to plant permanent crops, as this would interfere with the rule of uncertainty. He generally cannot produce cash crops or make improvements on his land. Arrangements between peasant and *hacendado* will always shift if they prove advantageous for the peasant. High fees may be charged for

[16] Adams, *The Second Sowing,* p. 92.

the use of a shanty, or the peasant may have to pay for use of the roads or paths. He may have to pay exhorbitant rates to have his corn ground at the *hacienda*'s mill, or he may have to work extra days for the *hacendado* to pay for alleged violations of *hacienda* rules.

As Feder notes, the *hacendado* makes his greatest profit not from his land, but from his workers, because they, in addition to being his labor force, are his borrowers, buyers, sellers, and tenants.[17] And there is no recourse from this system for the peasant once he is caught up in it, because even in the more advanced agricultural regions of Latin America the "right" of the *hacendado* to act in the capacity of jury, judge, and law enforcement agent is still usually taken for granted.

Before concluding this description of the hacienda, it should be noted that there are today in Latin America a growing number of "new-style" *haciendas,* sometimes referred to as "factories in the field." This modernized plantation, growing in numbers in, for example, the sugar areas of Brazil, Venezuela, and the Caribbean, is essentially corporate in nature. Its objective is profit, and it is generally run along "rational" lines by professional administrators. This type of *hacienda* also tends to be much more impersonal to the worker, similar to a typical urban corporation.[18] However, it should not be assumed that this type of operation has really changed that much for the peasant in material terms. As one study has remarked, even on the new *hacienda* the relationship between rural mass and rural elite, evolved from centuries of tradition, proves durable even in the most modernized sectors of agriculture.[19]

While the large estate accounts for most of the land in Latin America, many thousands of tiny villages and millions of small holdings do exist. The land tenure structure of the villages may be communal, as in the older Indian tradition, or it may reflect every variation lying between collective and individual ownership of plots. The village may lie next to a *hacienda,* but on the whole the pattern is for the *hacienda* to lie in the relatively rich valley and the village and its lands to lie on the more remote, and agriculturally poorer, mountainsides.[20]

The communal form of land ownership, largely limited to that part of the population that can still quite readily be described as "Indian,"

[17] See also Barraclough and Domike, "Agrarian Structure."

[18] See Adams, *The Second Sowing,* pp. 98–99, for a concise account of this modernized type of *hacienda.*

[19] See the article by John Duncan Powell, "Agrarian Reform or Agrarian Revolution in Venezuela?" in Arpad Von Lazar and Robert P. Kaufman (eds.), *Reform and Revolution: Readings in Latin American Politics* (Boston: Allyn & Bacon, 1969).

[20] Tannenbaum, "The Hacienda."

dates back to the times of the Aztec, Mayan, and Incan empires, since all of these followed some form of communal land tenure. It is based on another ancient institution, the extended family, and several families together claim a specific land area. The lands in this area are by custom (and today sometimes by law) nontransferable except to other members of the group. Many communities have actually subdivided and individualized their land holdings, but in most there remains a periodic reallocation of land among the members of the community.[21]

The Mexican *ejido,* whose members are generally *mestizo* rather than Indian, is today the major example of how a national government has attempted to combine farming traditions with modern economic and political requirements. The *ejido* has undoubtedly had considerable impact on the reorganization of farming in such countries as Cuba, Venezuela, and Bolivia—particularly when resettlement of peasants is involved.

The term *ejido* is itself an old Spanish term designating land on the outskirts of the Iberian village that was used in a communal fashion for such purposes as wool-gathering and pasturage, and over the years in Mexico it came to designate the typical Indian communal properties. According to the census there were 18,000 *ejidos* in Mexico in 1960, comprising an area of 45,000,000 hectares. The number of *ejidatarios* (*ejido* members) is estimated at somewhere between 2,225,000 and 2,300,000. Including their families, this means that one-third of the total Mexican population depend directly on the *ejido* for their daily life. The basic regulations which govern the *ejidos* and their members are contained in the Agrarian Code of 1942, as subsequently amended, and the Code itself is based on Article 27 of the Constitution of 1917.

Ejido lands cannot be sold, mortgaged, or leased. The *ejido* can lose its lands only under very specific and limited circumstances. An *ejidatario* may be deprived of his right to a parcel whenever he ceases to work it for two consecutive years. He may, in such circumstances, designate the transfer of his right to a parcel to a person economically dependent on him, and if he fails to do this the right will revert to his closest descendant or to the village itself for reallocation.

There are two types of *ejidos,* the one worked collectively and the other worked individually. In either case, the type is chosen by the *ejidatarios* themselves. On the collective *ejido* the land is worked and owned jointly by all members, all capital is under collective management, production is directed by the *ejido* administration and by elected work foremen, and all profits are distributed among members. On the whole, however, while there are some noteworthy exceptions to the rule, the collective *ejido* has not been successful either administratively or economically. This is

[21] See the article by Thomas Carroll, "The Land Reform Issue in Latin America," in Robert D. Tomasek (ed.), *Latin American Politics: 24 Studies of the Contemporary Scene* (Garden City, N.Y.: Doubleday, 1966).

probably due to the idea of total collective action which, however adaptable it may appear to be to communal holdings, is essentially foreign to the older traditions that include a strong element of individuality. In 1960 there were only 900 collective *ejidos* remaining in operation.

The individual or parcelized *ejido* is simply one in which the farming land has been allotted in individual parcels by the agrarian authorities. The plots are worked as family land and are handed down to heirs. Theoretically, the *ejidatario* does not permanently cultivate the same plot year after year, as lots are supposed to be cast annually to decide who will get which parcel of cropland (meadows, lakes, woodlands, and so forth, are used in common). In practice, the trend today on these *ejidos,* as in communal lands throughout Latin America, is toward more or less permanent "ownership" of a given plot of land.

While the agricultural techniques of the *hacienda* are generally fairly primitive, those of the small-holders, whether communal or "free" small-holders, are usually much worse. It tends strongly to remain a hoe-culture, whose motive power is human hands. That is, there is a great absence of work animals, and agriculture depends on hand tools which themselves are very primitive. When work animals are owned, more often than not they will be found pulling a crude, homemade wooden plow. In many of the remoter regions of Latin America the most primitive agricultural techniques of all are pursued. These include such things as "gathering"— for example, honey, rubber, or fiber—as well as "slash-and-burn" agriculture. The latter is the practice of slashing or burning the native vegetation from an area, planting a crop for a couple of years, and then moving on to another area when the original area has been destroyed by erosion. That this technique has totally destroyed the productive capacity of vast areas of Latin America is, of course, of no concern to the nomadic, primitive agriculturalist engaged in it.

This system of very small plots—generally termed *"minifundismo"* and the peasants involved in it *"minifundistas"*—has as its immediate goal (and in practice, its ultimate achievement) the bare living, the subsistence, of the peasants. Actually, this agriculture of poverty has endured for so long that it is not at all uncommon to find such farmers unwilling to raise cash crops even when these would better them economically. That is, there appears to be a marked tendency, culturally compelled, to raise such subsistence crops as maize, in order to achieve traditional food security, rather than to raise crops for sale which could in turn buy more maize than could be raised by the farmer himself. On the other hand, it has also been suggested that this attitude is largely the result of the small acreage available to the peasant, and that the main determinant of subsistence-versus-cash crops is the availability of suitable land.[22]

[22] See Michael Belshaw, *A Village Economy* (New York: Columbia University Press, 1967), p. 37.

In concluding this summary of *minifundismo* in Latin America, it should be noted that, in purely economic terms, it is harmful. While it allows the peasant to live, and while he could survive no other way, this type of agriculture, oriented toward the subsistence of the peasant with nothing left over for marketing, means that foodstuffs often have to be imported into countries with predominantly agricultural populations. As bad as the *hacienda* is economically, it does produce surpluses for the rapidly growing urban centers, while the subsistence farm by definition contributes nothing. This is why economists will argue for land consolidation as much as they will argue for land redistribution. Both the *latifundio* and the *minifundio* are agriculturally primitive, and there appears to be growing awareness among other sectors of the societies that industrialization cannot be rationally pursued without a corresponding development in the agricultural sector.

DESIRES

When asking the question "What do the rural people of Latin America want in terms of socioeconomic change?" it is easy to arrive at the simple conclusion that the large landowners want no change, and that the peasants want some sort of reform of the existing structure of land tenure throughout the area. This is the obvious conclusion given the extremes of richness and poverty that exist in the countrysides.

This answer gains additional credence from the fact that the "land question" is perhaps the dominant issue in most of Latin America today. All major political groups today espouse, either explicitly and in detail or vaguely, some notion of "agrarian reform." Every more-or-less popularly elected regime claims it is somehow attempting to safeguard the peasants' interests, and even the various dictatorial regimes insist that they are concerned with the plight of the vast majority of rural people. This is natural enough, since any regime, whether sincerely or cynically, is bound to pay at least lip service to such a huge section of the society as that constituted by the rural populace in every country in Latin America. Furthermore, foreign observers have in the last couple of decades commented so often and so disparagingly on the existing land tenure structure in each country that any regime attempting to put a good face on itself for the world to see —and for various reasons each country is concerned about its international image—will have to insist that it is interested in alleviating the situation.

The problem with "agrarian reform," or "land reform," or "agricultural reform" as it is variously called, is that it has very different meanings attached to it, depending on the person using the term and what he thinks the solution should be. In gross terms, for example, is every peasant to receive a plot of land of his own to till, regardless of the economic consequences this solution may have for the rest of the country? This is the solution sponsored by a good many reformers and intellectuals in Latin America who insist that the spiritual dignity the peasant will achieve as a result of possessing his own small plot far outweighs material losses for the rest of the society, which in any event is too materialistically oriented. Or, should the large estates be broken up to make parcels of an optimum size, which would allow for the introduction of modern agricultural techniques and technology, and which would provide work and sustenance for the peasants at the expense of large-scale land redistribution programs? This is a solution often proposed by dispassionate, rationally-oriented economists, both Latin American and foreign. Or should the land be redistributed so as to guarantee every peasant a family-sized farm, capable of being worked by the farmer with the aid of modern equipment? This is often proposed as a solution by North American critics of the current structure of Latin American land tenure.

The questions do not end here. Should, for example, the *minifundio* system be abandoned—which would involve force—so as to consolidate the small, economically unviable parcels into farms of sufficient size as to allow modernization of agriculture and the production of surpluses for the Latin American economies now spending their foreign exchange for foodstuffs rather than for capitalizing needed urban industry? Should the alleviation of rural poverty be accomplished by resettlement of over-populated areas and the colonization of virgin lands? Should the large estates be taken by force, or should they be bought peacefully by the government at good prices? If land is redistributed, should it be privately or collectively owned and, whatever the case, should it be privately or collectively worked? This is by no means intended as an exhaustive list of questions, but rather as an attempt to provide some idea of the complexities involved in the whole issue of agrarian reform in Latin America.

One of the most comprehensive—if unrealistic—examples of programs for agrarian reform was provided a decade ago in the Charter of Punta del Este, commonly known as the Alliance for Progress. In addition to provisions concerning fair and adequate taxation of large incomes and real estate, all the governments of Latin America, except Cuba, pledged themselves to encourage, in accordance with the characteristics of each country, programs of comprehensive agrarian reform leading to the effective transformation, where required, of unjust structures and systems of land tenure. With the help of timely and adequate credit, technical assistance, and facilities for marketing and distribution of products, the land was to become for the man who worked it the basis of his economic stability, the foundation of his increasing welfare, and the guarantee of his freedom and personal dignity.

However, while such questions and programs are certainly relevant in the abstract to the rural situation in Latin America, they do not necessarily reflect what the peasant himself is concerned with in terms of immediate or even ultimate desires. That is, the demands are the demands of agrarian reformers of various stripes who may not be, and usually are not, peasants themselves. Several studies of peasant organizations in Latin America have recently pointed out the need to distinguish between peasant desires and the desires of peasants as voiced by leaders. One study, for example, points out that four different types of peasant organizations can usefully be distinguished in Latin America, and that while three of these appear genuinely concerned with peasant desires, the fourth organziation is created by politicians and/or landowners themselves engaged in land speculation or political action.[23] In this case, peasants are the tools of the leaders and the flow of demands from the leader(s) downward is much more important than any flow of demands upward from the peasants.

Communist-organized peasant groups offer good examples of this type, although they are far from being the only ones who cynically attempt to manipulate the peasants for their own political purposes. (It has been suggested that Marxist intellectuals in general see agrarian reform as increased production rather than the break up of the *haciendas,* as the latter are regarded as a good basis for state-farms once the Marxists are in power.)[24] A case in point occurred in Mexico in the early 1960's with the formation of the Independent Peasant Central (Central Campesino Independiente, or CCI). The constituent congress, dominated by Communists, resolved that the CCI would fight to obtain the following: a return to observance of both the letter and spirit of the Constitution; expropriation of all *latifundios;* restitution to Indians and *ejidos* of all lands fraudulently taken from them; indemnification from the United States for the salinity of the Mexicali Valley; cheap water and credit for the peasants; diversification of crops; animal husbandry on the *ejidos;* guaranteed prices for farm products; nationalization of cotton gins, and of rice, olive, sugar, and henequen mills; extension of social security, medicine, education, potable water, and electricity to the countryside; and so forth. While these objectives were quite in keeping with a peasant organization seeking thoroughgoing agrarian reform, other provisions, as well as all subsequent action of CCI leaders, show the extent to which the peasants were tools of the Mexican Communist Party. Examples of some of these other provisions were: liberty for all political prisoners; denunciation of the cold war and of the United States for creating it; positive aid to the policy of peaceful coexistence; denunciation of the American policy toward Cuba; withdrawal of Mexico from such bellicose pacts as the Treaty of Rio de Janeiro; and so forth. It would be ridiculous to assume that the typical peasant, with

[23] Neale J. Pearson, "Latin American Peasant Pressure Groups and the Modernization Process," in *Journal of International Affairs,* Vol. 20, No. 2, 1966.

[24] See the introductory essay by T. Lynn Smith in T. Lynn Smith (ed.), *Agrarian Reform in Latin America* (New York: Knopf, 1965).

whom the CCI said it was concerned, understood in the least what these typically Communist political proposals were all about. For that matter, even many of the agrarian proposals themselves were probably quite irrelevant to the peasants. In short, even the basic program of the CCI indicated that the leaders were intent on manipulating the peasants for their own political ends, and this became absolutely clear when a few months after its creation the CCI joined with the Mexican Communist Party to form the abortive People's Electoral Front to participate in the 1964 elections.

Another typical example of demands expressed cynically in the name of the peasants was the organization by Francisco Julião in the early 1960's of peasant leagues in the state of Pernambuco in Brazil's Northeast. Julião, himself an owner of a large plantation, ostensibly aspired to lead the peasants concerned in a land redistribution program (although he took pains to ensure that organizational activities were far removed from the area of his own plantation). Actually, he was pursuing a political career, using this particular issue and his peasant organization to help him obtain national prominence and an "in" into the inner circle. His organizational activities were limited to the politically conscious, already relatively organized workers in the coastal sugar belt. For that matter, there is little evidence that the peasants involved actually wanted the land redistributed—rather, they essentially interested only in higher wages from the affluent plantations.[25] It is interesting to note that, probably because of Julião's apparent success through this method, between 1962 and 1964 representatives of the Brazilian Communist Party (Moscow oriented), the Communist Party of Brazil (Peking oriented), the Leninist Vanguard (Trotskyite), the administration of the state's governor, Migual Arraes, and the administration of President Joâo Goulart, were all competing to organize Pernambuco's peasants.[26] Throughout the entire competition to organize the peasants, the leadership never came from the peasants themselves. That is, the leaders and organizers, including Julião, were almost exclusively representatives of urban-centered interests and politics, even when agricultural products and landholding were the issues.[27]

While the desires of the relatively few urban-oriented peasants are open to question, all available literature suggests that the peasant typically does want land. The small-holder wants more land to add to his "starvation parcel." The peasant resident on the *hacienda*, like the landless sea-

[25] See the article by Anthony Leeds in Joseph Maier and Richard W. Weatherhead (eds.), *Politics of Change in Latin America* (New York: Praeger, 1966).

[26] See the article by Cynthia N. Hewitt, "Brazil: The Peasant Movement of Pernambuco, 1961–1964," in Landsberger (ed.), *Latin American Peasant Movements.*

[27] See the article by Leeds in Maier and Weatherhead (eds.), *Politics of Change in Latin America.*

sonal worker and the squatter, wants land of his own that he will have assurance of retaining.

While there is some literature explicitly dealing with the peasant's attachment to land, most of it is anthropological in nature; the attachment is perhaps best seen by inference. When he is aroused to violence the peasant will typically seize a piece of land for himself. This is seen, for example, in the case of the *paracaidistas* (squatters) in rural Mexico. Organizers from the cities will arouse peasants and incite them to move onto local (illegal) *haciendas*. While the government occasionally uses force to eject these squatters, it will often, depending on the local situation, take the steam from the movement by making some concessions in land to a sufficient number of peasants. No matter how small the amount of land thus redistributed, whether in the form of *ejido* or free-hold, the peasants generally appear content—until other agitators move into the area.

This is also what appears to have happened in the Cochabamba region of Bolivia, scene of much peasant unrest and organization prior to the revolution of 1952. The agrarian reform legislation that came out of this revolution was intended to divide the land among the landless, to protect medium-sized holdings efficiently farmed, and to provide technical assistance to aid farmers in raising production levels. Instead, the peasants simply took the land by force and divided it among themselves before the formal governmental apparatus was organized to administer the reform. Paying no attention to such considerations as size and efficiency of the estates they seized, nor to the size and efficiency of the parcels they created, they in effect replaced a *hacienda* system with a *minifundio* system. While today resettlement of much of the population of this area is necessary in any objective terms because of population density, it is impossible because of the terms in which the peasant sees the situation. He has his own plot of land, and he is apparently not going to give it up for any reason. For him, the "revolution" is over.[28] As one writer has put it, although still abysmally poor—not only by North American but by world standards—the life of Bolivia's peasant is much better than it was before the revolution;[29] that is, he now has an economically unviable parcel of land of his own. For that matter, the peasants in one region of Bolivia that has been studied actually have access to less agricultural land than they did before the revolution under the *hacienda* system, due to consolidation of plots into contiguous parcels in a region of considerable ecological variation.

[28] Richard W. Patch, *Bolivia Today*. American Universities Field Staff Reports: West Coast South American Series, Vol. 8, No. 4.

[29] See the article by Dwight B. Heath, "Bolivia: Peasant Syndicates among the Aymara of the Yungos—A View from the Grass Roots," in Landsberger (ed.), *Latin American Peasant Movements*.

The peasants' desire for land of their own can similarly be inferred from the results of a peasant "rebellion" in the valley of Convención, Peru, in the early 1960's. There, because of peasant unrest, the government promised to the peasants legal title of the small parcels they had been cultivating under the *hacienda* system. The peasants would pay the government for the parcels, and the government would pay the *hacendados*. As a study of this movement reports, from a traditional *hacienda* tenure pattern the entire valley was transformed into a new system of small landowners— again, a *minifundio* system was created.[30] A small parcel of land was all each peasant received, and he technically even had to pay for it, but he had his own land and the unrest ended.

Actually, as a recent study of Guatemalan peasants points out, the small-land-holder's parcel is really his only physical and psychological security. It ensures his family against starvation and against costs of illness and death. It also provides some form of security in old age as well as being the only substantive possession he can leave to his children. As a result, the shortage of land available to him not only represents an inability to provide for his family but also robs that family of any real security.[31]

On the other hand, it should not automatically be assumed that all *hacienda* peasants, or even the majority of them, want a life other than the one they have. Some obviously do, as evidenced by the occasional violent seizures of *haciendas* by peasants; but, at least until further evidence is available, it would be a ridiculous ethnocentric conclusion for us to insist that most feel this way. In other words, while alienation from the *hacienda* system is evident to some extent, that system is probably quite meaningful to many if not most *hacienda* peasants.

Despite "liberal" condemnation of the *hacienda,* despite the hundreds of English and Spanish-language polemics written against it and championing the peasants, and despite the its repugnance to "western, democratic" traditions, the fact remains that the *hacienda* system is a way of life in most of rural Latin America. The peasant accepts it as such, as, for example, most middle-class Americans accept capitalism, and there is no evidence that the bulk of the peasant populace wants something else. Some of the writers most in sympathy with the peasant concede that he knows no other way of life and as a result is scarcely capable of aspiring to one.

A recent study of rural communities in Peru, for example, states that the masses of the people, Indian and *mestizo* alike, are totally accustomed to being ruled by a small and dominant minority, and that the monopoliza-

---

[30] See the article by Wesley W. Craig, Jr., "Peru: The Peasant Movement of La Convencion," in Landsberger (ed.), *Latin American Peasant Movements.*

[31] Oscar Horst and Roland H. Ebel, "Land and Politics in Rural Guatemala," in Paulson, *The Community in Latin America.*

tion of power characteristic of the *hacendado*-peasant relationship has tended to forestall and discourage the peasants from even thinking about change.[32] Another study points out that the management of a huge American-owned *hacienda* in coastal Peru would like to remove itself from its paternal role, and allow the community to govern itself to a greater extent. The workers, however, do not want this, because the paternalistic role of the *hacendado* means something to them, while the benefits of the proposed new way do not.[33]

Powelson suggests that it is difficult to believe that the *hacienda* peasant would not have thrown off the rule of the *hacienda* if, after centuries of this way of life, he had really desired to do so. Most Indians, he says, and particularly the Incas, lived in paternalistic communal societies long before the Spaniard arrived, and the *hacendado* merely replaced the Inca and other rulers. Furthermore, the *hacendado* is not entirely or even necessarily an object of hatred, because he can provide comfort in time of illness or death, food when there is none, and spiritual guidance when it is needed. He concludes that while only the peasant can really say whether the peasant's lot is bearable, he himself suspects that it is.[34] It has also been suggested that the peasants resident on the *hacienda* consider themselves as better off than the rural seasonal laborer or landless peasant migrant who has neither the protection of the law nor of the *hacendado*.[35]

DEMANDS

This leads quite naturally to our second question: "What do the landowners and peasants demand from the political system?" It appears that the landowners demand much, but the demands of the peasants are not at all so clear. Actually, it is because of the peasants, more than any other socio-economic category in Latin America, that this particular question must be asked. Obviously, if the peasants aspire to nothing other than what they have, they will not make demands on the political system; less obviously, even when they do want something, they may be unaware of the political system as a means to pursue it.

[32] See the article by Allan R. Holmberg, "Changing Community Attitudes and Values in Peru: A Case Study in Guided Change," in Richard N. Adams et al., *Social Change in Latin America Today* (New York: Harper & Row, 1960).

[33] Richard W. Patch, *The Role of a Coastal Hacienda in the Hispanization of Andean Indians*. American Universities Field Staff Letter, March 15, 1959 (R.W.P.-2-'59).

[34] Powelson, *Latin America: Today's Economic and Social Revolution,* p. 42.

[35] Adams, *The Second Sowing,* p. 94.

In every country in Latin America with the exception of Cuba and perhaps Mexico, the *hacendado* is a major if not the *dominant* political actor. From the political system he demands that he and his peasants be left alone. The *hacienda,* as a socio-economic system or way of life, depends upon more or less total isolation from any extraneous influence or interference. This does not imply that groups of *hacendados* in any given country are not occasionally or even often at odds with one another over specific governmental policies—for example, tariff policies. However, ultimately all must be and are united on the issue of socioeconomic change in the countryside. They do not want it nor can they tolerate it; their very existence depends totally on maintaining the status quo.

The previous discussion of peasant desires should indicate that while some are aware of the potential efficacy of political action, the vast majority probably are essentially apolitical. It is almost entirely in those areas where agriculture has been to some extent modernized that the peasants are really politically active. That is, it is in those areas where, for one reason or another, the traditional social structure of the *hacienda* has already broken down that the peasants appear sufficiently motivated to make demands on the political system for what they want in terms of socioeconomic change. This is what Leeds, in his study of Julião, means when he states that the peasant leagues in Pernambuco are limited to the coastal portions of the Northeast—to the industrially organized coastal sugar belt. And, as he points out, the peasants there do not really appear to want the land redistributed, but rather want a greater share in the proceeds from production —similar to the typical demand of the urban laborer. These, Leeds insists, are fundamentally urban and politico-economic ends, to be achieved by political means; they are characteristic of societies organized in basically industrial-urban rather than rural patterns. Every study of Brazil's Northeast and its huge poverty-stricken peasant population finds that the vast majority of the peasants are apolitical; they do not see the political system or the government as something that potentially could or would listen to, and perhaps fulfill, their demands.

Other areas of Latin America illustrate this same phenomenon. A study of Guatemalan Indians, for example, showed that while many of them migrated seasonally to the Guatemalan Pacific coast for employment on plantations and thus were at least aware that something besides their own area existed, they nevertheless did not see the government in any light other than something to be mistrusted and feared. In the area studied, both Indians and *mestizos* showed their awareness of the government to the extent that they favored defenders of the status quo such as Presidents Armas and Ydigoras, and disapproved of Presidents Arévalo and Arbenz, who advocated change. Arbenz, for example, was disliked not only for his Communist reputation, but because of his administration's policy of intervening in local affairs in the name of social equality and justice. Communism itself was greatly feared, not on ideological grounds of which they knew very little, but because it promoted land reform. Neither Indians nor *mestizos* wanted the government to interfere in any way with the existing local *minifundio* system of land tenure, as each individual feared he would somehow lose the land he had. The study concludes that the peasants, including even the more articulate ones, have virtually no idea of how to go about electing one of their own number to political office or of giving effective support to persons friendly to their interests. They only want to be left alone, and avoid any political program, however beneficial it may abstractly appear to be, which would involve them in any form of social conflict or which would in any way limit their ability to control personally their own humble affairs.[36]

Another study of Guatemalan Indians states that Guatemala City is important to the community only insofar as it offers services instrumental in preserving the traditional Indian ways. The same study points out that this also was found to be true of a Peruvian Andean village, where wage labor allows the people to preserve their traditional institutions and values and helps them remain isolated from the national society. The study concludes that as long as Latin American peasant Indians can retain control of their miniscule plots in one way or another, and particularly if they do receive additional land as a result of reformist agitation, they will resist any change.[37] If this is the case, they will ask nothing of the political system except that it leave them alone.

Mestizo peasants, while more aware of and more likely to identify with the values of the national society, are essentially just as apathetic about government as are the Indian peasants. Neither appear to feel that the government, either national or local, can or will help him solve his problems, nor does he feel he can do anything about this situation.[38] In short, as Richard Adams has suggested, the problems of the community that demand solution are defined in terms of the community and its members, and not only will the problems be set but the solutions will be shaped by the culture and experience of the community.[39] If the culture and experiences of either the remote peasant villages or the even more isolated *hacienda* workers are negative toward the political system or do not include the political system, the peasants can scarcely be expected to act within the system in solving any problems they may recognize.

---

[36] Horst and Ebel, "Land and Politics in Rural Guatemala."

[37] Wagley, "The Peasant."

[38] Horst and Ebel, "Land and Politics in Rural Guatemala."

[39] Richard N. Adams, *A Community in the Andes: Problems and Progress in Muquiyauyo* (Seattle: University of Washington Press, 1959). pp. 50, 202.

The point just mentioned concerning the receipt of land leading to political apathy is particularly interesting in that it has great relevance to continued peasant political activity when such activity does occur. If peasant violence in Latin America can be viewed, at least for purposes of discussion, as political activity designed to force concessions from the political system, then the political activity tends to end once the system has granted a minimal amount of land to the peasants concerned. That is, while many peasant movements in Latin America have been described, and while great hope is usually placed by the author on the movement as an initial step in achieving socio-economic equality for the peasants, this hope is essentially in vain, at least for the present and the foreseeable future. As noted in the examples given above, once the peasant has received his small plot of ground he has achieved his goal and is once more apolitical.

This is probably the primary reason why Mexico, for example, has been so economically and politically stable for the last three to four decades. In the early 1920's a classic study of Mexican land tenure suggested that if the peasants remained unattached they would probably become to the countryside what the slum dwellers of Mexico's large cities were to those urban centers—a plague and a peril to society. Mexico's safety, therefore, depended in very large measure upon the success of the government in keeping the peasant on the land.[40] This, in essence, in what the Mexican government has done over the years. It has redistributed just enough land to keep down rebellions, and when peasant pressure builds up in a particular area (as it did, for example, in the early 1960's in Sonora), the government redistributes just enough land to relieve the pressure. While this device has built-in limitations, in terms of the land available for redistribution, it has allowed the government to pursue urban-industrial policies and even to mechanize much of the agricultural sector of the economy. It appears that this is also what the much-vaunted, "revolutionary" MNR did in Bolivia, and there is more and more evidence throughout Latin America that this tactic has been recognized by the governments as being a quite inexpensive and efficacious method of removing the peasants from political activity.

Finally, while peasant violence in Latin America has been viewed here as a form of political activity, this is not necessarily entirely or always true. A recent study of rural violence in Colombia indicates that perhaps a good deal of it is not "political" in any meaningful sense of that term. Since 1948, *la violencia*, as it is commonly called, has resulted in the death of 200,000 people in rural areas, and the study suggests that much of this might be the result of "psychopathic banditry." The peasant has become alienated from the society he has always known—the *hacienda* society—

---

[40] George M. McBride, *The Land Systems of Mexico* (New York: American Geographical Society, 1923), p. 171.

and he now has no norms, standards, customs, and in general no way of life to guide him. He is anomic in the fullest sense of that term.[41]

If this is true in Colombia, and if it is true to any extent in any other Latin American country, then the peasants engaged in violence under these circumstances cannot be considered to be acting politically. While the anomie may be the result of conflict between old and new ways, the peasant is actually rejecting the new as well as the old if he remains anomic. That is, he will be rejecting the political system as well as the *hacienda* system, so his activities cannot be construed as being the expression of demands on the political system.

This entire topic needs to be researched much further before we will be able to say much concretely about it. It is mentioned here only as a warning to the student of Latin American politics that the easy assumption about peasant violence being a form of demand on the political system, or a demonstration of a political resource in the political process, may be much too simplistic.

SYSTEM RESPONSE

The answer to the final question we are asking, "What do the peasants and the large landowners receive from the political system?" should be obvious from the entire foregoing discussion. In verbal or symbolic terms the peasant receives a great deal and the *hacendado* nothing. In material terms, however, the peasant, who is generally outside the political system, receives very little if anything from it. On the other hand, the *hacendado,* who is a major actor and force within the system, continues to receive his basic demand—retention of the status quo.

While peasants occasionally do receive land and other related material benefits, one has only to look at the distribution of land ownership in Latin America to realize that in none of the countries has land redistribution proceeded very far despite all the verbiage on "agrarian reform." In addition to the figures mentioned previously, other examples substantiating this conclusion are easy to find. In 1959 in Bolivia, for example, after eight years of "agrarian reform," 6.3 percent of all agricultural units still owned 91.9 percent of all land operated. This is particularly significant since the land redistribution program reached its zenith in 1962, and the land being redistributed since that time has been steadily declining. Actually, in Bolivia the *hacendados* seem to have regained their momentarily lost political position, because the governmental programs directed toward the peasants have been largely aimed at resettlement of unoccupied areas rather than expropriation of *haciendas.*

[41] Robert C. Williamson, "Toward a Theory of Political Violence: The Case of Rural Colombia," in Von Lazar and Kaufman (eds.), *Reform and Revolution.*

In 1959 in Costa Rica, which likes to consider itself as the most democratic country in Latin America, 8.9 percent of all agricultural units owned 70.0 percent of all land operated. In Ecuador, El Salvador, Honduras, and Panama 1.2 to 2.1 percent of all agricultural units operated from 35 to 65 percent of all agricultural land. *Minifundios* in these countries constituted between 12 and 19 percent of all land operated but accounted for between 72 and 89 percent of all agricultural units.[42] No matter how optimistic one is—no matter how intent one is on seeing peasant socioeconomic change—these and other figures of land ownership patterns in Latin America indicate that appreciable socioeconomic change is not occurring for the peasants, and therefore the large landowners must still be capable of extracting their demands from the various political systems.

Chile offers one final, major example of this conclusion, and is of special interest because many North Americans optimistically insist that Chile is one of the leaders of change and/or "reform" in Latin America. In Chile, the gap between haves and have-nots, instead of closing, is actually widening. The farm labor force, constituting approximately 87 percent of those involved in agriculture, earns only one-third of the income produced by agriculture. The top 1 percent of those engaged in agriculture receive 25 percent of that income. The gap is widening because the peasants have suffered a decline in purchasing power of approximately one-third between 1960 and 1965, and because the government has refused to raise minimum salaries to compensate for inflation. For that matter, the government has not been particularly active in ensuring that even the minimum rates are complied with by the *hacendados*.[43]

In terms of verbal benefits—what Almond and Powell call "symbolic outputs"—the peasants throughout Latin America receive a great deal. Most of the verbiage on agrarian reform is part of this type of benefit. Every country in Latin America today has some form of land reform program. Most also have laws concerning minimum wages, maximum hours, and such related items as rural education, sanitation, credit, and so forth. However, as Feder suggests, the countries have studied each other's legislation on such things as land reform very carefully, since a comparative analysis indicates that all such legislation contains similar or identical provisions that make the realization of land reform very difficult, if not impossible.

[42] João Gonçalves De Souza, "Aspects of Land Tenure Problems in Latin America," in *Rural Sociology*, Vol. 25, No. 1, March 1960. This article uses data compiled by the Inter-American Statistical Institute, an office of the Pan American Union.

[43] William C. Thiesenhusen, "Latin American Land Reform: Enemies of Progress," in *Nation*, January 17, 1966. See also the article by Robert R. Kaufman, "The Chilean Political Right and Agrarian Reform: Resistance and Moderation," in Von Lazar and Kaufman (eds.), *Reform and Revolution*.

Mexico offers a really excellent example of this type of verbal output. A constant theme of the ideology of the Mexican Revolution has been what might be called the "agrarian myth." The peasant is the protagonist of this myth, and his desires are its theme. He is symbolized by Emiliano Zapata, the official peasant hero of the Revolution. Mexican and foreign painters, sculptors, laywrights, moviescript writers, philosophers, historians, and social scientists have dwelt upon the peasant to the extent that virtually the entire world literati knows what he is supposed to look like and what he is supposed to desire. He wears a large straw hat, white pajama-like shirt and trousers, and is either barefoot or wears sandals. What he is said to desire can perhaps best be summed up in Zapata's slogan "tierra y libertad." Liberty is to be achieved for the rural masses through the attainment of social and economic equality and personal dignity, all of which will result from their possession of land. Over the entrance to the Ministry of Education in Mexico City are inscribed the words: "The land is for everybody, like air, water, light, and the warmth of the sun." To estimate the symbolic nature of this type of political output, one has only to look at the land distribution figures for Mexico given at the beginning of this chapter.

The rest of Latin America also finds it both expedient and inexpensive to give the peasants verbal benefits. When an agrarian reform bill is passed, it almost always must be done with the consent of the *hacendados*, and its intent is therefore suspect from the outset. The *hacendados* know, that is, that the legislation either cannot or will not be enforced. For that matter, as isolated as the typical *hacienda* is, it would be difficult if not impossible for even a sincere government to enforce agrarian reform legislation. Furthermore, the *hacendado* will strongly tend to control the local political structure, and will dominate such persons as the local military officers, the police, town mayor, the local agricultural officials, and so forth. Such legislation, then, generally cannot hurt the *hacendado,* and it allows the government to look good in the eyes of the relatively few peasants who are organized, as well as in the eyes of the world which watch the process of "agrarian reform" in Latin America.

The object of this chapter is to create not a mood of pessimism, but rather one of realism toward the entire rural situation in Latin America. That is, the only intent is to portray as objectively as possible certain conditions in Latin America that strongly tend to prevent socioeconomic change in rural areas.

When the Alliance for Progress was initiated, most Americans believed that Latin America—and in this case rural Latin America—would be dramatically altered socially, economically, and politically. Rural Latin America, however, remains essentially unchanged after ten years of the Alliance, and most North Americans are disillusioned and therefore cynical about the whole idea.

But the idea of agrarian reform in Latin America through the Alliance for Progress was unrealistic from its conception. While all the governments, except Cuba, agreed to the agrarian reform proposals of the Charter of Punta del Este, was it really realistic to expect that these governments would, or even could, implement agrarian reform? The Alliance for Progress was another symbolic output—no more, and no less. Again, with the exception of Cuba, in every country in Latin America the *hacendado* (and many *haciendas* are North American-owned) is a major if not dominant political actor. Under these conditions, is it realistic to believe that the "authoritative decision makers" will enforce, or even enact, legislation detrimental to the interests of the *hacendados*?

However, it is also unrealistic to believe that the political systems are totally unresponsive to peasant demands. The real problem for the peasants concerning socioeconomic change—and it is a problem that many North Americans refuse to recognize—is that relatively few peasants do place demands on the political system. There can and will be no change unless significant political forces demand it, and the Latin American peasants, generally unaware of or disinterested in their respective political systems, do not constitute a significant political force at this time. In short the *hacendado,* both by his own efforts within the system and by the peasants' lack of effort, dominates agrarian politics.

This does not mean that socioeconomic change cannot or will not occur. Some already has, as indicated, for example, by the organized sugar workers of Pernambuco. However, this change is itself a consequence of technological innovation in a rural area, which has transformed that area into something other than the traditional *hacienda* operation. More and more of this innovation is occurring, and as it progresses one can expect more and more change in the peasant sector. This however may not, and probably will not, take the traditional form of demands by peasants for land, but rather will have other goals. Change may also occur as the result of urban groups demanding development in the agricultural sector of the economy, in order to achieve some measure of balanced, overall economic development. But as long as the *hacienda* remains isolated and operating in the traditional fashion, major change cannot and will not occur.

FURTHER READING

ADAMS, DALE, "Colombia's Land Tenure System: Antecedents and Problems," in *Land Economics,* Vol. 42, No. 1, February 1966.

ADAMS, RICHARD N., *A Community in the Andes.* Seattle: University of Washington Press, 1959.

——————, *Rural Labor in Latin America.* Institute of Latin American Studies, Austin: University of Texas Offprint Series, 1964.

——————, *The Second Sowing: Power and Secondary Development in Latin America.* San Francisco: Chandler, 1967.

—————— et al., *Social Change in Latin America Today.* New York: Harper & Row, 1960.

ADIE, ROBERT F., *Agrarianism in the Mexican Political System.* Doctoral Dissertation, Austin: University of Texas, 1970.

ARANDA, SERGIO, *La revolución agraria en Cuba.* Mexico: Siglo Veintiuno, 1968.

BARRACLOUGH, SOLON L. and ARTHUR L. DOMIKE, "Agrarian Structure in Seven Latin American Countries," in *Land Economics,* Vol. 42, No. 4, November 1960.

BELSHAW, MICHAEL, *A Village Economy.* New York: Columbia University Press, 1967.

BEYER, R. C., "Land Distribution and Tenure in Colombia," in *Journal of Inter-American Studies,* Vol. 3 ,1961.

BOCK, PHILLIP K. (ed.), *Peasants in the Modern World.* Albuquerque: University of New Mexico Press, 1969.

BOGLICH, JOSÉ, *La cuestión agraria en la Argentina.* Buenos Aires: Editorial Pampa y Cielo, 1964.

BOORSTEIN, EDWARD, *The Economic Transformation of Cuba.* New York: Monthly Review Press, 1968.

BORTON, RAYMOND E. (ed.), *Selected Readings to Accompany Getting Agriculture Moving.* New York: Agricultural Development Council, 1966.

BRANDENBURG, FRANK, *The Making of Modern Mexico.* Englewood Cliffs, N.J.: Prentice-Hall, 1964.

CAMACHO-SAA, CARLOS, *Minifundia, Productivity and Land Reform in Cochabamba.* Thesis, Madison: University of Wisconsin, 1967.

CANELAS O., AMADO, *Mito y realidad de la reforma agraria.* La Paz: Editorial "Los Amigos del Libro," 1966.

CARROLL, THOMAS F., "The Land Reform Issue in Latin America," in Robert D. Tomasek (ed.), *Latin American Politics: 24 Studies of the Contemporary Scene.* Garden City, N.Y.: Doubleday, 1966.

——————, *Land Tenure and Land Reform in Latin America: A Selected Bibliography.* Washington, D.C.: Inter-American Development Bank, 1962.

CHONCHOL, JACQUES, "Land Tenure and Development in Latin America," in Claudio Veliz (ed.), *Obstacles to Change in Latin America.* New York: Oxford University Press, 1965.

The Community in Latin America. Lawrence, Kan.: U. of Kansas, Center of Latin American Studies, 1964, Occasional Publications Number 3.

COOK, HUGH L., "The New Agrarian Reform Law and Economic Development in Venezuela," *Land Economics,* February 1961.

CÓRDOBA BONICHE, JOSÉ, *Aspectos fundamentales de la reforma agraria en Nicaragua: Ensayo político-económico-social.* Mexico: Costa Amic, 1963.

CRESPO, TEODORO, *El problema de la tierra en el Ecuador.* Quito: Editorial Casa de la Cultura Ecuatoriana, 1961.

DALWART, LOUIS O., "Land for Venezuelans" in *Americas,* August 1961.

DE LA PEÑA, MOISÉS T., *El pueblo y su tierra: mito y realidad de la reforma agraria en México.* Mexico, D. F. Cuadernos Americanos, 1964.

DOMÍNGUEZ, OSCAR, *El campesino chileno y la acción católica rural.* Santiago de Chile: CIAS, 1961.

EDELMANN, ALEXANDER T., "Colonization in Bolivia: Progress and Prospects," *Inter-American Economic Affairs,* Vol. 20, No. 4, Spring 1967.

FAVRE, HENRY, CLAUDE COLLIN, and JOSÉ MATOS MAR, *La hacienda en el Peru.* Lima: Instituto de Estudios Peruanos, 1967.

FEDER, ERNEST, "Feudalism and Agricultural Development: The Role of Controlled Credit in Chile's Agriculture," in *Land Economics,* February 1960.

FERNÁNDEZ Y FERNÁNDEZ, RAMÓN, *Economía agrícola y reforma agraria,* 2nd ed. Mexico: Centro de Estudios Montarios Latinoamericanos, 1965.

FERREIRA, LUIS PINTO, *A reforma agrária.* Rio de Janeiro: Livraria Freitas Baston, 1964.

FLORES, EDMUNDO, "Balance de la reforma agraria mexicana," in *Visión,* 9 de Mayo de 1969.

——————, *Tratado de economía agrícola.* Mexico, D.F.: Fondo de Cultura Económica, 1961.

FORD, THOMAS R., *Man and Land in Peru.* Gainesville: University of Florida Press, 1955.

GALBRAITH, JOHN KENNETH, *El desarrollo económico y la política agraria.* Publicaciones del Instituto de Teoría y Política Económica: Montevideo, 1960, No. 20.

GERSDORFF, RALPH VON, "Agricultural Credit Problems in Brazil," in *Inter-American Economic Affairs,* Summer 1961.

GONCALVES DE SOUZA, JOÃO, "Aspects of Land Tenure Problems in Latin America," in *Rural Sociology,* Vol. 25, No. 1, March 1960.

GONZÁLEZ CASANOVA, PABLO, "Mexico: The Dynamics of an Agrarian and Semi-Capitalist Revolution," in James Petras and Maurice Zeitlin (eds.), *Latin America: Reform or Revolution?* Greenwich, Conn.: Fawcett Publications, 1968.

HEATH, DWIGHT B., "Land Reform in Bolivia," in *Inter-American Economic Affairs,* Spring 1959.

—————————, "Land Tenure and Social Organization: An Ethnohistorical Study from the Bolivian Oriente," in *Inter-American Economic Affairs,* Spring 1960.

————————— and RICHARD N. ADAMS (eds.), *Contemporary Cultures and Societies of Latin America.* New York: Random House, 1965.

HILDEBRAND, JOHN R., "Latin American Economic Development, Land Reform and United States Aid, With Special Reference to Guatemala," in *Journal of Inter-American Studies,* July 1962.

HIRSCHMAN, ALBERT O., *Journeys Toward Progress: Studies of Economic Policy Making in Latin America.* New York: Twentieth Century Fund, 1963.

Inter-American Committee for Agricultural Development, *Inventory of Information Basic to the Planning of Agricultural Development in Latin America.* Washington, D.C.: Pan American Union, 1963.

KALIJARVI, THORSTEN V., *Central America: Land of Lord and Lizards.* New York: Van Nostrand Reinhold, 1962.

KAUFMAN, ROBERT R., "The Chilean Political Right and Agrarian Reform: Resistance and Moderation," in Arpad Von Lazar and Robert R. Kaufman (eds.), *Reform and Revolution: Readings in Latin American Politics.* Boston: Allyn & Bacon, 1969.

Land Tenure Center, University of Wisconsin, *Agrarian Reform and Land Tenure: A List of Source Materials.* Madison, 1965.

—————————, *Bibliography: Agrarian Reform and Tenure, with Special Sections on Agricultural Finance, Taxation and Agriculture, Agricultural Statistics, and Bibliographical Sources.* Madison, 1964.

LANDSBERGER, HENRY A. (ed.), *Latin American Peasant Movements.* Ithaca, N.Y.: Cornell University Press, 1969.

Latin American USOM's Seminar on Agrarian Reform. Report of the ICA Seminar held in Santiago, Chile, in February 21–24, 1961. Washington, D.C.: ICA, 1961.

LEEDS, ANTHONY, "Brazil and the Myth of Francisco Juliao," in Joseph Maier and Richard W. Weatherhead (eds.), *Politics of Change in Latin America.* New York: Praeger, 1964.

LEWIS, OSCAR, *The Children of Sánchez.* New York: Random House, 1963.

LORD, PETER, *The Peasantry as an Emerging Political Factor in Mexico, Bolivia and Venezuela.* Madison: Land Tenure Center, University of Wisconsin, 1965.

MADDOX, JAMES G., *Land Reform in Mexico.* American University Field Staff Reports: Mexico and Caribbean Series, July, 1957.

MADSEN, WILLIAM, *The Virgin's Children: Life in an Aztec Village Today.* Austin: University of Texas Press, 1960.

MENDIETA Y NÚÑEZ, LUCIO, *Efectos sociales de la reforma agraria en tres comunidades ejidales.* Mexico: Universidad Nacional Autónoma de México, 1960.

MOSHER, ARTHUR THEODORE, *Getting Agriculture Moving: Essentials for Development and Modernization.* New York: Praeger, 1966.

MYREN, DELBERT THEODORE, *Biblography: Communications in Agricultural Development.* Mexico, 1965

NELSON, LOWRY, *Some Social Aspects of Agrarian Reform in Reform in Mexico, Bolivia, and Venezuela.* UP/ Ser. H/ VII, Pan American Union, 1964.

NICHOLLS, WILLIAM HORD and RUY MILLER PAIVA, *Ninety-nine Fazendas: The Structure and Productivity of Brazilian Agriculture, 1963.* Nashville: Graduate Center for Latin American Studies, Vanderbilt University, 1966.

PALOMO VALENCIA, FLORENCIO, *Historia del ejido actual.* Mexico: Editorial America, 1959.

PATCH, RICHARD W., Various American University Field Staff Reports, West Coast South American Series.

PEARSON, NEALE J., "Latin American Peasant Pressure Groups and the Modernization Process," in *Journal of International Affairs,* Vol. 20, No. 2, 1966.

PELLEGRINI, VICENTE, *Teoría y realidad de la reforma agraria.* Buenos Aires: Editorial Sudamericana, 1963.

POLEMAN, THOMAS T., *The Papaloapan Project: Agricultural Development in the Mexican Tropics.* Stanford, Calif: Stanford University Press, 1964.

POTTER, JACK M., N. MAY DIAZ, and GEORGE M. FOSTER, *Peasant Society: A Reader.* Boston: Little, Brown, 1967.

POWELL, JOHN DUNCAN, "Agrarian Reform or Agrarian Revolution in Venezuela?" in Arpad Von Lazar and Robert R. Kaufman (eds.), *Reform and Revolution: Readings in Latin American Politics.* Boston: Allyn & Bacon, 1969.

——————, "Peasant Society and Clientelist Politics," in *American Political Science Review,* Vol. 64, No. 2, June 1970.

POWELSON, JOHN P., *Latin America: Today's Economic and Social Revolution.* New York: McGraw-Hill, 1964.

QUIJANO OBREGÓN, ANÍBAL, "Contemporary Peasant Movements," in Seymour Martin Lipset and Aldo Solari (eds.), *Elites in Latin America.* New York: Oxford University Press, 1967.

QUIMBAYA, ANTEO, *El problema de la tierra en Colombia.* Bogota: Ediciones Sudamerica, 1967.

ROBOCK, STEFAN H., *Brazil's Developing Northeast: A Study of Regional Planning and Foreign Aid.* Washington, D.C.: Brookings Institution, 1963.

ROGERS, EVERETT M., *Modernization Among Peasants: The Impact of Communications.* New York: Holt, Rinehart & Winston, 1969.

SALVADOR PORTA, ELISEO, *Uruguay: Realidad y reforma agraria.* Montevideo: Ediciones de la Banda Oriental, 1961.

SAUNDERS, JOHN V. D., "Man–Land Relations in Ecuador" in *Rural Sociology,* March 1961.

SCHAEDEL, RICHARD P., *Land Reform Studies*. Austin: Institute of Latin American Studies, University of Texas, 1965, Offprint Series No. 19.

SEERS, DUDLEY (ed.), *Cuba: The Economic and Social Revolution*. Chapel Hill: University of North Carolina Press, 1964.

SENIOR, C., *Land Reform and Democracy*. Gainesville: University of Florida Press, 1958.

SIMPSON, EYLER N., *The Ejido: Mexico's Way Out*. Chapel Hill: University of North Carolina Press, 1937.

SMITH, PETER H., *Politics and Beef in Argentina: Patterns of Conflict and Change*. New York: Columbia University Press, 1969.

SMITH, T. LYNN (ed.), *Agrarian Reform in Latin America*. New York: Knopf, 1965.

—————, *The Process of Rural Development in Latin America*. Gainesville: University of Florida Press, 1967.

STAVENHAGEN, RODOLFO (ed.), *Agrarian Problems and Peasant Movements in Latin America*. New York: Doubleday, forthcoming.

STERNBERG, MARVIN JOHN, *Chilean Land Tenure and Land Reform*. Ann Arbor: University of Michigan Microfilms, 1965.

SUND, MICHAEL, *Land Tenure and Economic Performance of Agricultural Establishments in Northeast Brazil*. Madison: University of Wisconsin, Land Tenure Center, 1965, Research Paper No. 17.

TAX, SOL, *Penny Capitalism: A Guatemalan Indian Economy*. Chicago: University of Chicago Press, 1963.

THIESENHUSEN, WILLIAM C., *Chile's Experiments in Agrarian Reform*. Land Economics Monograph No. 1. Madison: University of Wisconsin Press, 1966.

—————, "Latin American Land Reform: Enemies of Progress," in *Nation*, January 17, 1966.

—————, *Survey of the Alliance for Progress: Problems of Agriculture*. Madison: University of Wisconsin, Land Tenure Center, 1968, Reprint No. 35.

United Nations Economic Commission for Latin America, *Problemas y perspectivas de la agricultura latinoamericana*. Buenos Aires: Solar/Hachette, 1965.

DE VRIES, EGBERT (ed.), *Social Research and Rural Life in Central America, Mexico, and the Caribbean Region*. Paris: UNESCO, 1966.

WAGLEY, CHARLES, "The Peasant," in John J. Johnson (ed.), *Continuity and Change in Latin America*. Stanford, Calif.: Stanford University Press, 1967.

WILLIAMSON, ROBERT C., "Toward a Theory of Political Violence: The Case of Rural Colombia," in Arpad Von Lazar and Robert R. Kaufman (eds.), *Reform and Revolution: Readings in Latin American Politics*. Boston: Allyn & Bacon, 1969.

WOLF, ERIC R., *Sons of the Shaking Earth*. Chicago: University of Chicago Press, 1959.

WOOD, GARLAND P., "Agriculture and Social Change," in William H. Form and Albert A. Blum (eds.), *Industrial Relations and Social Change in Latin America*. Gainesville: University of Florida Press, 1965.

YOUNG, MAURICE DE, *Man and Land in the Haitian Economy*. Gainesville: University of Florida Press, 1958.

YUDELMAN, MONTAGUE, *Agricultural Development in Latin America: Current Status and Prospects*. Washington: Inter-American Development Bank, 1966.

ZONDAG, CORNELIUS H., *The Bolivian Economy, 1952–65: The Revolution and Its Aftermath*. New York: Praeger, 1966.

CHAPTER **3**

BUSINESSMEN

THE CONTEXT: THE LATIN AMERICAN ECONOMIES, BUSINESS ATTITUDES AND PRACTICES

Businessmen, like the other socioeconomic groups we are discussing, are best seen in a particular context—and in their case the general economic setting seems most appropriate. However, the following discussion of the economy of Latin America—a subject on which hundreds of volumes in Spanish, English, and other languages have been written—is not intended as a sophisticated, comprehensive evaluation of the topic. Rather, only a few aspects of its past and present condition and development will be mentioned, in the expectation that these will aid in clarifying the complexities of how and the extent to which businessmen influence the operation of the various Latin American political systems and contribute to socioeconomic change in the region. Certainly, there will be no position taken here as to what Latin Americans "should" do in order to develop economically, as this is an issue upon which both Latin American and foreign economists are often diametrically opposed.

One of the best ways to study and to appreciate industrialization and its concomitant social and political changes in Latin America is to choose one of the countries—preferably one of the more economically advanced countries such as Argentina, Brazil, Chile, or Mexico—and trace historically the growth and change in economic pursuits over the course of, say, the 19th century. In this fashion one can much better understand the great importance to economic, social, and political development of such factors as discovery of mineral or nitrate wealth, a wave of immigration from Europe, adoption and adaptation of new technology, growth of a merchant marine or of railways, establishment of telegraph and then telephone networks, expansion of towns into sprawling urban centers, and so forth. However, portrayal of this process in even a single country in the area would by itself demand the space of a chapter; we will simply state that all of these and many other related factors are discernible to some extent in the nineteenth century history of every Latin American country. On the other hand, although some industrialization had occured in each country of the region, Latin America remained, until the first few decades of the twentieth century, essentially an exporter of raw materials. In economic terms, although benefits were distributed unequally among the various countries, the Latin American economies had only managed to achieve integration into the international economic system's division of labor[1] in the capacity of "hewers of wood and drawers of water."

The Depression of 1929 altered this picture considerably since markets for raw materials declined drastically, and as a result both capital and labor were more and more directed toward industrial pursuits. Due to inequalities in the domestic markets, the success of this reorientation varied considerably —the larger and already more economically advanced countries achieved relatively higher growth rates, while the smaller and less advanced countries experienced only a minimal effect. The advent of World War II accelerated this development momentarily, since it gave Latin America a very favorable export status and thus contributed to the accumulation of large foreign exchange reserves necessary for further capitalization. However, this particular impetus was very short-lived, as the immediate postwar years saw the loss of foreign markets due to renewed competition. Furthermore, the United States, as many Latin American writers still angrily point out, did not establish a Marshall Plan for Latin America. Such a plan, it is often asserted, would have maintained economic growth.[2]

The process of industrialization in Latin America after the Depression took the form of what economists term "import substitution." This means that the Latin American countries, rather than relying on their relative competitive advantage in the exportation of primary products, began to emphasize the establishment of national industries capable of satisfying domestic

---

[1] Celso Furtado, "Development and Stagnation in Latin America: A Structuralist Approach," in *Studies in Comparative International Development,* Vol. I, 1965.

[2] See Walter Kraus (ed.), *The Economy of Latin America* (Iowa City: Bureau of Business and Economic Research, College of Business Administration, University of Iowa, 1966), p. 151.

demands.[3] If seriously implemented, import substitution policies have the effect of favoring domestic industries—i.e., those protected by high tariffs—while leaving domestic producers of primary products to fend for themselves on the world markets. While domestic industry benefits from import substitution policies to a certain degree, it cannot go beyond the domestic market unless it is sufficiently competitive to enter the international market. Furthermore, the growth of industry itself is hindered by the depression of agricultural and other primary products, because of the relatively low (often nonexistent) ability of much of the populace to consume industrial output. In turn, this small-scale domestic market makes it very difficult for enterprises to mass produce low-cost surpluses to compete in the international market. As a result, industry in Latin America has been and is today severely hampered in developing its potential, and until the domestic scene somehow changes to allow much larger numbers of the general populace to enter significantly into the consumer market, it appears that the area will remain heavily dependent on exportation of primary products.

Uruguayan industrialization, perhaps an extreme example, has been dependent on import substitution policies, and much of the country's present economic stagnation is due to the total exploitation and subsequent exhaustion of this process. As a recent study points out, everything that can be economically produced in a market of only 2.5 million people is already being produced—and at a high cost. Most industrial material and energy sources are expensive because they are imported—a situation aggravated by the high cost of labor due to welfare and social security contributions by employers. Furthermore, because the enterprises protected from foreign competition tend to be monopolies, they do not experience domestic competition either. The end result is that Uruguayan industrial production is too expensive to compete internationally, and 95 percent of it is consumed domestically. Uruguay must, therefore, depend on export of ranch products to pay for its imports. These products, however, have remained at a fairly constant level for the last two decades. Since all the land is owned, increases in production cannot be achieved by exploitation of virgin lands, and there remains a strong, general unwillingness among ranchers to apply new, more efficient techniques to the land presently in production.[4]

Ecuador, with a population of approximately five million, of whom less than one-fourth have an annual income of over $112.00, offers another

[3] For a good summary of import substitution in Latin America see the article by Dwight S. Brothers, "Private Investment in Latin America: Some Implications for the Alliance for Progress," in Cole Blasier (ed.), *Constructive Change in Latin America* (Pittsburgh: University of Pittsburgh Press, 1968).

[4] Herman E. Daly, "An Historical Question and Three Hypotheses Concerning the Uruguayan Economy," in *Inter-American Economic Affairs,* Vol. 20, No. 1, Summer 1966.

good illustration of the problems of import substitution. First, because of low market expectations, factories are often established at less than economical (i.e., efficient) size. Second, even though one factory might eventually operate at full capacity, the profits resulting from protection attract other enterprises into the field. Third, entrepreneurs apparently feel much safer in entering a proven field than in taking risks in an unexplored area. As a result, factories operate at low capacity, are unwilling to be competitive, and sell at high prices. For example, a survey of sixteen Ecuadorean industries in 1961 showed only four operating at more than 60 percent of their capacity, and nine were operating at less than 50 percent. The textile factories provide a good illustration of this situation, since they contain only 1,400 to 2,500 spindles each, compared with the 10,000 which are considered to be the minimum number for efficient operation elsewhere. Furthermore, the 90 firms operating in textiles were unable to do so at more than 47 percent of their capacity despite the fact that factory units were originally uneconomically small.[5]

In summary of the economics of import substitution, it should be noted that most countries throughout the world have some form of tariff protection to stimulate the growth of domestic industry. However, protection in Latin America has tended to create very heavy dependence of industry on government, and lacking adequate domestic competition, industry does not even approach efficiency. As a result, most Latin American industry today cannot compete with foreign manufacturers, and as one study points out, even the Latin American subsidiaries of many United States-owned firms could not compete in the area with their parent companies if tariff protection for their products was removed.[6]

Finally, despite all programs of import substitution, the value of exports, almost entirely of primary products, is today 15 percent of the entire region's GNP, as compared, for example, with 5 percent for the United States.[7] For example, Venezuela's exports in 1963 represented 45 percent of its GNP, and petroleum accounted for 92 percent of these exports. In the same year, Argentina's exports were 14 percent of its GNP with grain and meat products representing, respectively, 25 and 22 percent of the exports. Chile's exports were 15 percent of its GNP, and these were comprised of 66 percent copper and 10 percent iron ore. Colombia's exports were 10 percent of its GNP, comprised of 70 percent coffee and 15 percent petro-

[5] Anthony Bottomley, "Imperfect Competition in the Industrialization of Ecuador," in *Inter-American Economic Affairs*, Vol. 19, No. 1, Summer 1965.

[6] See the article by Claude McMillan, "Industrial Leaders in Latin America," in William H. Form and Albert A. Blum (eds.), *Industrial Relations and Social Change in Latin America* (Gainesville: University of Florida Press, 1965).

[7] See the article by J. D. DeForest, "Latin America: The Economic Environment," in Kraus (ed.), *The Economy of Latin America*.

leum.[8] Furthermore, as noted above, the international market for primary goods constantly fluctuates, and as a result, Latin American long-term development plans that are dependent on foreign exchange earnings become very risky. For example, a one cent drop in the price of coffee on the international market nets Brazil a loss of $24 million in its foreign exchange reserves and Colombia a $6 million loss.[9] In summary of this situation, as one study puts it, less price instability in external markets would be advantageous for Latin America, but no amount of price stabilization by itself and by whatever international agency can really assure for the region what it expects. Raw materials marketed in the advanced countries can only expect to receive a declining proportion of the increasing income of these countries. The pessimistic implication of this—especially considering the population growth rate of the area—is a persistent widening of the gap between income in Latin America and income in the more developed countries.[10]

Partly a result and partly a cause of the economic situation of Latin America described here, another major problem of most of the economies of the area is inflation. During the period from 1953 to 1961, for example, the cost of living index in Argentina, Bolivia, Brazil, and Chile rose by approximately 500 percent,[11] a fact which greatly detracted from those countries' ability to attract investment even under the new import substitution programs. While these figures are the highest, most countries in the area experienced constantly high inflationary pressure, and the situation in most of Latin America today has changed very little. Without elaborating on this situation, it is obvious that constant inflation will adversely affect saving and investment, with consequent detriment to development. For example, it is a common observation (if not complaint) that Latin American businessmen have a strong penchant for investment in real estate, the value of which will rise with inflation, rather than for investment in industry. With inflation either rampant, or expected to become so at any time, this preference does not appear at all odd.

Foreign investment—particularly United States private investment—is another factor deeply affecting the Latin American economies. United States companies alone have an investment of $10 billion in the region. In Guatemala, for example, investment by United States firms totals approximately $127 million; in Brazil it is $1.5 billion; in Peru it is $605 million; in Panama it is $804 million; in Venezuela it is $2.5 billion; in Mexico it is $1.3 billion; and so on. Most of this investment is still concentrated in extractive industries—for example, of the $2.5 billion private United States invest-

8 DeForest, "Latin America."

9 Ibid.

10 Kraus, *The Economy of Latin America,* p. 157.

11 DeForest, "Latin America."

ment in Venezuela, $2 billion is owned by petroleum companies. In Chile, the total United States investment is $878 million, and $500 million of this was, until recent nationalization, invested in copper. Furthermore, the strong tendency is for United States firms to ship the raw materials they deal with, rather than establishing local processing facilities, and to send their profits to the United States. This, of course, deprives the countries concerned of much of the potential of their resources in that the money is removed from their economies rather than being used for further development.[12]

While it is not within the scope of this brief discussion to evaluate the contribution, or lack of contribution, that United States investment has made to the Latin American economies, it is relevant to point out that there is, rightly or wrongly, considerable and apparently growing resentment in Latin America over this investment. In a recent, nonpolemical article, for example, Ramón Ramírez Gómez states that the United States is responsible for the annual loss to Latin America of $1.5 billion because of the price difference that the United States establishes between products it sells and those it purchases. Furthermore, he insists, North American investors enjoy maximum profits in a minimum period of time—these profits always being far higher than those they would obtain in the United States. That is, in the areas of trade, primary industry, production of consumer goods, and mining and oil, they obtain annual profits of between 30 and 35 percent (and the companies themselves declare an average of 20 percent). Ramírez Gómez totally rejects a recent statement by Edwin Martin, an Undersecretary of State, to the effect that Latin American countries should remain producers and exporters of agricultural and mineral raw materials, and entrust their technical and industrial development to foreign private investors. According to Gómez, the latter are intent only on exhorbitant profits and care nothing for the country concerned. Again, the point is not whether Ramírez Gómez is correct in his analysis, but rather that he and many other Latin Americans *believe* it to be correct.[13]

Another major economic problem for Latin America, mentioned above only in passing, is the constantly deteriorating exchange price for raw materials. For example, it has been asserted by Raul Prebisch of the Economic Commission for Latin America that the effects of this deterioration of prices for raw materials resulted in a loss of $7.4 billion to Latin America between 1955 and 1960—an amount close to the total foreign capital received by the area in that period. Several reasons have been suggested for this deterioration in the terms of exchange. First, there is the privileged status of foreign

[12] See *Newsweek,* Vol. 73, April 14, 1969.

[13] Ramón Ramírez Gómez, "ECLA, Prebisch, and the Problem of Latin American Development," in *Studies in Comparative International Development,* Vol. 2, 1966.

capital invested in Latin America's natural resources. Second, there is economic dependence on the United States for most industrial materials. Third, there is the alliance between foreign capital and the national oligarchies, the latter being generally concerned only with high profits rather than with any national interests. Fourth, most foreign loans are conditioned to the purchase of machinery and other products from the lending country. Fifth, there is the lack of diversification and the rigidity of Latin America's foreign commerce. Sixth, Latin America's own industrialization has lagged greatly, in that during the last decade the area's rate of development was 1 percent compared to 4 percent in Western Europe and 6 percent in the "socialist countries." Seventh and last, there is the monopolistic nature of the United States' economic policy, which sets for exports a price even higher than for the domestic monopoly and also reduces the price for imports from Latin America.[14]

Again, the intent here is not to pass judgment on these allegations. Volumes could be (and have been) written on the subject, and there is no inclination here to enter the debate. Rather the point is that, rightly or wrongly, these and similar ideas are apparently not at all uncommon in Latin America, and thus impinge on private and governmental foreign relations. For that matter, the recent *Rockefeller Report on the Americas* not only recognizes these feelings but also suggests that they are at least partially warranted when it states that there is great resentment in the area because of the way United States aid programs have often been distorted to serve a variety of purposes in the United States which have nothing to do with Latin American interests and aspirations. In any event, some of the implications of these and similar assertions will become clearer in the discussion below on businessmen's attitudes in Latin America.

Finally, some mention should be made of regional integration, which many Latin Americans and foreigners believe will solve, or at least mitigate, the problems of economic development throughout the area. For example, this is the point that Victor Urquidi, a prominent Mexican economist, argues when he asserts that if Latin America wants to find solutions to problems that will assure progress, it must accept the concept of a single Latin America and a single Latin American economy.[15] In other words, it is argued that the economic isolation of Latin American countries from each other accounts for much of both past and present economic stagnation in the area.

Of the two regional economic organizations in the area, the Central American Common Market (CACM) appears to have enjoyed the greatest

14 Ibid.

15 For a discussion of this and other problems of development, see Ramón Ramírez Gómez, *The Challenge of Development in Latin America* (New York: Praeger, 1964).

degree of success—which may appear surprising given the small size of the five countries involved.[16] In 1955, for example, exports of the five countries to one another accounted for only 3.2 percent of all their exports, while by 1960 intra-zonal exports accounted for 7 percent and by the mid-1960s, 13 percent. Both local and foreign private investment has greatly increased, as have finances from the Bank for Economic Integration, the Inter-American Development Bank, the World Bank, and United States foreign aid programs. Common tariffs have been established around the zone, internal taxation is being harmonized, communications and transportation have been greatly improved, and so forth. As one study points out, in general the entire business climate in the area is rapidly changing,[17] although recent developments, such as the conflict between El Salvador and Honduras, have cast doubt on the viability of future progress.

The Latin American Free Trade Association (LAFTA) began functioning in 1961 in an aura of optimism and goodwill fostered by the Alliance for Progress. Its successes to date are reflected in such developments as the growth of intra-zonal trade from $650 million in 1961 to $1.5 billion in 1967; or in the 10,000 individual, item-by-item tariff concessions which have been negotiated under its auspices.[18] However, while LAFTA may have a much greater economic potential than the CACM, it has problems to overcome that are not shared by the smaller organization. These include such factors as the immense area it covers (most of Latin America), with the additional problem of Mexico's remoteness from the other major economic powers in the region; very formidable obstacles to communications and transportation, such as the Andes; the failure of an investment boom to develop; and the many reservations and special protective provisions contained in its legal base, the Treaty of Montevideo.

However, in the case of both the CACM and LAFTA there are major political problems to be overcome—and it is these, more than anything else, which make one hesitant to adopt an optimistic viewpoint toward these organizations' ultimate success. For example, common tariffs and intra-zonal industrial trade have only limited potential for economic development, if the same inefficiency in factory operation continues to be the norm within

[16] Costa Rica, El Salvador, Guatemala, Honduras, and Nicaragua.

[17] See the article by Robert A. Flammang, "Regional Integration," in Kraus (ed.), The Economy of Latin America.

[18] See the article by Walter A. Vela, "LAFTA and Regional Economic Integration," in Thomas A. Gannon (ed.), Doing Business in Latin America. American Management Association: 1968. For an up-to-date, in-depth discussion of the problems and poor prospects of both the CACM and LAFTA, as well as the projected Latin American common market see Miguel S. Wionczek, "The Rise and Decline of Latin American Economic Integration," in Yale H. Ferguson (ed.), Contemporary Inter-American Relations. Englewood Cliffs, N.J.: Prentice-Hall, 1972.

zone boundaries as it is now behind national boundaries. This is essentially a *political* problem, as are, to a considerable extent, such developmental factors as foreign economic domination, inflation, and so forth. What this means is that eventually there will have to be some form—however skeletal —of political union in order to resolve political problems reflected in zonal economic development problems. This is what creates pessimism about regional economic integration in Latin America, at least in the near future— and the pessimism includes, of course, the 1967 decision of the Latin American heads-of-states to create one huge common market by 1985. Within most of the Latin American countries there is little consensus on political legitimacy on a national basis, so it is extremely difficult to imagine a "union of political souls" on a regional basis. Furthermore, the strafing of one's neighbor's fishing boats, border wars, and similar incidents, while they may be smoothed over diplomatically with presidential handshakes and affirmations of faith essentially reflect deep-seated national interests which fit in very poorly with any form of regional integration.

Thus, while industrialization has occurred to some extent in every Latin American country, it should not be assumed that the post-Depression era has been in any sense magical; nor, for that matter, should it even be regarded rigidly, as it so often is, as a "watershed," since it is only one mark among many that could be noted. While as a result of the economic development that has occurred, groups continue to arise and strive for political position, the fact remains that every country in Latin America—although this remark is less applicable to some than to others—is to a large extent a traditional, agrarian society, and the traditional elite continue to constitute one of the strongest single groups in the various political systems.

The political power of the *hecendados* allows them to retain their system virtually intact (with the major excepton of Cuba and the more minor one of Mexico). Chile provides an excellent example of this situation because, as noted in the preceding chapter, it is often regarded, particularly by foreigners, as one of the most advanced, democratic, and socially progressive countries in the area. However, as a study of Chilean politics point out, the political position of the *hacendados* has scarcely been touched. For example, in the very bitter political battles in Chile that characterized the period between 1925 and 1933, when various social legislation was implemented, the Conservative Party, representing the *hacendados* and other wealthier groups, was the only party to emerge unscathed.[19] President-General Ibáñez (1927–32) made very significant noises about agrarian reform, but these ended when he married into a *hacendado* family. Even the Popular Front government elected in 1938, composed of Radicals, Communists, Democrats, Socialists, Radical Socialists, and the Chilean Labor

---

[19] Federico Gil, *Genesis and Modernization of Political Parties in Chile* (Gainesville: University of Florida Press, 1962).

Federation, did nothing to affect the *hacendados* in any serious manner. Only in the last few years has legislation been passed allowing the organization of Chilean peasants (*inquilinos*); it was previously legally forbidden. Whether or not this will remain a symbolic output of the political system, as it did during the Frei administration, will depend on the present administration of President Allende, who has to date been very cautious in his remarks about and implementation of agrarian reform.

In effect, as a recent study of the Chilean industrial bourgeoisie points out, historical analysis of Chilean industrialization and its concomitant social effects shows very different patterns than the industrialization process in, for example, Western Europe. That is, industrialization in Chile did not produce high social mobility and a genuine new class. Instead, all that occurred was a transfer of personnel and capital from commerce, agriculture, and services into industrial enterprises, a situation which precludes basic conflict between an agrarian and industrial elite. As the study points out, today in Chile industrialists invariably have a modest to substantial socioeconomic background connected to the business, professional, and landowning classes, and industrial activity has not been and is not today a significant avenue of social mobility.[20]

This point was recently made for Latin America as a whole by Fernando Henrique Cardoso when he stated that it would be a mistake to assume that the industrial process with its attendant social changes has given rise to an entrepreneurial elite opposed to the traditional elite. Rather, any major reorganization of Latin American societies which has occurred as a result of industrialization has produced a new synthesis which amalgamates the traditional oligarchy with an entrepreneurial sector.[21] In more specific studies, Helio Jaguaribe points to this phenomenon occurring in Brazil in the early 1930s, when the more radical revolutionaries lost out to those opposed to both rapid and profound changes in the society, and as a result the system of property and privilege remained unchanged.[22] Going even further into history, a study of Argentina suggests that many of the modern socioeconomic and political problems of that country are the result of the alliance formed between foreign capital and the local agrarian elite during the 1880s.[23] In Peru, Francis Borricaud points out, the rural elite are not entrepreneurs in any common definition of that term, but they do exercise

20 Dale L. Johnson, "The National and Progressive Bourgeoisie in Chile," in *Studies in Comparative International Development,* Vol. 4, 1968.

21 Fernando Henrique Cardoso, "The Entrepreneurial Elites of Latin America," in *Studies in Comparative International Development,* Vol. 1, 1965.

22 Helio Jaguaribe, "Political Strategies of National Development in Brazil," in *Studies in Comparative International Development,* Vol. 3, 1967.

23 Eldon Kenworthy, "Argentina: The Politics of Late Industrialization," in *Foreign Affairs,* Vol. 45, No. 3, April 1967.

close control over the national economic life. For example, most of the big coastal plantation owners are heavily represented in the management or administrative councils of the banks, and as a result they control to a great extent the agencies which in turn control credit as well as much of the import and export markets.[24] Unlike their counterparts elsewhere in Latin America, the Mexican agrarian elite were too rigid to accomodate change, and a violent revolution was necessary to establish the new social, industrial order—although one has only to look at the Mexican land tenure pattern discussed in the preceding chapter to realize that a rural elite, while not nationally dominant, still exists. For that matter, many of the traditional elite were forced into new economic pursuits by the rural violence and destruction of properties during the Revolution; while this doubtless spurred economic development, it also brought the traditional elite, with all their attitudes or general view of life, into the industrial sector. This congruence between modern business and traditional values and attitudes will be discussed shortly.

In sum, the developmental process in Latin America is in current terminology easily classifiable as "internal colonialism," two primary operational functions of which are to limit social mobility while maximizing participation in the developmental process. Furthermore, internal colonialism creates a situation wherein market forces coupled with low political participation and organization in subdeveloped areas, serve both to maintain a "dynamic of inequality" and to prevent the processes of egalitarianism characteristic of development in, for example, Western Europe, from emerging.[25]

Although it is quite impossible to provide a precise definition of the term "businessman," nevertheless some clarification appears necessary before proceeding to discuss business attitudes in Latin America. First, the term as used here at all times refers to individuals in the middle- and upper-income ranges, and does not include the "penny capitalist". That is, while such individuals as basket weavers and vendors, lottery ticket sellers, ice cream and softdrink street peddlers, prostitutes and procurers, tobacconists, shoe shiners and so forth are "businessmen" in a sense, they are not included in our operational conception of the term. Rather, with these individuals excluded, "businessman" as we use the term essentially reflects the Western European and North American stereotype of him. He may be a millionaire entrepreneur, but more typically, if he is an entrepreneur, he is on a smaller scale than this; he may be the president of a multimillion dollar corporate

24 François Borricaud, "Structure and Function of the Peruvian Oligarchy," in *Studies in Comparative International Development,* Vol. 2, 1966.

25 Pablo González Casanova, "Internal Colonialism and National Development," in *Studies in Comparative International Development,* Vol. 1, 1965.

structure but, again, he is typically of lesser stature. Whatever the case, however, he most definitely has middle or upper economic and social status and is engaged in commercial and/or financial pursuits.

The blending of old and new economic pursuits of the upper income groups in Latin America is, as previously noted, also reflected very clearly in certain attitudes prevalent among businessmen—for example, in their strong family orientation. A very common practice is their maintenance of wealth within the family. That is, even when they are not closely linked to a rural elite background, businessmen tend to think in much the same terms as the rural elite who have managed to maintain their estates intact to a great extent by maintaining their families intact. In fact, the elite family alliance pattern in Latin America has tended to operate historically through intermarriage to absorb the more important members of new groups as the latter arose in the course of gradual technological change within the societies. Furthermore, since the groups of greatest prestige were the rural traditional elite, it was their values to which the new groups aspired.[26]

In his study of Latin American businessmen, Albert Lauterbach suggests that there exists in Latin America a strongly felt desire for high social status, and in the case of businessmen this is supplemented by their need to differentiate themselves clearly from lower-status groups. Thus, the socialization process of the upper- or middle-class child tends to be dominated by the status needs of his family. The adult businessman with such a background—and, as noted previously, there are few who do not have such a background—continues to be dominated by the early values. As a result, he tends to view business not as an impersonal activity concerned with maximizing profits, but as an extension of his family's need for social status. Furthermore, it is through his family connections, which may and usually do include political connections, that he does business, so his and his family's social status becomes a constant, major consideration in determining business success.[27] That is, as a study of Peruvian business managers puts it, nonfinancial considerations are frequently identified as playing an important role in management decisions, and the profit motive, far from being the sole determining factor in such decisions, becomes only a limiting factor. Decisions are based on various values, and business strategy directed toward profits is determined by its congruence with these values.[28] In short, there is in Latin America a social climate in which the very rewards which have

26 See Cardoso, "The Entrepreneurial Elites."

27 Albert Lauterbach, *Enterprise in Latin America: Business Attitudes in a Developing Economy* (Ithaca, N.Y.: Cornell University Press, 1966).

28 Robert R. Rehder, "Managerial Resource Development in Peru: Directions and Implications," in *Journal of Inter-American Studies,* Vol. 10, No. 4, October 1968.

spurred on the entrepreneur in, for example, North America, are consistently deemphasized.[29]

Needless to say, perhaps, business firms operating on this basis tend strongly to become and remain "family firms," a tendency greatly reinforced by constant nepotism in recruitment and promotion norms. As Lauterbach notes, limited companies in Latin America may be quite prevalent, but actual ownership of the shares typically remains within the family, with perhaps the participation of some close and trusted friends. The family may or may not have professional managers to handle the business, but it is more frequently the case that management is largely comprised of family members.[30]

These and related attitudes and practices affect not only the manner in which business is structured and organized, but also impinge on its actual operation and potential in the developmental process. Frank Tannenbaum has quite correctly pointed out that the efficiency and single-mindedness of North American private enterprise does not take into account this general structure of values in Latin American business and that the North American ways of doing business are offensive to Latin Americans.[31] The point for socioeconomic development in Latin America, however, is that businessmen cannot automatically be assumed to play the same role characteristic of their counterparts in the already developed countries of the world. That is, the high esteem for personal dignity, family, and friendship, which are major normative orientations among Latin American businessmen, and which heavily influence their administrative and organizational behavior, can and often do conflict with the values of efficiency and profit quite characteristic of industrial development in Western Europe and North America. One does not have to make any personal judgment as to which set of values and norms is "best" in order to conclude that the role played by businessmen in economic development in one culture may be very different in another culture due to basic differences in norms and values.

For example, where a private business is relatively lacking in the profit motive, it will, as a matter of course, be affected in any expansionist activities, if indeed it does have expansionist plans. Actually, often the concern is *not* to expand, so as to allow firm control of the company to remain in the family. Or if business activity is closely linked to family and personal connections, the scope of the business is limited to the scope of the connections, which will tend strongly to limit otherwise advantageous business deals. Hiring of family members may easily lead to inexperienced, if

[29] See, for example, Aaron Lipman, "Social Backgrounds of the Bogota Entrepreneur," in *Journal of Inter-American Studies,* Vol. 8, No. 2, April 1965.

[30] See Lauterbach, *Enterprise in Latin America,* chapter 3.

[31] Frank Tannenbaum, *Ten Keys to Latin America* (New York: Knopf, 1962).

not incompetent, staffing of a business. Furthermore, a stock market in which large numbers of shares are constantly exchanged is a means of mobilizing capital; and where family firms predominate, such a market cannot effectively exist.

These considerations are not intended as an exhaustive discussion of the economic implications of cultural, social, and psychological attributes that appear to be fairly common among Latin American businessmen. Rather, the purpose is to point out that conceptions of business behavior that seem perfectly natural and valid in the context of, for example, Western Europe or North America, are not necessarily applicable to Latin American businessmen, and may in fact be entirely irrelevant. As a study of Colombian entrepreneurs puts it, in such countries as England and the United States, the very qualities that create successful entrepreneurship are culturally prescribed and are most highly rewarded, and the successful entrepreneur epitomizes the successful creature of his culture. The essence of success as defined by his culture is entrepreneurial and monetary success, and his socialization inculcates the motivational drive and defines the methods for achieving success. On the other hand, socialization in Colombia stresses traditional values which, rather than aiding, might actually detract from the individual's ability to become an efficient, rational, contemporary business leader.[32] (The problem here is, of course, that even the terms "efficient, rational, and contemporary" are defined, essentially, by the observer's own cultural viewpoint.) The North American and Western European entrepreneur has traditionally risked everything in order to achieve as his culture defines achievement, and has overall been willing to accept the consequences of his actions in terms of socioeconomic change. The Latin American entrepreneur, with considerably less profit motive in the first place, is much less willing to face the socioeconomic consequences of his economic activity, since these would endanger what he values more than profit. As a result, socioeconomic change dependent on business activities in Latin America cannot necessarily be expected to follow the same path as it has elsewhere.

As a final note before proceeding to businessmen's demands on and rewards from the political system, a not uncommon argument is that the infusion of new ideas into the culture by foreign entrepreneurs will aid in transforming business mentality in Latin America. Essentially, this does not refer to foreign businessmen investing in an enterprise in the area and occasionally visiting it to check on its operation—although there is an element of this thought implicit in some writings. Rather, the idea concerns immigrants who, with their different attitudes and techniques, enter Latin America to stay. Thus, for example, it is argued that foreigners entering the

[32] Lipman, "The Bogota Entrepreneur."

area have aided Latin America in achieving much of the industry present today through their example and their great ability to compete. Latin American businessmen see how well foreigners do, says this argument, and presumably will more and more be motivated to follow suit.[33]

There is no doubt that people of foreign origin are heavily represented in Latin American business. For example, in his study of Chilean entrepreneurs Petras found that their national origins were: 22 percent third-or-more generation Chilean; 19 percent Spanish; 5 percent Arabic; 12.5 percent Jewish; 37.5 percent Western European; and 2.5 percent Eastern European.[34] Similarly, a study of Peruvian social structure notes that although only 20,000 white immigrants have entered Peru since 1900, nevertheless most of these found their way almost immediately into business.[35] In fact, one has only to look at any Latin American "Who's Who" to realize the extent to which immigrants, first generation or otherwise, have been successful in economic, political, and intellectual pursuits.

However, as important as immigration appears to have been to Latin American industrialization, there is no certainty that immigrants have affected or will affect the "business mentality" of the area. For example, another study of Peruvian social structure admits that the great industrial initiatives have not been taken by the local oligarchy, but rather by newcomers, either immigrants or nationals of relatively low social origin. However, once the business is established and the greatest possible risk removed from it, it is generally taken over, through various means, by the oligarchy.[36] Even more convincing than studies such as this are the group of essays contained in the book *Doing Business in Latin America,* a book designed to help United States businessmen get along in Latin America with Latin Americans. Couched in various contexts and terms, the warning of "Don't buck the system" appears again and again.[37]

Despite the speculative interest of this topic, there is no convincing evidence to substantiate either side of it. Perhaps it is essentially a combination of factors, such as a high profit motive in immigrants who do not achieve until they learn local business practices. Form and Blum make this point in their study of industrial relations in Latin America when they argue that many instances can be found of immigrants building large,

[33] See, for example, Cardoso, "The Entrepreneurial Elites."

[34] James Petras, *Politics and Social Forces in Chilean Development* (Los Angeles: University of California Press, 1969), chapter 2.

[35] David Chaplin, "Industrialization and the Distribution of Wealth in Peru," in *Studies in Comparative International Development,* Vol. 3, 1967.

[36] Borricaud, "The Peruvian Oligarchy."

[37] Thomas A. Gannon (ed.), *Doing Business in Latin America* (American Management Association, 1968).

successful commercial and industrial concerns, but that perhaps the key to their success has been their marginality rather than social origin or nationality. As they point out, what is still necessary for any attempt to understand the problem is a series of case studies designed to show whether first and second generation immigrant entrepreneurs have handled their businesses differently than local entrepreneurs, and how immigrant businessmen have adapted to the nature of their host societies.[38]

DESIRES AND DEMANDS

In the preceding chapter a distinction was made between peasant desires and peasant demands on the political system because of their general inability to see the system as relevant to their desires. Businessmen, on the other hand, generally appear too aware of their environment and of the means to cope with it to allow belief that they are unaware of the relevance of the political system to themselves. This is evidenced in various widespread attitudes, including those discussed above, and their manner of doing business through a network of personal connections will almost inevitably involve political connections. For these and similar reasons, desires and demands are considered here in conjunction with the reasonable assumption that this will not too greatly distort reality.

Perhaps the most illuminating manner in which to discuss business desires and demands, particularly economic ones, is to look at the degree of economic nationalism present in the area—a subject of great importance given the arguments, discussed above, against foreign domination of the Latin American economies. However, in any discussion of economic nationalism there is always the argument that people use nationalist sentiment and ideology to cloak self-aggrandizement. Concerning businessmen, it seems, first, rather ridiculous to assume that just because they are businessmen, they are incapable of sentiment and basic beliefs, nationalistic or otherwise. That is, it seems reasonable to accept the argument made in a recent study that Latin American businessmen, like students, intellectuals, and politicians, are ideologically nationalists and that among them is widespread fear of foreign domination and exploitation, particularly on the part of the United States.[39] Second, with some reservations, the argument about selfish motivation behind economic nationalism is irrelevant in this discussion. A demand is a demand, whatever its motivation.

Albert Lauterbach's major study of Latin American businessmen

[38] William H. Form and Albert A. Blum, "Industrial Relations and Social Change," in Form and Blum (eds.), *Industrial Relations and Social Change in Latin America.*

[39] Brothers, "Private Investment in Latin America."

found that on specific points they evidenced considerable nationalist sentiment. That is, he found that the general attitude toward such things as
foreign investment appeared fairly favorable, and that practically all inter-
viewees thought that their countries needed capital from any source and
that foreign investment would long remain a necessity for national development. However, when more specific information was elicited, Lauterbach
found that most had significant qualifications to make about foreign involvement in the Latin American economies.

One of these qualifications or conditions was that such investment was
of only limited value to a country unless it was accompanied by industrial or
other skills not available in the country. This private technological assistance
actually appeared to be the main criterion for judging the value of foreign
investment. Second, it was stressed everywhere, but particularly in the more
developed areas, that foreign enterprise should receive no special privileges
as incentive to enter a country, even if this meant that foreign enterprise
would not enter. Third, many felt that foreign capital should be encouraged
to invest only in those business areas where there were no established domestic interests, although a minority felt that competition from any source
was necessary to stimulate efficiency. Fourth, many considered foreign investment essentially only in political rather than economic terms—asserting that
the history of foreign businesses' interference in domestic politics was no
longer tolerable. Fifth, foreign investment was felt to be good only if it was
not exploitative; it should not simply drain off a country's resources without
providing that country with corresponding benefits. Sixth, there was a
widespread negative attitude toward the idea of foreign capital not reinvest-
ing profits in the country in which they were earned. Seventh, related to the
last point, it was felt that the most desirable foreign investor was one who
came with his money and technology to live permanently in the country,
although some felt that if this did not occur loans from foreign capitalists
would be a suitable alternative. Eighth, there was almost total consensus that
the best enterprise was one which combined both foreign and domestic
shareholders, since the combination of foreign funds and technology with
local knowledge of markets and customs was seen as producing the best
business operation.

Apart from investment, there was widespread agreement that foreign
aid was necessary and desirable for development in the foreseeable future.
Some saw this aid in simple terms of money; others considered technological
assistance to industry and agriculture more important; still others saw it in
terms of aid for improvements in such fields as health and education. Usually, foreign aid was seen in terms of contributions from the United States,
although some mention was made of assistance from the United Nations
and from the International Bank for Reconstruction and Development. Finally, there was fairly general agreement that aid from any source should not

be used for stopgap measures or for maintaining ineffective governments.[40]

There is considerable similarity among many of these attitudes and some of the arguments presented in the introduction to this chapter in the discussion of some of the general economic conditions in Latin America. That is, business attitudes reflect dislike of such things as the exploitation of a country's natural resources by foreigners, particularly when the latter are granted special privileges as incentives to establish themselves, as well as dislike for noninvestment of profits. Furthermore, general unwillingness to compete, at least with foreigners, is evident. Economic dependence on the United States is seen in such factors as the almost automatic connection made between foreign aid and that country.

However, the arguments on these and other subjects in the introduction were made by individuals—economists and intellectuals—using their own special skills in reasoning to come to certain conclusions, right or wrong. The attitudes of the many businessmen surveyed by Lauterbach have much more significance than this. Economists can perhaps argue brilliantly, but it is the attitudes of businessmen on these subjects that create political relevance for the subjects. It is their attitudes, and the effects of these attitudes on politics, which will enter heavily into determining whether such business practices as more or less free competition actually occur. And it is their attitudes, and their political strengths and abilities, that will affect the form and amount of foreign aid, as well as the uses to which it is put. Of course, they are not the sole arbiters of such matters; for instance, bureaucrats' attitudes and desires, as discussed later in Chapter 8, definitely affect solutions as well as the administration of programs. However, brilliant economic analysis and bureaucratic developmental plans must, if they are to be realistic, at all times take into account the orientations of businessmen. Thus, whether as a result of nationalist sentiment or personal gain, business attitudes reflect current import substitution policies as well as other limitations on foreign participation in business enterprise in Latin America.

Another way in which to discuss businessmen's desires and political demands is to consider their attitude toward government. Oliveira Campos, for example, suggests that throughout Latin America there is an incongruous blend of thought which combines on the one hand a lack of faith in the regulatory abilities of government, and on the other hand a definite reluctance to take entrepreneurial risks without governmental protection.[41]

Businessmen in Latin America are capitalists, and show it in a variety of attitudes; but they have other attitudes not at all characteristic of their

---

[40] See Lauterbach, *Enterprise in Latin America,* chapter 7.

[41] Roberto de Oliveira Campos, *Reflections on Latin American Development* (Austin: Institute of Latin American Studies, University of Texas, 1967), p. 6.

Western European and North American counterparts. As Lauterbach points out, in North America and Western Europe emotional or dogmatic approaches to governmental intervention in the economy have long been the norm among private businessmen—even when government departments intervening in the economy are run by persons recognized as previously successful in private enterprise. That is, government intervention by definition is regarded as being improper, unsound, and probably immoral—despite all history of tariffs, subsidies, contracts, and so forth.[42] Although there is some similarity, generally, businessmen in Latin America are not at all so adamantly negative on the subject of government intervention in the economy.

First, concerning specific aspects of government intervention, Lauterbach found that state enterprises were generally viewed with nondogmatic disfavor. This attitude, perhaps inevitably, was particularly strong when government enterprises competed with private companies, and it was strongest of all when this occurred under unequal conditions—i.e., under rules set by the government. Government enterprises complementing private businesses were generally considered as acceptable. For example, communications, irrigation, low-cost housing, and so forth, were proper while nationalization of existing private enterprise or government entry into a field where private business was already active were improper. Nationalization was seen as good if it happened to foreign holdings in basic, especially extractive, industries.

Second, businessmen felt that the government should provide a proper infrastructure for economic development—that is, it should establish preconditions for successful business activity—and that unless the government did this, economic development would not occur. However, there was considerable variation on specific desires in this field. In some areas such things as roads, transportation, communications, water supply, power facilities, and land reclamation were stressed; in other areas the emphasis was on public health and education, judicial administration, and so forth.

Third, government aid to private enterprise was considered as legitimate and necessary, if not as a natural right. This aid was seen generally as technical assistance, research, and information. Provision for credit facilities at reasonable rates, if private facilities were not available, was considered a legitimate government function. So too, of course, was the establishment of protective tariffs, and these were often regarded as the only means by which industry could develop. Of particular significance here was the general acceptance, even in unprotected industries, of tariff policies. In short, on the subject of tariffs there was no apparent general sentiment supporting free trade.

Fourth, it was widely felt that the government should supply develop-

42 Lauterbach, *Enterprise in Latin America*, p. 101.

mental incentives beyond such things as tariffs and credit. It was taken for granted, for example, that new enterprises should have tax-free status for a substantial period of time; there was some belief that even old businesses should not be directly taxed, justified on the basis of a need for capital formation. The idea of taxing those who can afford to pay was rather unpopular, and it was definitely rejected regarding industrial and commercial profits.

Fifth, governmental developmental planning was considered legitimate in some areas but not in others. Reflecting previous arguments, it was believed that the government should provide the framework, infrastructure, supervision, and overall guidance for economic growth in agriculture and industry, but that the major role in this growth belonged to private enterprise.

Sixth, it was a fairly common feeling that the government could best aid economic development by fostering efficiency, democracy, and integrity within itself, since otherwise it could not perform these functions. For example, fairly common beliefs were that government did not understand business, that business was hampered by constant political favoritism, and that the civil service needed objective standards for its operation.

Seventh, land reform was often mentioned as a major function the government should perform, but specific ideas varied widely from country to country (probably reflecting the land tenure system of the areas concerned). Mexican businessmen wanted the *ejido* system revamped; in El Salvador, Argentina, and Uruguay, agrarian reform was scarcely mentioned; in Guatemala and Northeast Brazil colonization of unused land was emphasized. In general, the idea was expressed that the government should concern itself with financial, legal, and technological changes in agriculture so as to bring the peasants into the national consumers market.

Eighth, and finally, the contribution of private enterprise to public development was not considered to be a great concern. The government was generally regarded as something to grant concessions, rather than as something to receive contributions. The most positive contribution that business could make was to take an interest in better training opportunities for business executives, and this was seen mainly in terms of the individual firm's own interests.[43]

Although there are others of varying degrees of depth and specificity, Lauterbach's study is the only one described here. All, however, point to the essential conclusions which can be derived from the attitudes just described. Latin American businessmen are either elite or aspire to elite status, and they will in no way risk their position for whatever developmental goals. That is, they want everything from the government that will benefit themselves, but they are unwilling to give anything in return. Furthermore, they

[43] Ibid., pp. 102–15.

are willing to risk none of the traditional values such as status, prestige, or family, even if this would mean profit to themselves and/or to the society.

Their attitude toward reform in land tenure patterns perhaps best illustrates this conclusion, and it also suggests why the large landowners remain such a strong force in the region. For example, to elaborate on Lauterbach's findings on the point, Petras asserts that Chilean businessmen are quite aware of the need for larger domestic markets if business is going to expand and profit. This implies some radical alterations in the present structure of rural Chilean society. Petras states, however, that while 50 percent of the businessmen support the idea of "agrarian reform," this figure drops to a mere 12 percent when the idea of government expropriation of property is mentioned. This means that effective implementation of land reform is not supported by businessmen, since "voluntary" land reform is, as he suggests, pretty meaningless.[44]

This reflects the sharing of attitudes among businessmen and the traditional Latin American elite, previously emphasized, and it also suggests that, when it comes to specific issues, Latin American businessmen are opposed to economic development with its implied socioeconomic changes. Perhaps—and this is entirely speculative—Latin American businessmen's attitudes, which diverge from the capitalist norm in the developed countries, are essentially a reflection of the elitist nature of their societies. They apparently closely identify in many ways with the traditional elite, many objectively are and others subjectively want to be part of the elite; and in an elitist society what does an elite have to fear from government? In any event, the conclusion on this point—which may but not necessarily does contradict a previous point about the sincerity of economic nationalism—is that businessmen in Latin America, from all available evidence, do not appear to possess much in the way of "social conscience." As a result, their demands on the political system cannot be regarded as any sincere effort to achieve genuine socio-economic development in the region.

SYSTEM RESPONSE

One very easy way of illustrating the political success of businessmen in Latin America is to reconsider briefly the policies of import substitution so prevalent in the region. Every such policy, whether designed to create an industry or to protect an existing one, whether justified with nationalistic ideology or otherwise, benefits business and therefore businessmen. Under the capitalist system, definitely predominant in the region, this is the most immediate and obvious result. Whether such encouragement to business creates significant benefit to the society as a whole depends on such factors

[44] Petras, *Chilean Development,* p. 59.

as jobs created and wages paid, revenues the government receives from expanding business, and what the businessmen do with their increased corporate and personal wealth. Disregarding until the following chapter such questions as jobs and wages, the other questions are perhaps best answered in terms of taxation in Latin America.

The Charter of Punta del Este, which established the Alliance for Progress, committed the governments of Latin America to, among other things, programs designed to achieve a more equitable mobilization and use of domestic resources, including appropriate taxation of large income and real estate. The Charter also promised external assistance in improving tax administration, as well as tax-related items such as a more equitable distribution of national income and a greater percentage of national income devoted to investment. Other international agencies have also stressed the need for reform in order to expand government revenues and to make the distribution of the tax burden more equitable. As Raynard Sommerfeld points out in his major study of taxes in Latin America, both the Alliance for Progress and other international agencies have, with varying emphases, urged improvement of tax administration, and Sommerfeld himself feels that it is the most urgent need, since existing tax laws would be reasonably appropriate to achieve stated goals if they were actually implemented.[45]

Latin American businessmen, like their counterparts the world over, have a peculiar advantage regarding taxation, because even if a national bureaucracy can be assumed to favor genuine economic and social reform, and is willing to implement it, there is always the fear that increased taxation allowing for program implementation will endanger business activity and decrease the incentive to work and to invest. Furthermore, any assumption concerning governmental and bureaucratic willingness to enforce such a program is, in all countries of Latin America, a very risky one to make. As Sommerfeld asserts, his impression is not that the existing tax laws are poorly drawn, but rather that they are surprisingly sophisticated.[46] Thus the problem of taxation in the region is not legislative in nature: it is based on and reflects political and administrative realities. That is, the large-income groups—and these certainly include businessmen—do not want to pay taxes, personal or corporate, and their success in achieving their ends is seen in the general governmental unwillingness or inability to collect them.

Of particular benefit to businessmen is the norm of excluding capital gains, either partially or totally, from income tax provisions.[47] The rationale for this is, of course, the need to create investment and expansion incentive.

---

[45] Raynard M. Sommerfeld, *Tax Reform and the Alliance for Progress* (Austin: University of Texas Press, 1966), p. 45.

[46] Ibid., p. 65.

[47] Ibid., p. 90.

However, exclusion is not backed up with legislation preventing capital gains from being invested in purely speculative, nonproductive ventures. As Sommerfeld notes, the strong tendency to put money thus gained into speculation in foreign exchange, diamonds, or real estate only intensifies the shortage of capital for developmental purposes.[48] Finally, the effective rate of taxation on earned incomes in Latin America is generally not high to begin with, and Sommerfeld suggests that a great potential for increased taxation exists for at least the higher personal incomes. However, the liberal exclusions granted in legislation, as well as the accepted practices in business-income taxation, allow the wealthy taxpayer to evade truly progressive taxation even when it is attempted.[49] For example, in a country such as Venezuela 10 percent of the economically active population take over 60 percent of income, and the bottom 50 percent take only 11 percent. In Chile, 10 percent monopolize over 50 percent of income, and the lowest 50 percent of the population receive only 15 percent.[50] Nevertheless, in these countries as in most of Latin America, tax legislation and particularly tax administration make effective progressive taxation extremely difficult and often impossible to achieve.

In short, in the form of tax legislation there exists in Latin America considerable pressure on businessmen to contribute to socioeconomic development. However, as with legislation concerning the large landowners, this to a great extent is only a verbal, symbolic output of the various political systems. Regardless of whether or not they are essentially different in their attitudes toward taxation than their counterparts in other areas and cultures —perhaps a debatable point—businessmen in Latin America do not want economic development if this means significant cost to themselves in financing government's role in the process. Left to themselves to aid development on a capitalist basis, their potential is considerably hindered by their divergence from the capitalist "norm."

To conclude this topic it should be clearly acknowledged that Latin American businessmen have been portrayed here as very elitist, selfish, nondemocratic, and lacking in social conscience. Occasionally, generalizations probably overstate certain of these features. If one insisted on making a value judgment, the Latin American businessman's concern for family, friends and personal dignity, as well as his relatively relaxed manner of doing business, could easily be judged as much more human than the obsessional drive for profit allegedly characteristic of his North American counterpart. The point, however, is that two entirely different cultures are involved in

[48] Ibid., p. 91.

[49] Ibid., pp. 95–102.

[50] Dale L. Johnson, "Industrialization, Social Mobility, and Class Formation in Chile," in *Studies in Comparative International Development,* Vol. 3, 1967.

such comparisons. Thus, the assumption must not be made that the business-man in Latin America, whatever his personal merits, will contribute to economic development in the same fashion or to the same extent as has his counterpart elsewhere in the world. All evidence suggests that, given his values and his practices, the businessman is not and will not be a conscious force for socioeconomic change in Latin America. This does not mean, however, that all contingencies are or will be foreseen, or that those per-ceived are or will be controllable. It is inevitable that some socioeconomic change will occur as the result of very gradual, but perceptible, economic development. The point is, once more, that much of such change is and will be consciously resisted and hindered by businessmen.

FURTHER READING

Note—Many of the books and articles listed as further reading for Chapter 1 are relevant to this chapter.

AUBREY, HENRY G., "Deliberate Industrialization," Lyle W. Shannon (ed.), *Underdeveloped Areas*. New York: Harper and Brothers, 1957.

BAER, W. and I. KERSTENETZKY (eds.), *Inflation and Growth in Latin America*. Homewood, Ill.: Richard D. Irwin, 1964.

BORRICAUD, FRANCOIS, "Structure and Function of the Peruvian Oligarchy," in *Studies in Comparative International Development*, Vol. 2, 1966.

BOTTOMLEY, ANTHONY, "Imperfect Competition in the Industrialization of Ecuador," in *Inter-American Economic Affairs*, Vol. 19, No. 1, Summer 1965.

BRANCO, RAUL, "Brazilian Finances and their Implication for Economic Integra-tion," in *Inter-American Economic Affairs*, Vol. 19, No. 2, Autumn 1965.

BRANDENBURG, FRANK, "The Case of Mexico: A Contribution to the Theory of Entrepreneurship and Economic Development," in *Inter-American Economic Affairs*, Vol. 16, No. 3, Winter 1962.

——————, *The Development of Latin American Private Enterprise*. Washing-ton D.C.: National Planning Association, 1964.

BROTHERS, DWIGHT S., "Private Investment in Latin America: Some Implications for the Alliance for Progress," in Cole Blasier (ed.), *Constructive Change in Latin America*. Pittsburgh: University of Pittsburgh Press, 1968.

CARDOSO, FERNANDO HENRIQUE, "The Enterpreneurial Elites of Latin America," in *Studies in Comparative International Development*, Vol. 2, 1966.

——————, "The Industrial Elite," in Seymour Martin Lipset and Aldo Solari (eds.), *Elites in Latin America*. New York: Oxford University Press, 1968.

——————, *El proceso de desarrollo en América Latina*. New York: United Nations: 1965.

—————————, "The Structure and Evolution of Industry in Sâo Paulo: 1930–1960," in *Studies in Comparative International Development*, Vol. 1, 1965.

CHAPLIN, DAVID, "Industrialization and the Distribution of Wealth in Peru," in *Studies in Comparative International Development*, Vol. 3, 1967.

COCHRANE, JAMES D., "Central American Economic Integration: The 'Integrated Industries' Scheme," in *Inter-American Economic Affairs*, Vol. 19, No. 2, Autumn 1965.

DALY, HERMAN E., "An Historical Question and Three Hypotheses Concerning the Uruguayan Economy," in *Inter-American Economic Affairs*, Vol. 20, No. 1, Summer 1966.

DE OLIVEIRA CAMPOS, ROBERTO, *Reflections on Latin American Development*. Institute of Latin American Studies, Austin: University of Texas, 1967.

DUE, JOHN F., "The Retail Sales Tax in Honduras: A Breakthrough in Taxation for Economic Development," in *Inter-American Economic Affairs*, Vol. 20, No. 3, Winter 1966.

Economic Commission for Latin America, *Central American Integration and Development*. United Nations Economic and Social Council, March 28, 1961.

—————————, *Latin America and United Nations Conference on Trade and Development*. New York: United Nations, 1964.

Economic Survey of Latin America. New York: United Nations, 1964.

ELLIS, H. S. and H. C. WALLICH (eds.), *Economic Development for Latin America*. New York: St. Martin's, 1961.

FARMER, RICHARD and BARRY RICHMAN, *Comparative Management and Economic Progress*. Homewood, Ill.: Richard D. Irwin, 1965.

FAYERWEATHER, JOHN, *The Executive Overseas*. Syracuse, N.Y.: Syracuse University Press, 1959.

FELIX, DAVID, "Monetarists, Structuralists, and Import-Substituting Industrialization: A Critical Appraisal," in *Studies in Comparative International Development*, Vol. 1, 1965.

FILLOL, THOMAS R., *Social Factors in Economic Development: The Argentine Case*. Cambridge, Mass.: M.I.T. Press, 1961.

FRANK, ANDRÉ GUNDER, *Capitalism and Underdevelopment in Latin America*. New York: Modern Reader Paperbacks, 1969.

FURTADO, CELSO, "Development and Stagnation in Latin America: A Structuralist Approach," in *Studies in Comparative International Development*, Vol. 1, 1965.

—————————, "Political Obstacles to the Economic Development of Brazil" in Claudio Veliz (ed.), *Obstacles to Change in Latin America*. New York: Oxford University Press, 1969.

GANNON, THOMAS A.(ed.), *Doing Business in Latin America*. American Management Association: 1968.

GERMANI, GINO, "Mass Immigration and Modernization in Argentina," in *Studies in Comparative International Development,* Vol. 2, 1966.

GERSHENKRON, ALEXANDER, *Economic Backwardness in Historical Perspective.* Cambridge, Mass.: Harvard University Press, 1962.

GONZÁLEZ, ALFONSO, "Some Effects of Population Growth on Latin America's Economy," in *Journal of Inter-American Studies,* Vol. 9, No. 4, October 1967.

GONZÁLEZ CASANOVA, PABLO, "Internal Colonialism and National Development," in *Studies in Comparative International Development,* Vol. 1, 1965.

GORDON, WENDELL, "Capitalism and Technological Adaptation in Latin America," in *Journal of Economic Issues,* Vol. 3, No. 1, March 1969.

——————, "Orthodox Economics and Institutional Behavior," in Cary Thompson (ed.), *Institutional Adjustment.* Austin: University of Texas Press, 1967.

GRUB, PHILLIP D. and ARTHUR R. MIELE, "The Changing Marketing Structure in the Industrial Development of Venezuela: Part 2," in *The Journal of Developing Areas,* Vol. 4, No. 1, October 1969.

HAGEN, EVERETT E., *On the Theory of Social Change.* Homewood, Ill.: Dorsey Press, 1962.

HAIRE, MASON, EDWIN GHISELLI, and LYMAN PORTER, *Managerial Thinking: An International Study.* New York: John Wiley, 1966.

HANSON, SIMON G., "The Alliance for Progress: The Fourth Year," in *Inter-American Economic Affairs,* Vol. 20, No. 2, Autumn 1966.

HARBRON, JOHN W., "The Dilemma of an Elite Group: The Industrialist in Latin America," in *Inter-American Economic Affairs,* Vol. 19, No. 2, Autumn 1965.

HERRERA, F., "Latin America," in H. V. Prochnow (ed.), *World Economic Problems and Policies.* New York: Harper & Row, 1965.

HIRSCHMAN, ALBERT O., "Ideologies of Economic Development in Latin America," in Albert O. Hirschman (ed.), *Latin American Issues: Essays and Comments.* New York: Twentieth Century Fund, 1961.

——————, *Journeys Toward Progress.* New York: Twentieth Century Fund, 1964.

HOLMBERG, ALAN, and WILLIAM F. WHITE, "Human Problems of U.S. Enterprise in Latin America," in *Human Organization,* Vol. 15, Fall 1956.

IMAZ, JOSÉ LUIS, *Los que mandan.* Buenos Aires: Editorial Universitaria de Buenos Aires, 1964.

JAGUARIBE, HELIO, "Political Strategies of National Development in Brazil," in *Studies in Comparative International Development,* Vol. 3, 1967.

JOHNSON, DALE L., "Industrialization, Social Mobility, and Class Formation in Chile," in *Studies in Comparative International Development,* Vol. 3, 1967.

——————, "The National and Progressive Bourgeoisie in Chile," in *Studies in Comparative International Development,* Vol. 4, 1968.

KENWORTHY, ELDON, "Argentina: The Politics of Late Industrialization," in *Foreign Affairs,* Vol. 45, No. 3, April 1967.

KLING, MERLE, "Taxes on the 'External' Sector: An Index of Political Behavior in Latin America," *Midwest Journal of Political Science,* Vol. 3, No. 2, May 1959.

KRAUS, WALTER (ed.), *The Economy of Latin America.* Iowa City: University of Iowa, Bureau of Business and Economic Research, College of Business Administration, 1966.

LAUTERBACH, ALBERT, *Enterprise in Latin America: Business Attitudes in a Developing Economy.* Ithaca, N.Y.: Cornell University Press, 1966.

LENS, SIDNEY, "Uncommon Common Market," in *Commonweal,* Vol. 86, June 23, 1967.

LIPMAN, AARON, *El empresario industrial en América Latina.* New York: United Nations, March 1967.

——————, "Social Backgrounds of the Bogota Entrepreneur," in *Journal of Inter-American Studies,* Vol. 7, No. 2, April 1965.

LIPSET, SEYMOUR MARTIN, "Values, Education, and Entrepreneurship," in Seymour Martin Lipset and Aldo Solari (eds.), *Elites in Latin America.* New York: Oxford University Press, 1968.

—————— and REINHARD BENDIX, *Social Mobility in Industrial Society.* Berkeley: University of California Press, 1959.

LOWENTHAL, ABRAHAM F., "Alliance Rhetoric versus Latin American Reality," in *Foreign Affairs,* Vol. 48, No. 3, April 1970.

"A Matter of Vital Interest," in *Newsweek,* Vol. 73, April 14 ,1969.

McMILLAN, CLAUDE, "Industrial Leaders in Latin America," in William H. Form and Albert A. Blum (eds.), *Industrial Relations and Social Change in Latin America.* Gainesville: University of Florida Press, 1965.

MEDINA, ECHAVARRÍA, JOSÉ, *Consideraciones sociológicas sobre el desarrollo económico.* Buenos Aires: Solar-Hachette, 1964.

MEIER, GERALD M., "Export Stimulation, Import Substitution and Latin American Development," in *Social and Economic Studies,* Vol. 10, No. 1, March 1961.

PETRAS, JAMES, *Politics and Social Forces in Chilean Development.* Los Angeles: University of California Press, 1969.

PINTO, ANIBAL, "Political Aspects of Economic Development in Latin America," in Claudio Veliz (ed.), *Obstacles to Change in Latin America.* New York: Oxford University Press, 1969.

POWELSON, JOHN J., "Toward an Integrated Growth Model: The Case of Latin America," in Cole Blasier (ed.), *Constructive Change in Latin America.* Pittsburgh: University of Pittsburgh Press, 1968.

RAMÍREZ GÓMEZ, RAMÓN, "ECLA, Prebisch, and the Problem of Latin American Development," in *Studies in Comparative International Development,* Vol. 2, 1966.

REHDER, ROBERT R., "Managerial Resource Development in Peru: Directions and Implications," in *Journal of Inter-American Studies,* Vol. 10, No. 4, October 1968.

The Rockefeller Report on the Americas. Chicago: Quadrangle, 1969.

SILVERT, KALMAN H., *Expectant Peoples.* New York: Random House, 1963.

SOMMERFELD, RAYNARD M., *Tax Reform and the Alliance for Progress.* Austin: University of Texas Press, 1966.

STRASSMAN, PAUL W., "The Industrialist," in John J. Johnson (ed.), *Continuity and Change in Latin America.* Stanford, Calif.: Stanford University Press, 1967.

Towards a Dynamic Development Policy for Latin America. New York: United Nations, 1963.

URQUIDI, VICTOR L., *The Challenge of Development in Latin America,* New York: Praeger, 1964.

——————, *Free Trade and Economic Integration in Latin America.* Berkeley: University of California Press, 1962.

——————, "The Implications of Foreign Investment in Latin America," in Claudio Veliz (ed.) *Obstacles to Change in Latin America.* New York: Oxford University Press, 1969.

VERNON, RAYMOND, *The Dilemma of Mexico's Development.* Cambridge, Mass.: Harvard University Press, 1963.

WEEKLY, JAMES K., "Security Marketing in a Developing Economy: The Case of Colombia," in *Inter-American Economic Affairs,* Vol. 19, No. 2, Autumn 1965.

WITHERS, WILLIAM, *The Economic Crisis in Latin America.* London: The Free Press of Glencoe, 1964.

CHAPTER 4

URBAN WORKERS

THE CONTEXT: POPULATION AND URBAN GROWTH, SLUMS

Perhaps the most obvious context in which to discuss the urban worker is the historical development, features, ideologies, and so forth of the "labor movement" in Latin America. However, while the labor movement is mentioned briefly at a later point in this chapter, it seems more appropriate to try to place the worker in his current, general socioeconomic setting. This can best be done by looking at some of the demographic characteristics of Latin America as well as at certain aspects of the industrial process in the area. While such things as population growth and automation do not, of course, refer to and concern only the urban worker, they do very obviously affect his socioeconomic and political situation, and to a considerable extent they contribute to creating that situation.

This chapter also considers present-day labor unions and labor internationals. While organized workers in no way comprise even a majority of the urban lower classes, they are nevertheless particularly important to actual and potential socioeconomic change, in that only through some form of organization are workers capable of voicing significant demands to the political systems and extracting concessions from them. Finally, there is an examination of some of the desires and demands of both unorganized and organized workers, as well as an evaluation of their success in having their demands met.

Perhaps one of the most widely known facts about Latin America today is that the area in general is experiencing a population growth rate that is variously described by such terms as "very high," "phenomenal" and "frightening." For example, between 1961 and 1965 Brazil's population grew at the rate of 3.6 percent annually; Mexico's, 3.1 percent; Chile's, 2.4 percent; and Peru's, 2.0 percent. These rates for the same period are in considerable contrast to Italy's population growth rate of 0.5 percent; Japan's, 0.9 percent, and the United States', 1.7 percent.[1] As a whole, Latin America since World War II has been growing in population at a rate of nearly 3 percent per year, the highest rate for any world region. Its total population today is in the neighborhood of 250 million, and if it continues to grow at the present rate—and many demographers believe the rate will actually increase substantially—Latin America will have over 300 million people by 1975 and approximately 750 million by the year 2000.[2]

Various explanations have been advanced for this demographic explosion, and many of them are at least partially plausible. For example, it has been suggested that the growth owes much to poor people's love of children, as well as to their desire to achieve old age security for themselves by having many children to look after them. Or, the poor are said to be so casual about life that they do not see many children as a problem, and/or do not care what happens to them. Other suggestions are that they have no other form of recreation than sex, and/or that they are too Catholic to use birth control measures. Perhaps even the ideas of some public opinion leaders, such as certain intellectuals and editors, to the effect that the developed world wants to cut Latin America's growth rate in order to keep the area weak, and prevent it from becoming a "world power," have some bearing on the situation.[3]

Actually, one study suggests that most of these traditional explanations of the high birth rate ignore the fact that the poor would prefer *fewer* children, but that attitudes of male dominance, reluctance to discuss sexual matters, and apathy toward the future—in addition to sheer lack of reliable information on birth control—inhibit family planning and will continue to do so until the general cultural climate changes.[4] That is, old ideas, one way or another, will continue to contribute to a high birth rate, while new health techniques promoted by national and international agencies will continue to decrease the mortality rate. For example, Brazil has one of the highest

[1] Peter Ranis, "Modernity and Political Development in Five Latin American Countries," in *Studies in Comparative International Development,* Vol. 4, 1968.

[2] Moisés Poblete Troncoso, *La explosión demográfica en América Latina.* Buenos Aires: Editorial Schapiro 1967.

[3] Joseph A. Kahl and J. Mayone Stycos, "The Philosophy of Demograpic Policy in Latin America," in *Studies in Comparative International Development,* Vol. 1, 1965.

[4] Ibid.

mortality rates in the region, yet the number of births over deaths makes its population growth rate the highest in the region. That is, from 1920 to 1940 in Brazil there was a birth rate of 44 per thousand and a mortality rate of 25.3 per thousand, yielding a surplus of 18.7 per thousand, and during the period from 1950 to 1960 the surplus climbed to 30.5 per thousand.[5]

Whatever the reasons for the growth rate, it has great implications for Latin American social, economic, and political change. For one thing, the growth rate has fostered an economic problem among an increasingly youthful population. A little more than two-fifths of the population are younger than 15 years of age, while due to a relatively high mortality rate only about 3 percent of the population is older than 65. The result is that only about 55 percent of the population is in the economically productive ages (15 to 64), in contrast to approximately 60 to 65 percent in the more developed areas. The end result is that only approximately one-third of the population is economically active, compared to 40 to 45 percent in the more developed areas. Thus the dependency ratio—the number of persons dependent on each thousand of the economically productive population—is very high in Latin America, and it has been estimated that it will rise by the mid-1970s to around 890–940 as compared to the 500–650 estimated for the more developed areas.[6] Furthermore, the economy will be faced with providing literally millions of jobs per year as the young people enter the labor market.

Related to the population explosion in Latin America is the urban explosion—a constant, rapid increase in urban centers that is creating many current as well as potential socioeconomic and political problems in the area. While many view the area as being basically rural, Latin America nevertheless is considerably more urbanized than other regions of the world such as Africa and Asia, and it is even slightly more urbanized than Southern Europe—although it is definitely not as economically developed as the latter. In fact, Latin America is only somewhat less urbanized than the Soviet Union or Central Europe, and only North America, Northwestern Europe, Australia, and New Zealand are considerably more urbanized. Some Latin American countries are actually as highly urbanized as the latter— for example, Argentina, Chile, and Uruguay have more than one-half their populations in cities of 20,000 or more inhabitants, and are surpassed in this respect only by the United Kingdom, Australia, New Zealand, and the Netherlands. The extent of urbanization, however, is not at all even among the various countries: the percentage of population in centers of 20,000 or more ranges from approximately 12 percent in Honduras to about 30 per-

---

[5] Robert N. Dannemann, "Problems of Human Resources in Brazil," in *International Labour Review,* Vol. 94, No. 6, December, 1966.

[6] Alfonso Gonzalez, "Some Effects of Population Growth on Latin America's Economy," in *Journal of Inter-American Studies,* Vol. 9, No. 4, October 1967.

cent in Mexico and Brazil to 48 percent in Venezuela to 58 percent in Argentina.[7]

Much of this urbanization has occurred in major metropolitan complexes, and the ten cities of Buenos Aires, Rio, São Paulo, Mexico City, Santiago, Lima, Caracas, Bogotá, Havana, and Montevideo today have over one million inhabitants each, ranging from approximately 1,200,000 in Montevideo (about 46 percent of Uruguay's total population) to about 6,800,00 in Buenos Aires (approximately 34 percent of Argentina's total population). Argentina, for example, with about 46 percent of its population in cities of 100,000 or more is second only to Australia in this respect; while Chile, with about 34 percent of the population in cities of 100,000 or more, and Venezuela, with approximately 30 percent, are comparable with such countries as the United Kingdom, West Germany, and Belgium, and surpass the United States.[8]

In addition to the relatively high urbanization level in Latin America, there is the urbanization growth rate. That is, while urbanization occurred throughout the world in the 1950 to 1960 period, Latin America surpassed all other world regions, except Oceania, in enlarging the percentage of urban population. In the Dominican Republic, for example, the increase in population in centers of 20,000 or more was at the rate of 9 percent per year, and in Venezuela and Honduras it was at the rate of 8 percent. Compounded annually, an 8 percent growth rate doubles the urban population in only nine years.[9]

Put differently, the United Nations has projected that while Latin America had approximately 97 million urban dwellers and 110 million rural dwellers in 1960, this will increase to 215 million urban and only 148 million rural by 1980. That is, while the rural population will increase by approximately 32 percent from 1960 to 1980, the urban population will increase by over 100 percent. In other words, while the rural population will continue to expand, it is in the urban areas where the greatest expansion is occurring and will continue to occur.[10]

The differential in rural-urban growth rates may be partly due to factors such as health and sanitation facilities being relatively less emphasized in the countryside—thus affecting the ratio of births to deaths. However, the migration of people from rural to urban areas—to find employment or to

[7] For the data on the urban explosion in Latin America see the article by John D. Durand and Cesar Pelaez, "Patterns of Urbanization in Latin America," in Clyde V. Kiser (ed.), Components of Population Change in Latin America. Proceedings of the Sixtieth Anniversary Conference of the Millbank Memorial Fund: New York, 1965.

[8] Ibid.

[9] Ibid.

[10] See also Troncoso, La explosión demográfica, pp. 74–84.

enjoy the amenities of city life—accounts primarily for the higher growth rate in urban areas. For example, the total population of Latin America increased in the decade from 1950 to 1960 by 49.3 million, or by 31.7 percent. Urban dwellers increased by 33.9 million, or by 55.7 percent, and rural dwellers increased by 15.4 million, or by only 16.3 percent. If it is assumed that, in the absence of migration from rural to urban areas, the rural population would have increased in this decade by about the same proportion as the total population, the 1960 rural population would have been larger by approximately 30 million than in 1950, instead of only larger by 15.4 million. This means that, in very rough terms, between 14 and 15 million rural people migrated to towns during the decade.[11] In a more specific example, more than half the natural increase in Brazil's rural population was relocated in towns during the 1950s, raising the growth rate in urban areas in this decade to 79 percent.[12] In a still more specific example of this rural to urban movement, during the last 25 years Lima, Peru has tripled in population, and half this increase is comprised of first generation rural immigrants. Two new cities, Chimbote and Huancayo, chiefly composed of rural immigrants, are competing in importance with the old cities founded during the Spanish conquest.[13]

These millions of people are moving into the cities for a reason. Many may simply be lured by the idea of bright lights and so forth, but evidence suggests that perhaps most leave rural poverty with certain expectations of somehow bettering themselves. That is, this migration does not appear to be an anomic, mindless movement, but rather is based, explicitly or implicitly, on rational motivations. For example, a study of rural immigrants in Lima settlements found that many of them came in order to give their children a chance for a good education.[14] Thus, any discrepancy between their expectations and the cities' ability to meet those expectations, may create frustrations which produce political problems.

In an excellent summary of the entire problem of population growth, rural migration, and rapid urbanization, Louis Ducoff points out that underlying the massive dimensions of rural migration to urban centers that has occurred in the past 15 years, and is expected to continue for the next 15 at least, are the highest rates of natural increase of population recorded

[11] Louis J. Ducoff, "The Role of Migration in the Demographic Development of Latin America," in Kiser, *Population Change.*

[12] Gavin W. Jones, "Underutilization of Manpower and Demographic Trends in Latin America," in *International Labour Review,* Vol. 98, No. 5, November 1968.

[13] Julio Cotler, "The Mechanics of Internal Domination and Social Change in Peru," in *Studies in Comparative International Development,* Vol. 3, 1967.

[14] Alain Touraine and Daniel Pecaut, "Working Class Consciousness and Economic Development in Latin America,' in *Studies in Comparative International Development,* Vol. 3, 1967.

anywhere in demographic history. This is particularly true of rural Latin America where the growth in the labor supply far exceeds employment opportunities. For example, in Central America during the decade from 1950 to 1960, the estimated number of males reaching working age exceeded the number of job opportunities created by death and retirement by about 3 or 4 to 1 in the rural population, and 2 or 3 to 1 in the urban population. Aided by the poverty resulting from a per capita income of less than $100 per year, rural unemployment fosters migration to urban areas. Thus the historical concentration of the urban population in a few large centers has been greatly intensified by the heavy inflow of rural people.[15]

As a result, then, of both natural increase and rural immigration, urbanization is occurring at an intense rate in Latin America, and magnifying the tremendous problems of socioeconomic development in the region. These problems are not limited to transportation, potable water, streets, lighting, and refuse and sanitation disposal. If these were all, such problems could probably be reasonably managed, if not solved, by massive public works programs, foreign aid, and technical assistance. But the real problem rests on the inability of the industrial process to cope with urban population growth.

At first glance, those who are accustomed to relating urbanization and industrialization may find this statement of the problem to be quite peculiar. For example, the United States is heavily industrialized, and its huge urban population operates the technology that drives the industrial process. Thus, there is a tendency to assume that, because Latin America is urbanizing so rapidly, the industrial process must at least be well under way, if not actually in full swing. This assumption, however, is not really applicable to Latin America. Even in the United States, automation—substituting machines for men—can increase industrial capacity without increasing employment in industry, while the urban population may continue to grow as a result of industrial expansion.[16] That is, whether one thinks that the Latin American cities have come too soon, or regards them as having arrived far too late given the level achieved by the industrial process throughout the world, industrialization and urbanization in Latin America do not necessarily go hand in hand.

To elaborate on this point, the highest rates of urbanization in the United States occurred during the first half of the nineteenth century, when the rate rose from approximately 3 percent per year around 1810 to 5 percent in the 1830s, and has since declined progressively to approximately 0.4 percent annually. Recent and current urbanization rates in Latin America are comparable to the rate of the United States in the 1840s and 1870s, and

15 Ducoff, "The Role of Migration."

16 Dannemann, "Problems of Human Resources in Brazil."

several countries in Latin America have experienced urbanization rates comparable to, and in some cases far surpassing, the United States' rate at its highest. This does not mean, however, that Latin American industrialization is following the same path that North American industrialization followed, nor does it mean that the problems posed are at all similar in either scope or nature.[17]

One of the problems very different in both nature and scope is that North American urbanization occurred when the industrial process was quite young, and when technology was labor-intensive—that is, when the machine-age was still so young that many men were necessary for its functioning. On the other hand, today in Latin America, despite "primitive" machinery and methods of operation, industry (and particularly that industry resulting from foreign investment) is increasingly oriented toward capital-intensive technology at a time when capital is not only relatively scarce compared to the developmental results hoped for from it, but also when labor is in great and constantly increasing abundance.[18] Factories may cost millions, but they may require only a few persons to operate them—and those required are highly skilled, specialized individuals. Put differently, much of Latin American industry is veering away from labor-intensiveness in its production because of the shortage of *trained* manpower. In the mid-1960s less than 5 percent of the Latin American labor force had secondary education and less than one-fourth had completed 6 years of school. As a result, industry tends to concentrate on areas where neither skilled nor unskilled labor is necessary.[19]

Thus, for example, Venezuela's economy may be able to expand at the rate of 10 percent per year for 10 years, but at the end of that period the number of unemployed is as great as ever.[20] Or, for example, as a study of Brazil points out, although economic development may depend essentially on growth in industry, employment in industry has actually decreased—demonstrating its inadequate capacity to absorb manpower. Furthermore, in a developing country such as Brazil, when employment in an industrial sector is not planned, the rural migrants flocking to the cities only increase the ranks of the unemployed or underemployed. Thus, in Brazil during the 1950s, manufacturing and even construction (the latter is the greatest absorber of unskilled labor) actually decreased, and the influx from rural areas was added to the "tertiary" sector.[21] (Very crudely, this sector comprises all the various service industries of a complex economy).

[17] Durand and Pelaez, "Patterns of Urbanization."

[18] Barbara Ward, "The Poor World's Cities," in *Economist,* December 6, 1969.

[19] Jones, "Underutilization of Manpower."

[20] Ward, "The Poor World's Cities."

[21] Dannemann, "Problems of Human Resources in Brazil."

Concerning the "tertiary" sector of the economy, a large tertiary sector is supposed to be a sign of high economic development. As Barbara Ward points out, Latin America has a larger tertiary sector than the United States—but this does not mean anything in terms of economic development. In Latin America this sector is comprised to a very large extent of "penny capitalists" whose "business" provides fragile protection against complete destitution and starvation. In no important way do they contribute to economic development or to the acquisition of industrial skills.[22]

In short, public policy in Latin America, no matter how well-intentioned and altruistic, faces a major and perhaps insurmountable problem in altering, much less eliminating, the circumstances of the bulk of the burgeoning urban population.[23] As a vicious circle, and as noted in the preceding chapter, large-scale industrialization depends on large-scale markets, but the depressed nature of most of Latin America's rural economy, coupled with very high urban unemployment and great poverty, preclude such markets and therefore preclude more employment.

In view of all this, it is not at all surprising that urban Latin America is marked by extremes of affluence and poverty. For example, a current preoccupation in North America is the lack of what we consider to be "adequate" housing for urban people—defined, of course, in our own cultural terms. When these terms are applied to urban Latin America, there is an estimated housing deficit of approximately 15.5 million units, and this deficit is constantly growing. That is, the annual rate of new housing construction is only one-half of 1 percent, far below the 2 to 3 percent rate typical of the more developed countries—which also have far slower rates of population growth. The result is that the combination of poor existing housing and the urban explosion in Latin America is creating a virtually urbridgeable gap between adequate housing facilities and actual accomplishments in housing construction.[24] The final result of urban growth, unemployment, and inadequate housing construction is a tremendous growth in slums. Depending on the country concerned, these slums are known variously as *turgurios, ranchos, barriados, callampas, favelas,* and so on—but whatever the name, the vast and rapidly spreading slums harbor poverty-stricken people whose conditions often make the North American slum-and ghetto-dweller appear relatively fortunate by comparison.

For example, one study points out that in Lima, Peru one-half million people, approximately one-fourth of the city's population, live in slums. To eradicate the slums would entail the relocation of this great mass of people, a solution quite impossible since the slums themselves exist precisely because

22 Ward, "The Poor World's Cities."

23 Jones, "Underutilization of Manpower."

24 Gonzalez, "Some Effects of Population Growth."

better housing is not available at inexpensive rates. Moreover, the constant influx of migrants creates such a demand for even further housing that doing away with the slum dwellings is totally impossible—even if government leaders wished to do so.[25] Similarly, for example, the *favelas* of Rio de Janeiro have, according to the 1960 census, a population of 337,000 living in 79,000 dwellings, an increase of approximately 100 percent over the 1950 census. These people represent over 10 percent of the city's population. To put it differently, between the two censuses the population of the *favelas* doubled while the rest of the urban population increased by 35 percent. Actually, it has been estimated that the *favelas* of Rio already comprise from 600,000 to 1 million people—approximately one-third of the city's total population. For example, an estimate based on data collected by the National Service for Eradication of Yellow Fever suggests that a total of 830,000 people lived in Rio's slums in 1960.[26] But whatever the city, slums are growing rapidly as they absorb not only the rural immigrants, but also the surplus from natural urban population increase who cannot find reasonably remunerative employment. That is, they harbor heavily unemployed, essentially unskilled, and, to a great extent, culturally transitional people pursuing a marginal subsistence.

One of the features of the Latin American slums which distinguishes them from their North American counterparts is the "squatter" character of so many of them. That is, when North Americans think of slums they tend to see them essentially as urban ghettos, filled with tenements owned by rent-gouging landlords. While hundreds of such slums do exist in Latin America, an increasingly common phenomenon is the large group of hovels and shacks in most Latin American urban centers, built on private or public land—a riverbank, a boulder-strewn field, a swamp, a garbage dump, and so forth—and built without private or governmental permission. These settlements often grow rather slowly and "naturally," reflecting both the rural exodus and the gradual urban renewal that create supermarkets, high-rise apartments, and so forth; but more and more frequently they are the product of "invasion" of a piece of land by a more or less organized and coordinated group of squatters. The Chilean name for these, for example, is "callampa," meaning mushroom,—because like mushrooms they seem to appear overnight. As one study points out, these squatter invasions are the result of general urbanization and population growth which are not compensated for by provision of dwellings for the massive metropolitan lower classes. As crowding and rent-squeezing of the poor continues and increases,

[25] Frank M. Andrews and George W. Phillips, "The Squatters of Lima: Who They Are and What They Want," in *Journal of the Developing Areas,* Vol. 4, No. 2, January 1970.

[26] Manuel Diegues Junior, "Urban Employment in Brazil," in *International Labour Review,* Vol. 93, No. 6, June 1966.

the only outlet for hundreds of them is either to seize land for themselves or to rent tiny, makeshift quarters in clandestine settlements run as commercial enterprises.[27] Another study of Latin American slum neighborhoods points out that, to be sheltered, a person must have a house. To build a house (even of cardboard) he must have land, which he can obtain only by illegal seizure. To overcome the resistance of institutionalized authority to such seizure, cohesive associations of families are necessary, because it is much more difficult for the authorities to evict a large, well-organized group than to evict individuals or even a large number of unorganized squatters. Organized invasions, which are becoming more common, are premised on this strategy.[28]

Despite several excellent studies that have been made of these slums by private individuals and by national and international agencies—the squatter invasion appears to be a particularly interesting phenomenon—this area of research is still too new for much to be known about it. For example, although it is known that organized invasions occur and are becoming more common, it is not yet known how specific individual housing needs become translated into group action. Nor has the selection and roles of leaders yet been studied. The extent and nature of mutual help reflected in the formation of neighborhood associations has scarcely been touched.[29] Similarly, it has been discovered that squatter settlements represent a wide range of conditions, and cannot be stereotyped in such terms as apathy, misery, filth, crime, delinquency, prostitution, and family disintegration. For example, one study suggests that there are at least two types of squatter slums—one comprised of the poorest of the poor and essentially representing the stereotypical, total slum, and the other comprised of individuals with more drive to attain economic and psychological independence.[30] Again, however, why these differences exist and what their significance, if any, is for political action, has yet to be studied thoroughly.

Whatever the differences, however, the existence and constant expansion of slums reflects a large, marginal population with entirely inadequate educational and technological qualifications for an "industrializing" society. For example, a study carried out by the Economic Commission for Latin America has pointed out that the slum resident in Chile rarely has the security of a stable job, but rather more probably has a succession of poorly paid jobs of uncertain duration. A survey of Puerto Alegre in Brazil found

27 Daniel Goldrich, Raymond B. Pratt, and C. R. Schuller, "The Political Integration of Lower Class Urban Settlements in Chile and Peru,' in *Studies in Comparative International Development*, Vol. 3, 1967.

28 Lloyd H. Rogler, "Slum Neighborhoods in Latin America," in *Journal of Inter-American Studies*, Vol. 9, No. 4, October 1967.

29 Ibid.

30 Goldrich et al., "The Political Integration of Lower Class Urban Settlements."

that 40 percent of the family heads in slums worked only irregularly and another 55 percent were totally unemployed.[31] A study of 22 slums in Cali, Colombia found similarly poor conditions: 19 of the 22 had some electricity, although 4 of these were obtaining it by illegal tapping; 10 had water piped into homes, 7 had public spigots, and the others received it by mule-back; 10 had some sewage disposal; and none had any form of garbage collection.[32]

In other words, the standard of living in the slums is extremely low. In the slums of Santiago de Chile, the level of income is so low that the "adequate" family diet, as defined by the National Health Service of Chile, would cost well over 100 percent of the typical slum-dweller's income. And the situation of unemployment and low income is scarcely compensated for by social security benefits, since 61 percent of the slum residents are not covered by the social security system—although Chile is said to have the best social insurance system in Latin America.[33]

The rural migrant has particular problems with which to cope when he arrives in town—usually as a slum dweller. That is, in addition to the problems of unemployment, low wages, very inadequate housing, and so forth, his lack of knowledge of city ways and his own cultural orientations make his adjustment very difficult. Actually, the adjustment of rural people to urban ways is not well understood. In Chapter 2, a distinction was made between quite important attitudinal differences among the Indians, peasants, and plantation workers—the groups that make up the rural-to-urban migration wave—and each of these groups has, as a result of the differences, its own problems of adjustment. For example, a recent study has focused upon some of the psychological problems a peasant must cope with, one way or another, if he is to take his place in a "typical" urban society. He is accustomed to a very circumscribed life, with virtually no conception of individual advancement; the position of being inferior is a built-in feature of his culture. The paternalistic character of the *patrón-peon* relationship in no way equips him to cope with impersonal orders and situations. That is, his entire training has educated him to be servile and to accept his lot. Oriented to the patriarchal and extended family, the individual contributes his earnings to the common property of the family members, rather than having them at his own disposal. The Indian and the plantation worker share some of these attitudes and attributes, but they also have some peculiar to themselves.[34]

[31] See Andrew G. Frank, "Urban Poverty in Latin America," in *Studies in Comparative International Development,* Vol. 2, 1966.

[32] Rogler, "Slum Neighborhoods."

[33] See Frank, "Urban Poverty."

[34] See Manuel Zymelman, "Cultural Patterns of Labor and Latin American Industrialization," in *Journal of Inter-American Studies,* Vol. 5, No. 3, July 1963.

Thus, when the rural immigrant arrives in the city he brings with him a certain cultural package—and the extent of immigration has been such that it has led to what has been termed "urban ruralization"—a pattern consisting of an accomodation to the new habitat without eradication of the rural behavioral patterns. The rural areas continue to be reference points for the immigrants, and the slums they live in exhibit patterns of traditional behavior such as reciprocity, cooperative labor, and local fiestas.[35] Their backgrounds, and their attitudes in general, drive them into non-industrial and very unstable occupations—ranging from domestic service to basket weaving to construction work.

DESIRES

This is the social and economic milieu in which the urban worker lives, and it is this milieu of poverty, lack of education, and so forth that can, at least at times, create desires within him which in turn may become demands on the political system. Examination of some of these desires and demands is best done in terms of two types of organizations—formally organized unions, and small-scale, informal community organizations.

Latin American labor unions are, of course, one of the byproducts of the industrial process, and many of their characteristics today reflect the limited degree to which that process has advanced. Generally, the earlier unions were either outgrowths of workers' cooperatives of differing sorts, or the deliberate creation of various ideological groupings, particularly anarcho-syndicalists, socialists, and populists. They all tended to be quite ideologically oriented, but despite ideological differences the common thread binding them together in what might be termed a "labor movement" was the desire for a classless society, based on labor communities, as well as a deep distrust of the traditional ways of organizing government.[36] Gradually, however, as industrialization created the industrial worker, who stood apart from the former artisan or craftsman, the unions gave up the old, ideological emphasis and began instead to concentrate heavily on improving the immediate situation of the worker. That is, unions began to emphasize economic gain for their memberships, rather than total solutions for the entire society.[37]

While it would be useful to know the actual numerical strength of the union movement in Latin America, neither the governments nor the

[35] Cotler, "Internal Domination and Social Change in Peru."

[36] Victor Alba, *Politics and the Labor Movement in Latin America* (Stanford, Calif.: Stanford University Press, 1968), pp. 201 and 202.

[37] Ibid., p. 204. See also the article by Henry A. Landsberger "The Labor-Elite: Is it Revolutionary?" in Seymour Martin Lipset and Aldo Solari (eds.), *Elites in Latin America* (New York: Oxford University Press, 1967).

unions themselves have bothered much with collecting such basic information. For that matter, given their tendency to grossly overstate their memberships, statistics supplied by unions are notoriously unreliable, and government data on the extent of unionization is, for various reasons, little less suspect. In any event, Victor Alba in his major work on the Latin American labor movement suggests that 10 years ago total union membership was in the neighborhood of 7 million, while Moisés Poblete Troncoso and Ben G. Burnett, in a similar work, state that at that time there were 12 million organized workers.[38] A recent study of the Inter-American Regional Organization of Workers (ORIT) suggests that Latin American affiliates represent 15 million workers,[39] and not even ORIT spokesmen claim their organization represents *all* organized workers. In short, the data on union membership is totally unreliable, and the figures cited in various studies seem to depend on the degree of pessimism or optimism with which each study is written. Furthermore, although details are not available, it must be remembered that whatever estimate is chosen it will include many people who are not in any manner "workers"—that is, lower class—in Latin American terms.

The various governments of Latin America have been quite cautious toward unions, and occasionally have been overtly antagonistic. For example, in 1961 a majority of the governments had not signed conventions 87 and 98 of the International Labor Organization (ILO) which guarantee labor the right to organize. Labor may be—and, within certain limits, usually is—allowed to organize even if these documents are not agreed to, but this is a matter of government permission not backed by any moral suasion provided by international agreements. Actually, as far as such agreements are concerned, the governments have generally been quite reluctant to commit themselves. In 1961, of the then current one hundred-odd international labor conventions, Cuba had agreed to 64; Uruguay, 57; Argentina, 56; Mexico, 47; Chile, 36; Guatemala, 34; Nicaragua, 30; Brazil, 29; Peru, 26; Colombia, 25; Dominican Republic, 22; Venezuela, 19; Costa Rica, 17; Panama and Honduras, 11; Bolivia and Ecuador, 6; and El Salvador, 4.[40] And, of course, any formal agreements supply no indication of the degree to which they are actually enforced or are enforceable.

Furthermore, while national labor codes exist, they appear, more than anything else, to be attempts by the governments to control the unions. Union structure and operation are quite closely supervised. For example, unions must generally be recognized by the government if they are to speak

---

[38] Moisés Poblete Troncoso and Ben G. Burnett, *The Rise of the Latin American Labor Movement* (New York: Bookman Associates, 1960).

[39] Carroll Hawkins, "The ORIT and the CLASC: A Case of Conflicting Perspectives," in *Inter-American Economic Affairs*, Vol. 20, No. 3, Winter 1966.

[40] Alba, *Politics and the Labor Movement*, p. 214.

officially for their members, union constitutions must have government approval, union elections or strike votes must be attended by government officials, union funds are usually controlled by the government, and there are usually restrictions prohibiting the use of union funds for strike wages or political activities.[41] While such factors as government recognition of a union are necessary even in the United States before the union has a right to the protection of law, there is nevertheless an essential difference. In North America the basic rules are made and administered by the National Labor Relations Board, a quasi-judicial body fairly immune from overt governmental and other political pressure. In Latin America, on the other hand, the basic ground-rules are subject to the broad, discretionary authority of government ministries, and as a result the individual union tends to be at the mercy of government officials.[42] Furthermore, the need to obtain government recognition of a strike tends to undermine the effectiveness of the strike—or to make it illegal—and it makes labor dependent on the government for continued union operation.[43] In short, government constitutes the major external influence on Latin American union organization and activities[44] As one of the most suggestive studies of Latin American unions points out, this close relationship between government and unions reflects two basic characteristics. First, it shows the government's desire to control labor by keeping it weak and unable to exert pressure; and, second, it shows a continuing attempt to convert labor's gratitude into political support for those who grant some of its demands.[45]

Consequently, Latin American unions tend strongly to be what have been termed "political unions" as distinct from "economic unions."[46] That is, they tend to be dominated by political considerations rather than being primarily concerned with economics. One explanation of this phenomenon suggests that it is partly due to the financial weakness of the unions and their consequent need to look outside their own ranks for funding, and partly due to their political weakness, which necessitates obtaining strong political allies if they are to have any guarantee at all of security and freedom to operate.[47] Another, not necessarily contradictory, study suggests

[41] Robert J. Alexander, *Today's Latin America* (New York: Praeger, 1968). See also his article, "The Latin-American Labor Leader," in William H. Form and Albert A. Blum (eds.), *Industrial Relations and Social Change In Latin America* (Gainesville: University of Florida Press, 1965).

[42] Landsberger, "The Labor-Elite."

[43] Ibid.

[44] Troncoso and Burnett, *The Latin American Labor Movement,* p. 150.

[45] Landsberger, "The Labor Elite."

[46] Bruce H. Millen, *The Political Role of Labor in Developing Countries.* Washington, D.C.: Brookings Institution, 1963.

[47] Alexander, *Today's Latin America.*

that the political nature of unions is a consequence of government control over them. That is, because of many and stringent government regulations concerning union organization and activity, unions find their most basic concerns—such as wages and working conditions—determined by government, and therefore turn to the parties and groups in control of the government.[48] In any event, the result is that political parties tend to dominate unions. Therefore, party interests tend to supercede union interests, and the latter are often simply ignored. Union leaders tend to become party politicians and no longer maintain their members' interests as their primary concern.[49]

Concerning the Latin American union leader, there is some controversy over the degree to which the typical leader is corrupt—"corruption" being defined narrowly in terms of such things as acceptance of pay-offs and misuse of funds, as well as broadly in terms of sincerity, representativeness, and so forth. Alexander considers the union leader to be reasonably free of corruption but Alba seems to believe he is very corrupt. A compromise on this debate is suggested by Henry Landsberger in one of the few studies of the Latin American labor elite which seriously attempts to justify assertions with actual data—although, as he notes, the nature of corruption makes a really detailed study of it impossible. While pointing to widespread corruption in several major cases—early in the Mexican Revolution, in Brazil under Vargas, and in Argentina under Perón—Landsberger suggests that to classify all union officials as cynics pursuing personal gain is far too sweeping. Furthermore, whether or not they are cynics is, in one sense, beside the point, since the career of a labor leader is ultimately dependent on his relationship with his "constituents," and he cannot totally ignore their desires. As a result, even when he has considerable latitude, he must work to some extent for union membership as well as for personal gain.[50]

Like the industries of Latin America of which it is a result, organized labor in Latin America has been heavily influenced by foreign countries— again, particularly by the United States. While there are some national labor leadership training centers in Latin America, most of such training comes from foreign institutions. The Labor Institute of the University of Puerto Rico, for example, backed by United States funds, has a leadership training program which enrolls potential labor leaders from all over Latin America. The American Institute of Free Labor Development (AIFLD) is another major example. This institution, created in the early 1960s, today has a multi-million dollar budget financed by the United States government, and has branches throughout Latin America. Formed with AFL-CIO

---

[48] Landsberger, "The Labor-Elite."

[49] Alexander, *Today's Latin America*, p. 99.

[50] Landsberger, "The Labor-Elite."

encouragement, its formal purpose as stated by a recent chief executive of the institution, is to create an independent, free, labor union movement in Latin America.[51] Essentially this appears to mean the creation of unions similar to North American unions, following North American union ideology and techniques, to ensure that "alien" ideologies and techniques—particularly those of the Communists—are not pursued.

Another means by which the Latin American labor movement is influenced by North America is the Inter-American Regional Organization of Workers (ORIT), itself the Western Hemisphere branch of the International Confederation of Free Trade Unions (ICFTU). Founded in Mexico in 1951, the ORIT owes its creation largely to the efforts of the American Federation of Labor, and the ORIT, like the AIFLD, was and is essentially designed to frustrate communism in Latin American unions. ORIT is said to have some 30 million members, although one-half of these are members of American and Canadian affiliates. These affiliates are definitely the most affluent elements in the organization, and it depends quite heavily on their financial contributions for its operations. It also is dependent on financial assistance from the International Solidarity Fund of the ICFTU. A significant amount of aid comes directly from the United States government as well as from United States business firms. Ideologically, the ORIT states that it stands for social revolution, to be achieved, however, by such means as education, housing projects, hospitals, and so forth. It heavily endorses the Alliance for Progress and uses Alliance rhetoric as its own. At all times it carries on a quite massive anti-communist barrage. It is consistently friendly toward capitalism and free enterprise, and it is also consistently friendly toward the United States government.[52]

Another regional organization, the Latin American Confederation of Christian Trade Unions (CLASC), has been claimed to represent the greatest change in the Latin American labor picture during the 1960s. Furthermore, it is asserted that the outcome of the struggle between CLASC and ORIT for union allegiance will have great significance for the political, social, and economic development of the area.[53] Revolution is the basis of CLASC ideology, and CLASC sees revolution as involving a complete alteration of the Latin American social structure accompanied by a redistribution of wealth through a comprehensive social welfare system. Thus, the CLASC ridicules the ORIT for the latter's concentration on the strike

[51] Serafino Romualdi, *Presidents and Peons* (New York: Funk & Wagnalls, 1967).

[52] For this summary of the ORIT see Hawkins, "The ORIT and the CLASC."

[53] The following summary of the CLASC is based mainly on the article by Michael J. Francis, "Revolutionary Labor in Latin America: The CLASC," in *Journal of Inter-American Studies,* Vol. 10, No. 4, October 1968.

technique, since low wages are viewed as only one manifestation of the totally unjust socioeconomic system. While it advocates achieving the revolution by nonviolent means if possible, there is a constant suggestion in CLASC rhetoric that if the revolution is continually frustrated, violence will become an acceptable alternative.

Founded in 1954, the CLASC today claims to have influence over 5 million workers—although these are certainly not all or even mainly dues-paying members. Actually, even a sympathetic account of the organization places the membership, in terms of unions directly or indirectly affiliated with it, in the vicinity of 1 million.[54] Furthermore, a good proportion of these are members of peasant unions of various types, since the CLASC insists on the very problematical idea of moulding urban workers and peasants into a single movement with unified, coherent goals.

In terms of finances, the CLASC shares a basic, important characteristic with ORIT—it cannot support itself with membership contributions, but must look outside Latin America for support. The first and least important contributor is the International Federation of Christian Trade Unions (IFCTU), which helped to found the CLASC originally. The more important source of financial aid, however, is the International Solidarity Institute, which is itself financed directly by West Germany. Without aid from the Institute, the CLASC would probably collapse very quickly.

Actually, it is difficult to understand why some writers place so much confidence in the future of the CLASC—it certainly has not had resounding success to date. In fact, in the four largest, most industrialized countries of the area it has been quite unsuccessful in attracting membership. In Argentina, it has failed to attract the *peronistas,* since the latter are not at all revolutionary in the sense that the CLASC is, and even the Catholic hierarchy in Argentina is against it. In Brazil, the CLASC has (or, had) a major affiliate (the CNCO) but the latter has resisted CLASC efforts toward more cohesive organization, and the two organizations essentially rejected one another when the affiliate supported the Castello Branco coup. In Chile, which has had a strong element of Christian Democracy, the CLASC has had some success, but it is nevertheless far superceded by the FRAP coalition, both in terms of membership and in terms of control of key unions. The CLASC is also apparently often frustrated by the Chilean Christian Democrat Party, and has claimed that the latter is led by intellectuals not really interested in achieving basic social change. And in Mexico, the CLASC has been completely incapable of breaking the hold over organized labor of the Confederation of Mexican Workers (CTM), which essentially comprises the labor sector of the dominant PRI and which is affiliated with the ORIT.[55]

[54] Ibid.

[55] Ibid.

Both the ORIT and the CLASC represent deliberate foreign involvement as well as foreign influence in Latin American labor. And whether it is North American or European, this influence is a constant factor in the overall Latin American labor picture. The CLASC, for example, could easily be hurt, perhaps broken, by a shift in European politics which necessitated lack of friction between West Germany and the United States. Or, for example, any "revolutionary" stance adopted by the ORIT could be easily controlled by the definitely nonrevolutionary North American affiliates that support it—and could be seriously hurt if United States government and business support was withdrawn. Actually, neither of these two organizations' ideologies is really congruent with the Latin American culture. The CLASC preaches middle-class, intellectual ideas on social revolution to a lower class which is essentially very conservative and tradition-oriented in both its Iberian and indigenous bases. The ineffectual Latin American Confederation of Workers CTAL, a Marxist-oriented regional organization which includes Communist affiliates, has always suffered greatly from the same problem. While the ORIT has been relatively more successful, it too has been constantly faced with the difficulty and often the impossibility of selling a forward-looking, materialistic, essentially Protestant ideology to a tradition-dominated, essentially Catholic society.

In summary of organized labor in Latin America, there is in most literature on the subject a marked pessimistic attitude. Even when literature is definitely pro-labor—as, for example, various articles in the *International Labor Review* are—the pessimism tends to remain. While an occasional writer will attempt to be enthusiastic over some really very minor union triumph, this usually appears to be a whistling in the dark. That is, even those most in favor of labor in Latin America generally concede that it is very poorly organized, very inadequately financed, generally ineptly and often venally led, foreign-dominated, ideologically unappealing to the masses, and generally not very successful.

The lack of success of labor organizations in promoting revolutionary ideas essentially reflects the basic attitudes and desires of the typical Latin American worker. The typical union does not embrace workers who wish to see their society turned upside-down. To the contrary, evidence suggests that all they want is a better share in the benefits of existing society. That is, while it used to be the norm to regard Latin American labor as a revolutionary force teetering on the brink of profound—violent or nonviolent—social revolution, more recent studies suggest that this is basically a distortion of workers' attitudes. Workers may want such things as better wages, guaranteed employment, health insurance, unemployment insurance, and similar benefits, but these are desired so as to allow them to live a better life within the existing social systems.[56]

56 See, for example, Landsberger, "The Labor-Elite."

In one sense, this is quite incongruous, since it is the existing social and economic structures that have for years maintained urban workers in a state of economic deprivation and low social status. However, it appears to be essentially a matter of desires derived from basic cultural values. For example, it was for years believed that the emerging Latin American middle-income groups would prove to be the tool necessary to forge a new, more equitable, less elitist society throughout Latin America. That is, the Latin American pattern was to follow the apparent North American pattern insofar as socioeconomic change involving the middle-income groups was concerned. However, using various approaches, more recent studies of these groups in Latin America suggest quite strongly that they are not in any sense revolutionary and are very unlikely to become so since they possess traditional, elitist beliefs about the natural order of societies. The workers, in turn, seem to have the same attitudes. If they actually do aspire to higher status—the extent and depth of this desire is quite problematical—they aspire to that which is middle class, and they are not oriented toward destroying that which they want. Thus, for example, there is general lack of identity between semi-skilled and unskilled workers, between skilled and semi-skilled workers, between white-collar and blue-collar workers, and so forth. While this lack of identity or lack of solidarity among various types of workers is important to the potential success of the union movement in Latin America, the point to be made here is that the lack of identity essentially reflects cultural values which are not at all conducive to rapid and profound socioeconomic change.

This should not be taken to mean, however, that organized workers do not have some socioeconomic desires. Any organization, even if its leadership is totally venal, has to promise something to its membership, and promises, especially constantly reiterated promises, are bound to have some aspirational significance to the individual. Furthermore, the very fact that he is in an urban area, capable of observing various forms of affluence among the higher-income groups, will undoubtedly create some aspirations within the urban worker—however inchoate these may be and however minimal they may appear to most North American observers.

Even the unorganized worker appears generally capable of desiring a different, better life. That is, unlike so many peasants, whether Indian or *mestizo minifundistas*, or resident *hacienda* workers, the urban worker appears generally capable of seeing somewhat beyond the immediate situation and of aspiring to something else. For example, the individual leaving the *hacienda* to look for work in the city tends to be looked upon by those he leaves behind as a "betrayer," not only of the owner but of the *hacienda* community. Only a certain "bad" element migrates to the city, and those he leaves behind show his uniqueness by considering him a rebel against the society he knows.[57] If this is the case, he certainly does not have the

---

[57] See Zymelman, "Latin American Industrialization."

typical peasant mentality so totally conducive to acceptance of one's lot in life. Actually, various studies have found that rural migrants are often attracted to the city in the first place by some goal for the future, that they are capable of defining and organizing critical appraisals, and that they implicitly and explicitly formulate general orientations.[58] For example, a study of the squatters of Lima found that they were capable of quite definite desires regarding 26 public and private services, and were not at all hesitant about voicing their feelings. Intensive feelings of dissatisfaction were expressed over the location of medical services, availability of property titles, sewers, water supply, house and street lighting, and others.[59] Another study suggests that slum dwellers can be divided into three types. The first type simply withdraws—essentially he does not relate to the norms of industrial and urban life. The second type accepts and participates in industrial and urban life without much question, although he may harbor considerable dissatisfaction with the norms. And the third type openly questions work and urban norms, discusses and criticizes them, and so forth. It is the latter two types, particularly the third, that can become involved in the formulation of protest.[60] In short, the unorganized slum dweller is both a passive and manipulated person and a potential, occasionally actual, element in the formation of social movements of varying scope.[61]

DEMANDS

Despite any aspirations which can be shown or deduced, there is nevertheless a general lack of demands made by urban workers. That is, while many exceptions do exist, there is throughout Latin America a very low, often nonexistent politicization of the urban lower-income groups. When political action does occur, it has a strong tendency to reflect the older cultural tradition of the *patrón-peon* relationship, with, for example, organized political parties considered much less helpful than personalities such as major government officials or the President himself.[62]

One study suggests that this low level of political awareness is the result of a mixture of factors, such as poverty, restricted conception of time and space, a belief that the environment is unchangeable, the nature of lower-class occupations, vulnerability to sanctions, and others.[63] Another study points out that often gains by workers, in one form or another, are

[58] See, for example, Touraine and Pecaut, "Working Class Consciousness."

[59] Andrews and Phillips, "The Squatters of Lima."

[60] Touraine and Pecaut, "Working Class Consciousness."

[61] Ibid.

[62] See Goldrich et al., "The Political Integration of Lower Class Urban Settlements."

[63] Ibid.

achieved without their asking for them. That is, for various reasons based on workers' political potential, or feared political potential, many if not most major cases of labor achievements are concessions won without direct pressure from labor. For that matter, even labor leaders may not be consulted by the political authorities.[64] Again, one can view this as still another manifestation of the traditional *patrón-peon* system—a system of elitist noblesse oblige.

Given the low level of politicization of the urban worker, it is quite probable that many, if not most, of the more comprehensive demands actually made on his behalf do not really interest him. An outstanding example of such a demand is the one for participation in economic planning —a demand which the typical worker might be induced to support (if he is consulted), but which he is totally incapable of comprehending. For that matter, evidence suggests that even labor leaders often are incapable of understanding all that is involved in such a demand.

For example, the Fifth Congress of the ORIT in 1961 emphasized that labor should participate in national planning agencies.[65] That is, the ORIT was insisting that labor had to assume a heavier burden in protecting the rights of workers than just making wage demands. National organizations constantly voice the same demand. For example, the Confederation of Mexican Workers in 1965 stated that workers' organizations should share in all government activities concerned with planning and implementation of programs. In the same year the Chilean Federation of Workers insisted that workers' participation in planning at every level was absolutely necessary, since no problem left the workers unaffected. More specifically, the Colombian Workers' Union stated in 1963 that one of the national legislative chambers should be replaced by a Chamber of Labor in which workers, employers, and others would be represented.

However, as one study of union participation in economic planning points out, despite these and many similar statements the attitudes of Latin American unions, when it comes to actually creating a system of participation, are generally much less constructive. As the study indicates, the arguments for labor participation are essentially sound, but despite the enthusiasm of spokesmen, labor participation in planning is really quite low in their list of priorities. This in turn is due to several causes, among which are poor union structure and management, lack of representativeness, lack if solidarity, lack of leadership training, subservience to political parties, and

[64] Landsberger, "The Labor-Elite."

[65] The following discussion of labor involvement in planning is based mainly on Geraldo von Potobsky, "Participation by Workers' and Employers' Organizations in Planning in Latin America," in *International Labour Review*, Vol. 95, No. 6, June 1967.

subservience to government. Real planning inevitably involves basic conflict over goals, and labor leaders are generally unwilling to face such conflict.[66]

For example, a study of participation in planning in Chile has found that the trade union representative in the national body concerned with developmental planning (CORFO) generally has refrained from expressing his views, limiting himself to requesting information as to how various projects may possibly affect workers. Any explanations given to him are, of course, supplied by government officials or industrial representatives with whom he is supposed to conflict, if necessary, if he is going to really represent the workers' interests. The situation is repeated at the provincial level, and the study concludes on this point that workers' representatives generally lack a sense of responsibility, lack technical qualifications, speak only for themselves rather than for the unions they represent, and some of the unions are not really representative of the sector they claim to stand for.[67] Similar studies of labor participation in planning in other Latin American countries suggest the same general conclusions.

In the slums, such things as land invasions and even illegal tapping of electrical lines to obtain power for some in a community, can in one sense be regarded as a definite demand on the system. That is, as noted above, such activities are the end response of poverty-stricken people to an authoritarian and unresponsive system. However, they also seem capable of making demands in a fairly organized manner through fairly normal channels. For example, in a settlement on the outskirts of Lima, while invaders were first met with harrassment by police and military, the situation gradually stabilized, negotiations were carried on between the settlers' organization and government officials, and an agreement was finally reached to the effect that the government would provide certain services while the settlers would pay for the land they had usurped. Similarly, in Santiago, Chile an invasion occurred, negotiations were carried out, some settlers were allowed to stay, and others were moved with some government assistance to vacant government lands.[68]

However, whether involving unions or slum dwellers' ad hoc organizations, the demands of the urban worker in Latin America tend to be quite modest as well as ineffectual. As noted above, workers are quite vulnerable to sanctions, for a variety of reasons, and therefore they hesitate to incur them through positive action. They have generally low occupational skill and

[66] Ibid.

[67] Manuel Barrera, "Participation by Occupational Organizations in Economic and Social Planning in Chile," in *International Labour Review,* Vol. 96, No. 2, August 1967.

[68] Goldrich et al., "The Political Integration of Lower Class Urban Settlements."

low opportunity for employment. Unions are weak, and informal organizations are not only risky but are also short-lived even when successful. Distance between classes is so great that lower-class people in trouble with the government receive very little general social support. The bureaucracy is basically comprised of middle-class people who cannot identify with lower-class clients. And, finally, there is always police or military harrassment of lower-class "troublemakers."[69] The point is, then, that although expectations can lead to discontent and the voicing of demands, this occurs far less often than the North American observer might expect. That is, while there are many exceptions, there remains a strong tendency among the Latin American urban lower-income groups to accept their lot rather than make themselves conspicuous by political activities.

SYSTEM RESPONSE

Concerning rewards from the various political systems, the urban workers in Latin America receive a very great deal—in terms of formal legislation. Perhaps the best way to portray this is to look briefly at Article 123 of the Mexican Constitution of 1917. Article 123 and a few related articles, many Mexican writers proudly point out, preceded the humanistically-based constitutions of the Soviet Union and Weimar Germany, and provided a new concept of social life and law and a more comprehensive and generous interpretation of the meaning of distributive justice.[70] Certainly, this article, like other features of the Mexican Constitution, has been drawn on considerably in preparing labor codes and related legislation throughout Latin America.

Article 123 establishes such things as an eight-hour maximum working day (seven hours at night), a six-day working week, and severely limits overtime. The minimum wage must be more than a minimum that is, subsistence living wage. Equal wages must be paid the sexes. Wages are exempt from attachment, compensation, and deduction. Workers are entitled to participate in the profits of any agricultural, commercial, manufacturing, or mining enterprises. Children under twelve cannot be employed, and employees between twelve and sixteen years of age cannot work more than six hours per day. Various liberal provisions are designed to ensure the security, safety, and comfort of pregnant working women before and after childbirth. An employer cannot fire a worker without good cause, and workers are free to join unions and to participate in lawful strikes. A worker can leave his job and receive three months' wages in compensation

---

[69] Ibid.

[70] Fernando Yllanes Ramos, "The Social Rights Enshrined in the Mexican Constitution of 1917," in *International Labour Review,* Vol. 96, No. 6, December 1967.

if, for example, the employer has not been honest toward him. Workmen's compensation is provided for, and so forth.

In effect, Article 123 of the Mexican Constitution is a declaration of social rights for the worker. However, it and many provisions like it contained in Latin American constitutions and labor codes, essentially remain only a declaration—either a declaration in the abstract or a declaration of some future goal to be attained. That is, like agrarian reform laws which are so common in the region, this type of constitutional and/or legislative guarantee of workers' rights, privileges, and socioeconomic status is essentially only a verbal or symbolic output of the various political systems.

For example, all the Latin American countries have some form, however skeletal, of a social security program. However, as a recent analysis of these programs suggests, they are generally not to the advantage of workers with a low financial and social status. That is, rather than compensating the more economically and socially deprived segments of the populations, these schemes generally have exactly the opposite effect in that they give the advantage to the higher-income groups for whom the conditions of entitlement to benefit are less strict while the amount of benefit is greater. At the same time, because of the prices paid for goods and services and because of the regressive taxation systems, the burden of the contributions paid by employers and by governments is transferred to the entire population. As a result, the low-income groups, whose social security programs are the least advantageous or are nonexistent, are helping to finance the programs of the higher-income groups. In other words, while social security is generally considered to play an important role in redistributing national income, in Latin America this redistribution often takes a direction not usually considered to be socially just or, for that matter, economically desirable.[71] Actually, the very prevalence of differential programs for higher- and lower-income groups suggests the low political prestige and success of the latter groups.

In short, while there are some notable exceptions, urban workers are not very successful in having their demands met by the various political systems of latin America. If organized, they are captured and manipulated by leaders, politicians, and government officials. If unorganized, and most of them are, they have no effective voice. Unlike many peasants, most urban workers do have aspirations, but their generally low politicization tends strongly to suppress aspirational demands on the political systems. If they are not expressed, at least to the extent of grumblings which frighten the authorities, any desires will of course not be recognized. Furthermore, given the social systems of Latin America, as well as the low economic development

[71] Alfredo Mollet, "Diversification or Standardization: Two Trends in Latin American Social Security," in *International Labour Review,* Vol. 101, No. 1, January 1970.

that has occurred relative to the degree of urbanization that has taken place, there is considerable doubt that the political systems could meet strong, comprehensive demands from the urban workers—demands designed to give them a significantly higher standard of living.

FURTHER READING

ABRAMS, CHARLES, *Man's Struggle for Shelter in an Urbanizing World.* Cambridge, Mass.: M.I.T. Press, 1964.

ADAMS, RICHARD N., *The Second Sowing: Power and Secondary Development in Latin America.* San Francisco: Chandler, 1967.

ALBA, VICTOR, *Alliance without Allies: The Mythology of Progress in Latin America.* New York: Praeger, 1965.

—————, *Politics and the Labor Movement in Latin America.* Stanford, Calif.: Stanford University Press, 1968.

ALEXANDER, ROBERT J., "The Latin American Labor Leader," in William H. Form and Albert A. Blum (eds.), *Industrial Relations and Social Change in Latin America.* Gainesville: University of Florida Press, 1965.

—————, *Organized Labor in Latin America.* New York: Free Press, 1965.

—————, *Today's Latin America.* New York: Praeger, 1968.

ALMOND, GABRIEL, and SIDNEY VERBA, *The Civic Culture.* Princeton, N.J.: Princeton University Press, 1963.

AMARO, VICTORIA, NELSON, "Mass and Class in the Origins of the Cuban Revolution," in *Studies in Comparative International Development,* Vol. 4, 1968.

ANDREWS, FRANK M. and GEORGE W. PHILLIPS, "The Squatters of Lima: Who They Are and What They Want," in *Journal of Developing Areas,* Vol. 4, No. 2, January 1970.

ARCOS, JUAN, *El sindicalismo en América Latina.* Santiago: Feres, 1964.

BAIROCH, J., and J.-M. LIMBOR, "Changes in the Industrial Distribution of the World Labour Force, by Region, 1880–1960," in *International Labour Review,* Vol. 98, No. 4, October 1968.

BARRERA, MANUEL, "Participation by Occupation Organizations in Economic and Social Planning in Chile," in *International Labour Review,* Vol. 96, No. 2, August 1967.

—————, *El sindicato industrial: anhelos, métodos de lucha, relaciones con la empresa.* Santiago: Insora, 1965.

BARRET, RAYMOND J., "The Role of Trade Unions in Underdeveloped Countries" in *Labor Law Journal,* Vol. 13, December 1962.

BEYER, GLENN H. (ed.), *The Urban Explosion in Latin Amercia: A Continent in Process of Modernization.* Ithaca, N.Y.: Cornell University Press, 1967.

BISHOP, JORDAN, "Sprouting Slums," in *Commonweal,* Vol. 86, April 28, 1967.

Bonilla, Frank, "The Urban Worker," in John J. Johnson (ed.), *Continuity and Change in Latin America*. Stanford, Calif.: Stanford University Press, 1964.

Caballaro, Tamayo, Xavier, "The ILO and Development in the Americas," in *International Labour Review,* Vol. 100, No. 6, December 1969.

Campano, Arnoldo R., "The Minimum Wage Act in Argentina," in *International Labour Review,* Vol. 94, No. 3, September 1966.

Cardoso, Fernando H., and José Luis Reyna, "Industrialization, Occupational Structure, and Social Stratification in Latin America," in Cole Blasier (ed.), *Constructive Change in Latin America*. Pittsburgh: University of Pittsburgh Press, 1968.

Chaplin, David, "Industrialization and the Distribution of Wealth in Peru," in *Studies in Comparative International Development,* Vol. 3, 1967.

Cordova, Efren, "Collective Labor Relations in Latin American Ports," in *International Labour Review,* Vol. 100, No. 4, October 1969.

Cornelius, Wayne A. Jr., "Urbanization as an Agent in Latin American Political Instability: The Case of Mexico," in *American Political Science Review,* Vol. 63, No. 3, September 1969.

Cotler, Julio, "The Mechanics of Internal Domination and Social Change in Peru," in *Studies in Comparative International Development,* Vol. 3, 1967.

Dannemann, Robert N., "Problems of Human Resources in Brazil," in *International Labour Review,* Vol. 94, No. 6, December 1966.

de Imaz, José Luis, *Los que mandan*. Buenos Aires: Editorial Universitaria de Buenos Aires, 1965.

Diegues Junior, Manuel, "Urban Employment in Brazil," in *International Labour Review,* Vol. 93, No. 6, June 1966.

di Tella, Torcuato, "Populism and Reform in Latin America," in Claudio Veliz (ed.), *Obstacles to Change in Latin America*. New York: Oxford University Press, 1965.

Ducoff, Louis J., "The Role of Migration in the Demographic Development of Latin America," in Clyde V. Kiser (ed.), *Components of Population Change in Latin America*. New York: Proceedings of the Sixtieth Anniversary Conference of the Millbank Memorial Fund, 1965.

Durand, John D. and Cesar Pelaez, "Patterns of Urbanization in Latin America," in Clyde V. Kiser (ed.), *Components of Population Change in Latin America*. New York: Proceedings of the Sixtieth Anniversary Conference of the Millbank Memorial Fund, 1965.

Ferrero, Carlos, "Health and Levels of Living in Latin America," in Clyde V. Kiser (ed.), *Components of Population Change in Latin America*. New York: Proceedings of the Sixtieth Anniversary Conference of the Millbank Memorial Fund, 1965.

Fitzgibbon, R. H., "Political Implications of Population Growth in Latin America," in *The Sociological Review,* February 1967.

FRANCIS, MICHAEL J., "Revolutionary Labor in Latin America: The CLASC," in *Journal of Inter-American Studies,* Vol. 10, No. 4, October 1968.

FRANK, ANDREW G., "Urban Poverty in Latin America," in *Studies in Comparative International Development,* Vol. 2, 1966.

GALVIN, MILES E., *Unionism in Latin America.* Bulletin 45, New York State School of Industrial and Labor Relations. Ithaca, N.Y.: Cornell University, 1962.

GERMANI, GINO, *Política y sociedad en una época de transición: de la sociedad tradicional a la sociedad de masas.* Buenos Aires, Paidos, 1962.

GILLIN, JOHN P., "Changing Cultural Values of the Latin American Lower Classes," in Cole Blasier (ed.), *Constructive Change in Latin America.* Pittsburgh: University of Pittsburgh Press, 1968.

GOLDRICH, DANIEL, RAYMOND B. PRATT, and C. R. SCHULLER, "The Political Integration of Lower-Class Urban Settlements in Chile and Peru," in *Studies in Comparative International Development,* Vol. 3, 1967.

GONZALEZ, ALFONSO, "Some Effects of Population Growth on Latin America's Economy," in *Journal of Inter-American Studies,* Vol. 9, No. 4, October 1967.

GONZALEZ, GUSTAVO R., "The Migration of Latin American High-Level Manpower," in *International Labour Review,* Vol. 98, No. 6, December 1968.

GREENE, DAVID G., "Revolution and the Rationalization of Reform in Bolivia," in *Inter-American Economic Affairs,* Vol. 19, No. 3, Winter 1965.

HAUSER, PHILLIP M., *Urbanization in Latin America.* Paris: UNESCO, 1962.

HAWKINS, CARROLL, "The ORIT and the American Trade Unions: Conflicting Perspectives," in William H. Form and Albert A. Blum (eds.), *Industrial Relations and Social Change in Latin America.* Gainesville: University of Florida Press, 1965.

——————, "The ORIT and the CLASC: A Case of Conflicting Perspective," in *Inter-American Economic Affairs,* Vol. 20, No. 3, Winter 1966.

HEATH, DWIGHT B. and RICHARD N. ADAMS (eds.), *Contemporary Cultures and Societies of Latin America.* New York: Random House, 1965.

HOLLINGSHEAD, A. B. and LLOYD H. ROGLER, "Attitudes toward Slums and Public Housing in Puerto Rico," in Leonard J. Duhl (ed.), *The Urban Condition.* New York: Basic Books, 1963.

INKELES, ALEX, *Industrial Man: The Relation of Status to Experience, Perception and Value.* Indianapolis: Bobbs-Merrill Reprint Series in the Social Sciences, S-131.

JOHNSON, DALE L., "Industrialization, Social Mobility, and Class Formation in Chile," in *Studies in Comparative International Development,* Vol. 3, 1967.

JOHNSON, KENNETH FOX, *Urbanization and Political Change in Latin America.* Ann Arbor: Doctoral dissertation, University of Michigan Microfilms, 1964.

Jones, Gavin W., "Underutilization of Manpower and Demographic Trends in Latin America," *International Labour Review,* Vol. 98, No. 5, November 1968.

Kahl, Joseph A., *The Measurement of Modernism: A Study of Values in Brazil and Mexico.* Austin: University of Texas Press, 1968.

———— and J. Mayone Stycos, "The Philosophy of Demographic Policy in Latin America," in *Studies in Comparative International Development,* Vol. 1, 1965.

Landsberger, Henry A., "The Labor Elite: Is it Revolutionary?" in Seymour Martin Lipset and Aldo Solari (eds.), *Elites in Latin America.* New York: Oxford University Press, 1967.

Lewis, Oscar, *The Children of Sanchez.* New York: Random House, 1963.

Llosa Larrabure, Jaime, "Cooperación Popular: A New Approach to Community Development in Peru," in *International Labour Review,* Vol. 94, No. 3, September 1966.

Mangin, William, "Latin American Squatter Settlements: A Problem and Solution," in *Latin American Research Review,* Vol. 2, Summer 1967.

————, "Squatter Settlements," in *Scientific American,* Vol. 217, October 1967.

————, "Sociological, Cultural, and Political Characteristics of Some Rural Indians and Urban Migrants in Peru," in Edward M. Bruner and Aidan W. Southall (eds.), *Urban Anthropology.* Chicago: Viking Fund, 1967.

Maspero, Emilio, *América Latina: Hora cero.* Buenos Aires: Editorial Nuevas Estructuras, 1962.

————, "Latin America's Labor Movement of Christian Democratic Orientation as an Instrument of Social Change," in William D'Antonio and Frederick Pike (eds.), *Religion, Revolution, and Reform in Latin America.* New York: Praeger, 1964.

Micklin, Michael, "Demographic, Economic, and Social Change in Latin America: An Examination of Causes and Consequences," in *Journal of Developing Areas.* Vol. 4, No. 2, January 1970.

Millen, Bruce H., *The Political Role of Labor in Developing Countries.* Washington, D.C.: Brookings Institution, 1963.

Mintz, Sidney W., "The Folk Urban Continuum and the Rural Proletarian Community," in *American Journal of Sociology,* Vol. 59, 1953.

Mollet, Alfredo, "Diversification or Standardization: Two Trends in Latin American Social Security," in *International Labour Review,* Vol. 101, No. 1, January 1970.

Moore, Wilbert E., "Backgrounds of Social Change," in William H. Form and Albert A. Blum (eds.), *Industrial Relations and Social Change in Latin America.* Gainesville: University of Florida Press, 1965.

——————————, and ARNOLD S. FELDMAN (eds.), *Labor Commitment and Social Change in Developing Areas*. New York: Social Science Research Council, 1960.

MORRIS, JAMES O., "Consensus, Ideology and Labor Relations," in *Journal of Inter-Amercian Studies,* Vol. 7, No. 3, July 1965.

——————————, *Elites, Intellectuals, and Consensus*. New York States School of Industrial and Labor Relations, Ithaca, N.Y.: Cornell University, 1966.

MORSE, RICHARD, "Recent Research on Latin American Urbanization," in *Latin American Research Review,* Vol. 1, Fall 1965.

Organization of American States, *The Role of the Trade Unions in the Alliance for Progress*. Reference Document 17, July 21, 1962.

Pan American Union, *Social Survey of Latin America: 1963–1964*. Washington, D.C., 1965.

PAYNE, JAMES L., *Labor Politics in Peru: The System of Political Bargaining*. New Haven: Yale University Press, 1965.

PEATTIE, LISA REDFIELD, *The View from the Barrio*. Ann Arbor: University of Michigan Press, 1968.

RANIS, PETER, "Modernity and Political Development in Five Latin American Countries," in *Studies in Comparative International Development,* Vol. 4, 1968.

RATINOFF, LUIS, "Problems in the Formation and Use of Human Capital in Recent Latin American Development," in *Studies in Comparative International Development* Vol. 4, 1968.

ROGLER, LLOYD H., "Slum Neighborhoods in Latin America," in *Journal of Inter-American Studies,* Vol. 9, No. 4, October 1967.

ROMUALDI, SERAFINO, *Presidents and Peons*. New York: Funk & Wagnalls, 1967.

ROTTENBERG, SIMON, "Problems in a Latin American Factory Society," in *Monthly Labor Review,* July 1954.

RUBINGER, MARCOS M., "Social Participation as an Instrument for the Development and Formation of Society in Latin America," in *International Labour Review,* Vol. 97, No. 6, June 1968.

SHAPIRO, SAMUEL, *Integration of Man and Society in Latin America*. Notre Dame: University of Notre Dame Press, 1967.

SILVERMAN, BERTRAM, "Labor Ideology and Economic Development in the Peronist Era," in *Studies in Comparative International Development,* Vol. 4, 1968.

SIMAO, AZIS, "Industrialization, Planning and Occupational Organizations in Brazil," in *International Labour Review,* Vol. 98, No. 2, August 1968.

SMITH, PETER H., "Social Mobilization, Political Participation, and the Rise of Juan Perón," in *Political Science Quarterly,* Vol. 84, No. 1, March 1969.

SNOW, PETER G., "The Class Basis of Argentine Political Parties," in *American Political Science Review,* Vol. 62, No. 1, March 1969.

STYCOS, J. MAYONE, *Human Fertility in Latin America*. Ithaca, N.Y.: Cornell University Press, 1968.

SZULC, TAD, *The Winds of Revolution*. New York: Praeger, 1965.

THORN, RICHARD S., "The Alliance for Progress: The Flickering Flame," in Cole Blasier (ed.), *Constructive Change in Latin America*. Pittsburgh: University of Pittsburgh Press, 1968.

TOURAINE, ALAIN, "Social Mobility, Class Relations, and Nationalism in Latin America," in *Studies in Comparative International Development*, Vol. 1, 1965.

——————, and DANIEL PECAUT, "Working Class Consciousness and Economic Development in Latin America," in *Studies in Comparative International Development*, Vol. 3, 1967.

TRONCOSO, MOISÉS POBLETE, *La explosión demográfica en América Latina*. Buenos Aires: Editorial Schapiro, 1967.

——————, and BEN G. BURNETT, *The Rise of the Latin American Labor Movement*. New York: Bookman Associates, 1960.

TURNER, JOHN F. C., "Lima's Barriadas and Corralones: Suburbs vs. Slums," in *Ekistics*, Vol. 112, March 1965.

United Nations, *Statistical Bulletin for Latin America*. Vol. 2, No. 2, August 1965.

VON POTOBSKY, GERALDO, "Participation by Workers' and Employers' Organizations in Planning in Latin America," in *International Labour Review*, Vol. 95, No. 6, June 1967.

WAGLEY, CHARLES, *The Latin American Tradition*. New York: Columbia University Press, 1968.

WARD, BARBARA, "The Poor World's Cities," in *Economist*, December 6, 1969.

WHITEFORD, ANDREW HUNTER, "Impasse in Latin America," in *Christian Century*, January 17, 1968.

WHYTE, WILLIAM FOOTE, "Common Management Strategies in Industrial Relations: Peru," in William H. Form and Albert A. Blum (eds.), *Industrial Relations and Social Change in Latin America*. Gainesville: University of Florida Press, 1965.

WIARDA, HOWARD J., "The Development of the Labor Movement in the Dominican Republic," in *Inter-American Economic Affairs*, Vol. 20, No. 1, Summer 1966.

YLLANES RAMOS, FERNANDO, "The Social Rights Enshrined in the Mexican Constitution of 1917," in *International Labour Review*, Vol. 96, No. 6, December 1967.

ZUVEKAS, CLARENCE JR., "Economic Growth and Income Distribution in Postwar Argentina," in *Inter-American Economic Affairs*, Vol. 20, No. 3, Winter 1966.

ZYMELMAN, MANUEL, "Cultural Patterns of Labor and Latin American Industrialization," in *Journal of Inter-American Studies*, Vol. 5, No. 3, July 1963.

CHAPTER 5

THE UNIVERSITY

STUDENTS

THE CONTEXT: THE UNIVERSITY REFORM MOVEMENT, THE UNIVERSITY TODAY, THE STUDENTS, POLITICAL ACTIVISM

The Latin American university, the base if not always the scene of student politcial activity, is beset today with organizational and operational problems arising from its distant as well as its more recent past. Since these problems are quite often related to student political actiyity, some knowledge of the nature of the university is necessary in order to understand that activity.

The first university in the Western Hemisphere was established in Santo Domingo in 1513; the oldest in the hemisphere today is the University of San Marcos in Lima, Peru, which has functioned continuously since the 16th century. The colonial universities, a few dozen in number, were open only to a very privileged few, and were characterized by the traditional studies of art, law, medicine, and theology. While secular professors could, and occasionally did serve, these universities were essentially controlled and operated by the Catholic clergy and brotherhoods. Although this picture changed slightly toward the end of the 18th century—for example, a few studies in such disciplines as botany and mineralogy were introduced—the Latin American colonial university was predominantly a Church monopoly devoted to the traditional curricula.[1]

[1] For a concise history of the university in colonial Latin America see *The Student Struggle in Latin America*. Report of the International Student Conference Delegation, 1957.

The anticlericalism so generally prominent during and immediately following the wars of independence in Latin America soon led, among other things, to a bitter conflict between the new governments and the Catholic Church over control of the universities. The governments were triumphant in this struggle, and they assumed control over almost all universities. Theology was banned from curricula; priests were largely barred from teaching positions; many new, secular universities were established; and studies such as engineering and mathematics became more common. The Church, however, persisted in its efforts, and toward the end of the 19th century it had reestablished itself to a considerable extent in the field of higher education, mainly through creating its own, new institutions.

By the beginning of the 20th century the university in Latin America had become quite stagnant as a center for developing knowledge. Whether is was Church- or government-controlled, the essential character of the former colonial university remained. That is, the university in Latin America had not developed like its European and North American counterparts in its ability to contribute significantly to the cumulative knowledge possessed by the western world. Rather it had become extremely ideologically oriented, oppressively politically biased, and still placed very great emphasis on the traditional curricula. Thoughtful people were becoming increasingly disenchanted with university life in Latin America, which they understood to be intellectually conservative, if not reactionary. Positivism, for example, was perhaps the major philosophy of Latin America during the latter half of the 19th century; but rather than emphasizing the ability of man to cope with his problems, positivism in Latin America tended to emphasize various forms of social Darwinism to justify the elitist nature of Latin American society. For example, the regime of Díaz in Mexico was to a large extent characterized by the *cientificos,* who worshiped certain aspects of knowledge while blandly ignoring the conditions of 90 percent of the Mexican population.

Then in 1918 the University Reform Movement was initiated; this was to alter considerably the structure and operation of the Latin American university, as well as the university's and student's role in national politics. As one writer asserts, the effects of this movement have changed both the orientation as well as the character of education not only in Argentina, where the Reform began, but throughout Latin America as a whole.[2]

The Reform commenced officially on June 21, 1918, when students of Cordoba University in Argentina published their now-famous Manifesto, the much-quoted opening paragraph of which stated:

> We, members of the free republic, have just broken the last chain which in the 20th century still attached us to the old

[2] Richard John Walter, *University Reform and Student Politics in Argentina* (Ann Arbor: University of Michigan Microfilms, 1967).

monarchical and monastic dominion. We have resolved to call everything by its proper name. Cordoba has redeemed itself. From today on we can count in our country one less shame and one more liberty. The remaining miseries are the liberties we still lack. We do not think we are deceiving ourselves, since our hearts tell us we are not. We are making a revolution, and we are living a vital American hour.[3]

It is unnecessary here to reproduce the Manifesto in its entirety (approximately two thousand words in length) with its colorful, epic language. Essentially, it called for a major reorganization and basic reorientation of the university in Latin America. It insisted that the universities had become not only havens for mediocrity and ignorance, but also bases for tyranny and bigotry. Scientific inquiry, or pursuit of knowledge of any sort, simply could not flourish in such an environment. Not only the teaching, but the administration as well was judged anachronistic, self-perpetuating, and indifferent to changing times and needs. For these reasons, the Manifesto insisted, there must be a democratically-run university, which meant that the selection of the governing bodies must include the participation of professors and particularly, the participation of the students. The entire "archaic and barbarous concept of authority" had to be removed from university organization. This was to be accomplished through the revolutionary heroism of the Cordoba students, who, weary of tyrants, requested their colleagues throughout Latin America to cooperate in this revolutionary "work of liberation."

The students involved negotiated with the Argentine government, they eventually took over Cordoba University to lend weight to their demands, and the government finally acquiesced. Gabriel del Mazo, the Spanish-language authority on the history of the movement, suggests that what the government eventually agreed to were ten basic propositions, all of which were significant, and some of which were crucial to the future development of the movement.[4]

One of the major propositions concerned the autonomy of the university from the government. This particular proposition actually has great traditional significance to the Latin American university and is based on the medieval concept of the university as a guild with special privileges and exemptions.[5] If the university was to be reformed, it was mandatory to ensure its freedom from political influences. If this were not accomplished, unless the university was "sovereign" within its own sphere, other reforms

---

[3] The complete Manifesto is reproduced in English in David Spencer (ed.), *Student Politics in Latin America.* United States National Student Association, 1965.

[4] Gabriel del Mazo, "La nueva crisis de la universidades latino-americanos," in *Panoramas,* Vol. 10, July-August 1964.

[5] See the article by Luigi Einaudi, "University Autonomy and Academic Freedom in Latin America," in Spencer (ed.), *Student Politics in Latin America.*

intended to further the pursuit of knowledge would be hampered, if not thwarted, by politicians and groups interested in their own self-aggrandizement—whether in terms of political influence or material benefits.

Another major point concerned the participation of students and graduates, along with professors, in the government of the university (usually referred to as *co-gobierno,* or "co-government"). As del Mazo has pointed out, if the university was to be established as an autonomous democratic "republic," it was essential that all its citizens—not merely administrators, or administrators and professors, but students as well—participate in the election of the governors of the republic. This was also seen as the only means by which the university's autonomy could be guaranteed against the government.

Still another major proposition concerned the university's social orientation—its role vis-à-vis social problems and change. The Manifesto itself stated that the university must involve itself with the "great, national problems," rather than being, as the demand for autonomy seems to suggest, an ivory tower somehow removed from mundane considerations. Students were to assume responsibility for the people's destiny and to devote themselves to eradicating all evils, resolving all problems, and transforming the spirit of the people.[6] As one writer has pointed out, this proposition was clearly exemplified in the 1945 Constitution of Ecuador, which stated quite unequivocally that the universities were autonomous and would concern themselves particularly with studying and resolving national problems and spreading culture among the popular classes.[7]

Other basic propositions coming out of the Reform Movement were: free financial assistance for students; freedom of instruction and optional attendance at classes; competitive distribution of professorial chairs (that is, no tenure) ; publication of university actions; higher education for the masses; social aid for students; and the ability of each university to organize according to its specific circumstances instead of according to one set pattern.[8]

The great problem of these demands was that from the very beginning they tended strongly to be mutually contradictory. That is, the university was supposed to be free from political influence—free from all government control—while at the same time the university's concern for social problems and reforms would automatically make it a political agency participating in the political system. As Kalman Silvert has observed, the Cordoba Reform

6 See the article by Chris Hamilton, "Origin of the University Reform Movement: Student Politics in Argentina between 1918 and 1922" in Spencer; *Student Politics in Latin America.*

7 Einaudi, "University Autonomy."

8 del Mazo, "La nueva crisis."

was a symbol of academic independence and political intent.[9] The student had to be both a scholar eagerly pursuing knowledge and a political activist fighting for social reform. For that matter, perhaps Robert Scott is correct when he says that the principle of university concern for social conditions was unnecessary in order to politicize the students. They, in effect, had already entered national politics to challenge government-directed university authority and to fight for their own interests, so it was probably inevitable that they would become involved in politics outside the university.[10]

Fairly recently, this particular contradiction with all its problems was well displayed in Argentina itself. Article IV of the 1958 University Statute stated that the university was to be neutral in ideological, political, and religious matters, and would ensure within itself the greatest possible degree of liberty in research and expression. However, the article continued, the university could not be indifferent to social, political, and ideological problems. Instead, it was to study them scientifically. As one study notes, for those favoring the Reform, this naturally justified their participation in national politics, while those opposed to the Reform just as naturally insisted that national politics was not the university's concern.[11]

The other propositions also tended to pose major, almost insurmountable problems, perhaps for the very fact that they were designed to create a coherent, workable system. For example, the ideas of optional attendance at classes, freedom of choice of instructors, and nonpermanent appointment to chairs on the basis of merit, were all intended to bring out the best in a professor for the benefit of the students, or to dispense with his services if he proved inadequate. However, hindering one of these limits the realization of others. For example, censuring a professor by not attending his classes is nullified if attendance is made more or less obligatory by compulsory examinations, or if alternative courses are not available to the student.

Whatever the idealism and impracticality of its proposals, the Reform Movement quickly spread outside Argentina. As early as 1925, universities in Chile, Uruguay, Mexico, Peru, Cuba, Panama, Colombia and Bolivia had been touched by it.[12] Today, even if university authorities reject it, none of the hundred-odd universities in Latin America remains entirely untouched by it, although its greatest impact has definitely been felt in the "national"

[9] Kalman Silvert, *The Conflict Society: Reaction and Revolution in Latin America* (New York: American Universities Field Staff, Inc., 1966).

[10] Robert Scott, "Student Political Activism in Latin America," in *Daedalus,* Voll. 97, No. 1, Winter 1968.

[11] Ronald C. Newton, "Students and the Political System of the University of Buenos Aires," in *Journal of Inter-American Studies,* Vol. 8, No. 4, October 1966. This statute was greatly altered, away from autonomy, when the military deposed President Illia in 1966.

[12] Hamilton, "The University Reform Movement."

universities rather than in the Catholic or in the few, relatively uninfluential private institutions.[13]

The principle of university autonomy, one of the keys to the entire Reform Movement, has been recognized at least verbally throughout almost all of Latin America. It may be stated in the form of a constitutional provision, as in the case mentioned above of Uruguay, but it is more generally established in the opening articles of the statutes of the university.[14] However, despite this symbolic support for the principle, its application has never been complete even under the most benevolent of governments.

One of the greatest problems with the entire idea of university autonomy is the need for such independence to be achieved while the university remains financially dependent on the government. Except for a few relatively exclusive institutions, the university of Latin America, like its North American counterpart, depends heavily on the government to finance its expenditures. While in theory this does not necessarily mean that the government will control the university, in practice it means that the latter is circumscribed, often severely, in its ability to decide its own affairs. For example, it is impossible for the university to freely create new faculties, establish new courses, increase teaching and administrative personnel, or expand its activities in general, if such action depends on the willingness, and often the ability of the government to provide increased financial support. Occasional efforts have been made through statutes, and even through constitutions, to provide for university financial independence—for example, by allotting revenues from certain taxes to the university—but as one writer has stated, the poverty of the Latin American university has continually forced it to be at the mercy of the government for increases in funds.[15]

Furthermore, the governments of Latin America have at all times felt free to overtly violate university autonomy when they felt it necessary to their own interests. In the last decade alone, this has occurred quite openly with or without major violence in at least half a dozen countries. The actual need for this open government intervention in university affairs remains in Latin America as in North America, a matter of great controversy based on greatly differing points of view.

Argentina, the country in which the Reform Movement originated, has recently provided an excellent example of government intervention in the university. The example was dramatized because the institution concerned was the University of Buenos Aires, the largest (70,000 students) and perhaps most prestigious university in Latin America. In 1966 a

[13] Einaudi, "University Autonomy."

[14] Ibid.

[15] Ibid.

military coup headed by General Onganía deposed the civilian government. At the time, the administration of the University criticized the move, but publicly disassociated itself from any overt resistance. However, a month after its advent to office, the government issued a law which, among other things, abolished political activity within the University and subjected the University administration to the Ministry of Education. A thousand faculty members resigned, and the students protested, at one time occupying several buildings. In turn, police entered, and beatings and other forms of violence occurred.[16]

Overt repression of university autonomy has come to mean police or military on the campus, since other forms of government coercion tend to lead to this. Actually, some of the student activities vis-à-vis the police present comic aspects to the outside observer although the humor probably depends on one's point of view. For example, police or even troops will seal off a university or a building, leaving the rebellious students free in their fortress to dramatize themselves and the situation through speeches and proclamations concerning their own heroism, patriotism, and their undying opposition to government policy. One dormitory of Central University in Caracas, Venezuela, controlled by extreme-left students, has become known as "Stalingrad" because it is an armed camp to which the students escape when pursued by the police, at whom they can jeer once they are safely ensconced in their citadel.[17]

Often however, all humor disappears even for an outside observer, and is replaced by outright brutality and death. This was clearly shown in 1968 in Mexico, which possesses one of the stablest and least overtly repressive political systems in Latin America. In October of 1968 the "Battle of Tlateloco" occurred at the *Autonomous* National University of Mexico, where police and soldiers shot and killed students with apparently little more reason than to ensure a smoth opening for the Olympics which Mexico was hosting. Official government sources state that the army was brutally attacked by armed students and naturally defended itself. Students and observers, both domestic and foreign, insist that a poorly-attended rally was on the point of dispersing when police agents in the audience, wearing white gloves for identification, suddenly began shooting and then called to the waiting soldiers for assistance. According to the government, thirty-four civilians and one soldier were killed; common estimates place the number far higher than this figure.[18]

In short, while the principle of university autonomy remains very much a part of the academic scene in Latin America, it is not now, and has never

[16] Newton, "Students and the Political System."

[17] Francis Donahue, "Students in Latin American Politics," in *Antioch Review*, Vol. 26, No. 1, Spring 1966.

[18] Christopher Price, "Death on the Mexican Campus," in *New Statesman*, Vol. 78, November 28, 1969.

been, a reality. More than to any other cause, this situation is probably due to the conflict between the ideal of autonomy and the ideal of social involvement, which tends automatically to throw the university against the government. As a result of this conflict, the university is subjected to various government controls, either in the form of legislation which it and the students accept, or more violently in the form of police and soldiers on the campus when students will not accept an infringement on their "sovereignty." As one study puts it, it is always difficult to draw the line between justified and unjustified interventions, but any intervention is a violation of university autonomy,[19] and student reaction will be certain.

Unlike university autonomy, the reformist principle of student participation in university government has realized considerable success in its fulfillment. This does not mean, however, that the principle has not at times suffered the same fate as university autonomy, often for the same reasons, or that it is universally accepted in Latin American universities. It remains one of the major, underlying issues on campus today.

The relative extent of student participation in university government varies greatly from time to time and from country to country. In general, students, faculty, and alumni share in the formulation of basic university policies and subsidiary regulations, including scholastic and administrative matters. One estimate states that student representation ranges from approximately one-fourth to over one-third of the membership of the highest governing boards and the various faculty councils.[20] The governing board of the university, for example, elects the rector, who is the equivalent of a president of a typical North American university. As one study points out, while the rector may be elected for a specified term (usually two to four years) he can be turned out of office at any time if the students become sufficiently upset with him and adopt extreme measures—for example, a strike.[21] In the early 1960s the Autonomous National University of Mexico ceased functioning for a week due to a decision of the students that, among other things, university officials were not acting in the students' interests. Students occupied and barricaded themselves within buildings to defy regulations, and at one point actually kidnapped the rector. When the turmoil was ended, the rector resigned.[22]

Among those studies of the Latin American university that attempt to evaluate co-government, there is some disagreement as to its success. One study, for example, reports that professors in Central America say that stu-

[19] Einaudi, "University Autonomy."

[20] Donahue, "Students in Latin American Politics." See also Barbara Waggoner, George R. Waggoner, and Gregory B. Wolfe, "Higher Education in Contemporary Central America," in *Journal of Inter-American Studies,* Vol. 6, No. 4, October 1964.

[21] Ibid.

[22] Orlando Albornoz, "Student Opposition in Latin America," in *Government and Opposition,* Vol. 2, No. 1, October 1966–January 1967.

dent participation in university affairs causes little serious trouble, and that it has some value. Students, that is, are aware of university problems and are willing to face them. Even in Honduras, where student representation equals that of the faculty, and where some professors feel student influence is too great, it is still thought that students support development within the university more often than faculty. The study points out that hardly any person involved in Central American teaching or serious study advocates the abolition of co-government, and all agree that the main interest of students in university governing bodies is to improve curricula and faculty.[23]

On the other hand, one can consider situations such as in Bolivia where students are quite well organized—much more so than faculty and administrators—and where they attend meetings more regularly. As a result, they often exercise control over faculty and administrative appointments, tenure, suspension, dismissal, and course content. A study considering this situation states that professors can be quite bitter about, for example, an eighteen-year-old freshman's ability to cast the deciding vote on a proposal to alter the content of an advanced, highly technical and complex course.[24]

Perhaps the discrepancy in basic evaluations of student participation in university government is due to the emphasis placed by either the domestic or foreign observer on particular facets of that participation, as well as on the amount of student representation permitted on governing bodies by university statutes. If representation is low, and if the students are relatively unorganized, their ability to influence outcomes is also relatively small and will therefore be a less contentious matter. On the other hand, if student representation is high, as in the case of Bolivia, and if they are well organized, there is inevitably going to be bitterness among the out-voted professors and administrators who, probably with good reason, think they know better than the students in some matters. The particular aspect of student participation under study appears quite important for similar reasons. If students agitate for a larger share of the national budget, for erection of a new building, for creation of a new faculty, for student dining facilities, or for general university improvement, this is one matter. It is quite another matter, however, if they focus their attention on deciding curricula, insisting on optional attendance at classes, and censuring professors. Many North American exchange professors, accustomed to a much different system, have reacted very adversely to this aspect of student participation in university government.

In short, in evaluations of co-government the observer's personal criteria are always involved—that is, there is always an element of "should do" or the "good student" measured against some standard the evaluator holds. Since these standards can never be absolute, and are often hopelessly ethnocentric, an ultimate evaluation of co-government is impossible.

[23] Waggoner et al., "Higher Education."

[24] Donahue, "Students in Latin American Politics."

One further, perhaps more general, reaction to co-government is based on the manner and extent to which student campus organizations become involved in extramural political activities. This involvement essentially appears to be a natural or inevitable result of combining the two reformist ideals of co-government and university concern for social problems. For example, complaints are frequent that political activists who control campus organizations designed to further student participation in university government, use these bodies to advance their own political causes or careers in conflicts between memberships and political authorities. Consideration of this point, however, is better left for the discussion of actual student political activity.

Before completing this topic of the university, some mention of the professorate may be enlightening. On the whole, (although there are notable exceptions), a professorship is not a full-time career. That is, very few teaching positions in Latin American universities are full-time, and very few professors are sufficiently paid to allow them to live without other income.[25] The vast majority of contracts actually stipulate that professors will teach only on a part-time basis, and as Robert Scott has noted, most professors who earn their living only by teaching must hold three or more posts in order to do so. Most, however, are employed in government, industry, or are in private practice.[26] Teaching is also often a prestige hobby that has the benefit of some remuneration—a means whereby an individual retired from other employment can fill his days.[27]

As a result, professors do not have the time to acquaint themselves either with the students or with student problems and desires. They cannot, for example, really interest themselves in educational reform or university development, nor can they organize to collaborate with student organizations in order to contribute actively to university life.[28] Furthermore, this situation in no way contributes to professionalization of teaching and research, and almost ensures that the standard of both of these will be rather low.[29]

These factors are probably influential in activating at least some students, although there is no reliable data to substantiate this hypothesis. The most obvious way this could occur is through the attempts of the average university student to find his identity as an adult. This appears to be a sufficiently difficult process in the best of times, and it seems reasonable to assume greater difficulty if the student is not allowed any real personal,

---

[25] Einaudi, "University Autonomy."

[26] Scott, "Student Political Activism."

[27] George R. Waggoner, "Problems in the Professionalization of the University Teaching Career in Central America," in *Journal of Inter-American Studies,* Vol. 8, No. 2, April 1966.

[28] *The Student Struggle in Latin America* (see footnote 1).

[29] Scott, "Student Political Activism."

intellectual contact with his professors as he attempts to find answers to his personal problems. (It can be noted that it is mainly on the larger, increasingly impersonalized campuses that the most and strongest student political activity and violence is found in North America.) Furthermore, by having so little contact with the campus, the Latin American professor will probably be greatly hampered in comprehending and coping with such things as student idealism, and if he reacts to it with sarcasm or even bewilderment, he is liable to be automatically identified with the "establishment."[30] In such a situation, there is a good chance that the individual student will be drawn toward some political organization that has an embracing ideology with which he can identify.

The composition of the typical Latin American university student body tends to be quite elitist. That is, in terms of family background and his own orientations, the typical student is definitely a member of the middle class, and is often a member of the upper middle and upper classes, although this picture does vary considerably from country to country and between universities in the same country. Latin America today has an extremely high percentage of young people, but in 1960, of the total 17 million persons in the higher-education age groups, only .5 million persons were actually attending university.[31] Various surveys—they do not exist for all countries—show that in each case very few students belong to the lower socioeconomic groupings, however these are defined in each study. Nor, for that matter, do many belong to the most affluent, prestigious families, since the children of the latter, if they attend a university at all, tend to do so in select institutions in Europe or the United States. Furthermore, when a student could be said to belong to the lower class on the basis of North American socioeconomic indices, certain social and cultural factors in Latin America disallow the designation. As one study states, should the son of a peasant matriculate, by definition he ceases to be a peasant. A person of lower-class origin who attends a university, no matter how poverty-stricken his background, is no longer a lower-class person. Furthermore, the number of students who actually have a lower-class family background is extremely small indeed.[32]

[30] These points are elaborated on in same.

[31] Albornoz, "Student Opposition."

[32] For specific studies of the socio-economic backgrounds of students in various Latin American countries see Newton, "Students and the Political System," and Silvert, The Conflict Society. See also Ronald L. Scheman, "The Brazilian Law Student: Background, Habits, Attitudes," in Journal of Inter-American Studies, Vol. 5, No. 3, July 1963; Daniel Goldrich, Radical Nationalism: The Political Orientations of Panamanian Law Students. Bureau of Social Research, Michigan State University: 1961; and Frank Bonilla, "The Student Federation of Chile: 50 Years of Political Action," in Journal of Inter-American Studies, July 1960.

Given the elitist nature of the student body, it is in a way rather incongruous that they are so politically active, as they certainly are at times. That is, they are members of the socioeconomic and political "establishment," so why should they be so politically active, and why, in particular, do they so often articulate demands that are anathema to the establishment? Many studies have advanced explanations for this political activism. Most studies of Latin American student political activities appear to be undertaken in attempts to explain this phenomenon. Before beginning some of these explanations perhaps it should be pointed out that while some explanations appear very sound on a commonsensical basis and others appear quite specious, the fact remains that there exists so little hard data on the subject that any or all explanations may be partially correct or totally irrelevant. That is, while Latin American student political activities may be, and probably are, much more socially inspired, organized, and meaningful than were, for example, the former panty raids in North American universities, we as yet do not have much solid data unequivocally to demonstrate the assertion.

The most popular explanation of student political activism is definitely "youthful idealism," since in one form or another this is constantly alluded to. It has been asserted, for example, that during periods of dictatorships in Latin America the students have been the repositories of the ideals of the nations and have given expression to the grievances of the people.[33] Similarly, students are said to be heirs to the great traditions of European liberalism, nationalism, and rationalism.[34] Or a fairly common suggestion is that because of their youthful idealism, they are constantly moved by the oppression, poverty, social injustice, and ignorance that they see around them.[35] It has even been claimed, for example, that the University Reform Movement itself was greatly spurred by the desire of Latin American students to save their people from the destiny of Europe, then engaged in World War I.[36]

While such arguments may appear far too general, if not entirely superficial, they do gain credence from the fact that, as often as not, the students appear to see themselves in this rather heroic light, and perhaps act on this perception of themselves at least at times and to some extent. As the Cordoba Manifesto itself so definitely stated, youth is always surrounded

[33] See the article by Walter Washington, "The Students," in Robert D. Tomasek (ed.), *Latin American Politics: 24 Studies of the Contemporary Scene* (Garden City, N.Y.: Doubleday, 1966).

[34] Seymour Martin Lipset, "University Students and Politics in Underdeveloped Countries," in *Minerva,* Vol. 3, No. 1, Autumn 1964.

[35] See the article by Robert Alexander, "Evolution of Student Politics in Latin America," in Spencer (ed.), *Student Politics in Latin America.*

[36] del Mazo, "La nueva crisis."

by heroism, and is disinterested and pure because it has not yet had time to contaminate itself. The Manifesto proceeds to point out that certain violent acts at Cordoba University were the responsibility of the students implementing pure ideals. While the moral sense of the leading classes was obscured by their traditional hypocrisy and by a deplorable lack of ideals, the students had acted to create a new, pure spirit from among the ruins of Argentine life.

While it is impossible to state the extent to which feelings of this sort motivate Latin American students, it does seem reasonable to expect that, if they do fairly typically see themselves in this light, they will be quite politically active at times. One study of Brazilian students, for example, suggests that an important, if not major, cause of their political activism is their attempts to "actualize" their image. The study also points out that adult Brazilians often refer to students as defenders of freedom, social reformers, idealistic nationalists, and true democrats.[37]

Still another explanation of student activism which stresses idealism suggests that the activism springs from the curriculum. Today, as in the past, the typical curriculum is oriented toward theoretical, abstract studies, rather than to studies having definite, meaningful, and practical application. This, it has been argued, makes it easy for the student to think in idealistic terms, as well as to cloak personal ambitions in idealism.[38] On the other hand, it has also been suggested that the very impracticality of the curriculum, its inappropriateness for the country's needs which the student recognizes, as well as for personal employment needs, leads the student to react against it and thus become active against the government which helps to perpetuate it.

Of course, the entire idea of idealism tends to be negated if one views it instead as youthful irresponsibility—a viewpoint which is not at all uncommon.[39] For example, university students are said to be experiencing the only time in their lives when they are virtually free of responsibility, when they have no families to support, jobs to keep, and when they are at the same time receiving parental subsidies. In short, they feel free to take a position in the political spectrum which they might not otherwise adopt.[40] However, this particular argument loses much of its force if one considers the fairly high rate of employment among university students—often to ensure employment after graduation—as well as the fairly high number of students

[37] Robert O. Myhr, "The University Student Tradition in Brazil," in *Journal of Inter-American Studies and World Affairs,* Vol. 12, No. 1, January 1970.

[38] Washington, "The Students."

[39] See, for example, "Latin America Cracks Down on Student-Run Schools" in *U.S. News and World Report,* Vol. 64, No. 22, May 27, 1968.

[40] Alexander, "Evolution of Student Polities."

either living with their parents or having families of their own.[41] In fact, the exact opposite of the irresponsibility argument has been urged, based on child-rearing practices in Latin America. It is argued that a boy after eight or ten years of age enjoys a position in the family quite different from his North American counterpart, in the sense that he is encouraged to assert himself in political discussions in the home. As a result, he is said to be considerably more mature as a youth than is the North American youth.[42]

Closely related to, but distinct from, student idealism is the position of the intellectual in Latin America. As Germán Arciniegas has pointed out, the extent of the political participation of Latin American intellectuals in general is quite phenomenal if compared to that of their North American counterparts, and frequently the best known intellectuals of Latin America have also been renowned political figures.[43] And while Latin America does have its conservative intellectuals, those who have become the most famous have generally been of a liberal if not of a downright radical persuasion. Examples of such intellectuals are: Martí, Gallegos, Alegría, Vasconcelos, Rivera, Neruda, Lombardo Toledano, and Torres Bodet. To the extent, then, that the student is an idealist, is aware of social problems, and desires social change, he is supplied with much intellectual leadership and inspiration. For that matter, even the cynical student, motivated by personal ambitions, will be aided by the tradition of intellectual political leadership.

A second explanation of student political activism suggests that it is a springboard to a political career. This explanation is not necessarily the antithesis of the student idealism explanation, but it tends to be. It has been argued, for example, that students of lower socioeconomic status often see a political career as the best means of improving their position, and therefore use the campus as a springboard into the national political system.[44] Another study suggests that student activists often stir up and exploit otherwise quiescent anti-government feelings on campus in order to enhance their own political careers.[45]

Certainly, many politically active students have in their later years become prominent in the politics of their countries. Fidel Castro, for example, was an outstanding student activist long before he launched his military

---

[41] See, for example, Scheman, "The Brazilian Law Student."

[42] Washington, "The Students."

[43] See the article by Germán Arciniegas, "Intellectuals in the Politics of Latin America," in Cole Blasier (ed.), Constructive Change in Latin America (Pittsburgh: University of Pittsburgh Press, 1968).

[44] Washington, "The Students."

[45] David Spencer, "Latin America: The Need for Responsible Student Leadership," in Spencer (ed.), Student Politics in Latin America.

campaign against Batista. In Venezuela, the "Generation of 28" students, so active in the attempted overthrow of dictator-president Gómez in 1928, were prominent in the Venezuelan Student Federation, and among these students were Leoni (president of the Federation), Betancourt, Villalba, Galbaldón, Carnevali, and Tamayo, all of whom later became prominent in Venezuelan national politics. In Peru, Haya de la Torre, founder-in-exile of the once-major APRA (Popular American Revolutionary Alliance) was a prominent student political activist, and in Uruguay, Baltasar Brum stepped from leadership in student politics to national recognition.

However, despite all the major, as well as the hundreds of minor, examples of student political activists becoming part of the national political elite, the springboard argument of political activism is still not necessarily relevant. That is, university students are by definition part of the socio-economic elite in Latin America, and it is therefore not at all surprising that students, as well as nonstudent elites, achieve political prominence in their countries. Their student life may be a factor, but this has not been demonstrated. In fact, it has been suggested that disillusionment with the effectiveness of student political activism at the university level often results in a feeling of political anomie which may preclude later participation in politics.[46]

The same tenuousness prevails in other explanations of student political activism. It has been suggested, for example, that their concentration in large numbers on a campus automatically creates the situation necessary for political activity. Another explanation stresses the authoritarian nature of the family and related cultural factors, against which the young must rebel and, in the case of male students, assert their own masculine identity against the *machismo* of their fathers. Or, it has been argued that Latin American students are merely the children of their fathers, and thus are tempera-mentally aggressive, volatile, and opposed to authority.

Eventually, however, none of the explanations of student political activity in Latin America has any solid basis in empirical evidence. While a few good, but narrowly-focused, studies have been carried out in this direction, the results simply are not sufficiently conclusive to allow even very mild generalization about motivation—despite the fact that for years both Latin American and foreign scholars have been intrigued by the relatively high and observable degree of student political activism in the area.

Actually, one occasionally gains the impression from reading material related to Latin American students that virtually every student is politically embroiled. However, this is quite obviously not the case (although there is some evidence suggesting that student activism in Latin America is consider-ably greater than it is, for example, in the United States[47]). Robert Scott

[46] Albornoz, "Student Opposition."

[47] Ibid.

notes that a majority of students probably do not become political activists either in university or in later life.[48] While the majority may become involved from time to time in campus issues such as noncompulsory attendance at classes, they are not that strongly oriented toward politics in general, although student activists may seek to involve the entire student body in national issues when campus tempers are high. One study, focusing on Mexico, Panama, Puerto Rico, Colombia, Paraguay, and Uruguay, suggests that if only radicals are counted, the number of political activists in Latin American universities is indeed quite small. However, using a typology designed to distinguish varying degrees of political activism, the number of activists ranges from 26 percent of the student body in Colombia and Mexico to 42 and 43 percent, respectively, in Puerto Rico and Panama.[49] A study of Chilean university students suggests similarly relatively high percentages,[50] as do studies of Argentinean students,[51] and Brazilian law students.[52]

Such studies, however, do not supply any clear indication of the motivations of the political activists. It appears that general socioeconomic background can at times be a factor in political activism, as can urban rural background. Certain faculties seem more prone to student activism than others—perhaps substantiating, at least partially, a previous suggestion that curriculum content is responsible for activism. Parental involvement in politics also appears to be relevant to student activism, as do various peer group factors. In short, just about every factor that has been found relevant in the creation of political awareness and activism in North America is probably operative in Latin America also. Again, the problem is that while a few studies have been carried out in Latin America, they are indeed very few in number and, since they have been unrelated, it is impossible to generalize to any significant extent from their isolated observations.

A factor related to student political activism—and often claimed to be the motivating force behind it—is that of external organizations influencing and perhaps controlling student organizations. Almost every study of student politics in Latin America considers this factor to some extent, and almost every study insists that the outside influence exists. The differences among conclusions about this situation tend to concern the degree to which the influence is present. Some, notably the students themselves, insist that

[48] Scott, "Student Political Activism."

[49] Albornoz, "Student Opposition."

[50] Myron Glazer, "Student Politics in a Chilean University," in Daedalus, Vol. 97, No. 1, Winter 1968.

[51] See the article by Kenneth Walker, "Political Socialization in Universities" in Seymour Martin Lipset and Aldo Solari (eds.), *Elites in Latin America* (New York: Oxford University Press, 1967).

[52] Scheman, "The Brazilian Law Student."

students are their own agents operating on their own ideals and desires, and extramural organizations play a very minor role. Others—North American newspaper editors, for example—appear to believe that the student organizations are puppets in the hands of clever outside political puppeteers—Communists, or at least extreme leftists. All available evidence suggests, however, that student allegiance is a matter for great competition by almost all political groupings.

The claims that students are puppets appear to be based on several factors, a major one of which is the fairly high student representation in guerrilla movements. Fidel Castro and particularly Che Guevara seem to have become heroes for a certain type of student. After 1960, internal wars breaking out in, for example, Venezuela, Peru, Bolivia, Colombia, and Guatemala have had the active support of some students and the moral support of many more. One study suggests that universities continue to be the principal source of moral and material support for many guerrilla bands, and that contact with a band can often be expedited by going to the main university of the country rather than to the area in which the band is operating.[53]

These guerrilla movements have had very little real success. Unable to communicate with peasants, they have been destroyed or starved out, and the ones that remain, as one argument has it, have been forced into ineffective undergrounds where they are kept alive due to international and national political forces with no interest in their cause.[54]

This entire "conspiracy" (particularly "Communist conspiracy") argument has the fault of all such arguments. There is little, if any, evidence to support it. A very small minority of students do actually engage in guerrilla activities. Probably a majority of students are at least partly in sympathy with such activities—they appear to champion most lost causes. Probably most students also know Marxian terminology to some extent, and know bits and pieces of Marxian doctrine. The terminology, however, is part of the student vocabulary throughout the world, and Marxism, or parts of it, is common to all leftist or left-tending students. In short, the proponents of the argument that a huge conspiracy is constantly manipulating the Latin American student body for its own purposes will have to find further evidence if they are to be at all convincing.

Related to this is the idea of some that "professional students" are maintained in universities to promote the interests of external organizations. Most Latin American universities have generally lax rules concerning

---

[53] Albornoz, "Student Opposition."

[54] Luigi Einaudi, "Rebels without Allies," in *Saturday Review*, Vol. 51, August 17, 1968.

taking exams to finally complete a course, and a professional student is one who postpones such exams year after year, for as long as possible or until he himself decides to take them. Or he may have to take exams and fail them, but will then take advantage of generous provisions for repeating. Or he may take exams and pass, but for his own reasons will decline to graduate. One author cites as particular examples of the professional student the cases of Federico Muñoz, who at the age of thirty-one headed the Venezuelan Student Federation, and Efrén Capiz Villega, who at forty-one and after seventeen years of working for his degree, led a revolt against the University of Morelia in Mexico in 1963.[55] Even more significant than these individual examples was the fairly recent case in Venezuela where the administration of Central University decreed that a student of any faculty failing a course on two consecutive occasions is ineligible to continue in that faculty for two years. In the first application of the new regulation the Faculty of Engineering dropped some two hundred and sixty students.[56]

However, whatever the numbers of professional students—and there is considerable disagreement on this subject—and however gross individual examples may be, the argument that such students are maintained by outside organizations has yet to be substantiated. It is in the same position as the conspiracy argument: pat, but not verified. For that matter, there is no real evidence that great numbers of professional students who have been identified actually are political activists, much less fifth columnists for outside organizations.

It is fairly well documented, however, that most outside political organizations compete heavily for student support of their programs, and in this process the students can at times achieve an influential voice in determining organizational goals. The alliance may be formal or informal, depending on the organization and students concerned, and it can either be enduring or established for some special purpose. At times an alliance will appear incongruous, as in the mid-1950s when the Brazilian National Union of Students took the initiative in forming the Brazilian National Front with the National Federation of Industries, the Military Club, several trade unions, and the Higher Institute of Brazilian Studies.[57] However, the lines are usually much more finely drawn than in this example, and students must choose among the major power groupings in the country, or at least among the major ideological offerings.

In Peru, for example, both the Popular Action and the Christian Democrat parties have made great efforts to increase their student base in

---

55 Donahue, "Students in Latin American Politics."

56 Ibid.

57 *The Student Struggle in Latin America* (see footnote 1).

order to further institutionalize themselves. Until the military coup of 1968, Popular Action attempted to bolster its image on campus through such programs as University Popular Cooperation, a domestic, Peruvian-style peace corps.[58] In Venezuela, on the other hand, Democratic Action lost most of its youthful support in 1960 to the Revolutionary Left Movement, a radical-left organization, although apparently Democratic Action can still command some student support.[59] The Christian Social Revolutionary party of the Dominican Republic, coming to life after the death of Trujillo, has managed to capture a great deal of student attention. In Mexico, the dominant Institutional Revolutionary Party has a huge organizational and propaganda apparatus directed toward students, and although it has never been totally successful in capturing their allegiance, it continues to siphon off much student leadership, which in turn tends to bolster the left-wing of the party. A study of Brazilian university students argues that the four major student organizations are not actually campus oriented; rather they are national political organizations attempting to alter Brazilian society. In this case, however, the study asserts that politicians maneuver Brazil's 100,000 university students for goals that they, the politicians, decide upon.[60] A study of the University of Buenos Aires notes that the deans do not ask student centers within their faculties for knowledge of financial transactions since it is known that the centers must be subsidized to a considerable extent by outside organizations, and no embarrassment of either the students or the organizations is desired.[61]

The fact that knowledge of outside financial connections can be embarrassing emphasizes the entire problem of discussing students and their relationships with outside interests. We can recognize many more or less overt attempts of such interests to obtain student support, as we can see in many of the statements of student activists where their allegiance lies. However, this is really only the bare surface of the entire matter; we cannot discern all the political relationships, financial subsidies, organizational advising, and so forth that concern students. Many of these activities are by their very nature covert, whether for legal or strategic reasons. In short, on this point we can only say that many organizations of many political creeds compete for and win allegiance within the Latin American student body. Whether this competition is any greater than, for example, national party campus

[58] David Spencer, "The Role of Youth and Student Groups in Latin American Political Parties," in Spencer (ed.), *Student Politics in Latin America.*

[59] Ibid.

[60] Leonard D. Therry, "Dominant Power Components in the Brazilian University Student Movement Prior to April, 1964," in *Journal of Inter-American Studies,* Vol. 7, No. 1, January 1965.

[61] Newton, "Students and the Political System."

activities in the United States, is impossible to say. Some ability of students to influence national political organizations has been asserted here and this will become clearer in the discussion below of student political successes.

DESIRES AND DEMANDS

Both implicitly and explicitly in the foregoing discussion, the question of what students want from the political system has been answered to some extent. The majority of them, for example, want a considerable degree of autonomy for their particular university—freedom in their academic lives from the dictates of government. They also want to participate in the affairs of their university, whether in elections of governing bodies, selection of professors, or decisions on curricula. However, as important as these and related university concerns are to the students, and as much as they can become aroused over them, there appear to be other, major student desires underlying many of these "bread and butter" issues. That is, it is the socio-economic system against which they react and with which they desire the political system to cope.

One way of determining their basic political desires is to look at some of their major political orientations. David Spencer, who has written extensively on the student in Latin America, suggests that there are a dozen-odd political orientations found frequently enough in Latin American students to constitute types. There are, first, right-wing activist groups whose main concern is anti-Communism, although they possess a considerable degree of nationalist sentiment. This type may or may not be openly fascistic in nature. A second type is oriented toward the traditional liberal and conservative parties that dominated Latin America in the 19th century, and this type is still concerned primarily with the old battles of Church versus state and centralization versus decentralization. A third type is what Spencer calls Catholic Action, groups which have a quite conservative orientation and are controlled by the Catholic hierarchy. Fourth, there is the apolitical type, an orientation that sees only a minor role for students in politics, and concentrates instead on various welfare or service activities. Fifth, there are the Christian Democrat groups which emphasize the more liberal social doctrines of the Catholic Church but insist on freedom from the Church hierarchy. The sixth type is the "popular," non-Marxist and non-Catholic groups which have a liberal-socialist orientation. The seventh type, the independent groups, exist according to Spencer because they believe Marxism and Christian Democracy polarize politics too greatly in their attempts to gain mass support, and although this type is concerned with the betterment of the masses, they do not trust them. The eighth type, the undefined left, is distinguished not by any ideological line but by a virulent and romantic nationalism, as well as by a problem of reconciling leftist, revolutionary government with representative government. Ninth is the anarchist, a type of group that is heir to a long tradition of European-influenced anarchistic and anarcho-syndicalistic thought. This type is most commonly found in the early, most-idealistic stages of a student organization. The tenth type of orientation, the authoritarian, is also heir to a long tradition of Spanish and Latin American political thinking as well as actions. This, says Spencer, is often the orientation of students who are looking impatiently for total and rapid solutions to the underdevelopment of their countries. The eleventh type, the *fidelista,* is similar to the authoritarian but gives full support to Fidel Castro and the Cuban Revolution. The orientation is also similar to that of the undefined left in its concern for the mystique of revolution, but naturally it insists on a Cuban-style revolution for all Latin America. The twelfth type is the Soviet Communist, which is, quite simply, oriented toward Russia. And, thirteenth and finally, there is the Chinese Communist type, which although quite similar to the *fidelistas,* does not stress the Cuban Revolution.[62]

The problem with Spencer's categorization of Latin American students is that it is far too general. Even if the categories were refined to allow for more precision in classifying students, many serious drawbacks would remain. That is, its usefulness lies in suggesting the typical demands various categories of students will place on the political system, but the scheme provides no indication of the strength of the various groups, nor is it shown how one could discover the various strengths. Furthermore, as it stands it is far too general to allow discussion of the priorities given by the various types of groups to certain substantive questions—such as degree of democracy as opposed to economic development—although some of the categories do suggest partial answers to questions of this nature.

For example, Spencer's and other studies indicate a fairly constant, occasionally over-riding demand of many students that their countries remain free from foreign exploitation and control. This nationalistic desire apparently ranges from xenophobia on the political right through moderation in the face of needed foreign investment and other economic assistance for development, to xenophobia again on the political left. However, the orientation and depth of feeling among students on this issue appears to vary considerably depending on the time and circumstances, and not all studies of any given incident reach the same conclusion as to the degree of genuine nationalism involved. For example, in Lima and Caracas in 1958, when Vice-President Nixon was harassed by crowds in which students were very heavily represented, it was concluded by some observers that this was the result of a relatively few professional Communist agitators.[63] Others have

---

[62] David Spencer, "Political Positions in the Latin American Student Movement," in Spencer (ed.), *Student Politics in Latin America.*

[63] See, for example, Washington, "The Students."

concluded of the same event that it was one of the rare and authentic demonstrations that have occurred against United States involvement in Latin America.[64]

The moderation of the students regarding the subject of nationalism may, however, be greater than is generally credited. That is, we often get the impression that almost all Latin American university students are wild-eyed, fanatical nationalists, but specific studies of issues suggest that this is certainly not always the case. For example, despite the great controversy over foreign ownership and control of Chilean copper mines, a recent study of Chilean university students' attitudes found that only eight percent of the sample considered imperialism to be the major obstacle to Chilean economic development.[65]

As with nationalism, students can generally be counted upon to respond to some extent to certain domestic events and issues. Among most common of these are such things as any infringements on constitutionality and democracy (as they define these) in their counties, lack of social and economic equality, and Catholicism. Almost any military takeover is sure to incur great student opposition and vocal protest, as occurred, for example, in 1964 in Brazil and 1966 in Argentina. The only forceful overthrow of a government in recent years which has won widespread student support, at home as well as abroad, was Castro's movement in Cuba. In the same fashion, students will usually react strongly against authoritarianism on the part of the government, as has recently been demonstrated in Brazil as a result of torture of political prisoners and in Venezuela as a result of government attempts to control Communist activities. Demands for universal social and economic equality are perhaps incongruous given the typical socioeconomic background of the Latin American university student, but, odd or not, such demands are a constant feature in their various political programs and date at least from the Cordoba Manifesto. Today student activists typically attempt to associate their organizations with workers' movements and with agrarian reform. Finally, many students, even many practicing Catholic students, are quite anticlerical in the sense that they insist that while the Catholic Church has certain functions to perform in society, political activity is not one of them.

Of course, students respond to issues much more specific than these, such as to a particular foreign policy or agricultural program, a presidential veto or newspaper censorship. However, their demands can usually be subsumed under the broad concerns just described, even if such generalization lacks precision and clarity. Certainly, specific demands are usually presented in nationalistic, constitutional, equalitarian, and other such broad terms.

[64] See, for example, Albornoz, "Student Opposition."

[65] Glazer, "Student Politics in a Chilean University."

SYSTEM RESPONSE

Concerning the question of student success in having their demands met by the political system, there is again great difficulty in supplying unequivocal answers. First, since the demands students make have yet to be closely analyzed and are on the whole quite hazy, discussion about the realization of those demands are imprecise and tentative. Second, it is often quite impossible to determine, even tentatively, the influence students have in a given output of the political system. On the whole, students do seem to have some impact on the system, although the degree of this impact as well as the potential of student political activism is quite variously assessed and may perhaps be much less than is generally credited.

As with student political activities and demands, student political successes must be considered in two lights; success in achieving university-oriented demands, and success in achieving society-focused demands. The first type of success has been discussed above to a considerable extent. In their battles to maintain university autonomy the students have certainly not always been successful. Every recognizable infringement of this autonomy by the political authorities—and, as noted, there have been many overt infringements in the last decade—is an example of lack of success on the students' part. On the other hand, every vestige of autonomy that remains— and in some countries there remains considerable autonomy, both real and only formal—can in like manner be greatly attributed to successful student activism. The same argument applies to student participation in university government. This principle is also often submerged, usually as a result of loss of autonomy by the university, but co-government remains a basic principle throughout Latin American academic life. As with university autonomy, students have successfully achieved and maintained some degree of meaningful representation in most "national" Latin American universities, and often, as in some of the cases cited above, have achieved a decisive voice. The same conclusion can be drawn about other of the Reform principles.

Concerning the success of society-oriented student demands on the political system, some studies urge that it has been considerable. Speaking generally of Latin America, one study asserts that through their strikes and demonstrations students have been able to exert strong influence designed to guide, change, or even overthrow national governments.[66] Studies of specific countries have also arrived at this conclusion. A study of Cuba, for example, argues that students have historically been very influential in preserving some semblance of freedom, whether under Spanish rule or after the independence from Spain which they aided so greatly in achieving. Their success

66 Donahue, "Students in Latin American Politics."

was apparent also in the events leading up to the overthrow of Batista.[67] Two studies of Venezuela, one on the struggle against dictator Juan Vicente Gómez in the late 1920s and one on the overthrow of Marco Pérez Jiménez in 1958, suggest that students have been a constant and important, although not necessarily decisive, element in major political battles in Venezuela.[68] A study of Chilean university students suggests that their dedication to democracy, their willingness to protest injustice, and their resistance to political repression have helped keep Chile politically moderate.[69] In Brazil, a study has found that the students proudly consider themselves quite influential in national politics, and cite as instances of their successful demands such events as the return to constitutional prescription following the resignation of Janio Quadros in 1961, the results of the plebiscite in 1963 which returned presidential functions to Goulart, and the popular protests against the proposed declaration of a state of siege in late 1963.[70] Certainly the Castelo Branco regime considered student organizations sufficiently strong to warrant repressive measures against them, and the same can be said of police intervention in universities in Argentina and Mexico. In fact, every police or military intervention in a university can, in a sense, be regarded not only as an infringement of university autonomy, but also as a result and partial success of the other university reform principle of concern for social conditions. As another general study of Latin American university students concludes, in the last twenty years almost all political movements offering alternatives to repressive or unrepresentative government in Latin America have originated in the universities and have found their first expression through student organizations.[71]

Other studies, however, suggest a conclusion contrary to student political successes. That is, while certain successful activities can be noted, it is probably much more frequently the case that student demands are disregarded, that their strikes end with only token concessions, and that the instigators of actions that seriously demand significant change are imprisoned.[72] For example, in the Venezuelan, Brazilian, and Argentine cases the

[67] Jaime Suchlicki, "El estudiantado de la Universidad de la Habana en la política cubana," in *Journal of Inter-American Studies,* Vol. 9, No. 1, January 1967.

[68] John D. Martz, "Venezuela's 'Generation of '28:' The Genesis of Political Democracy," in *Journal of Inter-American Studies,* Vol. 6, No. 1, January 1964; and Walter Washington, "Student Politics in Latin America: The Venezuelan Example," in Spencer (ed.), *Student Politics in Latin America.*

[69] Bonilla, "The Student Federation of Chile."

[70] Therry, "The Brazilian University Student Movement."

[71] Kevin Lyonette, "Student Organizations in Latin America," in *International Affairs,* Vol. 42, No. 4, October 1966.

[72] Albornoz, "Student Opposition."

success of students was perhaps only recognizable to the extent that they irritated the authorities. That is, student political influence can perhaps be seen in forceful reactions by the authorities to their activities, but if the end result is repression of their activities, it is difficult to see in such cases, however much one might wish to, the achievement of anything politically significant.

Thus, for example, in Venezuela in 1963 Central University adopted a "no-repeating" regulation in a deliberate attempt to stifle, or at least reduce, student political activities. This measure, harsh for Latin America, provided that a student who failed more than twice would be dropped permanently from the University. A year later police entered the university to arrest certain students for alleged acts of terrorism, and violent demonstrations occurred to protest the arrests. The rector responded by threatening application of the new regulation, which until then had remained unenforced. Further strikes took place, involving both Communist and Christian Democrat organizations, but they terminated quite abruptly when the university administration announced that, if they continued, *all* students would lose a year's credit.[73] Similarly, Argentine student political activity achieved the result of police intervention, but as one study of the University of Buenos Aires concludes, the University is attempting to perform a role for which it is really not equipped. It has lost the prestige it once had as the domain of an acknowledged and, more importantly, accepted elite, and except in the minds of a few, very optimistic idealists, the University is no longer one of the holders of political power in Argentina.[74]

Actually, it has been argued fairly convincingly that while student political achievements were once quite discernible in Latin America, today student political activism in general, and therefore any possibility of political successes, is in strong decline. While the emphasis varies in such assessments, they all indicate that technological change and its attendant social and political consequences make student political activism much less likely.

For example, Robert Scott has argued that the original student activism in Latin America which initiated the Reform Movement was due to basic technological change in the late 19th and early 20th centuries, but as the technologization of Latin American countries proceeded, still further social changes occurred that made student activism irrelevant and unproductive. For example, he argues that there are now in Mexico many educated persons both in and out of government who share a national outlook, and consequently they replace the university student's former role in nation-building. Today, particularly because of the new skills needed in the economic life of the country, the university is returning to its role of education.[75]

73 Lipset, "University Students and Politics."

74 Newton, "Students and the Political System."

75 Scott, "Student Political Activism."

Luigi Einaudi comes to a similar conclusion when he argues that in Argentina since 1956 and even before that in Mexico, the old battle of whether or not the university should serve the country has been decided affirmatively, and the new emphasis in universities is on serving the country by providing competent professionals trained in the newer fields which are becoming increasingly important to the society. Furthermore, expansion of higher education and research facilities meets one of the major demands of the university reformists, and therefore weakens the drive of students to participate in university government. At the same time it removes a great potential source of discontent by providing the student with courses of study that are relevant to the present society and that give him some assurance of meaningful employment when he graduates.[76]

Using still another argument to arrive at the same conclusion, David Spencer suggests that as the societies of Latin America become more industrialized—more "modernized" in general—political parties will in turn become more institutionalized and much less personalistically oriented. As institutionalization becomes increasingly recognized as a means of obtaining mass support for programs, position and influence will become more achieved and less ascribed, and students will tend to lose much of their traditional prestige as politicians. That is, political leadership will become much more professionalized and much less personalistic and charismatic, and students will no longer automatically be considered as suppliers of ideas, programs, and leadership.[77]

These arguments appear quite convincing; however, their force is somewhat lessened by events elsewhere than Latin America. In the United States, for example, there is today fairly massive student unrest, although the United States, to use the criteria of the above arguments, is one of the most "modernized" countries in the world, its universities have long been oriented toward producing specialists in new fields, and its political parties have become extremely institutionalized. This is not intended as a rejection of Scott's, Einaudi's and Spencer's arguments, but rather as a cautionary note. In other words, the possibility that student politics in Latin America will increasingly lack relevance appears quite high, but it is not at all as yet demonstrable that industrialization and its attendant factors will indeed bring about student political quiescence. In fact it may bring about even further manifestations of activism—particularly if Latin American students, as North American students apparently are doing, continue to operate on idealistic, social reform-oriented principles.

In brief summary of this discussion of student political activism in Latin America, it can be restated that this activism is a phenomenon that

[76] Einaudi, "University Autonomy."

[77] Spencer, "The Role of Youth and Student Groups in Latin American Political Parties."

remains essentially unstudied by rigorous methodology, despite the interest it has piqued in many scholars. The evidence available on political motivations of students emphasizes their idealism and their readiness to act upon it. It also suggests a relatively high level of political activism (compared, for example, to the United States, even in these days). Much of their political activity apparently occurs as a result of attempts, implicit or explicit, to achieve the goals of the University Reform Movement, particularly in regard to university autonomy and student participation in university government, although their concern for the principle of solving social problems also constantly involves them in battles within the political system. They have often been successful in achieving the first two goals, but evidence is lacking as to their overall success in achieving solutions to social problems. Although some success seems apparent, it is often at the expense of gains made toward the other two goals, university autonomy and co-government. On the whole, then, whether because their role as political activists has been made increasingly irrelevant to national politics by modernization of their societies, whether they are co-opted by the social and political systems, or whether their demands are simply ignored with impunity by the political system, students do not appear to constitute a major force toward political and economic development in Latin America. Despite their self-image, and the image they present to the world, university students in Latin America appear, on the whole, to be followers rather than leaders, and if political and economic development does occur it will not be in spite of student political activity, but it also will not be because of it.

FURTHER READING

AGUIRRE BELTRÁN, GONZALO, *La universidad latinoamericano y otros ensayos.* Xalapa, Mexico: Universidad Veracruzano, 1961.

ALBORNOZ, ORLANDO, "Student Opposition in Latin America," in *Government and Opposition,* Vol. 2, No. 1, October 1966–January 1967.

ARCINIEGAS, GERMÁN, "Intellectuals in the Politics of Latin America," in Cole Blasier (ed.), *Constructive Change in Latin America.* Pittsburgh: University of Pittsburgh Press, 1968.

BARRERA ROMERO, MANUEL J., "Trayectoria del movimiento de reforma universitaria en Chile," in *Journai of Inter-American Studies,* Vol. 10, No. 4, October 1968.

BENJAMIN, HAROLD R. W., *Higher Education in the American Republics.* New York, 1965.

BONILLA, FRANK, "Promoting Political Development Abroad: Social Condition and Attitudes of Latin American Intellectuals," in *Studies in Comparative International Development,* Vol. 4, 1968.

——————, *Students in Politics: Three Generations of Political Action in a Latin American University.* Cambridge, Mass.: Harvard University, Doctoral dissertation, 1959.

——————, "The Student Federation of Chile: 50 Years of Political Action," in *Journal of Inter-American Studies,* July 1960.

CHIAPETTA, MICHAEL, "Education: The Baited Trap," in *The Nation,* Vol. 203, October 3, 1966.

CROUCH, COLIN, "The Universities for the 1970s," in *New Statesman,* Vol. 78, October 31, 1969.

DAME, HARTLEY F., MARGARET P. HAYS, and CHRISTY ANN HOFFMAN, *The Political Influence of University Students in Latin America: An Analytical Survey of Research Studies and Related Literature.* Washington, D.C., 1965.

DEHAINAUT, RAYMOND, "The Crisis in the Argentine University Reform Movement," in *Motive,* Vol. 27, January 1967.

DE IMAZ, JOSÉ LUIS, *Los que mandan.* Buenos Aires: Eudaba, 1964.

DEL MAZO, GABRIEL, "La nueva crisis de la universidades latinoamericanos," in *Panoramas,* Vol. 10, July–August 1964.

DILLON SOARES, GLAUCIO ARY, "The Active Few: A Study of Student Political Ideology and Participation," in *Comparative Education Review,* Vol. 10, No. 2, June 1966.

——————, "Intellectual Identity and Political Ideology among University Students," in Seymour Martin Lipset and Aldo Solari (eds.), *Elites in Latin America.* New York: Oxford University Press, 1967.

DONAHUE, FRANCIS, "Students in Latin American Politics," in *Antioch Review,* Vol. 26, No. 1, Spring 1966.

EINAUDI, LUIGI, "Rebels without Allies," in *Saturday Review,* Vol. 51, August 17, 1968.

ENARSON, HAROLD L., "University Education in Central America," in *Journal of Higher Education,* Vol. 34, April 1963.

GLAZER, MYRON, *The Professional and Political Attitudes of Chilean University Students.* Princeton, N.J.: Princeton University Doctoral dissertation.

——————, "Student Politics in a Chilean University," in *Daedalus,* Vol. 97, No. 1, Winter 1968.

GOLDRICH, DANIEL, "Panamanian Students' Orientations Toward Government and Democracy," in *Journal of Inter-American Studies,* Vol. 5, No. 3, July 1963.

——————, *Radical Nationalism: The Political Orientations of Panamanian Law Students.* Michigan State University: Bureau of Social and Political Research, 1961.

HAMUY, EDUARDO, *El problema educacional del pueblo de Chile.* Santiago: Editorial del Pacífico, 1961.

HARRISON, JOHN P., "The Confrontation with the Political University," in Robert N. Burr (ed.), *Latin America's Nationalistic Revolutions*. Annals of the American Academy of Political and Social Science, March 1961.

—————, "Learning and Politics in Latin American Universities," in *Academy of Political Science Proceedings*, Vol. 27, May 1964.

HATCH, W. B., J. LABBENS, and J. H. TERLINGERN, *Informe de la Misión Consultora de la UNESCO para las universidades centroamericanos*. Paris: UNESCO, 1962.

HUTCHINSON, BERTRAM, *Mobilidade e trabalho*. Rio de Janeiro: Centro Brasileiro de Pesquisas Educacionais, 1960.

"Latin America Cracks Down on Student-Run Schools," in *U. S. News and World Report*, Vol. 64, No. 22, May 27, 1968.

LIPSET, SEYMOUR MARTIN, "University Students and Politics in Underdeveloped Countries," in *Minerva*, Vol. 3, No. 1, Autumn 1964.

LYONETTE, KEVIN, "Student Organizations in Latin America," in *International Affairs*, Vol. 42, No. 4, October 1966.

MALDONADO-DENIS, MANUEL, "Challenge from the Intellectuals," in *The Nation*, Vol. 209, July 28, 1969.

—————, "The Situation of Cuba's Intellectuals," in *Christian Century*, Vol. 85, No. 3, January 17, 1968.

MANTOVANI, JUAN, "Idea, forma y misión de las universidades en los paises latinoamericanos," in *Política, Caracas*, Vol. 21, April–May 1962.

MARTZ, JOHN D., "Venezuela's 'Generation of '28:' The Genesis of Political Democracy," in *Journal of Inter-American Studies*, Vol. 6, No. 1, January 1964.

MYHR, ROBERT O., "The University Student Tradition in Brazil," in *Journal of Inter-American Studies and World Affairs*, Vol. 12, No. 1, January 1970.

NEWTON, RONALD C., "Students and the Political System of the University of Buenos Aires," in *Journal of Inter-American Studies*, Vol. 8, No. 4, October 1966.

PRICE, CHRISTOPHER, "Death on the Mexican Campus," in *New Statesman*, Vol. 78, November 28, 1969.

RIBEIRO, DARCY, "Universities and Social Development," in Seymour Martin Lipset and Aldo Solari (eds.), *Elites in Latin America*. New York: Oxford University Press, 1967.

SALERA, VIRGIL, "The Economics of Education: Latin America and California," in *Inter-American Economic Affairs*, Vol. 20, No. 3, Winter 1966.

SCHEMAN, L. RONALD, "The Brazilian Law Student: Background, Habits, Attitudes," in *Journal of Inter-American Studies*, Vol. 5, No. 3, July 1963.

SCHERZ-GARCÍA, LUIS, "Relations between Public and Private Universities," in Seymour Martin Lipset and Aldo Solari (eds.), *Elites in Latin America*. New York: Oxford University Press, 1967.

SCOTT, ROBERT E., "Student Political Activism in Latin America," in *Daedalus,* Vol. 97, No. 1, Winter 1968. Scott is currently preparing a book on Chilean and Mexican university students.

SHILS, E., "The Intellectuals in the Political Development of the New States," in Kautsky, J. (ed.), *Political Change in Underdeveloped Countries.* New York: John Wiley, 1962.

SILVERT, KALMAN, *The Conflict Society: Reaction and Revolution in Latin America.* New York: American Universities Field Staff, Inc., 1966.

—————, "The University Student" in John J. Johnson (ed.), *Continuity and Change in Latin America.* Stanford, Calif.: Stanford University Press, 1964.

Situação social da America Latina. Rio de Janeiro: Centro Latinoamericano de Pesquisas em Ciencias Sociales, 1965.

La situación educativa en America Latina. Paris: UNESCO, 1960.

SPENCER, DAVID (ed.), *Student Politics in Latin America.* United States National Student Association, 1965. Note: Individual contributors to this book of articles on student politics in Latin America are referred to in the footnotes of this chapter.

The Student Struggle in Latin America. Report of the International Student Conference Delegation, 1957.

SUCHLICKI, JAIME, "El estudiantado de la Universidad de la Habana en la política cubana, 1956–1957," in *Journal of Inter-American Studies,* Vol. 9, No. 1, January 1967.

THERRY, LEONARD D., "Dominant Power Components in the Brazilian University Student Movement Prior to April, 1964," in *Journal of Inter-American Studies,* Vol. 7, No. 1, January 1965.

WAGGONER, BARBARA, GEORGE R. WAGGONER, and GREGORY B. WOLFE, "Higher Education in Contemporary Central America," in *Journal of Inter-American Studies,* Vol. 6, No. 4, October 1964.

WAGGONER, GEORGE R., "Problems in the Professionalization of the University Teaching Career in Central America," in *Journal of Inter-American Studies,* Vol. 8, No. 2, April 1966.

WALKER, KENNETH, "Political Socialization in Universities," in Seymour Martin Lipset and Aldo Solari (eds.), *Elites in Latin America.* New York: Oxford University Press, 1967.

—————, "La socialisación política en las universidades latinoamericanos" in *Revista Latinoamerciano de Sociología,* 1965.

WALTER, RICHARD JOHN, *University Reform and Student Politics in Argentina.* Ann Arbor: University of Michigan Microfilms, 1967.

WASHINGTON, WALTER, "The Students," in Robert D. Tomasek (ed.), *Latin American Politics: 24 Studies of the Contemporary Scene.* Garden City, N.Y.: Doubleday, 1966.

WILLIAMSON, ROBERT C., *El estudiente colombiano y sus actitudes.* Bogotá: Monografías Sociológicas, Universidad Nacional de Colombia, 1962.

CHAPTER 6

ROMAN CATHOLIC

CLERGY

THE CONTEXT: POLITICAL HISTORY

As a group with institutional rather than categorical identity, the Roman Catholic clergy of Latin America have played and continue to play an important, if not decisive, role in the political, social and economic life of the region. The clergy, of course, derive this importance from their position within a formidable, traditional institution, the Roman Catholic Church, as well as from the informal prerogatives attached to such an institution. It is therefore impossible to evaluate the political role of the clergy without describing to some extent the institution within which they work. This does not mean that the clergy have no independence in determining the particular facets of their political role in Latin American life; but it does mean that the Church exerts tremendous influence on the outer limits of what is politically permissible. The personnel of the Church in Latin America—from a cardinal to the most obscure village priest—have some opportunities for performing differing and even contradictory political actions, but the doctrines, procedures, training and institutional power of the Church will not tolerate actions that threaten its own survival or that clearly jeopardize its position within Latin American societies.

In discussing the Roman Catholic Church in Latin America as background for an examination of the political role of the clergy in the process of socioeconomic change, it should be made explicitly clear that there is no interest here in the "rightness" or "wrongness" of theological doctrine, and no interest in condemning such past practices as religious intolerance or such present manifestations of Church upheaval as the case of the excommunicated rebel-priest Camilo Torres of Colombia. Instead, we are intent upon describing the historical role of the Church in the political life of Latin America, the organizational nature of the Church, which at least formally has remained largely unchanged over the years, and the impact of the Church as an institution on the current political scene in Latin America.

The history of the Roman Catholic Church in Latin America is closely entwined with the political history of the region itself. As one scholar has observed, the Church is the only formal organization that spans the four and one-half centuries of Spanish American history.[1] During much of that time, but especially during the immediate pre- and post-colonial period in Latin America, the Church was not only a major religious and cultural force but a primary economic and political power. At the time of Mexico's independence from Spain in the early nineteenth century, for example, the Church owned one-half of the country's land and many commercial enterprises,[2] and despite minor variations this was typical of the rest of Latin America during the latter part of the colonial era. In effect, the Church in the pre-independence period (1520–1810) shared power with the conquistadores, capitalists and officials of the Spanish Crown, and State and Church supplemented one another rather than having separate spheres of interest.[3] In this alliance of the sword and the cross for promoting the manifold interests of empire, the sword was generally the dominant partner. The colonizing process in and the extension of Christian civilization to Latin America were largely if not completely delegated to the Church. As an arm of State policy, the Church naturally acquired power as well as responsibilities. With civilizing and exploiting of the Indians came an educational system run by the Catholic Church. With promoting the economic interests of the State came the task of acquiring and using enormous amounts of the best land in the region. As one of the few formidable institutions upon which the Spaniards could rely, the Church was encouraged to perform a wide array of secular as well as sacred functions which, of course, lent political power to its other impressive privileges.

As a social and political force, the Church in Latin America was most important before rather than after independence, although even then it did not have an entirely free hand. As a result, the Church, as an important and powerful member of the traditional oligarchy in Latin America, was

[1] Ivan Vallier, "Religious Elites: Differentiations and Developments in Roman Catholicism," in Seymour Martin Lipset and Aldo Solari (eds.), *Elites in Latin America* (New York: Oxford University Press, 1967), p. 222.

[2] Alexander T. Edelmann, *Latin American Government and Politics* (Homewood, Ill.: Dorsey, 1965), p. 155.

[3] Francois Houtart and Emile Pin, *The Church and the Latin American Revolution* (New York: Sheed & Ward, 1965).

(and still is in some cases) committed to a defense of the economic, social and cultural systems that supported and justified its importance.[4] Then, as now, however, the Church's official policies diverged from the attitudes and practices of some of its priests. Just as Father las Casas earned a reputation for defending the rights of the Indians against exploitative treatment of both Church and State, so did priests, such as Father Hidalgo of Mexico, lead the independence movement that eventually threatened some of the bases of Church power.[5]

With the assertion of independence from Spain in the early nineteenth century came the effort by many independence leaders to end not only the intimate relationship which the Church enjoyed with the State but also, in many cases, the vast secular importance of the Church in general. As a political controversy, the separation of Church and State permeated Latin America throughout much of the nineteenth century, with the Liberals insisting upon a nonsecular and nonpolitical Church and the Conservatives arguing just as forcefully for a Church with its past powers and privileges largely intact. As the issue raged, it was clear at least to the Liberals, such as Juarez of Mexico, O'Higgins of Chile, and Battle y Ordoñez of Uruguay, that what was under attack was not Catholicism but the traditional political role of the Church, an institution that had aligned with a losing cause during the struggle for independence and that therefore had to adapt to a new situation of subservience under different masters.[6]

The separation of Church and State in Latin America—that is, the limitation of Church activities to principally the religious sphere and the delegation to the new governments of the region the secular roles previously performed by the Church—was and is an uneven and incomplete process. For example, although Colombia was the first country to endorse separation of Church and State, today the Church in Colombia is recognized as one of the strongest in the area.[7] On the other hand, Mexico, probably more than any other Latin American country, has a record of severe, if sporadic, persecution of the Church since the 1910 Revolution. Nevertheless, the country boasts a Church that ordained more priests, 211, in a recent year, 1967, than any other country.[8]

From such examples one can conclude that the process of separation

[4] Editorial, "Church and State in Latin America," in *A Journal of Church and State,* Vol. 8, No. 2, Spring 1966, pp. 173–85.

[5] Thomas G. Sanders, "Types of Catholic Elites in Latin America," in Robert D. Tomasek (ed.), *Latin American Politics,* second edition (New York: Doubleday, 1970), p. 181.

[6] Edelmann, *Latin American Government and Politics,* pp. 150–51.

[7] Editorial, "Church and State in Latin America."

[8] Luigi Einauldi et al., *Latin American Institutional Development* (Santa Monica, Calif.: Rand Corporation, Memorandum RM-6136—DOS), pp. 4–5.

of Church and State is not uniform throughout the area and therefore its concrete meaning depends upon the context and the particular country. In Argentina, Colombia, Costa Rica, Ecuador, Paraguay, Peru and Venezuela, the Church is, explicitly or implicitly, an established religion, the approved religion of the State. In a number of other countries (Bolivia, Brazil, Chile, Dominican Republic, El Salvador, Guatemala, Haiti, Honduras, Nicaragua, Panama, and Uruguay) the Church is more or less independent of the State and therefore does not greatly benefit or suffer under governmental auspices. Mexico, finally, lies at the other end of the continuum in the sense that great controls have been placed on the Church without the traditional benefits of Church and State cooperation. The Mexican clergy, for example, cannot engage in politics, vote or hold public office.[9] Less directly political, but no less restrictive, were other provisions of the 1917 Constitution that, among other things, made marriage a civil contract, deprived the Church of the legal right to own property, and gave the state legislatures the power to restrict the number of priests within each state.[10]

These variations in Church and State relations in Latin America are not easily explained. Perhaps of some validity is the notion that the political power of the church as a traditional institution will probably decline as the socioeconomic systems upon which it is based evolve. As noted in Chapter I, the socioeconomic changes within Latin America as a whole and within each country are uneven. Brazil, Argentina, Chile and Mexico, for example, have undergone greater industrialization, urbanization and economic growth than have the smaller countries of the Caribbean area. As development proceeds, the discrepancies within such countries multiply, making it difficult to discover a precise relationship between national economic development and the decline of the traditional Church. One can only suggest that there seems to be a general trend for the strength of the traditional Church to wane as socioeconomic development progresses. Not all changes undermine such institutions; indeed, the short-run effect may be to strengthen them (perhaps Argentina is an example of this). In any event, it is important to bear in mind that other factors are involved. For example, the Bolivian Church has not suffered the persecution common to Mexico and Cuba, although Bolivia did undergo a social revolution of sorts that struck at the power of the traditional oligarchy. Simply put, the Bolivian Church was never strong enough to be worth persecuting.[11] In sum, viewed from the long perspective of Church history since independence, socioeconomic development and secularization has tended to undermine the traditional bases of power of the

[9] Edelmann, *Latin American Government and Politics*, p. 162.

[10] Frederick C. Turner, "The Compatibility of Church and State in Mexico," in *Journal of Inter-American Studies*, Vol. 9, No. 4, October 1967, p. 598.

[11] Edelmann, *Latin American Government and Politics*, p. 168.

Church, and therefore have prompted a contemporary crisis of institutional identity.[12]

ORGANIZATION

One aspect of the Church that has remained basically unchanged over the centuries is the formal organization of its hierarchy. Institutions, especially those which operate on such bureaucratic principles as hierarchy, are prone to resist extensive internal reorganization—and the Church is no exception. But the lack of structural adjustments within the Latin American hierarchies of the Church is not solely due to the general tendency of many bureaucratic institutions to resist change. Whatever else may be said about it, the Church in Latin America is not simply a collection of several national hierarchies; it is also the extension of an international religious institution, with headquarters in the Vatican. The organizational and doctrinal ties of the Latin American hierarchies to an international loyalty naturally restrict the extent to which the national Churches may change their own structures, although they also have the advantage of providing a more or less coherent system of beliefs and practices that gives Catholicism a universal flavor. However, if the Vatican fails to take account of the serious strains upon the general societies of Latin America, then the organization of its national hierarchies will continue to be based upon a notion of society which is becoming increasingly irrelevant and out-of-date.[13]

Clearly, an attempt to describe the structure of the Catholic Church presumes an understanding of what exactly the term "Church" includes and what it excludes. A very broad definition has its drawbacks. With a large proportion of the world's Catholics, and with the prospect of accounting for one-half of the world's Catholics in the year 2000, Latin America is definitely Catholic in the sense that 90 percent of its population has been baptized in that faith.[14] However, of these Catholics, two-thirds never take first communion and most rarely if ever attend Church.[15] Many Latin Americans are Catholic in name only because they have not internalized Catholic teaching

[12] J. Lloyd Mecham, *Church and State in Latin America: A History of Politico-Ecclesiastical Relations,* rev. ed. (Chapel Hill: University of North Carolina Press, 1966), p. 417; and Donald Eugene Smith, *Religion and Political Development* (Boston: Little, Brown, 1970), pp. 160–61.

[13] Orlando Fals Borda, discussed in William L. Wonderly, "Social Science Research and the Church in Latin America," in *Practical Anthropology,* Vol. 14, No. 2, March–April 1967, pp. 161–73.

[14] Mecham, *Church and State,* p. 422; Einauldi et al., *Institutional Development,* p. 17.

[15] Mecham, *Church and State,* p. 422.

nor have they applied it to their everyday lives. Many Catholics (although this is less true of women, the very old and the very young) do not even practice the sacraments and other rituals which require little deep commitment.[16] A notion of the Catholic Church that includes these people would be so broad as to be meaningless.

Before proceeding in this discussion, it should be noted here that perhaps the most direct challenge for the Church in its failure to spiritually involve the masses of Latin America is the recent growth of non-Catholic religious movements, such as fundamentalist Protestant sects, the Caribbean cultic sects, and other sects that rely heavily upon the cultural heritage of African belief systems.[17] Although the growth of these religious alternatives is uneven in Latin America, with such countries as Brazil and Chile accounting for much of it, the adherents of such sects evidently gain what the Catholic Church has not generally been able to provide—spiritual involvement. Of course, one must not unduly overemphasize the significance of this challenge. Many times, the commitment to Protestantism is just as superficial as are older loyalties to Catholicism. But for a number of individuals, spiritual involvement is more likely with such sects than with the ritualistic Catholicism that often is out of touch with personal religious needs of the Latin American masses. In Brazil, for example, the three sects of Pentecostalism, Spiritualism, and Umbanda (the latter is a ritualistic combination of an African cult and Christianity which finds 12 million followers) diverge from Catholicism in that they do not passively accept the way things are, they use spiritual possession, and they largely recruit from the lower classes. But they also share compatible beliefs with Brazilian folk Catholicism and Messianism, which exalt the prophet as miracle worker. The spiritual satisfaction gained in such cults many times provides a release from frustration through nonpolitical means that Catholicism is either incapable or unwilling to supply.[18]

A more restrictive notion of the Catholic Church would emphasize the institution and its organization. For example, Sanders and Vallier focus upon what they call religious elites—the cardinals, the bishops, the clergy and the laymen who have internalized and applied Church teachings—rather than including all nominal Catholics (and therefore nearly all Latin Americans) without regarding their actual relationship to the institution. Such elites and their closer association with the Church as an institution are of principal interest here.

16 Thomas G. Sanders, "The Church in Latin America," in *Foreign Affairs,* Vol. 48, No. 2, January 1970, p. 286.

17 Vallier, "Religious Elites," p. 194.

18 Ibid., pp. 191–94.

The structure of the Church can partially be understood through an examination of its historical role.[19] In the seventeenth century, the Church forsook its religious functions in favor of its secular ones, a shift that required that the religious needs of the people were served in social groups such as the family, the community, and brotherhoods rather than principally by the priests and their sacramental authority. Another pattern that has existed since the beginning of the Church's history in Latin America is the subjection of Church elites to secular control. Even during its intimate alliance with the Spanish Crown, the Church had to work through and depended upon outside groups for its effectiveness and very survival. Consequently, the Church has always been "political" because it has had to form coalitions with other groups to ensure its institutional survival and well-being. Another pattern, and one that is closely related to the first two mentioned, is the failure to institutionalize a religious and moral code that effectively permeated the population. Since its inception as an important force in Latin American history, the Church depended not upon its success as a dynamic promoter of spiritual values but upon its role as an economic organization that, under the guidance and encouragement of the State, also fulfilled the task of providing social control. It is perhaps for this reason that outside observers are more impressed with the Church's history as a secular power than as a religious one. Recent strains on this traditional role suggest the possibility that the Church, if it is to find a sense of renewal in contemporary Latin America, will have to redirect its principal efforts toward the religious aspects of life, although this may involve political activities.

Finally, the Church's structure may be viewed in terms of its policy-making and administrative features. According to Vallier, the Church has undergone very few important structural changes. Traditionally, the Church manifested decentralization, lack of coordination and structural awkwardness. Lacking common religious objectives, the Church became an amorphous and internally divided institution, with confused lines of authority and with members working at contradictory purposes. All these patterns, especially this last one, exist today in the Church, defying simplistic stereotypes of the Church as a monolithic structure.

Given these and other considerations to be mentioned later, generalizations about the organizational nature of the contemporary Church must take account of formal appearances and informal realities. Like the Latin American societies of which it is an integral part, the Church is both old and new, national and international, local and cosmopolitian, bureaucratic and communal.[20] Such contradictions, which appear to be the price large social institutions such as the Church must pay for their importance, often

19 Ibid., p. 223.

20 Smith, *Religion and Political Development*, p. 178.

confuse image and reality. This is particularly true concerning the organizational nature of the institution. For example, the question arises: Is the Church hierarchy as monolithic and authoritarian as a formal interpretation of its legal foundations might suggest? Or is it a much more complex and subtle arrangement in which formal patterns of hierarchy are compromised within the context of Latin American society? Aside from those who favor either a narrow view of the Church or those who engage in polemical attacks against it, the most reasonable interpretation appears to be the second.

Looking at this claim in more detail, it cannot be denied that of the four major religions in the so-called developing world, Roman Catholicism as it exists in Latin America maintains a much less democratic structure and value system than do Islam, Buddhism or Hinduism.[21] This kind of structure is the legacy of both religious tradition and doctrine. Throughout the years, Church leaders generally not only condone but actively approve of such authoritarian structures. Church dogma reinforces the image of a devotion to rigid hierarchy. Since the Pope is the infallible representative of God, and the Church is the only church propagating absolute truth, authority is supposed to descend from the highest to the lowest members of the clergy— linking the Pope with cardinals, archbishops, bishops and parish priests— without formal recognition of national sovereignty.[22] According to the ideal Catholic model of organization, then, the Papacy makes broad policy that is to be applied through regional (but more likely through national) organizations of bishops. The Latin American Bishops' Council (CELAM) has thus provided regional direction to the national hierarchies, although the national hierarchies are directly charged with relating to Catholics within their respective countries. Lastly, the priests and laymen learn of and apply to their own situations the rulings of the higher Church authorities.[23]

This ideal view of Church organization requires further elaboration. The Church hierarchy within each nation is divided into a number of dioceses that are headed by residential bishops with independent authority under Canon Law and therefore the potential for diversity of opinions and behavior. Numerous dioceses headed by relatively independent bishops are an implicit concession to the variety of conditions and situations over which the Church hierarchy formally presides. But to ensure that the hierarchy has some restraint on this potential for diversity, the Pope has a representative in each country called an "apostolic nuncio," or titular bishop, who, although he has no independent authority over residential bishops, may challenge their actions and force the consideration of a controversy to a

21 Ibid., p. 178; and Einauldi et al., *Institutional Development,* p. 9.

22 Thomas G. Sanders, "The Church in Latin America," in *Foreign Affairs,* Vol. 48, No. 2, January 1970, p. 287.

23 Einauldi et al., *Institutional Development,* pp. 10–13.

higher council of the hierarchy, such as the Roman Curia, where the preferences of the apostolic nuncio generally prevail.[24] And yet, despite these symbolic resolutions of conflict, the fragmentation of authority and the diversity of personnel within the dioceses of each country contradict the authoritarian and monolithic image of the Church. The image is least accurate at the priest level where diversity, and therefore the potential for innovation in the Church, is most likely. Priests, who as secular priests are assigned to a particular diocese of a bishop, or who as members of religious orders are not necessarily under the immediate authority of the bishop of that diocese, are less likely to be influenced by formal aspects of the Church hierarchy and are more likely to be influenced by the informal features of society.

In other words, a formalistic examination of the Church hierarchy ill prepares the observer to understand how the Church and its personnel, especially those lower rather than higher in the hierarchy, respond to the pressures for change in Latin American societies. Of course, the Church viewed as a bureaucratic institution provides some insight into hierarchical resistance to change. But institutions like the Church are much more than their formal organization. They are also constituted of members whose particular activities vary with their place in the organization and with the multiple influences of a basically non-Church character. This and similar informal aspects of the Church must be examined to understand better the contemporary role of the Church in Latin American politics and society.

UPHEAVAL

Even a brief examination of the literature on the contemporary Latin American Church reveals a general sense of concern, if not anxiety, and of reassessment, if not despair, over the proper role of the Church. Some observers adopt an alarmist perspective in which the Church is viewed as one of the last moral bulwarks against the decadence of modernity and, more specifically, godless materialism. Consequently, these observers anxiously view the decline of the traditional Church as an indication of moral degeneration. Moreover, these conservative alarmists take a dim view of moderate, progressive and even a few radical clergy who are involving the Church in causes and activities that contradict traditional doctrine. Others view the upheaval within the Church as a sign of hope. They would argue that, although the Church as a vibrant and effective institution is seriously handicapped in many ways, it must adapt to changing conditions as a first step to regeneration. Implied in this perspective is a perhaps unfounded faith in diversity and pluralism within social institutions such as the Church. If the

24 For an elaboration of this argument, see Chapter 2.

Church in fact does—and it seems to—reflect the larger political and social forces which divide Latin American societies, this in itself does not necessarily mean that the Church will somehow become a modern institution promoting socioeconomic changes. In fact, the argument that has been suggested for Latin American politics and society in general might be extended to the Church in particular: the Church, as it comes more to reflect the current forces and divisions of contemporary Latin America, will suffer under, rather than effectively overcome, the immobility and inaction which typifies the region as a whole. This is not to belittle the argument that the Church must undertake a major reevaluation of its political role in contemporary Latin America. But it is an important warning to those who believe that the Church itself can make a significant contribution to the transformation of a kind of immobile society to which it is gradually becoming more similar.

As one surveys the recent concern with the renewal of the Church and the means to best pursue such regeneration, the tremendous gap between what many analysts think the Church can do and what is increasingly expected of it becomes abundantly obvious. In one sense, it seems reasonable to argue that one should always expect more of institutions than they can produce, since such expectations can encourage institutional growth. But there does appear to be a need to maintain a realistic and balanced perspective. For social institutions like the Church, as well as for governmental institutions, expectations that far exceed performance are likely to jeopardize the legitimacy of the institution. Unfulfilled expectations may aggravate rather than resolve frustration. As a matter of fact, the Church is handicapped by a number of impressive obstacles which severely limit its role in promoting socioeconomic change.

FINANCIAL RESOURCES

Although there is some variation throughout the national hierarchies of Latin America, the Church in general is not well supplied with the resources—financial or human—necessary to make a significant and unassisted assault on the problems of socioeconomic change. In some countries, such as Colombia, where the Church is relatively affluent, the conservative hierarchy is disinclined to use resources to promote such change. In other countries, such as Mexico, Bolivia and the Dominican Republic, the Church is either legally or financially unable to assume a major role in promoting change. Moreover, it is easier to document what the Church can legally do in Latin America than what it can financially do. Surprisingly perhaps, information concerning the assets of the Church is quite incomplete and inaccurate. As a landowner, for example, the Church in the various countries has never carefully surveyed or at least widely reported its holdings. We are therefore limited to vague estimates of magnitude—for example, that the Bolivian Church is not a "very large" landowner while the Colombian Church is a landowner of "considerable" importance. Where, as is still often the case, the Church manages its landholdings by the ancient and inefficient system of the *hacienda,* the use of this form of traditional wealth to promote development is severely restricted.[25] To some extent, of course, this is simply a specific illustration of the collapse of the traditional economic system upon which the Church was originally based. On the other hand, Chile, with some of the most progressive Catholic clergy in Latin America, has witnessed the development of a more socially aware hierarchy, concerned at least to some extent with social justice. Outspoken on social and political issues, many of the Chilean clergy have not only encouraged large scale social reform but have supported this verbal commitment by parcelling out Church lands to peasants. Implicit in this policy, however, is the realization that the Church itself is poorly equipped to use such a resource effectively and must therefore limit its role to providing the land and permitting other groups, perhaps Church-related or Church-inspired associations, to develop the potential of such a resource. In short, then, the availability and effective use of the economic resources of the Church—which may not be as great as one might expect—depend upon the situation of the particular national hierarchy and that hierarchy's relationships with other groups. With limited physical resources and often a financial dependence on the State, the Church in Latin America lacks a strong base from which to promote development in the area.[26]

HUMAN RESOURCES

The decline of traditional wealth, and the problem of effectively using what wealth remains is not the only, and perhaps not even the major, resource problem affecting the Church's ability to promote socioeconomic change. Perhaps of more immediate importance for the Church is the problem of its human resources—that is, the clergy who staff the national hierarchies of the region. One might expect that a region of the world that is so overwhelmingly Catholic would not lack sufficient personnel to minister to the religious and related needs of the population. But priests find it difficult to take care of the needs of the only 15 to 20 percent of the baptized Catholics in Latin America who do practice their religion.[27] This shortage

25 Einauldi et al., *Institutional Development,* pp. 3–4; and William V. D'Antonio and Frederick B. Pike (eds.), *Religion, Revolution and Reform* (New York: Praeger, 1964), p. 5.

26 Einauldi et al., *Institutional Development,* p. 19.

27 Edelmann, *Latin American Government and Politics,* p. 170; David E. Mutchler, S. J., "Roman Catholicism in Brazil," in *Studies in Comparative International Development,* Vol. 1, No. 8, 1965, p. 110.

of clergy at all levels, but especially at the priest level, has been and continues to be a major problem for the Church.

It may seem incredible to the North American who has not closely studied the situation in Latin America, but it is nevertheless true that there are more priests per Catholics in the United States—1 per 500—than in Latin America—1 per 5500.[28] Although the ratio varies considerably from country to country, with Colombia and Chile having the best ratios and Paraguay and Honduras being less fortunately endowed, the overall conclusion must be that the shortage of priests is a severe handicap for the Church.[29] This general lack of clergy tends to diminish the Church's influence on social matters because the priest is often the principal and many times the only educated person wielding much influence within local and especially rural communities. Religious personnel are also concentrated more in the urban than the rural areas, although rural Catholics are more often regular worshippers than urban Catholics. In addition, the failure to recruit new priests reflects the conservative influences within the Church.[30]

The shortage of priests directly affects the ability of the Church to reach the people. In Brazil, for example, 500 of the 5000 parishes have no permanently assigned priests[31]—and here, in the largest Latin American country, the ratio of priests to Catholics is approximately 1 to 5000–8000.[32] Moreover, the effective ratio is actually much greater because many priests lead essentially insulated lives within religious orders.[33] In other words, while the situation does vary from country to country, the great lack of clergy detracts significantly from the ability of the Church as a renovated institution to reach the Latin American masses and thereby play a significant role in promoting socioeconomic change.

Unable to counteract the growing shortage of personnel, national hierarchies in Latin America are placed in the unfortunate position of having to lessen the effects of the shortage of native clergy by importing clergy from outside the region. Today, one third of all priests in Latin America are foreigners.[34] Thus, paradoxically, while most Latin Americans are at least nominally Catholic, many priests are not Latin American in origin. One-half of the diocesan priests come from Spain and Italy.[35] Even the United States,

[28] Mecham, *Church and State*; Houtart and Pin, *The Church,* p. 150.

[29] Einauldi, et al., *Institutional Development,* pp. 19–23; Houtart and Pin, *The Church,* p. 167.

[30] Einauldi, et al., *Institutional Development,* p. 19.

[31] Mutchler, "Roman Catholicism in Brazil," p. 110.

[32] Ibid., p. 110; Charles Wagley, *An Introduction to Brazil* (New York: Columbia University Press, 1963), p. 237.

[33] Mutchler, "Roman Catholicism in Brazil," p. 110; Einauldi, et al., *Institutional Development,* p. 16.

[34] Einauldi et al., *Institutional Development,* p. 16.

[35] Houtart and Pin, *The Church,* p. 157.

which is basically Protestant rather than Catholic, supplies Latin America not only with money (about $10 million dollars a year) but with personnel (presently some 3,500 individuals, including lay volunteers).[36] Excepting Mexico, which expressly forbids the importation of foreign priests, most Latin American countries must count on immigrant priests to keep from falling farther behind in their priest-layman ratios. Even this is no guarantee that the ratio can be improved. For such countries as Venezuela, where nearly half the priests are foreigners, the prospect of overcoming the deficit is not at all encouraging.[37] Only a few countries—for example, Chile and Colombia—are able to recruit the bulk of their clergy from their nationals.[38] If, as one scholar insists, the Church in Latin America is a barometer of change in Latin America,[39] then the shortage and importation of priests in Latin America are symptoms of Church crisis.

An important question arises from this: Why is the Church in Latin America faced with such a crucial shortage of clergy? Several alternative answers to this question are available, but none of them, either individually or taken together, are sufficient to provide a really satisfactory explanation. Without dwelling on all or even most of the arguments, it seems more useful to consider the kinds of explanation offered for this shortage.

The first type of explanation is historical. It is said that the Church is today unable to adequately develop its human and other resources because of the separation from and persecution by the State in the past that have diminished its effectiveness. That is, the historical anticlerical attacks have left the Church in a disadvantaged position for recruiting the young.

Another kind of explanation focuses upon the basic shift of Latin American societies away from the traditional system upon which Church resources were founded toward more modern societies with different values. This argument suggests that the priesthood today, except in isolated rural villages, is not the only occupation of importance and upward mobility in urbanizing Latin America.

Another type of explanation is based upon a psychological and cultural assessment of Latin American masculinity. The term *machismo*, for which

[36] John J. Considine (ed.), *The Church in the New Latin America* (Notre Dame, Ind.: Fides Publishers, 1964), p. 105; Editorial, "Church and State in Latin America," pp. 173–85.

[37] Isidoro Alonso, et al., *La Iglesia en Venezuela y Ecuador*. Friburgo, Suiza: Oficina Internacional de Investigaciones Sociales de FERES, 1961, pp. 45–46.

[38] Isidoro Alonso, Renato Poblete, y Gines Garrido, *La Iglesia en Chile* (Friburgo y Bogota: Oficina Internacional de Investigaciones Sociales de FERES, 1962), p. 208; Gustavo Perez e Isaac Wust, *La Iglesia en Colombia* (Bogota, Colombia: Oficina Internacional de Investigaciones Sociales de FERES, 1961), p. 130.

[39] Jorge Lara-Braud, "Latin America: The Crisis and Signs of Hope," in *Catholic World*, Vol. 204, No. 1, January 1967, pp. 290–95.

there is no exact translation in English, is a dominant value of Latin American males, emphasizing manliness not only in a sexual sense but in social relations generally. This value, to the extent that it is accepted by most Latin American males, is highly incompatible with the accepted image of the priest. In its most extreme form, *machismo* may eventually diminish in importance as Latin American societies are permeated with more modern values. But, at present, the priest—who is regarded as neither male nor female—cannot expect to be regarded with masculine respect as he dons dress-like robes, forswears intimacy with the opposite sex and embraces other values which contradict rather than coincide with *machismo*. For example, supporting a concubine was one of the few ways that a Cuban priest could gain some respect from other Cuban men in the pre-Castro years.[40] To the extent that this unresolved contradiction is widely perceived and to the extent that the Church is unable or unwilling to change the image and substance of the priests' role, Latin American males are not likely to choose the priestly vocation in numbers sufficient to replenish Church ranks.

THE CLERGY IN PROFILE

The mere shortage of personnel is not the only problem in using the clergy as agents for promoting socioeconomic change. The clergy are actually a very diversified group of individuals who, within their specific roles in the Church hierarchy, and within their latitude to pursue different interests, have a complex and often poorly understood function as agents of change. To better comprehend this role, a variety of characteristics of the clergy must be examined.

Just as the shortage of clergy in most of the Latin American countries implies that the national hierarchies are not effectively dealing with institutional crises, the kind of clergy in the church generally suggests only a limited ability to promote change. Like most hierarchies, those at the top in the Church are old and tradition-bound. The Church's cardinals from Latin America, for example, averaged over 73 years of age, although half the population of Latin America is under 16 years of age.[41] This trend is reinforced at the lower hierarchical levels in that, for example, there is no policy requiring bishops to retire at a certain age. The infusion of young blood at the higher levels of the Church becomes very difficult and, consequently, there is a generation gap of major proportions between the older,

40 Leslie Dewart, *Christianity and Revolution: The Lesson of Cuba* (New York: Herder and Herder, 1963), p. 94; Andrew Weigert, S. J., "*Machismo* and The Priestly Vocation," in *Catholic World*, Vol. 199, June 1964, pp. 152–58.

41 Einauldi et al., *Institutional Development*, p. 16.

higher-placed clergy and the younger, lower-placed clergy who increasingly disagree over fundamental issues confronting the Church. Demands by some of the lower, more youthful clergy are often greeted with either open hostility or quiet disapproval by the high-placed clergy who set general Church policy. As a result, although the lower clergy are afforded some latitude by the 60 to 70 bishops—out of 600 in Latin America—who encourage progressive policies,[42] the prospect that the Church hierarchy will generally be apathetic or—and this is more likely—hostile to progressive programs may deter the recruitment and training of youthful priests. If, however, a young man still believes that the attempt to become a priest on those terms is worth the effort, he may soon find that the requirements in the seminary schools are irrelevant to current social problems and not what he expected.

Seminarians are subjected to a traditionalistic education in which values of pre-modern theology rather than the values of contemporary social justice are stressed. The conservative bastion of the seminary either produces clergy from upper or middle sectors working for the old order or discourages individuals from completing the seminary requirements.[43] Furthermore, many Latin American students view Christianity as equivalent to the Church and their lack of faith in the Church undermines most attempts to recruit a wide spectrum of seminarians.[44] The religious training of the seminary ill prepares the priest for the modern life to which many must adjust or face social ineffectiveness. For example, although claiming much concern for the family as an institution, the Church, through its seminaries, fails to provide the students with any practical knowledge about the family and its problems in today's world. Generally, then, the molding of the priest within the seminaries is inadequate for today's Latin America and is inadequate as a device to train Church personnel for effective roles in promoting changes in society.[45] The seminarian's understanding of the complex processes of change with which he may be required to grapple is at best faulty, because he has little practical involvement with them.

Those seminarians who eventually become priests are, despite some

[42] Lara-Braud, "Latin America."

[43] Margaret Bates (ed.), *The Lay Apostolate in Latin America* (Washington, D.C.: Catholic University of America Press, 1960), p. 6; Alonso et al., *La Iglesia en Venezuela y Ecuador,* p. 50.

[44] W. Stanley Rycroft, *Religion and Faith in Latin America* (Philadelphia: Westminster Press, 1958), p. 132.

[45] Jorge Ortiz Amaya, *El Sacerdote de Manana* (Buenos Aires: Ediciones Carlos Lohle, 1964) pp. 41–75; Camilo Torres Restrepo, "Social Change and Rural Violence in Colombia," in *Studies in Comparative International Development,* Vol. 4., No. 12, 1968–1969, pp. 277–78; Gustavo Perez Ramirez, *El Problemas Sacerdotal en Colombia* (Friburgo y Bogota: Oficina Internacional de Investigaciones Sociales de FERES, 1962); Robert H. Dix, *Colombia: The Political Dimension of Change* (New Haven, Conn.: Yale University Press, 1967), pp. 311–16.

exceptions, largely from the upper sector. Despite the relative influence of progressive clergy in such countries as Brazil and Chile, priests of lower-class origin still represent less than their class' proportion of the total population. Moreover, the shortage of clergy generally handicaps the efforts of the Church to readily recruit young men from the lower sectors into the priesthood. This class bias in the social origins of the Latin American clergy is symptomatic of the more general failure of the church to reach the masses.[46]

In addition to the personnel who staff the parishes, charitable institutions, hospitals, monasteries and convents of the Church, the clergy also maintain and serve in Catholic educational institutions, which still constitute an important cog in the educational process in Latin America. That is, while earlier anticlerical attacks curtailed the Church's dominant role in education, with only a few exceptions it remains a very important factor in the educational scene. In Brazil, for example, although the government supports secondary education, nearly half of this field is controlled by the Church.[47] In Venezuela, the Catholic schools use government-supplied textbooks in nonreligious subjects. In Colombia, where religious instruction is permitted in all public schools, the enrollment in Catholic schools is the highest in Latin America. At the opposite extreme, Mexico prohibits religious studies in public schools but provides textbooks to the religious elementary schools,[48] an occasionally controversial practice.[49] Thus, although the principal responsibility for education in contemporary Latin America resides with the State, five countries—Brazil, Mexico, Colombia, Argentina and Chile—each maintain 1,000 or more religious schools.[50] Catholic institutions also provide 15 to 20 percent of university education, 40 to 65 percent of middle school education, and 10 to 20 percent of primary school education. A recent conservative estimate indicates that students enrolled in Catholic schools account for about 10 percent of all Latin American students,[51] making it a preoccupation of the upper classes.[52]

[46] Renato Poblete Barth, S. J., *Crisis Sacerdotal* (Santiago de Chile: Editorial del Pacific, S. A., 1965) pp. 183–88; Isidoro Alonso, Renato Poblete, y Gines Garride, *La Iglesia en Chile* (Friburgo y Bogota: Oficina Internacional de Investigaciones Sociales de FERES, 1962).

[47] Einauldi et al., *Institutional Development,* p. 5.

[48] Mecham, *Church and State, passim.*

[49] Edelmann, *Latin American Government and Politics,* p. 161.

[50] Einauldi et al., *Institutional Development,* p. 26; Edward J. Williams, "Latin American Catholicism and Political Integration," in *Comparative Political Studies,* Vol. 2, No. 3, October 1969, p. 330.

[51] Einauldi et al., *Institutional Development,* p. 28.

[52] Margaret Bates (ed.), *The Lay Apostolate,* pp. 14–17; Houtart and Pin, *The Church,* p. 129.

The role of the Church in education is particularly important because the values generally propagated through Catholic educational institutions in Latin America are remnants of a dying era. The dissemination of these values is very intense within the rigid curriculum of Church institutions, and they also permeate, in less concentrated forms, other fields including politics. Catholicism, through its dogma, directive authority, and institutionalization, embodies the value of uncritical acceptance of religious authority. The transfer of this value to the secular and especially to the political realm serves to support rather than to challenge the traditional and conservative past by emphasizing submissive resignation to one's lot in life.[53] To the extent, then, that the influence of the Church in such matters is broader than its educational institutions, the impact of these values learned through Church-influenced education is static rather than dynamic. In short, although, as will be discussed later, some of the clergy disapprove of and seek to counteract the general institutional impact on education and the formation of key values, the Church as a whole supports an educational system which reinforces rather than challenges the immobility of contemporary Latin American society and politics.

One must not conclude from the foregoing discussions that the Church as an institution has been unaffected by the changes of the present century. But it must be repeated that the Church is poorly equipped as an institution to promote change. Plagued by fragmentation and institutional complexity, limited by human and financial resources, dominated by the rival power of the State, and restricted by a conservative hierarchy that belatedly reacts to change rather than actively promoting it, the Church is a clumsy and ill-constituted agent for effectively formulating a coherent policy toward change or even for assisting other groups and institutions to promote change.[54]

In summary, then, there is much confusion and disagreement within the Church between the minority of the clergy who want to promote change and the majority, active or passive, who want to retain the status quo. One thing does seem certain about the yet undefined role of the Church in contemporary Latin American politics: as clerical participation in politics increases, the divisions within the Church will likewise increase. With this development, the Church will lose much of the legitimacy it still retains to act as a nonpartisan moral force serving to integrate rather than to further divide Latin American societies.[55] But it seems highly unlikely that the Church can avoid playing a political and even a highly partisan role in the

[53] Smith, *Religion and Political Development,* pp. 178–84.

[54] Einauldi et al., *Institutional Development,* pp. 73–74.

[55] Frederic Hicks, "Politics, Power and the Role of the Village Priest in Paraguay," in *Journal of Inter-American Studies,* Vol. 9, No. 2, April 1967, p. 282; Mecham, *Church and State.*

present and the future. Individual clergy will find it increasingly difficult, and perhaps impossible, to live with the artificial distinction between the sacred and the secular.[56]

DESIRES

Turning now to the political desires, demands, and successes of the clergy in Latin America, the distinction between the Church as an institution and the clergy as a group of disparate individuals within it should again be noted. At the risk of some distortion of reality, the distinction nevertheless appears to be quite useful. The Church in the area of socioeconomic change can be regarded as an institution confronted with problems of resources and organization. The clergy, with various political orientations and often seeking a new role for the Church, represent to differing degrees nearly every point of view within the political systems of Latin America.

At first glance, the Church as an institution has much to lose and little to gain from the socioeconomic changes that are, at uneven rates, affecting Latin America today. With a premodern doctrine and a power base grounded upon a socioeconomic system that is slowly crumbling, the Church, until recently at least, has faced the prospect that change would undermine its traditional role and perhaps threaten its very institutional survival. Although some of the clergy, especially those in the higher echelons of Church authority, might candidly admit a fondness for the "good, old days," the reality and the challenge of socioeconomic change in contemporary Latin America does not present the realistic possibility that the Church can avoid the twentieth century; rather, it suggests quite imperatively that the Church must adapt to such changes if it is to survive as an institution.

No matter what the specific changes—for better or worse—that emerge, almost all members of the Church can agree that institutional survival must be maintained. Threats to institutional survival will be opposed by nearly all members, but threats are subject to different interpretations. The extreme cases are obvious to all. A Cuban or a Mexican revolution that seeks to eliminate an established oligarchy will seriously jeopardize if not totally eliminate the Church as a social institution. However, disagreement is more likely to develop over less clear-cut cases. For example, is the Church fundamentally threatened if the government prohibits an extensive parochial role in education? An answer to this type of question requires clarification of the role of the Church, and this is the source of considerable divergence of opinion among all clergy in Latin America. In Mexico, once the Church did not actively resist major restrictions on its secular activities, Church and

[56] Por un grupo de especialistas, *La Iglesia y la Politica.* (Santiago de Chile: Ediciones Paulinas, 1963), pp. 12–23.

State began to operate within compatible but largely different spheres of influence, allowing the Church to exist under less privileged conditions.[57] The national hierarchies of the other countries have not come under conscious or fundamental attack from the State in recent years. If these hierarchies do not insist upon usurping what has become the primary responsibilities of the State or prudently refrain from criticizing sensitive policies and personnel, the Church may expect toleration and perhaps some assistance.

The Church's strategies of survival in the past may provide some hint for the future, and the case of the Dominican Republic is quite illustrative. As a weak institution with little economic power but some moral suasion, the Church at first provided support to Trujillo in exchange for a number of governmental favors. But in 1959 the Church withdrew its support for the increasingly more aggressive and despotic regime, risking intimidation and harassment of its most activist clergy. Later, with the rise of Juan Bosch the Church's original support turned to opposition when the Bosch government established divorce, common-law marriage, and secular schools as constitutional provisions. Again, priests acting unofficially as individuals contributed to Bosch's overthrow.[58] Members of the clergy opposed Trujillo because his growing oppression was perceived as a basic threat to the Church and its members, and opposed Bosch because the latter threatened to deprive the Church of the prerogatives Trujillo had granted. The point is that the Church will generally provide at least tacit support of most governments until a perceived institutional threat stirs a significant number of clergy to opposition.

Aside from institutional survival, the clergy in Latin America share no common vision of the Church in a socioeconomically developed Latin America nor of how the Church can promote such development. Most of the clergy, but especially the more conservative in the higher positions within the hierarchy, want to maintain those institutional privileges, which, to varying degrees, the national hierarchies still exercise. In Colombia, for example, where the Church enjoys considerable privileges in the area of education, charities, and civil functions, the clergy generally maintain a stance of "defensive modernization" that emphasizes stability over change.[59]

---

[57] Frederick C. Turner, "The Compatibility of Church and State in Mexico," in *Journal of Inter-American Studies,* Vol. 9, No. 4, October 1967, p. 599; James W. Wilkie, "The Meaning of the Cristero Religious War against the Mexican Revolution," in *A Journal of Church and State,* Vol. 8, No. 2, Spring, 1966, pp. 214–33.

[58] Howard J. Wiarda, *Dictatorship and Development: The Methods of Control in Trunillo's Dominican Republic.* (Gainesville: University of Florida Press, Latin American Monograph Series, Ser. 2. No. 5); Howard J. Wiarda, "The Changing Political Orientation of the Catholic Church in the Dominican Republic," in *A Journal of Church and State,* Vol. 7, No. 2, Spring 1965, pp. 238–54.

[59] Dix, *Colombia,* p. 319.

As will be seen in more detail later, the military regime in Brazil has placed controls upon the political role of the Church but still provides financial assistance for its social welfare and educational programs.[60] In Argentina, where official religious tolerance has not yet led to religious diversity, the clergy are quick to complain about compulsory civil marriages and many if not all are conservative to the point of longing for a return to the Church's traditional secular privileges.[61] For example, when Peron legalized divorce and prostitution during his regime in the late 1940s and early 1950s, thereby violating Church doctrine and prerogatives, the Church exercised its strongest form of individual punishment for a Catholic: it excommunicated the Argentine dictator.[62] But despite the desire of many clergy for a restoration of traditional prerogatives, the chances that the State will reverse recent precedent are remote.

Most of the clergy also harbor some hopes that do not directly involve the Church as an institution. For example, although the family unit—which in Latin America is extended to include many more individuals than the smaller, nuclear family common in North America—does not give its undivided loyalty to the Church as it once did, the bulk of the clergy hope that, whatever the future brings, the family as a social unit will remain intact. Not unsurprisingly, the traditionally constituted family has supported the values which the Church, and especially the conservative clergy, eulogize. A decline in the family might suggest that external support for the Church is waning. Most Latin Americans, although they generally do not know the positions of the Church, probably agree with the official policy (recently reaffirmed by Pope Paul) which regards artificial birth control as an undesirable practice for protecting the stability of the family. Uneasiness over the apparent decline of traditional institutions and values—which is not as severe as some of the alarmists prefer to believe—becomes linked with the premonition that what will replace them is not only unknown but likely to be antagonistic to the values which the Church claims to hold sacred. For example, many clergy as well as laymen in such politico-religious movements as the Christian Democratic parties abhor the prospect that communism or capitalism may be the only alternatives for development, and denounce their inhumanity and materialism as "un-Christian." Some have suggested that, if these are the two alternatives for socioeconomic change, the sacrifice of spiritual values to such corruption may be too great to make.[63] Such argu-

60 Charles Wagley, *An Introduction to Brazil* (New York: Columbia University Press, 1963), p. 236.

61 John J. Kennedy, *Catholicism, Nationalism and Democracy in Argentina* (South Bend, Ind.: University of Notre Dame Press, 1958), pp. 171, 203.

62 Edelmann, *Latin American Government and Politics,* p. 166.

63 For a discussion of the Christian Democratic philosophy as an alternative, see Edward J. Williams, *Latin American Christian Democratic Parties* (Knoxville: University of Tennessee Press, 1967).

ments, self-serving and simplistic as they may seem to others, are nevertheless indications of the rampant confusion among the clergy about what to expect and what to want for the future.

Despite Pope John's *Mater et Magistra* (1961) (an encyclical seeking to modify institutional rigidity, anachronistic liturgy and indifference to problems of change within the Church), most clergy view the future warily, uncertain of their role in contemporary societies and, more basically, conscious of the fact that the Church itself has not resolved its own institutional crisis of identity. It is not difficult to find noble sentiments among some clergy about the need to help the lower classes. But the silence of the majority of the clergy is most accurately interpreted as indicating that conservative, rather than progressive, sentiments prevail.

DEMANDS

The demands made by the clergy on the political systems of Latin America can be seen to some extent in clerical participation in politics. Since the political participation of the clergy has increased rather than decreased the internal diversity of the Church, absorbing rather than resolving conflicts, the only generally agreed upon policy is that members of the Church, as a matter of "prophetic mission," should state what is just and good in the real world and try to attain it. Of course, the fact that the clergy generally cannot agree upon what is just and good in any particular situation is limited consolation to those who wish to see a unified Church. However, with the possibility of acting independently of the State, but trying to influence it as well, the clergy, championing different and sometimes conflicting causes, participate politically at different levels of intensity ranging from passive conservatism—which is the rule rather than the exception—to the moderate and even militant activism of a small minority.[64] Of course, politically apathetic clergy can have political consequences in that by remaining silent on a public issue they may tacitly endorse government policy or, more likely, serve the *status quo*. Beyond remaining silent, or doing nothing, there are a number of activities of different intensity. A priest may tell his flock to follow certain "guidelines of conscience." More intense, however, are such specific actions as telling a congregation of worshipers that voting for a certain political candidate or for a certain political party would be contrary to their religion if not a direct sin against God. Election to public office is a direct road to political participation by some clergy (as in Brazil) unless prohibited by law or constitutional provisions (as in Mexico). On an unofficial basis, the clergy form alliances with other political groups —on the right or on the left—to pursue such different goals as resisting

[64] Einauldi et al., *Institutional Development*, pp. 37, 48.

communism, setting up cooperatives, or operating charities. The most intense method of political participation, and one which the Church hierarchy generally opposes, is to join or actively support revolutionary groups such as guerrillas bent upon not only the overthrow of the government but also upon the complete transformation of society. Such extreme forms of clerical participation in politics are relatively rare but nevertheless interesting. Camilo Torres, for example, a Colombian priest, found that he could not promote rapid social change through the Church: he therefore joined a guerrilla band, giving up the privileges of an aristocratic heritage, a Ph.D. in economics, the priesthood, and a position at the National University. Killed at age 37 in his first skirmish, Torres nevertheless symbolizes the priest who became disenchanted with the Church's response to change, suggesting to romantics a desperate alternative for evading a serious dilemma.[65]

As noted previously, although the intensity of participation obviously varies, most clergy remain politically apathetic and inactive. But we are more concerned here with what the clergy actually do politically rather than with what they do not do. By emphasizing the activists, we may risk giving the impression that most clergy are highly involved in politics, which is certainly not true. Also, by emphasizing the activists, we risk giving more emphasis to the leftist clergy—the progressives and the radicals—than their actual importance warrants. That is, although the leftist clergy are generally portrayed as the only activists—perhaps because their beliefs are unorthodox by traditional Church standards—there are certainly also conservative activists who are perhaps more important because they are generally higher placed in the hierarchy than are the leftists.

One way of making sense of the vast jumble of clerical political activities is to classify the clergy as "reactionary," "conservative," "moderate," "progressive," or "radical." Although this categorization may occasionally create ambiguity and perhaps suggest negative connotations, this familiar classification of political activity has the advantage of simplicity and suggests orientations to change.[66]

Like most militant extremists, the reactionary clergy are probably more important than their scant numbers would indicate. Strongest in those countries which have undergone the least socioeconomic development, the reactionaries, in addition to their commitments to a traditional Church and to the oligarchy of a fading era, are highly disturbed by change of almost any scope or direction. The reactionaries, for example, find it difficult to discriminate between liberal reform and revolutionary upheaval. Particularly disturbed about the alleged threat of communism to Latin America, they

65 Lara-Braud, "Latin America," pp. 290–95.

66 For a more complex, but slightly different, classification scheme, see Vallier, "Religious Elites."

launch indiscriminate attacks on those who seek or even approve of changes of any kind. In Brazil, where a significant leftist movement in the clergy has promoted the development of a small band of reactionary clergy, the principal sources of external support for the reactionaries' sentiments are the large landowners, or *latifundistas* of the traditional oligarchy, and the large industrialists of the new oligarchy.[67] Insisting that there is a threat of socialism and a recent moral degeneration in Brazil, reactionary bishops have extended dogmatic and unqualified support to the principle of private property. While the reactionary bishops in Brazil are numerically or perhaps even politically not very important, their demands, especially when linked to those of the oligarchy, cannot be completely discounted. These rightists in the Brazilian Church clearly supported the military coup of 1964 and probably continue to support many of the regime's repressive measures, especially its attacks on leftists and dissenters. But it is much easier to argue that the reactionaries support the regime and its policies than it is to substantiate specifically what role, if any, the reactionary clergy have played in formulating government policy.

Somewhat more clear is the support the reactionaries gave to the demonstrations against the leftist civilian regime of João Goulart in 1964, just prior to the military coup that removed him from office. During these demonstrations—which were in part a reaction to Catholic leftists supporting Goulart—"hundreds of thousands" of upper- and middle-class women engaged in "Marches of the Family with God for Liberty," in which "communism" and "corruption" were denounced as vices infecting the Goulart regime. Once again, it is difficult to assess the influence of these demonstrations—supported by the reactionaries—upon the military's decision to intervene, but they probably had some effect. In the same year as the military coup, a reactionary Brazilian cardinal supported the action of the Governor of the State of Guanabara in using soldiers to break up the headquarters in Rio de Janeiro of the Basic Education Movement (MEB), a progressive Catholic organization.[68] However, although the reactionaries' demands for anticommunist measures, repression and limitation of social change have been implemented by the government, it is difficult to state that the reactionary clergy have gained much after the first few years of the military regime. The military has silenced all critics, including some friends of the reactionaries, and more importantly, has in several ways threatened the Church itself, the effect of which has been to move the hierarchy from right to left of center.[69] In Colombia, some clergy led violent attacks against

[67] Mutchler, "Roman Catholicism in Brazil," p. 104.

[68] Sanders, "The Church in Latin America," p. 287; Einauldi et al., *Institutional Development*, p. 65.

[69] Einauldi et al., *Institutional Development*, p. 66; *Time*, July 27, 1970.

Liberals. Lacking the official approval of—but not condemned by—the Colombian hierarchy, the attacks were generally the acts of local priests who felt threatened by Liberals and Protestants. In Mexico, the reactionaries waned as a political force not long after the Revolution. Climaxed by the "Cristero rebellion" which began in 1926, militant reactionary clergy provoked a violent test of the revolutionary government's will to restrict the Church. Church moderates were unable to prevail as a dominant influence over the reactionaries until 1929 when an armistice between Church and State was concluded. Having gained little and lost much, the Church became more docile and moderate as the violent Sinarquista movement, made up of clergy and the old oligarchy, became less important as an irritant to the revolution in general and to the government's policies toward the Church in particular.

In general, although located at the higher levels of the Latin American hierarchies, the reactionary clergy in Latin America can today only hope for a rear guard strategy. Favoring authoritarianism, clericalism, and divine will, the reactionaries have set themselves off as strident opponents of change. In most Latin American countries, the reactionaries make demands on the political systems according to an obstructive strategy that denies the Church and the State effective roles in promoting socioeconomic change—and therefore they aid the oligarchy's favored position in society.[70]

Less militant, rigid, and strident than the reactionaries, but still in basic agreement with their goals, are the conservative clergy. Whether political activists or inactivists, the conservatives constitute by far the largest proportion of Catholic clergy. And like most groups which constitute a majority, they are well represented at all levels of the Church hierarchy, but are especially dominant at the upper levels. As the dominant political faction within the Church, the conservatives are also the most effective in making demands on the political systems of the region. As defenders of religious orthodoxy and political conservatism, this faction is probably most responsible—rightly or wrongly—for the conservative and tradition-bound image of the Church.

Although some conservative clergy are politically involved, they are more likely to emphasize spiritual or institutional concerns rather than becoming overtly involved in politics. In fact, they tend to view greater clerical participation in politics as a mistake that the government should temper or totally eradicate; although, naturally enough, they tend to see clerical participation in politics as being those activities carried on by clergy to whose ideas they are opposed. Conservatives no longer must fight the anticlerical

[70] Thomas G. Sanders, "Types of Catholic Elites in Latin America," in Robert D. Tomasek (ed.), *Latin American Politics,* second edition (Garden City, N.Y.: Doubleday, 1970), pp. 183–86.

battles of the past but their principal contemporary problem is no less serious. Unconditionally loyal to an institution that is threatened by its failure to adapt to socioeconomic changes, the conservatives are largely responsible for perpetuating a Church increasingly out of touch with the masses. Like the reactionaries, the conservative clergy active in politics are more likely to do nothing to change Latin American society than they are to suggest concrete proposals for promoting change. If the situation becomes grave and something must be done as a last resort, the conservatives emphasize the importance of braking rather than accelerating change through public policy. Perhaps this attitude is as much a product of an unclear vision of the future as it is of ingrained tradition. In any event, most conservative clergy, unable to innovate and unwilling to apply new practices, simply find it easier to continue as before. In this sense, and perhaps better than the reactionary clergy, the conservatives symbolize the institutional crisis of the Church itself.

The conservative clergy, especially the activists, are not isolated within the physical and social boundaries of their institution, since they form coalitions with important power contenders in the political system. Rojas Pinilla of Colombia, Trujillo of the Dominican Republic, Batista of Cuba, and Perez Jimenez of Venezuela were all rightist dictators, who, for a time at least, enjoyed the support of the conservative clergy and therefore of the Church as a whole. Whether as a matter of timing or of cause, none of these dictators remained in power very long after they alienated important segments of the Church and especially the conservative clergy. Although the conservatives in control of the hierarchies will generally try to get along with any particular government in power, their opposition to agrarian reform, benefits for workers, and similar policies, generally prohibits their forming alliances with such groups as students, peasants, and urban laborers. For example, although the conservative bishops of Brazil (and they are a clear majority of the approximately 230 total) are abstractly aware of the necessity of social reforms, they prefer to refrain from advocating the obvious and instead seek spiritual answers to the secular problems of Brazil. Like the reactionaries, the conservatives view their surroundings as a morass of immorality accentuated by the atheistic influence of communism. During the 1964 turmoil, for example, one Brazilian cardinal, the Archbishop of Bahia, decided to suspend the activities of Catholic Action, a progressive yet hardly radical organization, on the ground that Communist infiltration had subverted the group. This anticommunism of the conservative clergy, however, is not supplemented with a prodemocratic bias. In addition to anticommunism, the conservatives embrace less directly political values such as hierarchy and authoritarianism from which a paternalistic condescension toward the masses is a principal consequence. The masses must be led, like the children they are in the eyes of God. This view, transferred to the political area, supports an antidemocratic paternalism among conservative clergy. Whether articulated or not, the conservatives favor a government that emphasizes control with a conservative bias. For this very reason, the conservative clergy are not likely to earn mass support for their traditionalistic elitism.

To put it differently, the Church conservatives are more concerned with immediate institutional problems and less concerned with the broader political issues which call into question the adequacy of the Church as an agent of social change. Less worried about the suspension or postponement of elections by a military junta, the conservative clergy are more likely to voice concern over the status of the Church within such a regime, especially with regard to such prerogatives as governmental subsidies, a role in education, and civic functions. The legal separation of Church and State—to the extent that it really exists—does not eliminate conflict over the kind and amount of support the State should provide or what the Church should do for this support. As the principal policy-makers within the Latin American hierarchies, the conservatives engage in the political struggle to receive governmental favors, competing with a number of other groups for limited public resources. Although the most influential faction of the Church clergy, satisfaction of their demands is not always possible, especially since the conservatives, due to self-imposed restrictions on strategy, refuse to form broad coalitions with groups whose demands contradict the orthodoxy the conservatives uphold.[71] Like the reactionaries, but perhaps less obviously, the conservatives pursue the opposite strategy: with the use of obstructionism, they encourage the government to do nothing or very little to upset their position. If that fails, they will follow rather than promote reforms.

The conservatives fear immediate radical change—especially through a Communist revolution—more than is probably warranted. Although some of their alarmist rhetoric is calculated to gain support rather than a statement of belief, most conservative clergy, and especially the activists, express an abiding horror for social revolution. It is true, of course, that such changes—unlikely as they are for most Latin American countries—would certainly threaten them and their concept of the Church. But they themselves admit their opposition to such change and must expect to be treated as implacable enemies if the leaders of such a revolution should ever triumph. Indiscriminately opposed to nearly all change, the conservatives in no way accept the argument that a flexible Church could contribute to moderate change, and could thereby make disruptive revolution less compelling an alternative. The case of Cuba is illustrative. Prior to Castro's ascension to power in 1959, the Cuban Church was different only in degree

---

[71] John J. Kennedy, "The Force of the Church," in John J. TePaske and Sydney Nettleton Fisher (eds.), *Explosive Forces in Latin America* (Columbus: Ohio State University Press, 1964), p. 51.

but not in kind from most conservative Church hierarchies in other Latin American countries. Isolated from the masses, financed by a few sugar mills, oriented to the past, the Cuban Church was divided over Castro's movement and could offer no viable alternative. As the storm approached, the hierarchy remained silent, drifting away from many of its lower clergy who offered Castro their support as individuals. Although it is impossible to argue unequivocally that the weakness of the Cuban Church directly contributed to Castro's success, the inflexibility of the Church prior to 1959 and its fate after that year are notes of warning to conservative clergy who find comfort in past verities rather than taking the difficult steps necessary to adapt their institution to the present.[72]

The term of "moderate" clergy is only a residual category that includes those individuals who do not actively—as do the reactionaries—or passively—as do many conservatives—insist on the past as a model for the present. Recognizing the need for reforms, the "moderates," unlike the progressives and the radical clergy, have not articulated or applied an alternative solution of their own. Rejecting the rightists and the leftists, and with some representatives within the hierarchy of such countries as Brazil, they appear to have no clear idea of how to proceed, what to demand from government, or how to rally support among other groups. The main purpose in mentioning them is that they do not fit into either side of the political continuum. Their awareness of this ambivalence has not encouraged sufficient activism to warrant much consideration.

The problem in discussing the leftist clergy—meaning the progressives and the radicals—is not a lack of activism but a deluge of attention directed at their numerous political activities. In order to keep a balanced perspective, however, it is important to recall that the spectacular exception often draws more attention than the dull generality. Whether the leftist orientation toward change is viewed as a problem or as a reason for hope, the progressive and radical clergy combined constitute an active, but nevertheless small, minority of all the Church's clergy.

Before exploring their demands on the Latin American political systems, it seems appropriate to define the "progressive" and the "radical" clergy by stating their similarities and differences. Both groups, for example, favor an active role for the Church in supporting and demanding policies that encourage fundamental socioeconomic change. Both are closely attuned to the needs of the underprivileged but, as a consequence, sometimes lack the contacts with important power groups in and out of government who could meet these needs. Both advocate socioeconomic reforms that, if adopted, would considerably change the dimensions of politics in Latin

72 Dewart, *Christianity and Revolution,* p. 183.

America. But these similarities—indeed one occasionally finds it difficult to distinguish between the progressive and the radical clergy—should not obscure some differences in emphasis. For example, while the progressive relies upon the documents of the Ecumenical Council (Vatican II) as a guide and tries to work within the framework of the Church, the radical is more likely to view himself as an innovator who must often operate outside the framework of the Church and away from the conservatives who largely dominate it. Moreover, the radical clergy view the Church as an unresponsive minority that, as an elite, has little understanding of the oppressed masses who, as Christians but also as multidimensional individuals, should define the directions of the future in Latin America. Although both progressives and radicals favor the development of small groups of Catholic laymen to involve the Church with external problems of social change, the radicals do not believe, as the progressives do, that these groups are suitable to "reconvert" society. Instead, the radicals assert that the groups simply represent nothing more than a Christian presence. Progressives, therefore, are fond of developing what they call "organizations of Christian inspiration," such as labor unions, cooperatives and Christian Democratic Parties while the radicals prefer alliances with non-Catholic, secular organizations which are largely unrestricted by the hierarchy. For example, the radical clergy suspected the hierarchy-controlled Catholic Action in Brazil and therefore prompted the formation of Popular Action as a political organization devoted to fundamental transformation of Brazilian society. Although Vatican II legitimized the independence of lay Catholic groups from the hierarchy, which encouraged such groups to reform the Church as an institution, the earlier complaint of the radicals stemmed from the belief that such associations were originally established to defend the Church as it was. Stated briefly, then, the principal difference between the progressive and the radical clergy is that the former are seeking to develop a uniquely Catholic strategy of evolutionary change directed from above while the latter emphasize revolutionary change from below, with Marxism as an ally rather than as an enemy.[73]

With their goal of making important changes through the existing political systems, the progressive clergy have become involved in a number of political activities which have, directly or indirectly, articulated demands they believe must be met if these systems are to be salvaged. The country which has received most attention as a stronghold of progressive influence—except perhaps for Chile—is Brazil. One of the first Latin American countries to develop a small but not uninfluential band of progressive clergy at

---

[73] Sanders, "Types of Catholic Elites in Latin America," pp. 187–93; Smith, *Religion and Political Development,* p. 275.

the priest and at the bishop levels, Brazil has witnessed a number of clerical pronouncements on the need for reform in such areas as education and agriculture.[74] Constituting at most 10 to 20 percent of the Brazilian clergy, the progressives, borrowing from European experience, began a lay group in 1935 called Catholic Action, a Church-affiliated association to promote socioeconomic change. Not very successful, Catholic Action was somewhat eclipsed by the youth movement within the program, which emphasized a more dynamic and militant approach to creating alliances with student, peasant, and working class youth.[75] Advised by the clergy, especially secular clergy and the religious order of the Dominicans, Catholic Action supported the leftist regime of Goulart in 1961, much to the displeasure of the conservative clergy. In 1962, Catholic Action yielded its leadership of the Catholic left to Popular Action, which pursued humanistic and socialistic alternatives of development without the direct participation and control of the clergy. In 1961, a similar development occurred when a Brazilian Archbishop gave permission to four priests to create rural Catholic labor unions which, with 200,000 members, gradually came under the control of lawyers rather than of the clergy. Also during the early 1960s, an apparent era of progressive development, the "Basic Education Movement," or MEB, a fairly independent lay association, attempted to attack illiteracy and bring a progressive and sometimes revolutionary message to the program. Most of these activities were curbed or eliminated either by the Church hierarchy or by the conservative military coup of 1964.

In Colombia the paternalism of the progressives was more evident. The hierarchy established and controlled a program called Popular Cultural Action which was designed to foster a Christian education of rural adults but did so with little or no independence from the hierarchy.[76] Despite their diversity, all of these programs symbolize the progressive's concern for paternalistic mobilization of the lower sectors which have numbers if not political importance. Simple urgings that the government should undertake certain programs are often seen by the progressives as insufficient. Although the progressive clergy do make demands regarding these kinds of policies

[74] Emanuel de Kadt, "Religion, the Church and Social Change in Brazil," in Claudio Veliz (ed.), *The Politics of Conformity in Latin America* (New York: Oxford University Press, 1967), pp. 207–8.

[75] de Kadt, "The Church and Social Change," pp. 209–10; Einauldi et al., *Institutional Development,* p. 34; Thomas G. Sanders, "Catholicism and Development: The Catholic Left in Brazil," in Kalman H. Silvert (ed.), *Churches and States: The Religious Institution and Modernization* (New York: American Universities Field Staff, Inc., 1967), p. 85.

[76] Sanders, "Catholicism and Development," pp. 88–98; de Kadt, "Paternalism and Populism: Catholicism in Latin America," in *Journal of Contemporary History,* Vol. 2, No. 4, 1967, p. 92; de Kadt, "The Church and Social Change," p. 214.

and occasionally cooperate with the government to implement them, their eventual goal is to mobilize the masses into effective organizations of more than transitory political importance.

The efforts of the progressive clergy have also led, in some countries, to the development of Christian Democratic parties which, although relying upon the recent ideological developments in Catholicism, are not generally considered to be the political arm of the Church hierarchy. Although in such countries as Chile and Venezuela, where their electoral success has been recent, the progressive clergy do not directly affiliate with these parties, but they did provide much of the original impetus for the development of party ideology and electoral success. That is, while the progressive clergy exercises no policy or other such controls over the political parties, they nevertheless are able to support political leaders who, if electorally successful, will be receptive to the demands of the progressive clergy and, more than that, will do what they can to implement the demands through their official positions in government.

In Chile, where the progressive clergy contributed to the origins of the first important movement of Christian Democracy in Latin America, the Jesuits, and especially Fathers Fernando Vives and Alberto Hurtado, worked with young laymen who in 1938 established the Falange National, the predecessor of the Christian Democratic Party. Also of not inconsequential importance was the emergence of the Centro Bellarmino, a research center sponsored by the Jesuits that is devoted to reevaluating the socioeconomic problems confronting Chile and Latin America. In addition to providing a catalyst for progressive clergy and concerned laymen, perhaps most significantly, the Center contributed heavily to the ideological development of Chile's Christian Democratic Party. In 1962, perhaps in partial response to this activity, the Chilean Bishops issued a pastoral letter advocating rapid change of Chile's socioeconomic structures, at the same time condemning Marxism. With considerable independence from a friendly hierarchy, as well as a growing base among Chilean voters, the Christian Democrats, under their leader Eduardo Frei with his slogan "Revolution in Liberty," were able to capture the presidency in the 1964 elections. However, as a humanistic movement dedicated to constructive and nonviolent revolution, the Christian Democrats once in power confronted a number of obstacles. Some of these problems were also the direct concern of the progressive clergy. For example, the Christian Democrats adopted the suggestion of Roger Vekemans of the Centro Bellarmino that the marginal 50 percent of the Chilean population must be encouraged to act in their own interests. But soon paternalism reappeared when the government bureaucracy, staffed by Christian Democrats, exerted control from above and therefore undercut their original intent. With a not unblemished past and an uncertain future after their defeat in the 1970 elections, the Christian Democrats in Chile may have learned that their moderate progressivism cannot easily resist the divisive tendencies stemming from the mounting pressures for more rapid reforms.[77]

Except for Venezuela, the Christian Democrats have not scored major electoral successes outside Chile. In the presidential elections of 1968, the Christian Democratic Party in Venezuela defeated Democratic Action, and Rafael Caldera, the party's founder, became the second Christian Democrat in Latin America to be elected to a national presidency. Although the Venezuelan Christian Democrats gained original support from the progressive clergy, their relations today are cemented more by common Christian values inspired through recent Church encyclicals than by a partisan coalition in which the party does the Church's political bidding.[78] The progressive clergy nevertheless have a powerful ally which, once in power, agrees basically with their notions of the kinds of changes which should be initiated to promote the socioeconomic development of Venezuela. Without this informal alliance of shared beliefs, the pleadings of the few progressive clergy for change-oriented public policies would have little or no effect. However, recent evidence suggests again that once in power, Christian Democrats face a great difficulty, if not an impossibility, in implementing their programs.

In addition to organizing lay groups and stimulating the growth of the Christian Democratic movement, the progressive clergy have become involved in politics in other more sporadic and less easily categorized ways. Much of their activity does not directly involve the making of demands on government because the progressive clergy are busy organizing the lower sectors, a stage of mobilization that must precede effective influence on public policymaking. Examples abound of both individual as well as organized attempts of the progressive clergy to influence the course of political events. With Trujillo's harassment of the Church in the waning years of his dictatorship, individual priests attacked his regime at considerable personal risk. Ecuador, a country not renowned for large numbers of progressive clergy, nevertheless has witnessed priests urging the elimination of *latifundios* and *minifundios* so that the government could expropriate the land for the common good. In Mexico, Ivan Illich, before he withdrew under Vatican pressure from his sacerdotal functions, was, and in some ways continues to be, a leading critic of Latin America's archaic social structure and the role of the United States in supporting its continued existence. Also from Mexico, the bishop of Cuernavaca, Don Sergio Mendez Arceo, has actively joined those who seek an alliance of Christians and Marxists to "liberate" Latin America.

---

[77] Smith, "Religion and Political Development," pp. 208–10; de Kadt, "Paternalism and Populism: Catholicism in Latin America," pp. 96–97; Einauldi et al., *Institutional Development,* pp. 62–63.

[78] Williams, *Christian Democratic Parties,* pp. 15–19, 22, 163–64, 168.

In Colombia, some priests support the return to power of ex-dictator Rojas Pinillas because he has promised a redistribution of the wealth to the lower sectors.[79] In Chile, the progressive clergy, more than any other in Latin America, actually authored, as well as played a role in implementing, public reform policies of the Frei government.[80] In Brazil, progressive bishops such as Dom Helder substantially contributed to the development of peasant leagues in the northeast, but have suffered a decline of influence since the military regime has curtailed such activities. And in Peru, where the conservatives, especially at the higher levels of the hierarchy, clearly outnumber the progressive clergy, the progressives are simply trying to obtain the right to speak out and act freely under the somewhat progressive but authoritarian military regime that came to power in 1968. Small numbers of progressive clergy and their Catholic laymen contributed to the Castro movement to overthrow Batista in 1959. According to Dewart, Castro owes his life to the intervention of Monsignor Perez Serantes, who argued against Castro's execution for participating in the attack on the Moncada army barracks in 1953. Later, other clergy joined or supported the movement as much in response to Batista's repression as to Castro's promises. One priest in Santiago de Cuba helped the movement by inserting coded messages into his radio broadcasts that were intended for Raul Castro, Fidel's brother. As conditions deteriorated, the sporadic support of individual clergy was supplemented with the organized support of Catholic laymen. In April, 1958, Catholic labor unions obeyed Castro's request for a general strike. However, despite these indications of clerical support, Castro, it is commonly believed, never did gain the loyalty of the majority of the clergy or of the laymen in Cuba.[81]

Finally, the progressive clergy of Latin America have a regional forum for expressing demands for reform. The Latin American Bishops' Council (CELAM) provides the progressive bishops of the region, who are a distinct but vocal minority, with an opportunity to advocate if not implement suggestions for socioeconomic reform within the various countries. In exercising its function of interpreting papal pronouncements and recommending to the national hierarchies how they should be applied, CELAM has tended to advocate revolutionary, if not violent, change in Latin America. The significance of CELAM's rhetoric is somewhat misleading, however. Most of the bishops are silent conservatives rather than vocal leftists, leaving the false impression that CELAM is generally constituted of revolutionary

[79] Edelmann, *Latin American Government and Politics,* pp. 177–78; Howard J. Wiarda, "The Changing Political Orientation of the Catholic Church," J. Gordon Chamberlin, "Ecumenical Tangle," in *Christian Century,* Vol. 85, No. 3, January 17, 1968; Einauldi et al., *Institutional Development,* p. 57.

[80] Einauldi et al., *Institutional Development,* pp. 61–62.

[81] Dewart, *Christianity and Revolution, passim.*

clergy. In Medellin, Colombia, the bishops released pastoral recommendations advocating: that Church and State cooperate on matters of justice,
morality, and the abuse of power; that the Church collaborate with Latin
American governments on constructive programs but shun intimate alliances
with particular regimes; and that the Church promote changes in attitudes
among the elites through religious movements and the Church's educational
institutions. The Medellin recommendations are certainly a statement of
common purpose for progressive clergy but they cannot be interpreted as
representing the views of most of the bishops or even as being a direct attempt to influence the national governments of the region on specific
programs.[82]

Unlike the progressive clergy, the radicals are prone to form coalitions
with Marxists and other extremists, the demands of which are more likely
to provoke governmental hostility than governmental compliance. The radicals are not uninfluential in some ways; their small numbers underrepresent
their impact. However, given their militancy and fondness for utopian
remedies, the radical clergy have tended to present polemical, rather than
concrete, demands which the leaders of Latin American political systems
generally cannot meet, even if they were inclined to do so. As innovators at
one extreme of the political spectrum, the radicals are intent upon dis-
covering new directions, preferring to leave to the progressive clergy the task
of making the practical compromises with power groups to ensure that at
least a few, if not all, of their preferences are converted into public policy.
Much more than the progressives, the radical clergy emphasize a strategy
for mobilizing the masses. Without such mobilization, radicals argue, effective demands for fundamental change in policy and in the system itself
are unlikely. To make effective demands for rapid change, the masses must
acquire an awareness of who they are, what they want and how to get it.
This romantic task is monumental, if not completely impossible, to achieve.
As Paulo Freire, a noted Brazilian intellectual, has argued, the illiterate
adult faces his environment with resignation, pessimism, and fatalism, attitudes that power groups have traditionally encouraged through paternalistic manipulation. The radical clergy must somehow awaken the individual and social consciences of the masses to their historical destiny as an
oppressed class. This awakening—or *conscientizacão* as it is called in Brazil
—must occur if the masses are to wrench the future of Latin America from
the control of the important power groups.[83] In pursuing such a long-range

82 Einauldi et al., *Institutional Development,* pp. 43–46; Sanders, "The Church
in Latin America."

83 Edward J. Williams, "Latin American Catholicism and Political Integration," in *Comparative Political Studies,* Vol. 2 No. 3, October 1969, p. 340; Sanders,
"The Church in Latin America," pp. 296–97; Smith, *Religion and Political Development,* pp. 166–67.

strategy, the radical clergy forego the possibility of making demands upon the system because their goal is eventual transformation of the system through convulsive and massive participation of an aroused populace. By emphasizing a vision of revolution, the radicals risk, and must be prepared for, at best, governmental indifference, and at worst governmental hostility and repression.

Because the radical clergy do not play the game of political influence like most groups that accept the current system, their activities have identifiable and sometimes counter-productive results. In Brazil, where the radical clergy have played a more important role than in some other Latin American countries, the military regime has persecuted them, and also others who cannot really be classified as radicals, for their criticisms of policies and personnel. But the radical clergy have been one of the military regime's prime targets because they openly advocate alliances with communist forces to foment a violent revolution.[84] Harassment of the radical clergy had also prompted progressive clergy to make more cautious and vague statements about Brazilian reforms. In Chile, on the other hand, a more lenient, civilian government has not seriously obstructed such leftist groups as *Iglesia Joven* (Young Church), constituted of radical clergy and laymen who advocate immediate revolution—with or without violence—based upon a Christian concern for the spiritually and materially poor. In Colombia, despite a conservative Church and a less than sympathetic government, some clergy have abandoned rhetoric for action. One priest took part in efforts of Bogota's poor to squat on and occupy land. In Guatemala some Maryknoll missionaries, a group of American clergy, were expelled from the country after they were accused of encouraging peasants to seize control of the land they worked and to defend their actions with arms if necessary. In a more famous case mentioned earlier, ex-priest Camilo Torres died as a guerrilla, but his symbol of humanism and revolution may mean more in death than his brief life did.[85] But most radical clergy in Colombia are still struggling just to express their ideas within a hierarchy which is more antagonistic than most to leftist sentiments.[86] Although the seeds of populistic radicalism among the young clergy also exist to some extent in such countries as Peru and Argentina, nourished by the ambiguities of Pope John's encyclicals, the political climate of Latin America in general, except in Chile and excluding Cuba from the discussion, is hostile to the immediate satisfaction of radical demands for change and even to the existence of the radical clergy as a group.

[84] Mutchler, "Roman Catholicism in Brazil," p. 111; de Kadt, "The Church and Social Change in Brazil," p. 208.

[85] Smith, "Religion and Political Development," pp. 238–41; Einauldi et al., pp. 58, 61.

[86] de Kadt, "Paternalism and Populism," p. 100.

SYSTEM RESPONSE

In this survey of the demands of the various political factions within the Latin American clergy, some success has been implied or made explicit. When examined in more detail, it becames clear that the different factions vary in effectiveness, for different reasons. For the reactionary clergy, government is rarely responsive to most of their demands, except under stress when anticommunism and instability become the key concerns of troubled conservative regimes. More importantly, the reactionaries receive some of what they want due to an immobilized political system unable to promote socioeconomic change. This ineffectiveness is not the result so much of any specific demands of the reactionary clergy but is simply a fundamental feature of Latin American politics which favors obstructive tactics. The recognition of specific demands of the reactionary clergy is more likely to come if the clergy is aligned on a particular issue with members of the traditional and modern oligarchy. In this alliance, which includes large landowners and large industrialists, the reactionary clergy are clearly the junior partners.

Of all the political factions of the clergy, the conservatives receive the most from the political system, except perhaps in Chile. Not only are their articulated demands in tune with the status quo, and hence more acceptable to leaders in power, but, if a nondemand may be considered as a type of demand, the political apathy of the majority of conservative clergy enables governments to use limited resources to ward off threatening demands from less satisfied and more insistent political groups. Although rarely supported by symbolic rewards of government, the conservative clergy, like the reactionaries, benefit from the immobility of the Latin American political process, in which changes are smothered rather than directly opposed. Matters such as institutional survival, anticommunism, law and order, and stability are all policies that attract the concern of the conservative clergy. If they do require positive government action, conservative-backed policies are at least less difficult to implement than complex policies of reform. Many conservatives will settle for symbolic government support for reform demands, recognizing that concessions must occasionally be made to groups who oppose the views of the conservatives. On balance, then, the political immobility in Latin America, and the fact that an obstructive strategy to preserve the status quo is convenient and effective in such a context, means that the conservative clergy receive much of what they want from government because a government that is not requested to promote change is being asked to do little or nothing that is different from what it has always done.

The progressive and radical clergy, while asking much of their political systems, receive the least—and what they do receive is often symbolic, and generally ineffective commitment to gradual reform. Both factions—but especially the progressives—have had and will continue to have a direct and positive impact on public policy. For example, governments must deal with clergy-instigated if not always clergy-controlled groups such as unions, peasant leagues, literacy and education movements, and the Christian Democratic movement. Thus, minimal advances have been recorded, but the current climate of conservative militarism and reaction does not provide an encouraging sign that the future success of these two factions —and especially of the radical clergy—will be assured. In some ways, the obstacles confronting the Church as an institution promoting socioeconomic change are similar to, if not identical with, those facing the progressives and the radicals. Except for a few bishops, neither faction can find much solace or active encouragement from the hierarchy and must therefore turn to the masses who are, in the long run, supposed to benefit from the demands that the leftist clergy, a relatively privileged group itself, make on the political systems of the region. Mobilization of the masses by these two factions of the clergy is a long-term, and not always predictable, strategy. Increased mass participation may eventually provide the needed support for the demands voiced by the progressives and radicals. But the immediate prospects in contemporary Latin America are to control and carefully limit the growth of participation, especially through military regimes as in countries like Brazil, supported by the middle and upper socioeconomic sectors. Although the two leftist factions can continue to expect grudging and minimal response to their demands for socioeconomic change, the radical clergy can expect continued intolerance. Indeed, especially in military-controlled countries, the radicals face the prospect not only of a lack of positive response to their demands but also governmental hostility toward, if not outright elimination of, their political activities. By their militant and revolutionary rhetoric, the radicals, unlike the progressives, can not realistically expect that a system they are trying to destroy should be responsive to their demands which, if implemented, would hasten its end. By the nature of their goals, then, the progressives and radicals, although using different methods, cannot expect responsiveness or even toleration for their demands for significant socioeconomic changes.

In conclusion, the Church as an institution and its clergy as a fragmented political force are not as prepared to contribute as much to socioeconomic change as some optimists suggest.[87] For example, Williams asserts that the Church and its inspired social movements can legitimize governments bent on development, that the clergy can bridge the gap between elites and masses, and that the Catholic lay movements will be able to integrate the Church's premodern theology with modern thought.[88] And

[87] David E. Mutchler, *The Church as a Political Force in Latin America* (New York: Praeger, 1971).

[88] Williams, "Latin American Catholicism," especially p. 329.

Vallier advances a sophisticated argument to support the view that the Church can make a contribution to the socioeconomic development of other groups and then can follow up the changes begun by others. Mostly, Vallier hopes that the Church, and especially the elite that runs it, can bring together universal religious values and more modern secular ones in the hearts of laymen who will accept Christianity and continuous change.[89] However, the realization of these hopes is still quite distant. The Church as an institution is poorly equipped to lead or even to follow the banners of rapid change. As individuals, most clergy are generally apathetic and conservative. Handicapped by impressive obstacles, the few clergy who are actively trying to promote socioeconomic change are committed to a long-run and somewhat romantic strategy of awakening the masses, the success of which is by no means inevitable.

FURTHER READING

ALONSO, ISIDORO, et al., *La Iglesia en Venezuela y Ecuador.* Friburgo, Suiza: Oficina Internacional de Investigaciones Sociales de FERES, 1961.

——————, Renato Poblete y Gines Garrido, *La Iglesia en Chile.* Friburgo y Bogota: Oficina Internacional de Investigaciones Sociales de FERES, 1962.

BATES, MARGARET, (ed.), *The Lay Apostolate in Latin America.* Washington, D.C.: Catholic University of America Press, 1960.

CHAMBERLIN, J. GORDON, "Ecumenical Tangle," in *Christian Century,* Vol. 85, No. 3, January 17, 1968.

CONSIDINE, JOHN J., (ed.), *The Church in the New Latin America.* Notre Dame, Ind.: Fides Publishers, Inc., 1964.

D'ANTONIO, WILLIAM V. and FREDERICK B. PIKE (eds.), *Religion, Revolution and Reform.* New York: Praeger, 1964.

DE KADT, EMANUEL, "Religion, the Church and Social Change in Brazil," in Claudio Veliz (ed.), *The Politics of Conformity in Latin America.* New York: Oxford Unviersity Press, 1967.

——————, "Paternalism and Populism: Catholicism in Latin America," in *Journal of Contemporary History,* Vol. 2, No. 4, 1967.

DEWART, LESLIE, *Christianity and Revolution: The Lesson of Cuba.* New York: Herder and Herder, 1963.

DIX, ROBERT H., *Colombia: The Political Dimension of Change.* New Haven: Yale University Press, 1967.

EDELMANN, ALEXANDER T., *Latin American Government and Politics.* Homewood, Ill.: Dorsey, 1965.

[89] Ivan Vallier, *Catholicism, Social Control and Modernization in Latin America* (Englewood Cliffs, N.J.: Prentice-Hall, 1970), pp. 104, 158.

EDITORIAL, "Church and State in Latin America," in *A Journal of Church and State*, Vol. 8, No. 2, Spring 1966.

EINAULDI, LUIGI, et al., *Latin American Institutional Development*, Santa Monica, Calif.: Rand Corporation, Memorandum RM-6136—DOS.

FALS BORDA, ORLANDO, discussed in William L. Wonderly, "Social Science Research and the Church in Latin America," in *Practical Anthropology*, Vol. 14, No. 2, March–April 1967.

HICKS, FREDERIC, "Politics, Power and the Role of the Village Priest in Paraguay," in *Journal of Inter-American Studies*, Vol. 9, No. 2, April 1967.

HOUTART, FRANCOIS and EMILE PIN, *The Church and the Latin American Revolution*. New York: Sheed and Ward, 1965.

KENNEDY, JOHN J., *Catholicism, Nationalism and Democracy in Argentina*. Notre Dame, Ind.: University of Notre Dame Press, 1958.

——————, "The Force of the Church," in John J. TePaske and Sydney Nettleton Fisher (eds.), *Explosive Forces in Latin America*. Columbus: Ohio State University Press, 1964.

LARA-BRAUD, JORGE, "Latin America: The crisis and signs of hope," in *Catholic World*, Vol. 204, No. 1, January 1967.

MECHAM, J. LLOYD, *Church and State in Latin America: A History of Politica-Ecclesiastical Relations*, rev. ed. Chapel Hill: University of North Carolina Press, 1966.

MUTCHLER, DAVID E., S. J., *The Church as a Political Force in Latin America*. New York: Praeger, 1971.

——————, "Roman Catholicism in Brazil," in *Studies in Comparative International Development*, Vol. 1, No. 8, 1965.

ORTIZ AMAYA, JORGE, *El Sacerdote de Manana*. Buernos Aires: Ediciones Carlos Lohle, 1964.

PEREZ, GUSTAVO and ISAAC WUST, *La Iglesia en Colombia*. Bogota, Colombia: Oficina Internacional de Investigaciones Sociales de FERES, 1961.

PEREZ RAMIREZ, GUSTAVO, *El Problema Sacerdotal en Colombia*. Friburgo y Bogota: Oficina Internacional de Investigaciones Sociales de FERES, 1962.

POBLETE BARTH, RENATO, S. J., *Crisis Sacerdotal*. Santiago de Chile: Editorial del Pacifico, S. A., 1965.

Por un grupo de especialistas, *La Iglesia y la Politica*. Santiago de Chile: Ediciones Paulinas, 1963.

RYCROFT, W. STANLEY, *Religion and Faith in Latin America*. Philadelphia: Westminster Press, 1958.

SANDERS, THOMAS G., "Types of Catholic Elites in Latin America," in Robert D. Tomasek (ed.), *Latin American Politics*, second edition, New York: Doubleday, 1970.

——————, "The Church in Latin America," in *Foreign Affairs*, Vol. 48, No. 2, January 1970.

—————, "Catholicism and Development: The Catholic Left in Brazil," in Kalman H. Silvert (ed.), *Churches and States: The Religious Institution and Modernization*. New York: American Universities Field Staff, Inc., 1967.

SMITH, DONALD EUGENE, *Religion and Political Development*. Boston: Little, Brown, 1970.

TORRES RESTREPO, CAMILO, "Social Change and Rural Violence in Colombia," in *Studies in Comparative International Development*, Vol. 4, No. 12, 1968–1969.

TURNER, FREDERICK C., "The Compatibility of Church and State in Mexico," in *Journal of Inter-American Studies*, Vol. 9, No. 4, October 1967.

VALLIER, IVAN, *Catholicism, Social Control and Modernization in Latin America*. Englewood Cliffs, N.J.: Prentice-Hall, 1970.

—————, "Religious Elites: Differentiations and Developments in Roman Catholicism," Seymour Martin Lipset and Aldo Solari (eds.), *Elites in Latin America*. New York: Oxford University Press, 1967.

WAGLEY, CHARLES, *An Introduction to Brazil*. New York: Columbia University Press, 1963.

WEIGERT, ANDREW, S. J., "*Machismo* and The Priestly Vocation," in *Catholic World*, Vol. 199, June 1964.

WIARDA, HOWARD J., *Dictatorship and Development: The Methods of Control in Trunillo's Dominican Republic*. Gainesville: University of Florida Press, Latin American Monograph Series, Ser. 2, No. 5.

—————, "The Changing Political Orientation of the Catholic Church in the Dominican Republic," in *A Journal of Church and State*, Vol. 7, No. 2, Spring 1965.

WILLIAMS, EDWARD J., "Latin American Catholicism and Political Integration," in *Comparative Political Studies*, Vol. 2, No. 3, October 1969.

—————, *Latin American Christian Democratic Parties*. Knoxville: University of Tennessee Press, 1967.

CHAPTER 7

MILITARY OFFICERS

The military in Latin America, except in Costa Rica, Mexico, and Uruguay, plays a pivotal role in the various political systems of the area. It performs this role not only as an institutional interest group seeking to influence public policy, but also as a political elite that either places its own members in high positions within the systems or determines which civilians will occupy those positions. Thus, the military is a formidable and often decisive force in determining the nature of Latin American politics as well as the prospects for socioeconomic change.

The Latin American military has attracted the interest of scholars the world over. However, knowledge of why and how the military performs its role in the political systems of the region remains at best fragmentary. Actually, both Latin American and foreign scholars find it difficult to discuss the military in a neutral fashion in that there is a strong tendency to view it either as a fascist destroyer of democratic values or as a firm savior of the nation in the face of disorder and uncertainty. Thus, although a great deal of literature exists on the military and politics in Latin America, a neutral assessment of its role is difficult because of the frequent need to rely for information on polemical accounts.

In order to overcome this difficulty to some extent, it seems best to look briefly at the military as an institution existing in every country of the world, with particular reference to the military of all, or at least most, underdeveloped countries. This overview is necessary to illuminate military politics in Latin America.

THE CONTEXT: THE MILITARY IN DEVELOPING SOCIETIES

The military is a politically important factor in virtually every country of the world. Contemporary history is littered with major events involving the military—international wars, civil wars, guerrilla operations, missile crises, and so forth. Even today, the military establishments of developed countries help to guarantee the continued existence of their respective nations. However, even in the developed countries the military does more than just attempt to guarantee national security. Large and important military establishments are also influential in domestic politics because national security requires vast expenditures of public funds which, if not allocated to military affairs, could be used to provide for domestic needs. Thus, with the question of priorities in government spending, the military must become involved in politics and policy. However, although the military of the developed countries has an important impact on domestic politics, its main role, both actual and perceived, is to secure the nation against foreign enemies by maintaining effective offensive and defensive strategies.

National security, however, is not generally the principal role of the military in many of the developing countries of the world. Indeed, a crucial distinction between the political role of the military in the developed and in the developing countries is that the military in such countries as the United States, Western European nations and the U.S.S.R. justifies its existence because it defends the nation against external aggression, while the military in such countries as Brazil, Argentina and Peru justifies its existence because it claims to defend the nation against internal enemies. Consequently, the principal role of the military in many underdeveloped countries is not defense against external aggression but control over the people and the politics of their own nations.[1] As a former president once remarked, with some exaggeration, "Each Latin American country is being occupied by its own army."[2]

---

[1] For general works on military politics especially in developing countries, see Samuel P. Huntington (ed.), *Changing Patterns of Military Politics* (New York: Free Press, 1962); S. E. Finer, *The Man on Horseback: The Role of Military in Politics* (New York: Praeger, 1962); Morris Janowitz, *The Military in the Political Development of New Nations: An Essay in Comparative Analysis* (Chicago: University of Chicago Press, 1964); John J. Johnson (ed.), *The Role of the Military in Underdeveloped Countries* (Princeton: Princeton University Press, 1962); Samuel P. Huntington, *The Soldier and the State: The Theory and Politics of Civil-Military Relations* (Cambridge, Mass.: Harvard University Press, 1957); John H. Kautsky, "The Military in Underdeveloped Countries," in *Economic Development and Cultural Change,* Vol. 12, January 1965.

[2] Quoted in Willard F. Barber and C. Neale Ronning, *Internal Security and Military Power: Counterinsurgency and Civic Action in Latin America* (Columbus: Ohio State University Press, 1966), p. 67.

Thus, in Latin America as in other underdeveloped areas, the military, with its principal concerns turned inwards, assumes a political role of heightened importance. Its manpower, organization, and resources come to play a direct role in the domestic politics of the individual nations. For example, military technology becomes a power factor in conflicts of domestic politics rather than a more traditional means of defending the country against external enemies. In short, the military in underdeveloped areas tends to be first and foremost a privileged power wielder in domestic politics and only secondarily is it a defender against external aggression.

Actually, military domination of politics is closely related to the general problems of governing in socially, economically, and politically underdeveloped areas. In order to comprehend the role of the military in this context, one must appreciate the kinds of societies in which such military institutions operate. Consequently, it is necessary to elaborate to some extent upon the discussion in Chapter 1 dealing with development, decay, and immobility.

In attempting to suggest reasons for the obvious importance of the military in the politics of the developing areas of the world, several observers are drawn to the concept of the "praetorian state."[3] Indeed, the "praetorian state" in many ways describes the features of politics in Latin America and other developing areas, because the concept basically involves military intervention in and potential military domination of politics.[4] Unlike the politics of modern democracies, the politics of the praetorian state encourage the development of military rule because civilian institutions and groups—the presidency, legislature, courts, political parties, interest groups and such—are incapable of operating a political 'system that can effectively meet demands for socioeconomic change. In other words, the politics of immobility, as described here, provide the conditions that nourish the praetorian state.

Many developing countries face the prospect of becoming praetorian states because military domination of civilian politics seems to be almost an integral part of the breakdown of old societies and the imperfect construction of the new. For those who live in modernized democracies, military domination over civilian politics is unlikely because when civilian institutions are generally regarded as legitimate, military intervention assumes a

[3] Samuel P. Huntington, *Political Order in Changing Societies* (New Haven: Yale University Press, 1968); Samuel P. Huntington (ed.), *Changing Patterns of Military Politics* (New York: Free Press, 1962), especially the essay by David C. Rapoport; Amos Perlmutter, "The Praetorian State and the Praetorian Army: Toward a Taxonomy of Civil-Military Relations in Developing Politics," in *Comparative Politics*, Vol. 1, April 1969, pp. 382–404.

[4] Huntington, *Political Order in Changing Societies*, p. 195; Perlmutter, "The Praetorian State and the Praetorian Army," p. 383.

negative connotation. It is just this lack of legitimacy of civilian institutions and political processes which encourages military intervention in the developing countries of Latin America, Asia, and Africa. And while the military state may be a poor vehicle to promote change,[5] the military usually ventures into politics partly in response to the stagnation and immobility existing under civilian politicians.

Related to this is the fact that many underdeveloped societies are severely divided, and the resulting fragmentation helps to make government and other social institutions ineffective. The fragmentation of society as a whole, in which a lack of basic agreement on the rules of the game is a major roadblock to effective and stable politics, also permeates the groups of such a society. For example, as mentioned here in Chapter 1, it is somewhat of a distortion to imply that the "groups" discussed are coherent, more or less organized, unified entities; rather they are fairly arbitrary "social categories" designed for purposes of discussion. Concomitantly, except for a few notable exceptions, strong, effective, and permanent political parties do not exist to aggregate the demands of the many and disparate groups.

In such societies even the military cannot escape completely from a tendency to fragment, especially when specific political issues affect it as an institution. During the 1965 Dominican crisis, for example, the situation was considerably exacerbated by violent divisions within the armed forces. However, although the military is not immune to fragmentation, it is nevertheless usually sufficiently isolated from the most severe schisms to provide the degree of unity necessary to operate the affairs of government for a time. When civilian politicians cannot provide this, the military is there to step in.

Another factor often alleged to be influential in leading to the praetorian state is the absence, weakness, or fragmentation of a middle class (or sector). The argument generally suggests that if the underdeveloped country concerned had a large middle class such as in, for example, the United States, it would be much more politically stable and thus would offer far less excuse for a military takeover. However, while this idea has many distinguished proponents, the matter does not appear to be quite so simple. Latin America has the largest middle class sectors of any developing area, but it also has a long as well as recent history of military rule. Thus, it can and has been very ably argued that it is *because* of the existence of significant middle class groups that the military will depose civilian regimes.[6] This may be because in a society not far advanced along the development continuum, the emergent middle sector is challenging the traditional elite, or because in a society further advanced along the continuum, the established middle class is resisting the ambitions of the lower class groups. Some of

---

5 Huntington (ed.), *Changing Patterns of Military Politics,* p. 72.

6 Perlmutter, "The Praetorian State and the Praetorian Army."

the reasons for this connection between the military and the middle class will become apparent in later discussion.

Many other factors may be involved in achieving praetorianism in the underdeveloped countries, but the point should be clear: the political importance of the military in the underdeveloped areas of the world is not just due to the military establishment itself, but is in great part due to the unresolved problems of incomplete development. In Latin America, at least, the fragmented societies place a premium on one form of political power—violence of one type or another. And the threat or actual use of violence becomes a political resource of tremendous importance. Since the concentration of violence in Latin America, legitimately or not, lies almost exclusively with the military establishments, the military's political importance is greatly magnified.

In the fragmented societies of Latin America, the concentration of the tools of political violence in the hands of the military is generally so overwhelming that they rarely need be used directly. The means of violence may be demonstrated in some way without actually using it upon a political group or person: the threat of military action is generally sufficient to obtain the desired compliance. On the other hand, less privileged and powerful groups must exercise and display their tools of violence if they wish to force a response from the political system. Some violence is not consciously political. A spontaneous, anomic riot of urban laborers, for example, may have no clear political purpose although it may have some political consequences. Still other groups, that lack the channels of influence with the government that the military enjoys, may use violence to represent and call atention to their demands. Guerrillas in Uruguay, students in Mexico, and miners in Bolivia have used violence to represent their demands and to bolster their statuses as worthy power contenders. Finally, the military is not likely to use violence aimed at revolutionary goals. In fact, in the three countries—Mexico, Bolivia, and Cuba—where social revolutions did occur, the military establishment in the beginning was counter-revolutionary and later was either destroyed or considerably restrained. More likely, segments of the military are prone to form coalitions with other groups to depose governments. Such a standard feature of political instability is nevertheless not indicative of basic social revolution.[7]

7 For further reading on political violence in Latin America, see Merle Kling, "Toward A Theory of Power and Political Instability in Latin America," in *Western Political Quarterly*, Vol. 9, No. 1, March 1956; William S. Stokes, "Violence as a Power Factor in Latin American Politics," in *Western Political Quarterly*, Vol. 5, No. 3, September 1952; Edward W. Gude, "Political Violence in Venezuela: 1958–1964," in James Chowning Davies (ed.), *When Men Revolt and Why* (New York: Free Press, 1971); Victor Perera, "Guatemala: Always Violencia," in *New York Times Magazine*, June 13, 1971, p. 12; Martin C. Needler, *Political Development in Latin America: Instability, Violence and Evolutionary Change* (New York: Random House, 1968), pp. 43–51.

THE MILITARY AS AN INSTITUTION

It must also be noted that in most underdeveloped areas the military, when compared to other institutions and groups, is relatively modern and efficient. That is, in addition to its monopoly of effective violence, the relative "modernity" of the military tends to make it predominant in developing societies. However, it must also be taken into account that the military organizations of underdeveloped countries possess only in an incomplete or amended form the general features of their counterparts in more developed areas. Thus, for example, in terms of bureaucratic organization—hierarchy, chain of command, salaried employees, efficiency, rationality, professional careerism, expertise, discipline, regulations, and so forth—the military of underdeveloped areas only roughly approximates the military of the more developed areas. This is due greatly to the fact that the military cannot be totally isolated from the stresses and strains characteristic of developing societies. The military must compromise with its social setting.

The extent to which the military of any particular developing country approximates the ideal of bureaucratic organization depends somewhat upon the general level of development of the country. The Honduran military, for example, is farther from the ideal than the Chilean military. But the principal standard for judging whether the military of a developing country approaches the bureaucratic ideal is the concept of "professionalism." Despite some disagreement about what exactly this term means, most observers conclude that the military establishments of the underdeveloped areas generally rank low in "professionalism" compared to those in the developed areas, although there is considerable variation from country to country.

"Professionalism" generally implies more than a full-time commitment to military service. According to Huntington, "professionalism" also includes an emphasis on expertise, responsibility (to civilian control), and a sense of unity within the establishment.[8] But if this is true, then the creation of military "professionalism" is an extremely awkward and uneven process. For example, although standards of competence are being more frequently demanded for promotion, the military in Latin America has not necessarily become less political or more subservient to civilian politicians. In other words, both the emphasis on expertise and military dominance in civilian politics have increased in many countries. If one insists that all these conditions be present in order to consider a military institution to be "professional," then most underdeveloped countries, and even some of the so-called developed countries, are without "professional" military organizations. Put differently, although many officers in Latin America believe in the

[8] Huntington, *The Soldier and State,* p. 15.

importance of order and hierarchy, of functional divisions, of the nation-state and power, of realism and conservatism, most view themselves not as servants of civilian leaders but as servants to the nation which is often viewed as betrayed by these civilian leaders.[9]

In summary, supported by the public treasury, sustained partially by a fragmented society that places a premium on violence, benefited by resources of organization, manpower, and technology, the military establishments of Latin America and other underdeveloped areas are formidable if not always unified institutions that enjoy generally unrivaled superiority over other power contenders. Consequently, in all but a few Latin American countries, the military plays an important and sometimes predominant role in the various political systems.

Given the political importance of the military, it seems appropriate to look more closely at various features of the Latin American military, concentrating particularly on the individuals who occupy its most important ranks and their relationships to their institution and to the larger society in which that institution operates.

THE MILITARY MAN IN LATIN AMERICA

It has been a political tradition in much of Latin America that military men—meaning individuals from the army, navy and, more recently, air force—are either presidents themselves or determine which civilian politician is acceptable as the chief executive. Peron of Argentina, Batista of Cuba, Trujillo of the Dominican Republic, Rojas Pinilla of Colombia, Perez Jimenez of Venezuela, Cardenas of Mexico, Somoza of Nicaragua were all chief executives with military backgrounds. More recently, Argentina, Brazil, Bolivia, Ecuador, and Peru have also experienced military rule, and not merely the rule of chief executives with military backgrounds. Thus, there is obviously no neat distinction between civilian and military careers; the latter is certainly an asset for the former in many Latin American countries.

Clearly, the military officers of today are different from those of the post-independence period in the early nineteenth century. During the earlier period, military leaders were locally-oriented *caudillos* with a personal band of followers. Without any commitment to nationalism or professionalism, the control of any particular area fell into the hands of the *caudillo* who was frequently a large landowner and member of the traditional oligarchy. But, as changes in Latin American societies began to transform its traditional structure, the military became less the domain

9 Huntington, *The Soldier and the State,* pp. 76, 96; Lucian W. Pye, *Aspects of Political Development* (Boston: Little, Brown, 1966), pp. 172–87.

for the upper class member and increasingly became the domain of a more professional, middle class officer who was considerably more oriented to the nation and modernization. This gradual shift occurred first in Chile, Mexico, and Brazil and only in the most recent decades has it begun to spread to the rest of the region. The modernization of the military has also made officers more closely allied with newer groups rather than with the traditional oligarchy.[10] At the end of the last century, officers, especially lower-ranking officers, were being recruited from the emerging middle sectors and to some extent even from the lower sectors. Merchants, small farmers, craftsmen, and military men rather than members of the traditional oligarchy began to supply their sons as members of the military establishment. Today, for example, two-thirds of the officers in Argentina are of middle class background with generals coming from the urban areas, the upper middle class, and possessing considerable university education.[11] And military officers from the middle sectors have come to identify most closely with, and to protect the interests of, other occupational groups of the same general level—teachers, administrators, lawyers, white collar workers and others.

In addition to their middle sector backgrounds, Latin American military officers also tend to reflect in other ways recent economic and social changes. Although the ranks may still include large numbers of rural draftees, the officer is likely to be more urban and cosmopolitan than in the past. In Mexico, for example, nearly 40 percent of the officers come from the Mexico City area. Given this increasing metropolitan emphasis in background, the officers are increasingly likely to take a more contemporary view of their nation and its future. However, the fact that many military officers are frequently stationed slightly apart from, but within the immediate vicinity of, the most populous centers of their nations suggests that the military, more than other groups, are *of* but not always *in* the nation.[12]

The composition of the military officers in Latin America in other ways reflects the aspirations of the middle sectors. The military provides opportunities for upward mobility. For example, General Velasco of the Peruvian army, who helped depose President Belaunde in 1968, rose through the ranks without identifying himself with plutocrats, foreigners, civilian leaders, and other elites.[13] Although by many standards most military officers

10 John J. Johnson, *The Military and Society in Latin America* (Stanford, Calif.: Stanford University Press, 1964), p. 237.

11 Jose Luis de Imaz, *Los Que Mandan: Los Fuerzas Armadas en Argentina* (Buenos Aires: EUDEBA, 1964), pp. 55–58.

12 Jess P. Unger, "The Military Role in Nation-Building and Economic Development," *CAG Occasional Papers,* Bloomington, Indiana, 1963, p. 13.

13 Luigi Einauldi, *The Peruvian Military: A Summary Political Analysis* (Santa Monica, Calif.: Rand Corporation, 1969).

are mediocre, the greater emphasis on better trained professionals has stimulated the chances for middle sector officers to move up the ranks. In the past, for example, most officers were old-line types, or "barracks officers," who obtained their rank through political connections and activity. Although still a conservative and influential segment of the military today, this type of officer is declining in importance. Of growing significance are the "school officers" who have attended training institutes and who regard themselves as career professionals in the middle- and lower-ranking positions. Despite their greater training, however, the "school officers," like the "barracks officers," have not renounced intervention in politics. Indeed, the top leaders of the military coup which ousted President Belaunde of Peru in 1968 were members of the same graduation class at their military academy. And last, the "laboratory officers" are the youngest and lowest in rank but have received the most training, generally in the United States. Although they are less politically inclined than older officers, the "laboratory officers" can become, especially as they move up the ranks, an important political force in the military.[14]

If anything, then, the technological competence of the Latin American officer corps has improved but their inclination to intervene in politics has not substantially declined. Indeed, the career fortune of the military officer in contemporary Latin America may require a complex and sometimes bizarre combination of political pull and technical competence. In some countries—for example, Argentina—promotions depend more upon the political affiliations of the officer than on his professional qualifications.[15]

Although military officers in Latin America can differ considerably in educational and class backgrounds, they do appear to share a wide array of general sentiments about their nation and their institution. Actually, many military attitudes fuse the idea of the nation and the military. Consequently, what is good for the military is also good for the country. The close identity that most military officers have with the nation-state is quite understandable, considering that their very existence depends upon a rationale in which they view themselves as defenders and guardians of the nation against all enemies, external and internal. As compared with the traditional oligarchy that ruled in the past, this military attitude is "modern." But this must not be confused with the idea that the military corps of these countries favor the development of modern nation-states based upon democracy and egalitarianism. If anything, the values to which most officers subscribe incline toward just the opposite. Attachment to order, dignity, and hierarchy and to the concept that the opposition is an intolerable enemy are military values contradicting the free play of forces required in the democratic process. Given these

14 Victor Alba, *El Militarismo: Ensayo sobre un Fenomeno Politico-social Iberoamericano* (Mexico: Institucion de Investigaciones Sociales UNAM, 1959).

15 Perlmutter, "The Praetorian State and the Praetorian Army."

values, most military officers demonstrate an unwavering concern for political stability, although, paradoxically, they are often the principal weapon used to overthrow governments. In other words, it is quite understandable that the values of order, discipline, hierarchy and stability are enshrined in the military establishments of most countries in Latin America. No military in any country can be exempt from these principles without considerable jeopardy to its effectiveness. However, given the political importance of the individuals who believe that these principles should be extended to the operation of the entire nation-state, it becomes obvious that the military attitude contradicts some features of democratic politics.

Other values that help define military attitudes on specific issues are closely related to these nearly universal values of order, stability, discipline and hierarchy. Over the years, military officers have assumed for themselves the duty of safeguarding the nation. Since his mission is to defend his nation and his institution, the military officer is likely to interpret his actions as defending the constitution, and those who disagree with him—and especially civilians—are regarded as undermining his interpretation of what is good and bad for the country. For example, the self-righteousness with which many officers regard their actions is especially apparent when the leaders of a military coup attempt to legitimize their actions by arguing that they have saved the country from corruption, communism, or some other threat. Their duty, it is claimed at such trying moments, is to the nation and not to the civilian leaders who have, in their opinion, done such a bad job of running the country. And, of course, such ideals as "duty" and "mission" leave much room for interpretation. Is it the duty of a military officer, or a group of them, to conspire against a government, which is contrary to the constitution, in order to uphold the constitution? In effect, then, the military often says what the constitution means and how it will be protected.

Another military attitude, which is related to increasing professionalism, is the notion of corporate unity and interest of the military. Under this notion, the officer is a member of a corporate body to which he owes his undivided loyalty in the performance of some high duty and tradition. Such an institution with its responsibilities and privileges naturally must be protected, especially from the encroachments of outsiders. This corporate self-interest is a dominant concern of the military and of the civilians who must appease it.[16] What exactly is included within this corporate self-interest varies with the particular military establishment and its society. At

[16] Lyle N. McAlister, "The Military," in John J. Johnson (ed.), *Continuity and Change in Latin America* (Stanford, Calif.: Stanford University Press, 1964), p. 149; Samuel E. Finer, *The Man on Horseback*, p. 47; Samuel P. Huntington, *The Soldier and the State*, p. 79; Eric A. Nordlinger, "Soldiers in Mufti: The Impact of Military Rule upon Economic and Social Change in the Non-Western States," in *American Political Science Review*, Vol. 64, No. 4, December 1970, p. 1134.

the least, it includes a jealously for its status and privileges which, if provoked, may lead the military to assume the role of ultimate decision-maker in military affairs as well as in foreign and domestic policy. In Latin America, however, protection of the corporate self-interest of the military does not merely concern the maintenance of narrow institutional interests, but often involves the expansion of its own interests at the expense of other groups, and perhaps identifying its own interests with those of the nation to the extent that it takes control of the government.

Obviously, construed narrowly or broadly, a threat to the corporate self-interests of the military will provoke a defensive response directly involving the military in politics. Among other things, for example, the growing strength of the paramilitary Peronist urban workers led to the military overthrow of the Argentine dictator in 1955. That is, such a large group as this threatened to deprive the military of some of its privileges and power. A cut in, or even a failure to sufficiently increase military expenditures may also provoke military intervention in order to preserve the corporate self-interest. Although, as will be seen later, there are considerable divisions within the Latin American military as it becomes more deeply involved in politics, its corporate self-interest serves as a rallying point and may actually be used by its more political leaders as a symbol of considerable political potency.

In addition to the attitudes closely related to the military's operations and its corporate self-interest, most military officers have broader attitudes that extend to the nature of development and change in their societies. Most officers in Latin America, but especially those with more technical training and sophisticated education, favor the industrialization of the economies of the region, if only because industrialization is required to support the domestic production of military weaponry and to sustain military power independent of foreign suppliers. That is, in the contemporary period of costly and more sophisticated weapons, officers tend to see industrialization as a symbol of military strength and an indispensable foundation for military power in relations with other nations. Furthermore, as a modern elite in their own countries, the officers regard technical progress and industrialization generally as mandatory for all developing nations,[17] and particularly the younger and better trained officers may become greatly frustrated when the politicians are unable to overcome rapidly the economic obstacles to industrialization and economic progress.[18]

[17] John J. Johnson, "The Latin American Military as a Politically Competing Group in Transitional Society," in Johnson (ed.), *The Role of the Military in Underdeveloped Countries,* p. 111; Mario Horacio Orsolini, *Ejercito Argentino y Crecimiento Nacional* (Buenos Aires: Ediciones Arayu, 1965), pp. 279–80.

[18] Victor Alba, *El Ascenso del Militarismo Tecnocratico* (Estudioa y Documentos, 1963), p. 7.

The technocratic faith of the officers is linked to a preference for nationalistic policies against foreign entrepreneurs and for interventionist policies of the national government to promote economic development. The nationalist sentiment, which can often border on xenophobia, is not only a natural attribute of any military organization, but also reflects the strong, similar feelings of the middle sectors from which officers are largely recruited. For example, although dramatically expressed, the hostile attitude of the Peruvian military in 1968 toward foreign control of oil production is not basically different from officers' attitudes in most other Latin American countries. Moreover, officers tend to be in substantial agreement with many groups in the middle sectors over specific aspects of nationalism. They do not, for example, identify the nation with any particular civilian regime in power, and they are also generally agreed that nationalism itself should be suplemented with considerable government intervention in the economy. As public bureaucrats with a particular specialty, officers tend to place limited faith in private enterprise just as they tend to view civilian governments as inefficient and occasionally expendable factors in national life. Concerning national development in general, they favor a gradual expansion of all goods and services rather than the rapid redistribution of these goods and services.[19]

Although the general attitude of officers toward development is permeated with conservative gradualism, their faith in education, if extended to many in Latin America, contains the possibility of stimulating change. For example, military officers must command individuals of the nonofficer ranks who have a minimum level of education. When a shoeless, formally ignorant, parochial, politically unaware peasant is drafted, the experience tends strongly to change him quite basically, perhaps even making him a patriotic citizen aware of a national identity, of modern life styles, and of his potential ability to participate politically in order to pursue his own desires. If, upon release from service, the draftee chooses to remain in the mainstream of national life, he is certainly a different person from the peasant who knew little of and cared even less about contemporary national society. Even if he returns to his former life, he takes with him some education and experiences that may subtly affect those in his village.

The attitudes of military officers toward their institution, nation, and the future are certainly more complex than portrayed here. Obviously, what individual officers believe in a specific instance will be affected by other factors, such as personal and political rivalries. But no one can deny John J. Johnson's argument that what officers feel or believe will probably for some time continue to be decisive factors in the formation of national goals and aspirations.[20] As an elite in most Latin American countries, and the ruling

[19] Johnson, *The Military and Society in Latin America,* pp. 135–49.

[20] Johnson, *The Military and Society in Latin America,* p. 3.

elite in some, military officers are committed to general attitudes which reflect their privileged position over other power contenders in Latin American politics.

POLITICAL ROLES OF THE MILITARY

Having argued that military officers in Latin America comprise one of the most important political elites, it is appropriate to shift from a focus upon those who are individual members of this elite to the nature of the elite as a political, if not always united, group in Latin American politics. Earlier, it was argued that the Latin American military, like the military of other developing areas, is principally geared not to external defense but to a variety of political roles and activities that have direct domestic consequences. Given this fact of political life in Latin America, the nature of this political participation of the military must be explored in order to evaluate what the military officers want, demand, and receive in the Latin American political systems.

It is clear that the military in Latin America performs more than one political role. According to one observer, the military acts as an institutional interest group that helps or harms the interests of other groups; it serves a military purpose, but only if viewed broadly; and it performs various public service functions, such as building highways, or conducting civic action programs involving community participation, if for no other reason than to limit the appeal of guerrilla activity.[21] But the key problem is to understand why the military breaks out of these fairly limited roles and assumes the tasks of overtly running the government, heavily dominating those who do run it, or participating in important ways in daily government operations. In any event, military intervention in politics increases rather than declines during the intermediate stages of development as problems of change escape solution by political institutions.

One role of the military in Latin America is that of an institutionalized governorship in which military officers, apparently feeling that they can run the government better than can the civilians, assume control without the intention of sooner or later returning it to civilians.[22] The military regimes which came to power in Brazil in 1964 and in Peru in 1968 seem to have acted in this fashion. Closely related to this, and sometimes difficult

---

[21] McAlister, "The Military," pp. 136–58; Richard N. Adams, *The Second Sowing: Power and Secondary Development in Latin America* (San Francisco: Chandler, 1967), Ch. 12.

[22] Gino Germani and Kalman Silvert, "Politics, Social Structure and Military Intervention in Latin America," in *European Journal of Sociology,* Vol. 3, 1961, pp. 62–81; Janowitz, *The Military in the Political Development of New Nation,* p. 85; Thomas M. Millington, "The Latin American Military Elite," in *Current History,* Vol. 46, No. 333, May 1969, p. 352.

to distinguish from it, is the role of trustee governorship in which the military apparently intends to seize and run the government until such time as it feels the civilian politicians are capable of supplying a coherent and stable regime. This role is what most leaders of military coups claim as theirs, although not all have enough faith in the civilian political processes to return the government to civilian hands. For example, in Peru the military is particularly antagonistic toward the APRA, the party led by Haya de la Torre. As the *de facto* ultimate judge of elections, the military in 1962 seized the government to prevent Haya de la Torre from assuming the presidency.[23] Until recently, most coups have been of this type, but military impatience with civilian politics has threatened to shift the emphasis to institutionalized and relatively permanent governorships rather than the more temporary trusteeships.

The other roles of the military in civilian-military relations do not involve the military as directly as occupying positions of executive power generally reserved for civilians. According to Germani and Silvert, the military may orient national policy without directly assuming policy-making positions. That is, the military sets the broad limits within which the civilians must confine their policy-making. Failing to remain within these limits may bring on military wrath in the form of a coup in which the military becomes an institutionalized or trustee governor. Prior to the military takeover in Argentina in 1966, the military exercised this role, overtly containing the policies of the government and limiting the power of the Peronista workers.[24]

Still more limited but also less frequent, the military may serve as a pressure group with veto power. It can prevent civilian policies that threaten it as an institution but it cannot initiate policies that lie outside its institutional interests, as in Chile. Having even less political importance the military may act as a pressure group within a setting largely dominated by civilian political groups, as in Uruguay. Costa Rica has a military that plays the role of a simple police force completely dominated by the civilian government. With a small, 5,000 man civilian guard, the Costa Ricans are reluctant even to call it an army. Finally, the military role may involve the military as a political arm of the state. This role is generally restricted to the regimes of the revolutionary left, of which there have been very few in Latin America. The principal contemporary example of this role is Castro's Cuba where the professional army was disbanded and its functions turned over to civilian militias. Those army officers not purged were highly indoctrinated in the revolutionary ideology of the Castro regime.

[23] Victor Villanueva, *El Militarismo en el Peru* (Lima: Empresa Grafica T. Scheuch, S. A., 1962), p. 198.

[24] Ruben Bortnik, *El Ejercito Argentino y el Arte de lo Posible* (Buenos Aires: Ediciones Guemes, 1967), p. 40.

It should be made clear that more than one of these roles, including those involving the military as governor, may be found in one military establishment at the same time and over time.[25] In Argentina, for example, several kinds of military intervention have been used since the 1930s, ranging from the veto role to the governor role.[26]

The military, however, does not itself escape disruption as it intervenes in politics, because as it intervenes, in whatever way, it becomes more divided. Younger officers may be aligned against the older ones; one branch of service may be pitted against another branch (for example, the navy is generally more conservative than the army); regional and personal rivalries will become exaggerated as political questions become primary; conflicting civilian groups will attempt to use different members of the military to intervene on their behalf. Overall, a politically active military leads to a decline in unity of command and professionalism.

Actually, the close political relationship between different sectors of the officer corps with different sectors of the civilian populace means that it is somewhat misleading to view military politics simply as a problem of intervention because, in effect, the Latin American military is not politically isolated from other groups. That is, the Latin American military interacts with other groups, not just against other groups. The political interests or elements within the military become identified with those of the middle sector and other more specialized groups. The question then becomes not one of the military posed against everyone else, but of certain groups within the military aligning with certain civilian groups for mutual protection of interests.

DESIRES AND DEMANDS

In describing the political importance of the Latin American military, the members of the officer corps, and their methods of intervening in Latin American politics, the foundation has been laid for a discussion of what the military officers want, demand and get from the political systems of the region. It is difficult to separate these aspects of the military officers because what the officers desire, they generally demand, and what they demand, they generally receive.

Above all, the military in Latin America wants to be certain that despite whatever socioeconomic changes occur, its own corporate self-interest will be served. Of course, in Latin America exactly what constitutes the corporate self-interest of the military is not determined generally by the civilian politicians but by the military officers themselves. In marginal cases

[25] Germani and Silvert, "Politics, Social Structure and Military Intervention in Latin America." Cf. p. 201.

[26] de Imaz, *Los Que Mandan,* pp. 47–51.

in which misunderstanding between the military and the civilians crops up, a civilian government may inaccurately assess the military's regard for its corporate self-interest. In such cases, the continued viability of the civilian government becomes extremely doubtful. For example, President Goulart's challenge to the principle of military discipline in March, 1964, triggered, although it was not the principal cause of, the military coup which deposed him.[27] Therefore, the corporate self-interest is of primary importance not only to the military but also to the civilian government which depends for its continued existence upon a relatively satisfied military establishment.

Of the various aspects of corporate self-interest which the military seeks to protect, its own survival as a relatively autonomous institution is the most vital but generally the least threatened. There are very few cases in which the military as a relatively autonomous and even dominant institution has been jeopardized or threatened by the civilians. (Uruguay and Costa Rica never did have important military establishments.) More than once the military has used the argument that it must intervene to protect its very survival. For example, the Dominican Republic army toppled Juan Bosch as president in 1963 with the justification that his regime presented a "Communist" threat to eventually destroy the army and its leadership.[28] However, Mexico stands as a valid, but partial, exception. During the 1930s, President Cardenas professionalized the military, incorporating it as one of the four countervailing sectors of the revolutionary party, which ultimately became the present PRI. By the 1940s when the revolution had become clearly institutionalized, the military had no important voice in policies that did not directly concern it. Instead of basically dismembering the military, President Cardenas, himself an old revolutionary general, was able with the help of the junior officers to oust those revolutionary generals who wanted to play the traditional power role, leaving behind a relatively professional army concerned principally with economic development, community projects, and support for orderly government.[29]

27 Thomas E. Skidmore, *Politics in Brazil, 1930–1964: An Experiment in Democracy* (New York: Oxford University Press, 1967).

28 Howard J. Wiarda, "The Politics of Civil-Military Relations in the Dominican Republic," in *Journal of Inter-American Studies,* Vol. 3, No. 4, October 1965, p. 480.

29 Karl M. Schmitt, "The Roles of the Military in Contemporary Mexico," in A. Curtis Wilgus (ed.), *The Caribbean: Mexico Today* (Gainesville: University of Florida Press, 1964), pp. 55–57; Irving Louis Horowitz, "The Military Elites," in Seymour Martin Lipset and Aldo Solari (eds.), *Elites in Latin America* (New York: Oxford University Press, 1967), p. 168; Edwin Lieuwin, *Arms and Politics in Latin America* (New York: Praeger, 1961), pp. 101–21; Peter Calvert, "The Institutionalisation of the Mexican Revolution," in *Journal of Inter-American Studies,* Vol. 9, No. 4, October 1969; Edwin Lieuwin, *Mexican Militarism* (Albuquerque: University of New Mexico Press, 1968).

The only major example of a basic threat to the survival of the military as an institution is Castro's Cuba. Before Castro's rise to power in 1959, the military, of course, generally supported the Batista government. Batista himself was a sergeant in the 1930s, using a revolt of the young officers and enlisted men to rise to power. As the conflict with Castro's forces continued in the 1950s, it became obvious that Batista's government suffered from a number of weaknesses that infected the military's enthusiasm to pursue an aggressive campaign against Castro. When the end came, the government's army was eventually dismantled, many of the officers were dismissed and/or shot, and even those officers in Castro's own army were not immune from the purge. In the Cuban case, given Castro's peculiar brand of Communist revolution, the fate of the government army as it had been was almost predetermined. The elimination of the old army officers and the establishment of the military as a militia functioning as a political arm of a Marxist state are prospects that most officers in the rest of Latin America regard as totally unacceptable.

The Cuban experience also reinforces the uncompromising anticommunism of the region's top military officers. Fearing that radical changes of a similar type would jeopardize their position (even their lives) as well as their institution, they will use every available method to ensure the continued existence of their institution and its relative autonomy from the domination of revolutionary politics. Fortunately for such officers, the threat is more imagined than real, but it is a useful weapon against less radical opponents demanding changes.

The corporate self-interest of the Latin American military concerns not only institutional survival, but extends far beyond to include such things as the maintenance and expansion of their wealth and prerogatives, both as individual officers and as an elite group.[30] Despite the obvious economic drain that these desires place on the economic system in general and on other groups in particular, the military officers often want and demand a continuous growth of military expenditures for large and small arms, equipment, personnel, and such. Whenever a military government exists, the officer corps is in a very advantageous position to increase its own resources through the public treasury. In those Latin American countries dominated by the military, 18.5% of the government expenditures go to the military compared with 9.3% in those countries with a politically uninvolved military.[31] Even if the formal responsibility for allocating the budget lies in the hands of nonmilitary men, what the military wants and demands as a minimum cannot be ignored. For example, when President Betancourt assumed office in 1958, he was very careful, as Venezuela's first civilian pres-

[30] Nordlinger, "Soldiers in Mufti," p. 1134.

[31] Ibid., p. 1135.

ident in ten years, to provide liberal allotments for jet aircraft and fringe benefits in return for military support of his moderate reform programs.[32] Similarly, the average percentage of the gross national product spent for defense in those countries with military rule was 3.6 between the years 1957 and 1962. Even when the military does not overtly seize control of government, the percentage of the gross national product is still impressive— 3.4%.[33] In short, although the corporate self-interest of the military is often an ambiguous concept, at least one thing is clear: the military desires and demands a sizable portion of the public treasury and the country's productivity.

As in many large organizations, some of the corporate desires are expressed for individual gains. Actually, one of the reasons why the military attracts ambitious, middle sector individuals is that it provides a regularly-paid salary. In Brazil, for example, where the government very generously responds to the budgetary demands of the military, the salaries and benefits of the officers are better than those of the average civilian of comparable education and experience.[34] In Mexico, officer salaries are modest but comfortable, with annual increases. In addition to the usual privileges of power such as bribes and kickbacks, the military officers, especially those in positions of political importance, often have ready access to low interest loans which are not available to other groups. Retirement pensions are also relatively generous. For example, Argentina retires its officers at full pay after thirty years.[35]

In some countries, the salary scale, even for officers, is insufficient, but officers are expected, and often encouraged, to search for additional sources of income. In Guatemala, for example, there are two principal ways of obtaining extra income.[36] Additional stipends are provided for serving in certain high posts which, of course, leads to much political competition for the extra income. But, also, officers in the Guatemalan military are allowed to engage in private enterprise, and many do so, especially by investing their capital into absentee-landlord operations. Or, for example, under military dictator Rojas Pinilla, Colombian officers, especially those of higher ranks, profited from post exchanges, rebates on wholesale commodity prices, and bank loans on dubious security.[37] In Brazil and other countries, officers in

[32] Ibid., p. 1136.

[33] Ibid., p. 1135.

[34] Johnson, *The Military and Society in Latin America*, p. 236.

[35] Ibid., p. 103.

[36] Richard N. Adams, "The Development of the Guatemalan Military," in *Studies in Comparative International Development*, Vol. 4, No. 5, 1968–1969, p. 92.

[37] J. León Helguera, "The Changing Role of the Military in Colombia," in *Journal of Inter-American Studies*, Vol. 3, No. 3, July 1961, p. 355.

certain posts are permitted to hold extra jobs. In those countries, such as Guatemala and Colombia, where the level of military professionalism even by Latin American standards is still quite low, such methods of raising the income of officers may compromise their potential professionalism but nevertheless make a military career relatively lucrative.

In addition to institutional survival—which is rarely in doubt—and generous budgetary requests, the military also expresses, implicitly or not, desires for a key role in the operation of governmental affairs and politics in general. Sometimes, this is expressed by demands for staffing largely civilian posts with military officers. Even in those countries where the military does not directly run the government or occupy the position of the chief executive, it often demands that its personnel hold positions not only in the military ministries but also in autonomous and semi-autonomous agencies which perform largely civilian tasks. In other words, despite considerable variations throughout the countries that have important military establishments, military men many times demand positions in civilian administration. These demands are not limited simply to appointive, bureaucratic posts with the central government. Even in Mexico, for example, which has bridled its military much better than most Latin American countries, officers hold a large portion of the governorships of the states and a similarly impressive number of national legislators in the Senate and in the Chamber of Deputies carry military titles.[38] In other countries officers also occupy key positions requiring technical skills involving economic development, public works, banking, construction and education. With its skepticism toward civilian ability, it seems inevitable that the military insist that its officers be permitted to exercise civilian duties in the name of the national interest. And with the frequent inability of civilian politics to solve problems, coupled with the military's self-confidence nourished by training and administrative experience, many government agencies come to rely upon the military officer corps to staff important, technical positions.[39]

As an institution, the military seeks to maintain if not increase its political role in the developing countries of Latin America. Paradoxically, however, this aspect of corporate self-interest, upon which most officers agree, often becomes the source of severe internal disagreement regarding specific political issues and especially regarding the military's role in promoting or retarding socioeconomic changes. Despite its advantages of organization, once it enters the political arena, the military often becomes acutely divided. As in Argentina, these divisions may be magnified into national crises.[40]

[38] Johnson, *The Military and Society in Latin America,* pp. 129–31.

[39] Ibid., pp. 198–206, 212.

[40] Robert A. Potash, "The Changing Role of the Military in Argentina," in *Journal of Inter-American Studies,* Vol. 3, No. 4, October 1961, p. 571.

Explanations of motivations behind military desires and demands are quite varied. Lieuwin, for example, argues that military intervention, as the expression of a demand for participation and for a particular policy, is due to self-interested motives.[41] Similarly, looking at the Ecuadorian military coup of 1963, Needler found that the personal motivations of the coup leaders were more important than ideological justifications. Only later was the argument used that the military had to overthrow President Arosemena to protect the national interest.[42] This line of argument also stresses that military intervention to protect its corporate self-interest and to enhance personal ambitions has been greatly stimulated by the perceived threat of "communism" which favors the abolition of the traditional army in favor of a popular militia. For example, the Bolivian commander-in-chief, after the successful overthrow of President Paz Estenssoro in 1964, claimed that important segments of the President's support came from individuals who, as part of a Communist tactic, wanted to disband the army.[43] The case of Cuba, and even of Bolivia in 1952 and Mexico in 1914, provides sufficient evidence to already suspicious officers in Latin America that revolutionary change means the elimination of their institution.[44] From this perpective then, military officers are viewed principally as demanding, through intervention, a wide array of personal or narrow institutional wants. And since the military generally occupies a highly favorable position within the Latin American political systems, satisfaction of these demands is regarded as serving conservative rather than progressive ends, spending money that could be spent for more reformist programs, and serving the interest of the relatively privileged elite rather than serving the interests of the lower sectors.

Contrasted to this view is the tendency to regard the military as a reformist group that wants and demands comprehensive but gradual changes for the socioeconomic development of their nations. Instead of stressing the relatively narrow corporate self-interests of a privileged elite, the military, in this view, allows, when it does not actually lead, the national

41 Lieuwin, *Arms and Politics in Latin America;* Edwin Lieuwin, *Generals vs. Presidents: Neo-Militarism in Latin America* (New York: Praeger 1964); Edwin Lieuwin, "The Military: A Force for Continuity or Change," in John TePaske and Sydney N. Fisher (eds.), *Explosive Forces in Latin America* (Columbus: Ohio State University Press, 1964).

42 Martin C. Needler, *Anatomy of A Coup d'Etat: Ecuador 1963.* (Washington, D.C.: Institute for the Comparative Study of Political Systems, 1964).

43 Martin C. Needler, "The Latin American Military: Predatory Reactionaries or Modernizing Patriots," in *Journal of Inter-American Studies,* Vol. 11, No. 2, April 1969, p. 241; William H. Brill, *Military Intervention in Bolivia: The Overthrow of Paz Estenssoro and the MNR* (Washington, D.C.: Institute for Comparative Study of Political Systems, 1967), p. 60.

44 Lieuwin, "Militarism and Politics in Latin America," p. 146.

pursuit of industrialization, technological progress, educational advancement, political stability, and the development of modern life styles for the general populace. Sometimes this argument starts from the idea that the good soldier is a modernized man himself because he must break with the past in order to function as a member of his institution. Within his institution, the soldier is given new foreign models for his personal development. Borrowing from the West, the soldier ideally becomes one of the most modern segments of Latin American society. As an administrator and politician, the military officer may become that rare individual in Latin America who can combine political power with the inclination to use it for modernizing purposes.[45]

There is, of course, something to be said for both views. That is, what the military officers of Latin America want and demand may consist of narrow selfishness with a conservative bias and it may also consist of nationalistic and patriotic demands for development and modernization. Military intervention in Latin American politics may be motivated by both these narrower institutional interests and broader concerns of socioeconomic change. But given our interest in the problems of socioeconomic change in Latin America, the question of just what role military officers play in promoting or retarding such changes must be more thoroughly evaluated.

Those who view the Latin American military chiefly as promoters of socioeconomic change and development begin with the relatively advanced backgrounds of the officer corps. From this beginning, observers such as John J. Johnson argue that the military favors development because it is oriented to industrialization, nationalism, state intervention, technological progress, and education. However, advocates of this view do not seriously deny that the military in Latin America favors only gradual change and that it is ambivalent to agrarian reform and sometimes openly hostile to other reform programs. Moreover, they admit that the military does not equate development with democracy. Such concepts are apparently foreign to many military officers who prefer that change be directed or controlled from above rather than accelerated from below. Besides, the military has a jaundiced view of elections in which civilian politics often confuse and sometimes threaten the preferences of the military for orderly and stable conduct in public affairs.

In the past, various military groups and individuals have supported socioeconomic changes. Earlier in this century, some military officers were reformers aligned with the middle sectors against the ruling oligarchy.[46] Calles of Mexico, Ibanez of Chile, Peron of Argentina, Franco of Paraguay,

---

[45] Lucian W. Pye, *Aspects of Political Development* (*Boston*: Little, Brown, 1966), Ch. 9.

[46] Johnson, "The Latin American Military as a Politically Competing Group in Transitional Society," pp. 110–13.

Busch and Villaroel of Bolivia, Remon of Panama, Arbenz of Guatemala and Cardenas of Mexico were to some extent reformers opposed to the oligarchy and to the oligarchy's colleagues in the military.[47] But in most of Latin America today, the middle-sector military is no longer the reformist and democratic group it once might have been. In a number of countries, the military has actually intervened to protect the middle sectors against the growing numbers of the urban working sector.[48] In Argentina in 1962, military officers divided into factions: those who were moderate toward the *peronista* labor-left; those who felt they owed something to the *peronistas;* and those who strongly opposed *peronistas*. Although these factions split the military on the issue of the middle versus the lower sectors, the hardliners have generally prevailed against the *peronistas* and in favor of the middle sectors.[49] The problem of participation was raised in slightly different fashion. An open election there often presents the possibility—as it did in 1962—that the *peronistas,* if allowed to assume the numerous positions in Congress and the governorships that they won in that election, would gain a nightmarish advantage over the middle sectors and their spokesmen within the military. In Brazil, alleging threats of communism, as well as pointing to corruption and inflation, the military leaders of the 1964 coup initiated an effort to protect the middle sectors, as well as businessmen and landowners, who felt threatened by the greater participation of the lower sectors under the leadership of President João Goulart. Lacking the unity and numbers to counteract the growing threat of mass participation, the military intervened as institutionalized govenors on behalf of these groups by abolishing the political rights of opponents and voiding the powers of civilian institutions.

In these cases, by intervening through coups and remaining in power as institutionalized governors, the military has attempted to nullify the threat of organized and possible armed urban labor and to slow down the chances for rapid reform or threats to privileged groups. Of course, the middle sectors have not always been implacable enemies of the working sectors in these countries. In fact, the middle sectors have at times aligned with parts of the lower sectors to contest the control of the traditional oligarchy.[50]

[47] Lieuwin, *Arms and Politics in Latin America,* p. 129; Marvin Goldwert, "The Rise of Modern Militarism in Argentina," in *Hispanic American Historical Review,* Vol. 48, No. 2, May 1968, pp. 189–205.

[48] Jose Nun, "A Latin American Phenomenon: The Middle-Class Military Coup," in James Petras and Maurice Zeitlin (eds.), *Latin America: Reform or Revolution?* (Greenwich, Conn.: Fawcett Publications, 1968), pp. 145–85.

[49] Lieuwin, *Generals vs. Presidents,* pp. 13–17; James W. Rowe, "Argentina's Restless Military," in *American Universities Field Staff Report,* May 1964.

[50] For a description of one of these earlier episodes, see Jordan Young, "Military Aspects of the 1930 Brazilian Revolution," *Hispanic American Historical Review,* Vol. 44, No. 2, May 1964.

But in countries like Brazil, Colombia, and Venezuela the political potential of the lower sectors is growing rapidly and they are not easily susceptible to control by the fragmented middle sector. It is at such a point in time that the military, prompted by some particular event or situation, intervenes to represent the desires and demands of the insecure and vulnerable middle sectors against the peasants and urban workers. In Uruguay, Chile, and Mexico, moreover, the military helped the middle sector achieve the stability it lacks in most of Latin America. But such intervention by the military in most of Latin America only temporarily alleviates the problem because it maintains the system in which similar crises of participation by new groups will sooner or later arise.[51] The middle-sector military coup, then, both manifests and promotes immobility in Latin America.

Despite the conservative nature of the desires and demands of most military officers—emphasizing restricted rather than mass participation, modernization rather than reform, and stability over change—the desires and demands of some military officers in contemporary Latin America seem, on the surface at least, to be rather progressive. Perhaps the most obvious example of military reformism is in Peru. In 1968, a military coup led by reformers, but having the support of more conservative officers, toppled the well-meaning but ineffective government of President Belaunde. There does not seem to be much doubt that the military has made changes of political importance since then, but it is too early to be sure what these changes mean and how important they really are.

What the military regime of Peru wants and demands in terms of socioeconomic change is not at all clear to everyone. On the one hand, there are those who claim that the Peruvian military has brought a nonviolent, but nonetheless genuine, revolution to the country. There are others who are not quite so sure. Although not all the facts are known, what is known tends to deny complete support of either view.

Despite the unclear impact of the military regime on Peru's political system in general, most agree that the Peruvian military is itself not the same institution that it was years ago. Antiforeign, antioligarchical, anti-private enterprise, the military wants to free the country from its dependence on outside interests and from the immobility of its archaic social structure. Sincerely concerned with the ineffectiveness of civilian politics to promote development and to quiet the discontent of guerrilla insurgents, the military has begun to make long overdue adjustments to make the present system more workable.[52] The military has pushed land reform and cooperatives in the coastal estates, profit sharing, joint-ownership, the restriction

[51] Nun, "A Latin American Phenomenon," pp. 145–85.

[52] Luigi R. Einauldi, *Peruvian Military Relations with the United States* (Santa Monica, Calif.: Rand Corporation, 1970), p. 10; Luigi R. Einauldi and Alfred C. Stepan, *Latin American Institutional Development: Changing Military Perspectives in Peru and Brazil* (Santa Monica, Calif.: Rand Corporation, 1971).

and the expropriation of foreign investment (as in the IPC affair), government-control of minerals, and greater public control of foreign exchange transactions and utilities. The general intentions of these policies are clear: to bring a more egalitarian and just society to one that has never had much of either.

Judged on this alone, the Peruvian military would be an important exception to the idea that Latin American military officers play a conservative role on behalf of the middle sectors within their complex and fragmented societies. But, from what has happened so far and/or may take place in the future, the role of the Peruvian military in promoting socioeconomic change may not be so different after all. Some see these reforms as inherently limited and even necessary to keep things from changing completely under a Castro-like revolution. For example, the land reform attacked the old landed oligarchy but it also attacked the influence of the military's only comparable competitor for political power—the APRA party. Moreover, the land reform allowed the rural elites to move into the industrial sector.[53] It also undermined APRA's influence in the rural areas. The reforms are limited in another important way: these policies come from above and exclude broad participation by the masses. By using military and bureaucratic dominance of developmental policy, the military is falling under the conservative institutions that cannot govern Peru.[54] By demanding that a few at the top of the bureaucracy make decisions about national development, the military may place intolerable burdens on government that it does not have the capabilities to carry.[55] As the military more and more gets involved in specific policies of development, disunity and factionalism may split the military as a disciplined institution and water down its reformist inclinations.[56] Its political authoritarianism and centralized control of the economy may eventually make the middle sectors restive and the emphasis on social justice and rapid development, if carried too far, will be opposed by the civilian elites.[57] So, despite a reformist beginning, the Peruvian military may find that their desires and demands for further socioeconomic change may undermine their own institution and the system

[53] Julio Cotler, "Political Crisis and Military Populism in Peru," in *Studies in Comparative International Development,* Vol. 6, No. 5, 1970–1971, p. 107.

[54] Einauldi, *Peruvian Military Relations with the U.S.,* p. 24; Luigi R. Einauldi, *Revolution From Within? Military Rule in Peru Since 1968* (Santa Monica, Calif.: Rand Corporation, 1971), p. 14.

[55] Richard Lee Clinton, "The Modernizing Military: The Case of Peru," in *Inter-American Economic Affairs,* Vol. 24, No. 4, Spring 1971, p. 56.

[56] Ibid., p. 64; Einauldi, *Peruvian Military Relations with the U.S.,* p. 22.

[57] Einauldi and Stepan, *Latin American Institutional Development,* p. 138.

which assures its political importance. Unlike Brazil, where economic development has gone farther than anywhere else in Latin America and where the military is suspicious of social justice and rapid change, Peru, which has undergone less development, has a military establishment that is progressive compared with other Peruvian elites, but that is an establishment nonetheless. As such, it cannot be as radical as some would hope nor can it run the country regardless of the factors that elevated it to such power.

Sometimes, the military unintentionally broadens political participation. This was the case in Colombia when Rojas Pinilla took over the government in the early 1950s from the Liberals and Conservatives who were unable to control civil disorder.[58] In order to build popular support for his government, Rojas made some appeals to the lower sectors; when their expectations were not met, due in part to the military's inability to run a government once in power, he was forced to relinquish his position.[59] Furthermore, in order to build the support necessary to take over a government, political arrangements must frequently be made within the military itself which include conservative, moderate, and progressive officers within a ruling coalition. In the Brazilian coup of 1964, for example, the "hard-liners" among the officers spent considerable effort trying to convince the older moderates of the need to oust Goulart.[60]

However, when officers expressing relatively progressive and reformist demands constitute or help to constitute a military government, their demands may legitimize their actions in the eyes of the lower sectors, but once in power their ability to achieve what they claim is very limited. Moreover, ambitious junior officers may use the banners of modernization and reform to legitimize their efforts to move up the military hierarchy, and once successful, forget their pronouncements in favor of their own particular interests.[61] In short, although the military does include some younger, progressive officers who become involved in military intervention to express liberal desires and demands, their success, as will be seen later, is severely compromised once they achieve power.

More generally, the military officer corps will simply fail to act as an agent of development or, through intervention, actively oppose socio-economic changes where the middle sectors are relatively wealthy, as in Brazil and Argentina. That is, where the middle sectors and the military have a relatively large stake in society, the military will intervene conserva-

---

[58] Vernon Lee Fluharty, *Dance of the Millions: Military Rule and the Social Revolution in Colombia* (Pittsburgh: University of Pittsburgh Press, 1957), p. 311.

[59] Lieuwin, "Militarism and Politics in Latin America," pp. 152–54.

[60] Skidmore, *Politics in Brazil, 1930–1964*.

[61] Nordlinger, "Soldiers in Mufti," p. 448.

tively to protect such interests against the peasants and workers of the lower sector. If socioeconomic change has not yet developed to the point that there is no serious threat from below, the military will be more inclined to promote economic change. In more traditional societies, such as Nicaragua, Honduras, and Haiti, the officer may be progressive and even radical. But, as participation in politics increases throughout the political system of a developing country, such as in Brazil, the military arbitrates the interests of middle sector groups while at the same time attempting to prevent mass participation from threatening the existing order to which the military is committed.[62]

Despite the fact that the Brazilian military shares some of the same desires and demands of the Peruvian military, the military government of Brazil is very cautious and suspicious of rapid change.[63] True enough, the military in Brazil and Peru both see the problem of national security within the broader context of economic development and political ineffectiveness. Moreover, both insist that the military become deeply involved in politics in lieu of the bankruptcy of civilian institutions. Both favor a minor (if any) role for political participation of the masses. Nevertheless, aside from the shared conviction that the military must play some political role, the Brazilian military diverges quite markedly from the Peruvian military over questions of change. For one thing, the Brazilians favor a corporate-style, mixed economy in which the military government and the economic elites agree that industrial growth is more important than social justice. On related questions, the Brazilians also are conservative, adhering to a pro-U.S. foreign policy, economic favors for big business and the landed elite, and prefering order enforced from above rather than change from below. Since 1968, the military government has been unable to set up a consistent policy that fosters ordered change in the country. In large and complex Brazil, the military is finding out that the fragmented politics of Brazil are highly resistant to even the desires and demands of the country's most formidable institution. If the military does not find a formula for blending its demands for control and change, it may become more isolated than ever and may have to go back to its old role as political moderator.

Put differently, in the fragmented societies of Latin America, limited participation is most likely to guarantee at least temporary political stability. And while some groups can pressure the government to reduce instability

[62] Nordlinger, "Soldiers in Mufti" pp. 1143–44; Huntington, *Political Order in Changing Societies,* pp. 221–22.

[63] This comparison draws from Einauldi and Stepan, *Latin American Institutional Development,* and Alfred C. Stepan, *The Military in Politics: Changing Patterns in Brazil* (Princeton, N.J.: Princeton University Press, 1971).

and change, the military can demand and secure the replacement of the government if—as has frequently happened—the government cannot *guarantee* stability. So despite its desires for modernization, the military's intervention, as a form of expressing substantive demands, serves more to limit participation that is ultimately necessary in a modern and developed political system.[64] As participation rises faster than economic development, the military acts as a conservative force to prevent the satisfaction of demands of the newly participating lower sectors for drastic social change.[65]

As the size of the middle sectors has increased, the military has carried out fewer coups of a reformist nature. Between 1935 and 1944, 50 percent of all successful coups were reformist. In the 1955 to 1964 period, the percentage of reformist coups dropped to 17.[66] Actually, the majority of coups in more recent years were aimed at preventing popular leaders from meeting the demands of the lower sectors.[67] In short, only when the civilian political institutions of Latin America can, in a stable fashion, handle demands for mass participation will the military, as in Uruguay and Mexico, assume a relatively nonpolitical and more professional role.[68] But since mass participation inhibits the possibility of successful military intervention, the military will likely attempt to restrict great political involvement of the lower sectors.[69]

The desires and demands of most Latin American military establishments will continue to be important for the political life of their respective countries. But, although there are some common desires and demands from country to country, the impression should not be encouraged that these are constant within each establishment. Personal, generational, political, and inter-service rivalries permeate the military organizations of all these countries. Also, as a natural consequence of the praetorian state and its

[64] Martin C. Needler, "The Latin American Military," pp. 243–44; Martin C. Needler, *Political Development in Latin America* (New York: Random House, 1968), p. 64; Ernest A. Duff and John F. McCamant, "Measuring Social and Political Requirements for System Stability in Latin America," in *American Political Science Review,* Vol. 62, No. 4, December 1968.

[65] Martin C. Needler, "Political Development and Socio-Economic Development: The Case of Latin America," in *American Political Science Review,* Vol. 62, No. 3, September 1968, 889–97; Martin C. Needler, "Political Development and Military Intervention in Latin America," in *American Political Science Review,* Vol. 60, September 1966, 616–26.

[66] Needler, *Political Development in Latin America,* p. 65.

[67] Nordlinger, "Soldiers in Mufti," p. 1148.

[68] Huntington, *Political Order in Changing Societies,* p. 222.

[69] Robert D. Putnam, "Toward Explaining Military Intervention in Latin American Politics," in *World Politics,* Vol. 20, No. 1, October 1967, p. 97.

particular form of immobile politics in Latin America, the military is fragmented although it is more unified as an institution than are the middle sectors as a categorical group. Therefore, the desires and demands of officers will depend not only upon certain common features of the military, but upon the alliances that factions of them form with external groups. Such alliances may want and demand change. Or they may favor stability, order, and immobility. In any event, the military officers of Latin America in many ways express their desires to their political systems. How the systems respond to their demands may determine not only who will be allowed to fill important positions, but also the future directions these political systems will take.

SYSTEM RESPONSE

Having considered the desires and demands of the military officers, especially as expressed through various forms of intervention in politics, there remains the question of how successful they are in achieving their demands. In most of Latin America, the military as an institution wants a great deal and, on the whole, consistently receives much of what it demands. In fact, of all the important political groups in Latin America, the military is perhaps the most successful in achieving what it wants from politics. Of course, the fortunes of individual military officers are more variable, depending upon political gamesmanship, career opportunities, and a number of other considerations. Therefore, we have the common situation in which one military commander, in alliance with a certain faction, deposes another military officer who occupies the chief executive position. The basic strength of the military as a political institution has not been threatened but the fate of particular officers has changed. The price of such manueverings to the military institution, however, may be somewhat high because the unity of the officer corps is severely hampered.

Perhaps the most impressive and visible indication that the military of Latin America receives much of what it demands is the substantial sums of money allocated for military spending. As noted earlier, the percentage of the government budget allocated to military spending is quite high, whether or not the military overtly controls the government.[70] Moreover, the highest expenditures for arms are in those countries that have high economic growth rates.[71] In 1967, total military expenditures in Latin America came

[70] Irving Louis Horowitz, *Three Worlds of Development: The Theory and Practice of International Stratification* (New York: Oxford University Press, 1966), p. 269.

[71] Thomas A. Brown, *Statistical Indications of the Effect of Military Programs, 1950–1965.* (Santa Monica, Calif.: Rand Corporation, 1969), p. 19.

to $2,268,000,000, with Brazil, Argentina, Cuba, Mexico, Venezuela and Peru being the largest spenders. Overall, Latin America spent about 2 percent of all its gross national product on military expenditures that year.[72] Looked at differently, military expenditures in Latin America have grown significantly from the late 1930s despite the lack of wars in the area, although the actual percentage of the total government burget devoted to military spending has declined somewhat.[73] In the early 1960s, Haiti, Paraguay, the Dominican Republic, Colombia and Peru had the highest percentages alloted to military expenditures, averaging about 20 percent of their budgets.[74] In some countries, such as Chile, defense spending as a percentage of total government spending has been declining since the late 1950s.[75] In others, like Mexico and Venezuela, the defense budget is quite stable at 7 percent and 10 percent, respectively.[76] On the other hand, Colombia has experienced unstable military budgets, ranging within a four year period between about 16 percent to 23 percent of the total government budget.[77] Depending upon the situation in a particular country, the military claims from a moderate to a large portion of the government budget.

Related to general military spending are the numbers of officers and enlisted men in the armed forces, estimates of which vary considerably. Joseph E. Loftus suggests that in 1965 the armed forces in Latin America— excluding Cuba—totalled 694,000 men, including officers, enlisted men, and draftees.[78] By far the largest armed forces were in Brazil (200,000) and Argentina (132,000), with Peru (70,000) and Mexico (60,000) a poor third and fourth. In 1967, the total number of the armed forces has been estimated at 944,000 (a substantial increase over the earlier approximation) or four members of the armed forces per 1,000 of the general population of the area. Cuba, Honduras, and El Salvador maintained about 20 or more

[72] U.S. Arms Control and Disarmament Agency, *World Military Expenditures, 1969.* (Washington, D.C.: U.S. Government Printing Office, 1970), Table 2, p. 12.

[73] Charles Wolf, "The Political Effects of Military Programs: Some Indications from Latin America," in *Orbis,* Vol. 8, No. 4, Winter 1965, Table 5, p. 889; Barber and Ronning, *Internal Security and Military Power,* Table 4; Joseph E. Loftus, *Latin American Defense Expenditures* (Santa Monica, Calif.: Rand Corporation, 1968), p. vii and Tables 5, 6, and 8.

[74] Loftus, *Latin American Defense Expenditures,* Table 6.

[75] Alain Joxe, *Las Fuerzas Armadas en el Sistema Politico de Chile* (Santiago de Chile: Editorial Universitaria, S.A., 1970), p. 90.

[76] Lieuwin, *Mexican Militarism,* p. 146; Loftus, *Latin American Defense Expenditures,* p. vii.

[77] Loftus, *Latin American Defense Expenditures.*

[78] Ibid., Table D-4.

members of the armed forces for every 1,000 of their citizens, but the rest of the countries did not exceed 9 members for every 1,000.[79] While it can and has been argued that these figures indicate relatively low military spending in Latin America compared to Africa and Asia, nevertheless, as John D. Powell has pointed out, these defense expenditures are highly concentrated under the control of a very tiny minority of the total population.[80]

Military spending and force levels can reveal much about the privileged consideration the governments of Latin America extend to their military establishments. But this is not the entire story. In addition to these domestic rewards, the Latin American officer corps can count upon foreign governments, and especially those of the United States and other developed countries, for weapons and other programs of military assistance. With this direct assistance from foreign countries, as well as being supplied with arms through purchases in other countries, the political position of military officers in Latin America is further enhanced domestically.

In July, 1962, for example, a Sherman tank rammed the gates of the Pizarro Palace in Lima, Peru when the President of the Republic, Manuel Prado y Ugarteche was deposed by a military coup. The officer who engineered the capture of the palace was trained at the Ranger School at Fort Benning, Georgia. Another key figure had graduated a month earlier from the United States Naval Academy.[81] Such incidents are frequent enough to provoke considerable controversy in the United States and in Latin America regarding the political effects of military assistance programs to the armed forces of the region. Those concerned with the maintenance of democratic, change-oriented governments in Latin America are particularly prone to criticize United States military assistance programs. These critics argue that such programs, begun during World War II to defend against threats from outside the hemisphere, have actually had the political effect of increasing the power of the military in the domestic affairs of the Latin American region.[82]

Although the original purposes of military assistance to Latin America were hemispheric defense, defense against communist subversion, and other problems, the purposes to which this assistance has been actually directed are considerably different. As early as the 1920s, the United States created

[79] U.S. Arms Control and Disarmament Agency, *World Military Expenditures*, Table 2, p. 12.

[80] John Duncan Powell, "Military Assistance and Militarism in Latin America," in *Western Political Quarterly*, Vol. 18, No. 2, June 1965, p. 384.

[81] Ernest Gruening, "The 1962 Peruvian Coup," in Paul E. Sigmund (ed.), *Models of Political Change in Latin America* (New York: Praeger, 1970), p. 196.

[82] Powell, "Military Assistance and Militarism in Latin America," p. 382; Lieuwin, *Arms and Politics in Latin America*.

the first standing army in the Dominican Republic, which was later used for about 30 years by Trujillo as a weapon to maintain his dictatorship.[83] Furthermore, the Latin American military is often concerned with obtaining sophisticated weapons which have little utility in fighting subversion but which do add something to the prestige of their military establishments. The political uses rather than the military uses of arms received through such military assistance programs seem to be of most concern to the officer corps of Latin America. This increases the military's domestic power in civilian politics, although the civilian sector does not directly finance it.

The military assistance provided to Latin America has grown over the years. Between 1952 and 1960, the United States has provided $237 million in various programs, the leading recipients being Brazil, Chile, Peru, Colombia, and Uruguay.[84] Steadily increasing through the 1960s, military assistance to such countries as Ecuador, Venezuela, and Bolivia—where the military is occasionally dominant in politics—accounts for a considerable portion of the defense budgets of those countries.[85] Most of the aid is dispensed through grants which allow these countries to purchase American-made arms. In Haiti, Nicaragua, El Salvador, and Paraguay, where the military always dominates national politics, defense expenditures go for infantry-type armaments and some tanks purchased in the United States. Such acquisitions seem reasonable, given the intention of the military to effectively control the civilian populace. In the countries where the military occasionally dominates politics, the governments devote more of their budgets to military expenditures and they receive a relatively greater amount of U.S. military assistance than those countries in which the military always dominate. But generally speaking, the proportion of United States military assistance in the defense budgets of Latin American countries is quite small, although large enough to make a difference in countries where the civilians have even fewer resources.[86] Until recently, the arms, aircraft and other military goods provided in these aid programs have been quite ancient, but the governments of some of the more advanced countries such as Brazil,

[83] Howard J. Wiarda, "The Politics of Civil-Military Relations in the Dominican Republic," in *Journal of Inter-American Studies,* Vol. 7, No. 4, October 1965, p. 467.

[84] Geogrey Kemp, "Rearmament in Latin America," in *The World Today,* Vol. 23, September 1967, p. 379; Barber and Ronning, *Internal Security and Military Power,* Table 2, p. 36.

[85] Powell, "Military Assistance and Militarism in Latin America," Table 2, p. 385.

[86] Powell, "Military Assistance and Militarism in Latin America," p. 387. For analyses of the roles of the military and military assistance, see Millington, "The Latin American Military Elite"; Theodore Wyckoff, "The Role of the Military in Latin American Politics," in *Western Political Quarterly,* Vol. 13, No. 3, September 1960.

Argentina, Peru, and Venezuela are intent today upon acquiring modern jets and other sophisticated equipment and weaponry.

In addition to grants for the purchase of arms, the United States provides other assistance that bolsters the military and its conservative role. For example, military assistance advisory groups, or MAAG's, advise the host country on such military matters as civic action; this is intended to improve community development in order to head off efforts of guerilla insurgents by eliminating the causes of insurgency. A number of United States training centers, such as the U.S. Army School of the Americas, the Army Special Warfare Center, and the Army Civil Affairs School, have provided training in counterinsurgency, civic action and other techniques to Latin American officers. Without social reforms in the Latin American countries, however, such programs probably nurture the military's inclination to support the *status quo*.[87] But there is no completely convincing evidence that such educational and training programs are related to the desire for the military to intervene in the domestic politics of their countries.[88]

The Latin American military can also get what it wants in the world arms market. The Kennedy and Johnson administrations in the 1960s were reluctant to sell costly and highly sophisticated aircraft, weapons, and other material to Latin American nations, because even if such sales or military assistance did not contribute to the overthrow of duly elected governments, scarce government resources would be shifted away from such inadequately funded areas as education, economic development, and reform programs. With the self-imposed limit of $75 million per year in arm sales, the United States simply forced the Latin American military establishments to shift their purchases to other countries, especially to France and other European countries. Chile, Argentina and Brazil went to Europe to buy warships. As a result of recent border conflicts, Honduras has purchased jets and rifles from private European manufacturers to defend against El Salvador. Moreover, Cuba under Castro has not totally relied upon the Communist countries for arms. At the time of the Bay of Pigs invasion in 1961, Castro purchased automatic weapons from a private Belgian firm. The military dictator of Paraguay, General Stroessner, also shops at the same firm.

Military purchases clearly indicate that the military receives much of what it wants. Having convinced itself that it needs these prestigious symbols of military power, the Latin American military has contributed its share to the world's arms market, spurring competition among the developed countries to corner at least some of this profitable trade. By refusing to sell

[87] Barber and Ronning, *Internal Security and Military Power,* pp. 144–80.

[88] Putnam, "Toward Explaining Military Intervention in Latin American Politics," p. 106.

jet planes to Peru, the United States, in this and other cases, has cut itself out of the market, forcing such countries to secure jet planes from France and other countries. Today, some military establishments in Latin America are seeking to produce some of their own hardware needs. For example, Argentina is building a plane which can be used for military purposes and has also purchased a French tank production line. Brazil is producing its own rifles and has bought an aircraft assembly line from Italy. Latin American self-sufficiency in weapons is still a long way off, but the military of the region seems more willing than ever to go elsewhere if the United States is unable or unwilling to supply the weapons desired.

Observing that the Latin American military was indeed going elsewhere to purchase the hardware it wanted, the Nixon administration has tried to get around the Congressional limits on U.S. arms sales, although the government is still reluctant to sell supersonic Phantom jets and other sophisticated weapons to the Latin American military. Apparently, the prospect of being cut out of the market no longer appeals to the United States government, although such sales have little or nothing to do with helping to eliminate conditions conducive to insurgent activities. What disturbs some observers is that all of these expensive purchases, although not great in absolute terms, do not contribute to, and indeed may detract from, the possibilities for promoting successfully programs of development and reform. With no important external threats or threats of communism and insurgency, the military assistance to and spending in Latin America serves to drain resources from other, under-funded programs. In this sense, the military receives what it wants but this, in turn, slows down the pace of socioeconomic changes promoted by governments in Latin America.

As was noted previously, with the threat or use of force as the ultimate tactic, the military can *limit* the rate of socioeconomic change but, even if so inclined, the military reformers find it difficult, once in power, to *promote* rapid changes. Consequently, Samuel P. Huntington discounts the possibilities of a Nasser-like reformist military emerging in Latin America because most Latin American societies are too complex and too economically developed. The military instead plays the conservative role of defending the middle sectors.[89] The modernizing elements within the officer corps are not likely to get what they want because they are only one of the elements in most takeovers of government. Once in power, the more conservative elements become dominant. Also, once in power, the loose coalition of modernizing and conservative elements of the military leadership disagree on specific courses to follow, resulting in delay and perhaps a diluted approach to reform. Furthermore, the military modernizer must have skills

89 Needler, "The Latin American Military," p. 242; Huntington, *Political Order in Changing Societies,* p. 228.

in negotiation and compromise, but given the military mind and its peculiarities discussed earlier, it is obvious that the officers are often ill-suited to
run the government once they have seized it, especially if their intention
is to make changes in past policies. Being by nature against radical change,
military officers are by temperament unable to provide those political skills
necessary to lead a government toward gradual changes and reforms. The
leaders of coups are generally united in their opposition to those people in
control prior to the coup and to their policies. After it gains power, the coup
coalition splits apart, immobilizing reformist programs which require a
unity of strategy among the reformers. Reformist tendencies of military
coups are also cut back by conservative technicians upon whom the military
innovators must rely for advice. In addition, a modernizing military regime
will be opposed by those civilian groups with power, namely the conservative elements of the political system.[90] Finally, according to more than
one observer, military reformers will be bought off by the system, enrich-
ing themselves, obtaining the privileges of high rank and position and
generally forgetting—if indeed they ever really believed in—their earlier
modernizing rhetoric.[91]

All this is not to argue that the military officers, especially when in
control of the government, have no impact on promoting socioeconomic
change. But as with other groups in Latin America, the institutional nature
of the military, its elitist position within society, and its roles within the
political system combine to blunt much change of lasting success by
reformers. Despite a general commitment to improve a society, to develop it
economically, to correct its inherent inequalities, the Latin American
military, when it does intervene in politics, does not achieve rapid change.
Instead, the dominant values and desires within the military officer corps
are satisfied—needs for order, political stability, anti-communism, protection
of corporate self-interests, gradual (if any) change and protection of the
middle sectors from the uncertainties of rapid change affecting their
recently acquired privileges. Military officers cannot escape their roles as
long as the military is deeply embedded in the politics of immobility. Unable
to insulate themselves politically from general outside forces, military officers
check rather than promote change. The political stagnation of Latin
America, or the failure of government to promote rapid socioeconomic
changes, on balance, favors the interests of most military officers in the
short run. As a privileged group, military officers then receive generally

[90] Needler, "The Latin American Military," p. 242; Huntington, *Political
Order in Changing Societies,* pp. 228–31, 233–36; Needler, *Political Development in
Latin America,* pp. 68–69.

[91] Lieuwin, *Arms and Politics in Latin America,* Chapter 5; Nordlinger,
"Soldiers in Mufti."

what they want in terms of private demands and public policy. Unintended changes in Latin American society may eventually transform its institutions, including the military. But as socioeconomic change proceeds—and in Latin America such change is often so small as to elude detection—the military will probably become even more conservative, following the history of its counterparts in the developed countries. As of now, neither the military nor other groups, together or separately, are able to promote change consistently and effectively. Instead, the military elite assumes the role of protecting the civilian elites who have something to fear from the consequences of change, especially the rise in the political participation of the masses. In other words, the military officers of Latin America are practitioners as well as victims of the politics of immobility.

FURTHER READING

ADAMS, RICHARD N., "The Development of the Guatemalan Military," in *Studies in Comparative International Development*, Vol. 4, No. 5, 1968–1969.

——————, *The Second Sowing: Power and Secondary Development in Latin America*. San Francisco: Chandler, 1967.

ALBA, VICTOR, *El Ascenso del Militarismo Tecnocratica*. Estudios y Documentos, 1963.

——————, *El Militarismo: Ensayo sobre un Fenomeno Politicosocial Iberoamericano*. Mexico: Institucion de Investigaciones Sociales UNAM, 1959.

ARTHUR RIOS, JOSE, "Los Militares y el poder en Brasil," *Mundo Nuevo*, No. 31, January 1969.

BARBER, WILLARD R. and C. NEALE RONNING, *Internal Security and Military Power: Counterinsurgency and Civic Action in Latin America*. Columbus: Ohio State University Press, 1966.

BORTNIK, RUBEN, *El Ejercito Argentino y el Arte de lo Posible*. Buenos Aires: Ediciones Guemes, 1967.

BRILL, WILLIAM H., *Military Intervention in Bolivia: The Overthrow of Paz Estenssoro and the MNR*. Washington, D.C.: Institute for Comparative Study of Political Systems, 1967.

BROWN, THOMAS A., *Statistical Indications of the Effect of Military Programs, 1950–1965*. Santa Monica, Calif.: Rand Corporation, 1969.

CALVERT, PETER, "The Institutionalization of the Mexican Revolution," in *Journal of Inter-American Studies*, Vol. 9, No. 4, October 1969.

CHILCOTE, RONALD H., *Military Intervention and Development Tendencies: Preliminary Analysis for Study and Research of the Argentine Experience*. Riverside: University of California at Riverside, Latin American Research Program, 1966.

COTLER, JULIO, "Political Crisis and Military Populism in Peru," in *Studies in Comparative International Development*, Vol. 6, No. 5, 1970–1971.

CLINTON, RICHARD LEE, "The Modernizing Military: The Case of Peru," in *Inter-American Economic Affairs*, Vol. 24, No. 4, Spring 1971.

DE IMAZ, JOSE LUIS, *Los Que Mandan: Los Fuerzas Armadas en Argentina*. Buenos Aires: EUDEBA, 1964.

DUFF, ERNEST A. and JOHN F. McCAMANT, "Measuring Social and Political Requirements for System Stability in Latin America," in *American Political Science Review*, Vol. 62, No. 4, December 1968.

EINAUDI, LUIGI R., *The Peruvian Military: A Summary Political Analysis*. Santa Monica, Calif.: Rand Corporation, 1969.

——————, *Peruvian Military Relations with the United States*. Santa Monica, Calif.: Rand Corporation, 1970.

——————, *Revolution from Within? Military Rule in Peru Since 1968*. Santa Monica, Calif.: Rand Corporation, 1971.

—————— and ALFRED C. STEPAN, *Latin American Institutional Development: Changing Military Perspectives in Peru and Brazil*. Santa Monica, Calif.: Rand Corporation, 1971.

FINER, S. E., *The Man on Horseback: The Role of the Military in Politics*. New York: Praeger, 1962.

FLUHARTY, VERNON LEE, *Dance of the Millions: Military Rule and the Social Revolution in Colombia*. Pittsburgh: University of Pittsburgh Press, 1957.

GERMANI, GINO and KALMAN SILVERT, "Politics, Social Structure and Military Intervention in Latin America," in *European Journal of Sociology*, Vol. 3, 1961.

GOLDWERT, MARVIN, "Dichotomies of Militarism in Argentina," *Orbis*, Vol. 10, No. 3, Fall 1966.

——————, "The Rise of Modern Militarism in Argentina," in *Hispanic American Historical Review*, Vol. 48, No. 2, May 1968.

GRUENING, ERNEST, "The 1962 Peruvian Coup," in Paul E. Sigmund (ed.), *Models of Political Change in Latin America*. New York: Praeger, 1970.

GUDE, EDWARD W., "Political Violence in Venezuela: 1958–1964," in James Chowning Davies (ed.), *When Men Revolt and Why*. New York: Free Press, 1971.

HEARE, GERTRUDE E., *Trends in Latin American Military Expenditures 1940–1970*. Washington, D.C.: Department of State, 1971.

HELGUERA, LÉON, "The Changing Role of the Military in Colombia," in *Journal of Inter-American Studies*, Vol. 3, No. 3, July 1961.

HOROWITZ, IRVING LOUIS, "The Military Elites," in Seymour Martin Lipset and Aldo Solari (eds.), *Elites in Latin America*. New York: Oxford University Press, 1967.

——————, "The Military in Latin America," in *Economic Development and Cultural Change,* Vol. 12, January 1965.

——————, *Three Worlds of Development: The Theory and Practice of International Stratification.* New York: Oxford University Press, 1966.

HUNTINGTON, SAMUEL P .(ed.), *Changing Patterns of Military Politics.* New York: Free Press, 1962.

——————, *Political Order in Changing Societies.* New Haven: Yale University Press, 1968.

——————, *The Soldier and the State: The Theory and Politics of Civil-Military Relations.* Cambridge, Mass.: Harvard University Press, 1957.

JANOWITZ, MORRIS, *The Military in the Political Development of New Nations: An Essay in Comparative Analysis.* Chicago: University of Chicago Press, 1964.

JOHNSON, JOHN J., *The Military and Society in Latin America.* Stanford, Calif.: Stanford University Press, 1964.

—————— (ed.), *The Role of the Military in Underdeveloped Countries.* Princeton: Princeton University Press, 1962.

JOXE, ALAIN, *Las Fuerzas Armadas en el Sistema Politico de Chile.* Santiago de Chile: Editorial Universitaria, S.A., 1970.

KAUTSKY, JOHN H., "The Military in Underdeveloped Countries," in *Economic Development and Cultural Change,* Vol. 12, January 1965.

KEMP, GEOFFREY, "Rearmament in Latin America," in *The World Today,* Vol. 23, September 1967.

KLING, MERLE, "Toward A Theory of Power and Political Instability in Latin America," in *Western Political Quarterly,* Vol. 9, No. 1, March 1956.

LIEUWIN, EDWIN, *Arms and Politics in Latin America.* New York: Praeger, 1961.

——————, *Generals vs. Presidents: Neo-Militarism in Latin America.* New York: Praeger, 1964.

——————, *Mexican Militarism.* Albuquerque: University of New Mexico Press, 1968.

——————, "The Military: A Force for Continuity or Change," in John TePaske and Sydney N. Fisher (eds.), *Explosive Forces in Latin America.* Columbus: Ohio State University Press, 1964.

——————, "The Changing Role of the Military in Latin America," in *Journal of Latin American Studies,* Vol. 3, No. 4, October 1961.

LOFTUS, JOSEPH E., *Latin American Defense Expenditures.* Santa Monica, Calif.: Rand Corporation, 1968.

McALISTER, LYLE N., "Changing Concepts of the Role of the Military in Latin America," *The Annals,* Vol. 360, July 1965.

—————— "Civil-Military Relations in Latin America," *Journal of Inter-American Studies,* Vol. 3, July 1961.

—————, "The Military," in John J. Johnson (ed.), *Continuity and Change in Latin America*. Stanford, Calif.: Stanford University Press, 1964.

MILLINGTON, THOMAS M., "President Arturo Illia and the Argentine Military," *Journal of Inter-American Studies*, Vol. 6, No. 3, July 1964.

—————, "The Latin American Military Elite," in *Current History*, Vol. 46, No. 333, May 1969.

NEEDLER, MARTIN C., *Anatomy of A Coup d'Etat: Ecuador 1963*. Washington, D.C.: Institute for the Comparative Study of Political Systems, 1964.

—————, *Political Development in Latin America: Instability, Violence and Evolutionary Change*. New York: Random House, 1968.

—————, "Political Development and Socio-Economic Development: The Case of Latin America," in *American Political Science Review*, Vol. 62, No. 3, September 1968.

—————, "The Latin American Military: Predatory Reactionaries or Modernizing Patriots," in *Journal of Inter-American Studies*, Vol. 9, No. 2, April 1969.

NORDLINGER, ERIC A., "Soldiers in Mufti: The Impact of Military Rule upon Economic and Social Change in the Non-Western States," in *American Political Science Review*, Vol. 64, No. 4, December 1970.

NORTH, LIISA, *Civil-Military Relations in Argentina, Chile and Peru*. Berkeley, Calif.: Institute of International Studies, 1966.

NUN, JOSE, "A Latin American Phenomenon: The Middle-Class Military Coup," in James Petras and Maurice Zeitlin (eds.), *Latin America: Reform or Revolution?* Greenwich, Conn.: Fawcett Publications, 1968.

—————, "The Middle-Class Military Coup," in Claudio Veliz (ed.), *The Politics of Conformity in Latin America*. New York: Oxford University Press, 1967.

ORSOLINI, MARIO HORACIO, *Ejercito Argentino y Crecimiento Nacional*. Buenos Aires: Ediciones Arayu, 1965.

PERERA, VICTOR, "Guatemala: Always Violencia," in *New York Times Magazine*, June 13, 1971.

PERLMUTTER, AMOS, "The Praetorian State and the Praetorian Army: Toward a Taxonomy of Civil-Military Relations in Developing Politics," in *Comparative Politics*, Vol. 1, April 1969.

POTASH, ROBERT A., "The Changing Role of the Military in Argentina," in *Journal of Inter-American Studies*, Vol. 3, No. 4, October 1961.

POWELL, JOHN DUNCAN, "Military Assistance and Militarism in Latin America," in *Western Political Quarterly*, Vol. 18, No. 2, June 1965.

PUTNAM, ROBERT D., "Toward Explaining Military Intervention in Latin American Politics," in *World Politics*, Vol. 20, No. 1, October 1967.

PYE, LUCIAN W., *Aspects of Political Development*. Boston: Little, Brown, 1966.

Rowe, James W., "Argentina's Restless Military," in *American Universities Field Staff Report,* May 1964.

Schmitt, Karl M., "The Roles of the Military in Contemporary Mexico," in A. Curtis Wilgus (ed.), *The Caribbean: Mexico Today.* Gainesville: University of Florida Press, 1964.

Skidmore, Thomas E., *Politics in Brazil, 1930–1964: An Experiment in Democracy.* New York: Oxford University Press, 1967.

Stepan, Alfred C., *The Military in Politics: Changing Patterns in Brazil.* Princeton, N.J.: Princeton University Press, 1971.

Stokes, William S., "Violence as a Power Factor in Latin American Politics," in *Western Political Quarterly,* Vol. 5, No. 3, September 1952.

Unger, Jess P., "The Military Role in Nation-Building and Economic Development," *CAG Occasional Papers,* Bloomington, Ind., 1963.

U.S. Arms Control and Disarmament Agency, *World Military Expenditures, 1969.* Washington, D.C.: U.S. Government Printing Office, 1970.

Villanueva, Victor, *El Militarismo en el Peru.* Lima: Empresa Grafica T. Scheuch, S.A., 1962.

Weaver, Jerry L. "Las Fuerzas Armadas Guatemaltecas en la politica," in *Aportes,* No. 12, Abril de 1969.

——————, "The Political Elite of a Military-Dominated Regime: The Guatemalan Example," in *The Journal of Developing Areas,* Vol. 3, April 1969.

Wiarda, Howard J., "The Politics of Civil-Military Relations in the Dominican Republic," in *Journal of Inter-American Studies,* Vol. 3, No. 4, October 1965.

Wolf, Charles, "The Political Effects of Military Programs: Some Indications from Latin America," in *Orbis,* Vol. 8, No. 4, Winter 1965.

Wood, David, *Armed Forces in Central and South America.* London: Adelphi Papers, April 1967.

Wyckoff, Theodore, "The Role of the Military in Latin American Politics," in *Western Political Quarterly,* Vol. 13, No. 3, September 1960.

Young, Jordan, "Military Aspects of the 1930 Brazilian Revolution," in *Hispanic American Historical Review,* Vol. 44, No. 2, May 1964.

CHAPTER **8**

BUREAUCRATS

Like military officers and the Catholic clergy, Latin American bureaucrats are an important political group with an institutional identity. However, they are different in at least one sense—the bureaucrats have only recently achieved power as the role of government itself has increased. As Latin America experienced the multitude of changes associated with development, national bureaucracies were created to meet new demands and perform tasks related to development. Although their importance is not the same throughout Latin America, bureaucracies have become politically more important as economic change has occurred. However, one must not automatically assume that bureaucrats want rapid changes just because their importance is due to earlier changes. Such an assumption would be too simple, given the complex role that bureaucrats play in the politics of today's Latin America.

The recent growth of national bureaucracies in Latin America generally, and in such countries as Brazil, Mexico, and Chile in particular, reflects to a great extent the common Latin American view that government should assume broad responsibilities for society and its members. For example, on the political right and left in Latin America there is general agreement that government should have an active role in promoting economic development, although disagreement exists over specific policies.[1] This permissive attitude toward an active government role in the promotion of

[1] Charles W. Anderson, *Politics and Economic Change in Latin America* (New York: Van Nostrand Reinhold, 1967), p. 3.

. socioeconomic change helps to provide an atmosphere conducive to a highly influential position for bureaucrats in Latin American politics.

The executive branch of Latin American government, to which bureaucrats belong, has traditionally been more important than the legislative branch. Even today, the single executive or a coalition of executives (involving civilians, military men, or both) dominates the legislative and judicial branches. However, in countries such as Mexico, Chile, and Brazil, which have evolved large national bureaucracies to promote development and provide services in response to popular or elite demands, bureaucrats enjoy considerable importance in determining not only the day-to-day operation of government but also the concrete meaning of governmental goals. Although the size and importance of national bureaucracies vary considerably throughout Latin America, the increasing tendency of governmental leaders to rely upon bureaucracy to fulfill the government's role in development promises a growing if not well-defined role for bureaucrats.

Before pursuing a detailed examination of bureaucrats as a political group in contemporary Latin America, some consideration must be given to the term "bureaucrat" as it is used here. This is particularly necessary if one is to avoid misconceptions and hasty, ethnocentric conclusions about the bureaucrat's political role.

THE CONTEXT: AN INTRODUCTION TO BUREAUCRACY

As in North America, when the general public in Latin America thinks about the term "bureaucrat," their first reaction is commonly negative, strongly contrasting with the image which the term "public servant" evokes. So when one term rather than another is chosen to identify something, there is always the risk of clouding with value-laden symbols an otherwise dispassionate examination of the topic. However, the term "bureaucrat" is used here as a natural and convenient derivative of "bureaucracy," and it in no way implies any form of blame or praise. That is, while most bureaucrats see themselves in a very favorable light, and while many Latin Americans see most bureaucrats as a parasitic and incompetent group rendering virtually no valuable service to the nation and having no worthwhile commitments,[2] we are attempting to use the terms "bureaucracy" and "bureaucrat" in a neutral, descriptive sense.

Terminology is not a minor consideration because it also raises the issue of the "proper" role of bureaucrats in the political process of Latin American countries. Latin American thinking on this topic has been greatly influenced by North American beliefs concerning public administration. Of

---

[2] See Jose A. Silva Michelena, "The Venezuelan Bureaucrat," in Frank Bonilla and Jose A. Silva Michelena (eds.), *A Strategy for Research on Social Policy* (Cambridge, Mass.: M.I.T. Press, 1967), p. 86.

particular importance has been the orthodox and enduring myth in the United States that "politics" and "administration" can be and should be separated. That is, it is felt that some people should fill principally political roles and other people should fill principally administrative ones. This view, to which many specialists in public administration still adhere, emerged in earlier North American reform movements; it aimed at eliminating political corruption, favoritism and inefficiency and instituting instead efficient and impartial administration in the public interest.

Most will agree that this reformist goal reflects admirable intentions. However, the complete separation of "politics" and "administration" remains an impossible goal not only in such a "developed" country as the United States but also in such "developing" countries as those of Latin America. It is true that certain programs, such as recruitment and promotion policies based upon the merit system, have improved the quality of bureaucrats and have somewhat insulated them from external political pressures. In applying this principle to foreign countries such as in Latin America, however, the reformers did not achieve the intended results. Instead, in many Latin American countries that have attempted to pattern programs after the North American experience, bureaucrats continue to be hired for political reasons and then cannot be dismissed because of tenure provisions. Actually, the lack of trained personnel makes Latin American civil service programs based upon a merit system nothing more than a legal charade. Under such conditions the merit system introduces an inflexible policy that enshrines old practices while failing to institute constructive changes. That is, the transplantation of civil service reform, with its assumptions of a nonpolitical bureaucracy, from the North American context to Latin America has promoted the development of an often unresponsive but still very political bureaucracy. Imitating these North American practices is a vain exercise for Latin America. Moreover, such efforts may further worsen the situation, as will be discussed later.

A rigid separation of "politics" and "administration" in developing countries such as the Latin American nations is impossible to achieve for other reasons. A basic assumption behind this separation is that certain structures must specialize. Interest groups "articulate" or express demands; political parties "aggregate" or bring together demands; and bureaucracies are supposed to process demands mechanically without becoming otherwise involved. However, if we examine Latin American bureaucracy, and even those of the more developed countries, this assumption is clearly questionable. For one thing, specialization has not occurred to the extent that we can find well-defined interest groups expressing demands on government, nor can we find political parties that bring these various demands together.

As was argued in Chapter 1, interest groups and political parties do not exist in developing countries in the same ways as they do in such developed areas as Western Europe or North America. Or if they do exist, they are too weak to perform the specialized roles that the "politics-administration" dichotomy requires.[3] Instead, what we find in many Latin American countries is the existence of powerful national bureaucracies which not only meet demands but make demands, which assume the roles interest groups and political parties are supposed to perform in developed countries, and which serve as centers of political power rather than as efficient mechanisms for carrying out the specialized duties that external political groups have demanded. Indeed, in some countries that have not progressed far along the road of development, the top executives and their bureaucracies are, for most purposes, *the* political system. Even more than in developed countries, bureaucracies in Latin America have a disproportionate importance in making policy and in wielding power, if only by default.[4] In short, whatever may be the case in the more developed countries, virtually no bureaucracy in Latin America can mechanically meet demands and do nothing more. Consequently, it is futile to believe that bureaucrats in Latin America are basically nonpolitical and that they perform strictly administrative tasks.

In addition to their domination of the political process, Latin American bureaucrats differ from those of developed countries in other ways. They have less professional training; they may only be part-time officials who, due to low pay scales, must work at other jobs and therefore jeopardize their impartiality and independence; the official position may be less important than the particular person filling it; positions may be obtained more through personal connections than by standards of competence; laws and formal regulations may be less important for defining administrative behavior than are traditional customs and personal influence; bureaucrats may be more responsive to powerful political groups than to the individuals they are legally supposed to serve. In other words, bureaucrats in Latin America as well as in other developing regions cannot be defined as a group in the same terms that Max Weber used to describe his "rational-

---

[3] For a survey on this and other problems of public administration in Latin America, see Pan American Union, *Administracion Publica en America Latina* (Washington, D.C.: Secretaria General, OEA, 1967).

[4] There is a growing literature concerning the nature of bureaucratic power in developing countries: Ferrel Heady, *Public Administration: A Comparative Perspective* (Englewood Cliffs, N.J.: Prentice-Hall, 1966); Fred W. Riggs, *Administration in Developing Countries: The Theory of Prismatic Society* (Boston: Houghton Mifflin, 1964); S. N. Eisenstadt, "Bureaucracy, Bureaucratization and De-Bureaucratization," in *Administrative Science Quarterly,* Vol. 4, December 1959; Joseph LaPalombara, *Bureaucracy and Political Development* (Princeton: Princeton University Press, 1963); Lucian W. Pye, "The Political Context of National Development," in Irving Swerdlow (ed.), *Administrative Development: Concepts and Problems* (Syracuse, N.Y.: Syracuse University Press, 1963).

legal" bureaucracy. When discussing Latin American bureaucrats, care must be taken to resist thinking that they are exactly the same kinds of political actors that exist in, for example, the United States. Inappropriate analogies may lead to confusion and, even worse, to fundamental misunderstanding of an important segment of Latin American politics.

Still another problem in defining the term "bureaucrat" in the Latin American context is introduced by the central importance of military participation in national bureaucracies. Usually, the term "bureaucrat" in the United States conjures up the image of a civilian or at least a public official whose professional training is used to fulfill some civilian task. This image sometimes betrays reality in the United States, and it is even less accurate for Latin America. The military in Latin America is not merely an institutional interest group, but is also sometimes a ruling elite that uses its personnel to staff administrative agencies performing largely nonmilitary functions. In Brazil, Argentina and Peru, for example, various ministries and assorted agencies of the national bureaucracies are staffed partially if not totally with military officers. In some matters, such personnel are acting as extensions of the military leaders who control the government. However, in other matters, they act as bureaucrats within a particular agency, occupying positions previously held by civilians, and they are not principally concerned with serving as direct conduits to the military leadership. Thus, some bureaucrats are military men, but not all military men, particularly not those who occupy only military positions, are considered to be "bureaucrats" in the sense that the term is used here.

A bureaucrat, then, is any individual who occupies a position of responsibility within the bureaucratic structures of the Latin American countries. He need not be a military officer, but he may be. He is appointed to his position rather than elected. He is neither the most important nor the least important member of an agency. He is typically a person of middle income with some policy-making responsibilities. The bureaucrat, or *funcionario,* has the formal responsibility to decide what advice given by technicians should be accepted and what advice should be ignored. In addition to those mentioned, he may also perform other political roles—for example, he may be a party official, or he may be a part-time bureaucrat who formally represents within the bureaucracy the interests of some external group. In other words, the Latin American bureaucrat is a political actor of considerable variety, and it is difficult to speak of him as possessing well-defined characteristics. However, from bureaucracy to bureaucracy and from country to country, he is to varying degrees either a formulator of public policy or at least a public official who poses the alternatives of policy decisions that others make.

These explorations into the problems of defining the term "bureaucrat" are not meant to be definitive. In any event, the rewards in pursuing such an exercise diminish with extended effort. Since definitions are primarily devices for explaining the use of the words rather than explaining what these words represent, it seems appropriate not to give undue emphasis to this kind of discussion. However, before moving on to related matters, it does seem necessary to recall that Latin American bureaucrats, as well as those in other developing countries, cannot be viewed in entirely the same way as bureaucrats are, for example, in the United States. No matter how much North American public administration specialists urge Latin American bureaucrats to emulate North American administrative behavior, Latin American bureaucrats will still reflect in belief and in deed the peculiar features of their own society and political system.

EXTERNAL INFLUENCES

Latin Americans believe that government is the decisive factor in promoting and creating socioeconomic change.[5] Without substantial governmental efforts, socioeconomic changes, it is felt, will either not take place or will occur too late. And the fairly common expectation that the government will assume the task of developing socioeconomic assets places the bureaucrat in a crucial position in the political process. He becomes the target for demands from such opposing groups as landowners and peasants, businessmen and labor, military and students. He is confronted at all times with contradictory demands and in his mediatory efforts he often determines which demands shall be recognized and met.[6]

How bureaucrats decide which demands to meet and which to ignore is greatly influenced by the general society in which this process takes place. And more often than not, these influences hamper Latin American bureaucracy in promoting socioeconomic development. That is, they often obstruct the bureaucracy in its formal task of transforming the larger society. This is due to the mixture of the modern and the traditional in developing countries, which often paralyzes effective administration despite the fact that administration is relatively unopposed by external political groups such as mass political parties and interest groups. Thus, instead of the bureaucracy having an important impact on society as a promoter of socioeconomic changes, certain factors of society often penetrate bureaucracy in such a way as to dilute its efforts to transform the society.

One of these social factors is that individuals with financial resources, social status, or personal connections can compromise the bureaucracy's

[5] Richard N. Adams, *The Second Sowing: Power and Secondary Development in Latin America* (San Francisco: Chandler, 1967), p. 177.

[6] Robert E. Scott, "The Government Bureaucrats and Political Change in Latin America," in *Journal of International Affairs,* Vol. 20, No. 25, 1966.

goals. That is, instead of providing services to all who are legally entitled to them, bureaucrats are more often responsive to those who can afford them. For example, the Mexican bureaucrat often demands a bribe (*mordida*) before he will perform a service that he is legally supposed to perform. This source of income, by North American standards of administrative morality, is an example of corruption. However, in a developing society like that of Mexico, such practices are accepted as normal. The client gets more or less what he wants and the bureaucrat's meager salary is consequently supplemented. While the bribe in Mexico can be, and has been, considered more egalitarian than social status and personal connections (which are the norm, for example, in Chile), in the sense that money is more easily come by, nevertheless the problem in promoting socioeconomic change through bureaucracy is that bureaucrats are more responsive to those who already have more than to those who do not have much.[7]

It is not true that bureaucracy is totally unresponsive to the larger society in Latin American counties—but it definitely is more sensitive to those who have privileges to protect than to those who would most benefit from rapid socioeconomic changes in the society, which bureaucratic policy-making could promote. Latin American bureaucrats are not alone in their susceptibility to such influences. In the developing countries of Latin America, however, bureaucratic favoritism to clienteles with wealth, social status, and personal contacts is particularly important, because it militates against bureaucracy's potential to promote further development. If the public bureaucracy cannot act, there is a good chance that no other institution will fill the vacuum.

Latin American society also influences bureaucracy by weakening administration concerned with change. If bureaucrats, monetarily or otherwise, are persuaded to perform services, they are probably circumventing the formal lines of authority within the bureaucracy. Thus, in agencies created to promote such goals as agrarian reform, responsiveness of bureaucrats to influential landowners will dilute the effectiveness of the reform program and will also mean less concern for the formal goals of the program and for their implementation. As noted in Chapter 3, for example, it is a common practice in Latin America for members of powerful economic groups, in violation of the law, to evade payment of direct taxes. This results in low resources for government institutions, which results in low salaries for bureaucrats, which in turn increases the financial vulnerability of bureaucrats to bribery and other pressures. This vulnerability then helps

---

[7] Charles J. Parrish and Jorge I. Tapia-Videla, "Welfare Policy and Administration in Chile," in *Journal of Comparative Administration,* Vol. 1, No. 4, 1970. The authors argue that welfare bureaucracy in Chile has been more responsive to the middle class than to the lower class whom it is supposed to serve.

these powerful economic groups obtain special privileges. Discussion of similar structural weaknesses of bureaucracy in Latin America will be returned to later in this chapter.

Another effect that society has on bureaucracy lies in the exercise of power by individuals in bureaucracy. Earlier, the argument was made that bureaucracies in developing areas such as Latin America often occupy a powerful position relative to other political institutions. This favored position is largely due to a lack of strong institutions such as legislatures, and to a lack of strong, informal groups such as political parties and interest groups. Without the direction that strong institutions and external groups can provide, the bureaucracy is the inheritor of considerable discretion in making policy.[8] That is, while bureaucracy does not, of course, have total discretion, the weakness of other institutions, political parties, and interest groups enhances the opportunity for bureaucrats to exercise their personal judgment in making decisions which in more developed countries are made outside bureaucratic circles. And since bureaucrats are quite vulnerable to various other external pressures, they naturally use this discretion for favoring certain kinds of individuals and groups over others. Special exceptions to rules are commonly made, violations of procedure are overlooked, and irregularities go unnoticed. In other words, bureaucrats become an interest group which exchanges the application of general policy for favors and other forms of support from those groups in society that can afford them. To put it differently, without general control and direction from a broad spectrum of social groups, bureaucrats are in an advantageous position to help some and hurt others—and their general vulnerability to specific demands for privileged consideration contrasts sharply with a lack of bureaucratic responsiveness to demands for socioeconomic change.

This vulnerability of bureaucrats coincides with the fact that bureaucrats are hired for personal reasons, although almost all Latin American countries have laws designed to establish a merit system of recruitment. As things generally turn out, bureaucrats are hired for almost every reason except competence. Personal connections, loyalty to individuals within the bureaucracy, and other such considerations tend to be much more important than an aspirant's ability to perform the tasks required. Once a person is hired, the civil service laws usually prevent him from being fired. In many Latin American countries (and notably in Chile) bureaucracies are overstaffed with people hired through friendship and other connections: government employment has become a dole.[9] Friends and family are hired so that

8 See footnote 4 and Guy Benveniste, *Bureaucracy and National Planning: A Sociological Case Study in Mexico* (New York: Praeger, 1970).

9 James Petras, *Politics and Social Forces in Chilean Development* (Berkeley: University of California Press, 1969).

"bureaucratic families" exist over the years.[10] In other words, bureaucrats who are hired for personal reasons and are vulnerable to compromising deals weaken the effectiveness of the bureaucracy.

Mentioned earlier, but deserving of more attention, is another factor permeating Latin American bureaucracy. This is the systematic exclusion of certain minorities from participating in bureaucracy or from influencing bureaucrats. Often observed in developing countries generally, this phenomenon seems to be quite common in Latin America. Much of Latin America has experienced the emergence of different groups. While in the colonial and the immediate post-independence periods the landowners, the military, and the church were the primary groups of political importance, more recently other groups such as urban workers, peasants, students, bureaucrats and businessmen have come to have some importance. However, this has not led to equal influence of these groups in the councils of government, nor has it brought about fundamental consensus on the legitimate goals of these groups or the proper methods for pursuing them. And so, some of these groups have much more influence on the formulation of bureaucratic policy than do others. Gomez, for example, claims that Indians, who constitute a large bulk of the Peruvian population, received less than 1 percent of the budget between 1964 and 1967. Any other budgetary expenditures that affected Indians were unintended, and the reformist regime of military officers which assumed power in 1968 may or may not be able or willing to change this situation.[11] In addition, some groups are more effective than others in placing their representatives, formally or informally, in positions of bureaucratic power. Successful groups are likely to have middle or upper class origins, and their principal concern will be to maintain or to enlarge what they already have. Furthermore, those groups which have thus far benefited most from bureaucratic policies are those most likely to have a continuing impact on bureaucratic policy-making.

The mixture of old and new cultural norms also has an impact on bureaucracy. As was argued in Chapter 1, Latin American societies are neither old nor new, but rather are a bewildering mixture of both. Naturally enough, the bureaucracies of these societies reflect this confusing blend. For example, bureaucrats are as likely to be hired because they come from the same part of the country as does the department chief as they are to be hired on the grounds that some particular expertise is needed. A few "workhorses" may do most of the work for any department but the rest simply view their jobs as more or less a sinecure. Moreover, this mixture of old and new norms does more to obstruct than to help bureaucracy in promoting socioeconomic change. Often the wide variety of old and new

10 Scott, "The Government Bureaucrats."

11 Rudolph Gomez, *The Peruvian Administrative System* (Boulder: University of Colorado Press, 1969), pp. 56–57.

norms serves to promote such unofficial goals as providing patronage and job security, and creating islands of special influence which frequently interfere with the realization of change-oriented policies. The formal norms, which are often if not always "new," are violated by higher and lower officials alike who are operating on the basis of older values.

What all these effects of society on bureaucracy indicate is that, even with change-oriented political leaders, the bureaucracy cannot be isolated from the society that it is supposed to transform. Of course, some bureaucrats in Latin America may be able to elude some of the impact of traditional norms on the effectiveness of their agencies. However, most bureaucrats must work under conditions that undermine the effectiveness of change-oriented agencies. The hope that such bureaucracies can be isolated from some of these social influences rests on a feeble optimism that ignores the compelling arguments against the possibility of the separating "politics" (defined as governmental policy-making for the whole society) and "administration" (defined as the mechanical implementation of policies).

INTERNAL INFLUENCES

Factors within bureaucracy as well as factors outside bureaucracy hinder its effectiveness in pushing for change. External and internal factors influencing bureaucracy are hard to separate. Some things could be interpreted as being both external and internal, such as an official hiring a relative. So, to some extent, deciding what is external and internal is the same problem as saying where bureaucracy ends and the general society begins. It is perhaps best to keep in mind that bureaucracy is influenced by both external and internal factors. For example, a bureaucrat is much more likely to view his superior as having legitimate authority over him—an internal matter—if this relationship of authority is complemented through family ties—an external matter.

The chief executive of the national bureaucracy in Latin American countries is usually the president. Through various devices such as budgetary controls, appointment power, personal favoritism and his traditionally dominant role in Latin American government, the president has the opportunity to exercise considerable influence over the major activities of the various ministries and agencies within the national bureaucracy. However, in Mexico, Chile, and other countries the president and his closest political associates have yielded some of their control over a growing bureaucracy.[12] With the gradual expansion of activities in such fields as education,

[12] L. Vincent Padgett, *The Mexican Political System* (Boston: Houghton Mifflin, 1966), pp. 161–62.

welfare, economic development, public works, health, agriculture, and so forth, new agencies have been created to handle new functions. These new agencies are quite often semi-independent of the president, and conduct many of their activities without his direct or constant supervision. In the smaller and more underdeveloped countries of the Caribbean and Central America, this gradual increase of bureaucratic power has proceeded much more slowly, and therefore the president and his most immediate associates have been able to retain closer control of a smaller and less independent bureaucracy. However, the trend seems to be general: the growth of bureaucracy in Latin America has created more problems in controlling its expanding influence in making policies on matters involving socioeconomic change.

In addition to the sheer growth of bureaucratic apparatus, factors within any particular bureaucracy operate to slow the effectiveness needed to solve problems of socioeconomic change. For one thing, as White notes in his study of Peru, workers in organizations avoid individual, face to face confrontations and instead resolve conflicts by appealing to higher authority.[13] This is inflexible and inefficient and places a great load on the physical and mental resources of higher officials. Thus this attitude toward authority is a major obstacle to organizational effectiveness. The exalted position of the *jefe* is also reinforced because bureaucrats in Latin America want to be on very good terms with a superior. Although this relationship is akin to the traditional *patron* relationship mentioned in connection with peasants and workers, its consequences in bureaucracy are not always known, but certainly it may foster severe competition among individuals of equal rank to the extent that inefficiency and ineffectiveness result. Moreover, the superior is less likely to have his ideas challenged by underlings when they should be.

Such problems of authority also stem from personal rather than institutional loyalties. Bureaucrats are more likely to cooperate with individuals of equal rank with whom they share some common personal bond than with others who lack this bond. Since such loyalties are not very broad, a breakdown of legitimate authority throughout the entire bureaucracy takes place.

Another factor within Latin American bureaucracies which chronically obstructs socioeconomic change is an administrative mentality that resists adjustments to new problems. Worldwide, bureaucrats are accused of this failing, and Latin American bureaucrats are probably no more guilty than others. In Latin America, however, the importance of this failing is magnified because bureaucrats are one of the few political groups that have

---

13 William Foote White, *Organizational Behavior: Theory and Application* (Homewood, Ill.: Richard C. Irwin, and Dorsey, 1969), p. 725.

an opportunity to aid (or to impede) the socioeconomic transformation of their countries.

The attitudes of bureaucrats toward change are not at all clear. Bureaucrats may maintain a generally conservative position within the political system, since their task is to manage conflict rather than to promote it. Some have argued bureaucrats generally are committed to the modernization of their countries. In Chile, for example, bureaucrats have been found to favor gradual agrarian reform and increased education. However, such changes, if abruptly introduced, could threaten the positions of many bureaucrats who have benefited from the present system. For example, since most bureaucrats owe their position, wholly or in part, to family connections or other traditional ties, the rapid introduction of hiring on the basis of merit would be an attack on their own security. Consequently, it is in the interests of many Chilean bureaucrats to voice demands for change but not to implement them if their position is jeopardized. According to Petras, Chilean bureaucracy is a socially conservative influence because it has adapted to a relatively stagnant society, rather than making major attempts to transform it. It remains to be seen whether the Allende government, founded on a shaky coalition of assorted leftist groups, will be able to use bureaucracy effectively to promote major changes in Chilean society.[14]

How bureaucrats view their job is also of some importance. For example, bureaucrats often view their agency as a provider of jobs, rather than as an achiever of goals of socioeconomic change.[15] That is, many administrators are concerned more with their status, privileges, security and patronage than with organizational purpose. For example, as privileged members of society, bureaucrats in Chile are generally aware of the inequality of opportunities that pervades their society, but few want to make the sacrifices necessary to eliminate the inequality.[16] Similarly, Daland found in Brazil that administrators realize that the implementation of formal plans would threaten the system of patronage and benefits from which they have profited. In short, major administrative reforms designed to achieve efficiency and effectiveness have failed in Brazil as well as in other Latin American countries because they strike at the personal security of bureaucrats as well as at the political power of important groups. Since most administrators are aware of their personal vulnerability to pressures for maintaining a patronage-oriented rather than service-oriented position, the

14 Petras, *Politics and Social Forces in Chilean Development,* p. 288.

15 Robert T. Daland, *Brazilian Planning: Development, Politics and Administration.* (Chapel Hill: University of North Carolina Press, 1967), pp. 198–99, and Petras, *Politics and Social Forces in Chilean Development,* pp. 293–300.

16 Petras, *Politics and Social Forces in Chilean Development,* p. 149.

safest attitude among bureaucrats becomes a prudent and conservative strategy of survival.

Bureaucrats also bring mixed motivations to their work and this tends to foster disunity within. Hopkins' study of the government executive of Peru revealed that there are many different kinds of motivations among bureaucrats.[17] For example, the "classic executive," who receives high job satisfaction, is devoted to public service. The "manager," on the other hand, has a specific skill but no prior governmental experience. He is impatient to get the job done and therefore is frustrated by the stagnation and inaction of bureaucratic procedure. The "career executive" is more concerned with simply making a living and views his job not as a challenge to meet the government's formal goals of change and development but to get along through preserving his security and welfare. Bureaucrats with such varied motivations naturally have different attitudes toward the bureaucracy and their job in it.

Another internal division occurs between bureaucrats and technicians (*técnicos*). The professional bureaucrat generally occupies a formal position of some importance in policy-making—for example, he may be a department head or an assistant to an administrative director. A *técnico,* on the other hand, obtains authority not from a formal position explicitly granting policy-making powers but from his expertise and education. As a group in Brazil, for example, the *técnicos* are generally younger and more aware of themselves as an emerging elite in the government than are the older and more satisfied bureaucrats. With the institutionalization of Brazilian politics, the *técnicos* have begun to challenge the power not only of the professional bureaucrats but also, to a limited extent, of the chief executive. As the tasks of bureaucracies become more complex, the power of the capable *técnico* may increase. His growing importance comes not merely from his knowledge, but from his ability to select the particular alternatives from which the professional bureaucrats must choose a policy.[18]

The internal obstacles to effective bureaucracy are complex. Administrative fragmentation, red tape (*papelería*), departmental jealousy, bureaucratic attitudes, divided loyalties and a number of other factors all impede the effectiveness of bureaucracy. It is impossible to insulate bureaucracies from these general factors or from the specific demands of important groups that seek to compromise the goals of change that bureaucracy is supposed to achieve. Even with semi-autonomous, decentralized agencies, the lesson is clear: such agencies cannot be effectively insulated from their environment.

---

[17] Jack W. Hopkins, *The Government Executive of Modern Peru* (Gainesville: University of Florida Press, 1967).

[18] Nathaniel H. Leff, *Economic Policy-making and Development in Brazil, 1947–1964.* (New York: John Wiley, 1968), p. 143–53.

This survey of Latin American bureaucracy is only meant to be a brief preface for better understanding the desires, demands, and rewards of bureaucrats. Without virtually restating the entire foregoing discussion, we can conclude that the bureaucracies of Latin American governments reflect the cleavages of transitional societies, the stagnation of societies that have not been integrated, the mixture of traditional and modern which often serves to blunt bureaucratic action and, in general, the immobility of bureaucracy in promoting socioeconomic changes.

DESIRES

Before asking "What do bureaucrats in Latin Amesica want in terms of socioeconomic change?" it should be simply stated that the bureaucrat has personal as well as professional desires, and while these certainly overlap, they can for present purposes be separated. The personal wants of bureaucrats are likely to involve salaries, privileges, status symbols, security, welfare and other amenities. His professional wants have broader and more complex implications, in that his role in making important policies, setting organizational goals, meeting the demands of external groups, and achieving his conception of progress, is broadly political.

As is the case with most occupational groups, the Latin American bureaucrat first and foremost wants to receive certain basic rewards from the bureaucracy in which he works. For example, salary is often an important, if not the sole, reward he seeks to maximize. However, salaries for most bureaucrats in Latin America are relatively low compared to their counterparts in more developed countries. In fact, many salaries are so low and so restricted by budgetary limitations that many Latin American bureaucrats supplement their salaries through multiple job-holding as well as through such illegal activities as accepting bribes. Low salaries are important for two reasons. First, they make bureaucrats more vulnerable to those who have money to buy favors, and this compromises the willingness of the bureaucrat to work for change as well as creating divided loyalties in an already fragmented structure. Second, low salaries attract the incompetent. To become a bureaucrat involves the notion that one deserves a minimum salary without regard to qualifications. Low salaries also encourage the belief that employment in a government agency is a right which should be provided to as many friends and relatives as possible. Thus, instead of paying one individual a good salary, three individuals may be employed for the same amount, thereby guaranteeing an annual minimum wage and a hedge against financial insecurity. The so-called middle class of Latin America has particularly benefited from this form of welfare.

Bureaucrats want more than just an income: they want a secure income. It is very difficult to fire any bureaucrat, and most bureaucracies also have some form of welfare system which provides medical, social, and other benefits to employees and their families. Compared to more marginal groups such as peasants and workers, these benefits place many bureaucrats in an enviable position.

Prestige is another intangible, personal desire. It is an important feature of Latin American culture to have certain symbols and privileges attached to one's employment. For example, a persistent, widespread value among Latin Americans is that a gentleman does not perform manual work and while the tasks of bureaucrats vary considerably, it is certainly the case that most of the work they perform is not manual. The nonmanual character of bureaucratic work makes it most sought after by Latin Americans, especially those in the so-called middle class. Another example of prestige in bureaucracy stems from the exercise of power. Anyone who spends much time around the offices of important bureaucrats in Latin America will soon realize that the anteroom or outer office is often jammed with people waiting to see some particular functionary. A waiting line in the outer office is a sign of status. Bureaucrats want these symbols of power, and naturally resist the delegation of such work to others, particularly to those they might not trust.[19] The professional desires are less vital to some bureaucrats. Many bureaucrats at the lower organizational levels, for example, have little or no conception of their agency's goals in the developmental process of their countries. Moreover, they are more likely to choose personal desires if these conflict with organizational goals. For those bureaucrats at the higher levels of their agencies who do have some interest in doing their job and are concerned with fulfilling the goals of their organizations, professional wants may be just as important.

The professional desires of Latin American bureaucrats become directly involved with the role of bureaucracy in promoting socioeconomic changes. Most bureaucrats, especially those in agencies dealing with education, welfare, and land reform, verbally support the view that their job in the long run is to promote socioeconomic progress. However, as with other political groups, there is less agreement among bureaucrats concerning the specific role bureaucracy should play in promoting change at the present time. That is, some bureaucrats are more imbued with a change-oriented ideology than are others, and those more concerned with financial viability in such ministries as Finance or Treasury may be more conservative than are those in agricultural ministries who are concerned with promoting agrarian reform. So it is very difficult to categorize the ideology of bureaucrats in Latin America as simply "conservative," "liberal," or "radical." There are simply too many opinions concerning the proper role of bureaucracy in promoting change. However, on the whole, one generalization can be suggested: Latin

---

[19] Daland, *Brazilian Planning,* p. 125.

American bureaucrats are much more likely to favor gradual change over a long period of time than abrupt and perhaps disruptive change in a short period of time. In other words, most bureaucrats want to see socioeconomic changes come to their countries, but they want these changes to evolve through the present system which not only provides them with personal security, but also allows them considerable importance in making policy.

Bureaucrats are also likely to disagree among themselves about the immediate strategies for socioeconomic development. Some argue that the government should emphasize capital development, private investment, development of roads, highways and similar elements of economic infrastructure. Others are more concerned with redistribution of wealth under governmental auspices, rather than with absolute economic growth. Sometimes this difference in emphasis depends upon the kind of agency in which the bureaucrat works, while at other times it is dependent upon the division between the older bureaucrats and the younger bureaucrats and *técnicos*. In any event, bureaucrats, like military men, Catholic clergy and other institutional groups, are far from united in their views on immediate strategies for development.

Another professional desire of Latin American bureaucrats is a major role in the policy-making process. As mentioned earlier, bureaucrats are different from most political groups in Latin America because they directly formulate policy—although most bureaucrats recognize the right of others to participate in the policy-making process. At present, and probably for the near future, however, bureaucrats will continue to exercise disproportionate influence on policy-making. They will certainly oppose any major reduction of their role.

In general, the professional desires of Latin American bureaucrats are complicated and not simply understood, particularly since many of these wants are contradictory. That is, the pursuit of a particular desire by some bureaucrats may conflict with similar or different desires of others, thus engendering political conflict within and between bureaucracies. However, they do maintain some abstract commitment to improvement and change as long as this socioeconomic change does not help other groups at the expense of themselves or important groups with whom they are aligned. How well they resist the dilution of their position in the future will depend upon the weakness of their competitors and the degree of their own insulation from external influences.

DEMANDS

Latin American bureaucrats make demands differently than most other political groups. Groups such as peasants, urban workers, businessmen, clergy and others do not always have formal representation in the deliberative bodies of governments in Latin America. Even if they do, such groups cannot make and meet their own demands upon government; they need at minimum the consent and active cooperation of those who occupy formal positions of power. Even if these groups have this cooperation, the implementation of policies designed to meet their demands does not completely depend upon these officials. It also depends on the cooperation of bureaucrats and on other groups in the society who may or may not support their demands.

Since they are themselves a formal part of the government, bureaucrats do not have to make the special efforts other groups do in order to present their demands to the government, nor do they have to take the same steps to guarantee that government officials will comply with the demands. Furthermore, bureaucrats as a group not only make demands upon government from a privileged position, but they also make their demands a matter of public policy. Certainly a demand for increased salaries and pensions for Latin American bureaucrats would require approval of the chief executive, and in such countries as Chile and Costa Rica where the legislature is relatively strong, approval of the legislative branch. Nevertheless, many of the demands which bureaucrats make do not require the active approval of other groups because the demands can be met simply through the day-to-day operation of government, which in such countries as Mexico, Chile, and Brazil, lies largely in the hands of the bureaucrats themselves.

Despite the general power of Latin American bureaucrats, demands for personal rewards in public service are tempered by a lack of abundant resources. Pay increases, for example, may not keep pace with high rates of inflation, which places the bureaucrats in the same general financial situation as other members of the so-called middle class. In addition, many bureaucrats must cope with crowded and inadequate offices, untrained assistants, slow communications, ancient machinery, and other inadequacies common to many organizations, public or private, in Latin America. Nevertheless, bureaucrats make numerous demands, many of which are intended to ensure the welfare, security and income of the person making the demand, and many of these are met. For example, pay scales for most Latin American bureaucrats are set by the laws governing bureaucracy in general or a particular agency, but an informal proliferation of new positions allows individual bureaucrats to receive different salaries. As long as such demands are met through formal and informal means, bureaucrats will generally have more reason than not to support the present system under which they benefit.

It is often difficult to determine whether bureaucrats are expressing demands for themselves, or acting as mediators or even as a political party, or making demands for individuals or groups outside the organization. For example, a demand by an administrative assistant to the head of an agency that a road be improved in a certain district may be the product of external pressure. Actually, pressures may even originate outside national borders. For example, an international aid agency might require the road improvement as part of an aid agreement. In general, the permeation of bureaucracies by outside influences makes it very difficult to identify the sources of such demands.

Bureaucrats in Latin America sometimes create demands on behalf of various groups or categories of persons who, for one reason or another, do not voice their desires to the political system. For example, Chilean bureaucrats have sought to organize peasant unions and organizations where none previously operated so that such organizations could make demands which would support the goals of their agencies. This tactic of creating and mobilizing popular support is a rather common device upon which bureaucrats depend. Not only can demands be made to the bureaucracy apparently from some external source, but such groups are also controlled by the bureaucracy. Of course, this tactic is not used solely by bureaucrats, but it is a technique that particularly favors the ability of the bureaucrat to control demands on his agencies among lower class and poorly organized groups. The advantages are obvious: support is mobilized for the bureaucracy and an appearance of responsiveness to outside demands is given to a process which, in reality, is generally controlled by the bureaucrats. (Naturally, such powerful groups as landowners, businessmen, and the military are not as susceptible to this tactic as are peasants, laborers and, to some extent, students). Thus, by controlling demands in this way bureaucrats can better maintain their influence in making policy for socioeconomic change. Occasionally, however, a newly created group will become independent and make demands which the bureaucracy is unwilling or unable to meet.

SYSTEM RESPONSE

The implication of the preceding discussion is that bureaucrats have been quite successful in having their demands met by the political systems. That is, as government officials deeply involved in policy-making and other activities, Latin American bureaucrats receive demands of groups, including those of their own group, and within some limits, decide which demands will be met. This task is of crucial political importance because bureaucrats, by default in some cases and by delegation in others, have responsibilities for resolving conflicts, a task which politicians are more likely to perform in more developed areas of the world. Consequently, Latin American bureaucrats have considerable influence on the direction and rate of political change, so it is necessary to speak not only of how the political systems of

Latin America respond to the demands of bureaucrats, but also of how bureaucrats shape the response of these systems.

Many bureaucrats have a conservative or braking effect on the direction and rate of change promoted through governmental policies.[20] As Scott notes, for example, a common practice for ensuring that bureaucracy acts as a brake on socioeconomic change is the creation of new agencies as a means for controlling the disruptive and unsettling conditions of unintegrated societies.[21] The attainment of goals is therefore more apparent than real. In one sense, at least, Latin American bureaucracy came on the scene too early and has therefore controlled change in some countries before important changes could take place. In some of the developed countries, on the other hand, bureaucracy emerged after some fundamental changes in society had already occurred. Thus, the premature emergence of bureaucracy in Latin America has often had the effect of retarding what it is formally supposed to promote.

The political systems of Latin America are more responsive to bureaucrats' personal and narrow professional interests than to their ideological commitments to gradual change. This is not to cast doubt on the sincerity of all bureaucrats who have some influence in promoting their ideologies of nationalism, development, and democracy. However, bureaucrats are getting much, if not all, they want under the present system. Commitments to socioeconomic change in the long run are less satisfied through the present system. In Mexico, for example, the Revolution has been institutionalized not only through the PRI, the dominant party, but through a proliferating and important bureaucracy. Scott, for one, has some doubts about the success of the Mexican bureaucracy in promoting an integrated, national society.[22] Despite their verbal commitments to change within an integrated, modern society, Mexican bureaucrats may have hindered rather than promoted the changes necessary to achieve a well-integrated society in which modernity and development permeate all sectors. In Mexico, as elsewhere, bureaucrats are likely to be dominating and semi-authoritarian with the general public which they are supposed to serve, while as an elite themselves, they are most responsive to elite groups who are less interested in social development.

Bureaucrats are less likely to implement programs which attempt to redistribute the wealth within developing economies. For example, a study of the Social Security Institute of Mexico, a decentralized, semi-autonomous agency that provides social security services to eligible workers, reveals that

20 Scott, "The Government Bureaucrats:" see also Petras, *Politics and Social Forces in Chilean Development.*

21 Ibid.

22 Ibid.

those groups best served under the agency are the organized workers of urban areas rather than the unorganized, and especially rural, workers. Rural workers have been eligible for the social security system for years but they simply cannot afford to belong. In other words, this agency, as well as many similar ones scattered throughout the administrative structures of the Latin American countries, is incapable of adequately serving those citizens who most need its services.[23] This, again, is not to argue that the leading bureaucrats of such agencies have no ideological commitments to the formal redistributive goals of their institutions. To the contrary, and especially in Mexico, such bureaucrats express dissatisfaction with the progress their agency has made in providing the benefits of development to all their people. Nevertheless, they are responsive to many pressures that slow the implementation of policies in bureaucracies that are supposed to provide more of these benefits to increasing numbers of Latin Americans.

In summary, bureaucrats, like most political groups, must be willing to accept less than what they would like to receive, but bureaucrats have a distinct advantage for achieving both their personal and professional demands through their central role in the making and meeting of demands for the entire political system. They have obviously benefited disproportionately from the expansion of governmental services and tasks during recent Latin American history. Most of the countries suffer from expensive and inefficient bureaucracy. Inadequate to the tasks of socioeconomic change, bureaucracy provides voice and support only to the powerful.

What are the prospects for socioeconomic changes made possible through bureaucracy? The future seems brighter than the present, a judgment which might be based more on optimism than evidence. Bureaucrats, despite formidable obstacles and their own defects as promoters of socioeconomic change, have nevertheless contributed something to the process of change. Moreover, newer methods and younger, better trained personnel may eventually free the bureaucracy from its conservative impact on developing societies. But one should recall that the influences on bureaucracy and bureaucracy itself are powerful obstacles to the effective use of public administration as a device for promoting major change. The immobility of the political systems of Latin America also permeates its bureaucracies. And yet there is the fortunate possibility that changes not welcomed by the elites may take place in spite of the general role of bureaucrats in Latin American politics. In addition to those few bureaucrats who want major change but cannot bring them about are those many bureaucrats who do not want major changes but cannot foresee the gradual and unintended consequences of their own policies. They may not always know what they do.

[23] Guy E. Poitras, "The 'Bureaucratic Politics' of a Welfare Agency in a Developing Political System: The Case of the Mexican Institute of Social Security," (Ph.D. dissertation: University of Texas, 1970).

FURTHER READING

ADAMS, RICHARD N., *The Second Sowing: Power and Secondary Development in Latin America*. San Francisco: Chandler, 1967.

ANDERSON, CHARLES W., *Politics and Economic Change in Latin America*. New York: Van Nostrand Reinhold, 1967.

BENVENISTE, GUY, *Bureaucracy and National Planning: A Sociological Case Study in Mexico*. New York: Praeger, 1970.

DALAND, ROBERT, *Brazilian Planning: Development, Politics and Administration*. Chapel Hill: University of North Carolina Press, 1967.

EISENSTADT, S. N., "Bureaucracy, Bureaucratization and De-Bureaucratization," in. *Administrative Science Quarterly*, Vol. 4, December 1959.

GOMEZ, RUDOLPH, *The Peruvian Administrative System*. Boulder: University of Colorado Press, 1969.

HEADY, FERREL, *Public Administration: A Comparative Perspective*. Englewood Cliffs, N.J.: Prentice-Hall, 1966.

HOPKINS, JACK W., *The Government Executive of Modern Peru*. Gainesville: University of Florida Press, 1967.

LAPALOMBARA, JOSEPH, *Bureaucracy and Political Development*. Princeton: Princeton University Press, 1963.

LEFF, NATHANIEL, *Economic Policy-making and Development in Brazil, 1947–1964*. New York: John Wiley, 1968.

MICHELENA, JOSE A. SILVA, "The Venezuelan Bureaucrats," in Frank Bonilla and Jose A. Silva Michelena, *A Strategy for Research on Social Policy*. Cambridge, Mass.: M.I.T. Press, 1967.

PADGETT, L. VINCENT, *The Mexican Political System*. Boston: Houghton Mifflin, 1966.

PAN AMERICAN UNION, *Administracion Publica en America Latina*. Washington, D.C.: Secretaria General, OEA, 1967.

PARRISH, CHARLES J. and JORGE TAPIA-VIDELA, "Welfare Policy and Administration in Chile," in *Journal of Comparative Administration*, Vol. 1, No. 4, February 1970.

PETRAS, JAMES, *Politics and Social Forces in Chilean Development*. Berkeley: University of California Press, 1969.

POITRAS, GUY E., "The 'Bureaucratic Politics' of A Welfare Agency in A Developing Country: The Case of the Mexican Institute of Social Security." Unpublished Ph.D. dissertation: University of Texas at Austin, 1970.

———————— and CHARLES F. DENTON, "Bureaucratic Performance: Case Studies from Mexico and Costa Rica," in *Journal of Comparative Administration*, Vol. 3, No. 2, August 1971.

Pye, Lucian W., "The Political Context of National Development," in Irving Swerdlow (ed.), *Administrative Development: Concepts and Problems.* Syracuse, N.Y.: Syracuse University Press, 1963.

Riggs, Fred W., *Administration in Developing Countries: The Theory of Prismatic Society.* Boston: Houghton Mifflin, 1964.

Scott, Robert E., "The Government Bureaucrats and Political Change in Latin America," in *Journal of International Affairs,* Vol. 20, 1966.

White, William Foote, *Organizational Behavior: Theory and Application.* Homewood, Ill.: Richard C. Irwin and Dorsey, 1969.

CHAPTER 9

THE POLITICS
OF IMMOBILITY

Whether one views it in terms of a century or of the last few decades, Latin America has undergone considerable socioeconomic change. Discovery of minerals, whether oil or less spectacular industrial metals, has greatly added to the region's economic potential. With similar result, various changes have occurred to some extent in agricultural techniques and products. Gradual industrialization, particularly through the introduction of new technology, has not only increased the size and political importance of older urban centers, but has created new ones. Although these and many similar changes have resulted largely from external influences (such as technology developed in and for the more economically advanced countries), no one can seriously deny today that such change makes it impossible to consider Latin America as simply a collection of more or less totally traditionalistic societies.

The important question, therefore, focuses not on the past but on the future. Granted that changes of uneven scope and effect have permeated much of Latin America, it is still quite evident that they have sometimes been stalled, and they have not always promoted economic, social, and political development in the region. Given this, the question arises as to the future possibility of such development, as well as to the direction it will take if it occurs. It may or may not occur, and if it does occur, it may very well not take the form and direction experienced by the so-called modernized countries of the world.

One cannot begin to understand the problems Latin Americans face in developing their countries without some knowledge of the various economic, political, and social aspects of development. On the other hand, one cannot hope to take into account every conceivable economic, political, and social factor that might affect the prospects, form and direction of development. Therefore, the principal concern here has been to focus on several major groupings in Latin American society, discussing them in a particular context in order to provide some idea of their socioeconomic and political situation, and then examining what each grouping desires, demands, and receives from the various political systems. Hopefully, from this discussion have emerged the major problems involved in socioeconomic and political development in the region. Since this is the fundamental concern here, a brief reexamination of each grouping appears in order.

First, rural Latin America is characterized by great extremes of wealth and poverty, partially as the result of the prevailing land tenure structure whereby most land, and certainly most productive land, is owned by relatively very few individuals and families. These large estates (*latifundios*) depend on a variety of means to ensure a labor force to work the land, but primarily it is the existence of the estates themselves that ensures a lack of arable land for the millions of peasants and therefore ensures a surplus of labor for work on the estates. This labor surplus, in turn, is the real basis of the estate's ability to maintain its workers in a condition of poverty. At the same time, while some change is apparent in the form of modernized, mechanized, and profit-run agricultural enterprises, the virtual monopoly of land by the large estates tends to ensure continued great inefficiency in the agricultural sectors of the various economies. For that matter, underutilization of its lands by the estate also contributes to the labor surplus that allows the estate to persist as a way of life in rural Latin America. At the opposite extreme, the other basic land tenure pattern in Latin America is the *minifundio* system, a system of very small plots that allow their millions of owners or holders to scrape a bare existence from the soil, but that produce virtually nothing for the domestic and/or foreign markets. As a final result of both the *latifundio* and *minifundio* systems, the agricultural sector of almost all Latin American economies is at best only poorly integrated into the national economy, and no country in the area has a really "balanced" agricultural sector. Thus foreign exchange which is badly needed to pursue developmental goals is consumed in buying foodstuffs for countries with predominantly rural populations.

Given all this, it might be expected that rural Latin America is hovering on the brink of profound social disorder and violence—a situation often suggested by foreign journalists outraged at socioeconomic conditions in rural areas. But this kind of thinking ignores the essentially conservative nature of the rural areas—conservatism on the part not only of the *hacendado* but also of the peasant. While the *hacendado* can naturally be expected to wish and to fight to maintain the traditional way of life, the peasants appear to be generally lacking in revolutionary aspirations. The *hacienda* is a way of life to them too, and there is no real evidence that the peasants aspire to anything much different. Similarly, the *minifundistas* do not apparently aspire to a life basically different from that which they have. They may, and probably do, want more land, but considerable evidence suggests that they would much rather forego this possibility than become politically involved in order to achieve their desire. In other words, most of the rural populace in Latin America can be classed as more or less outside the political systems of the region in the sense that they do not perceive the national systems as relevant to furthering any interests they may have. In fact, when relevance of the political system is perceived by them, attempts are often made by peasants to use it to maintain customs and traditions not at all in keeping with what we consider to be a "modern" society.

In considering demands on the political systems from rural Latin America, it is easy to see where the relatively sophisticated and often very politically astute *hacendado* makes considerable demands to maintain the status quo of his society—particularly in the countryside—while the peasant by not making counter-demands essentially supports these demands. Apathy, that is, induced by whatever means, is a strong supporter of existing conditions. Demands are, of course, often made in the peasant's behalf under various circumstances, but these mainly appear to be made cynically by some individual or group aspiring to influence the political system for personal ends, or by isolated and ineffectual humanitarians.

Most of what the peasant receives from the political system is essentially in the form of symbolic support—for example, in the form of unenforced and/or unenforceable agrarian reform legislation. The *hacendado,* on the other hand, essentially receives what he demands, if the continuing land tenure pattern of Latin America is any indication at all. The peasant *might* receive much more than symbolic rewards from the system *if* he strongly demanded change—but if rural change is not demanded on a fairly widespread basis, it will, of course, not materialize.

Second, Latin American businessmen have been discussed in the context of general economic conditions in the region. Since the depression, industrialization has occurred to a considerable extent throughout the region, although the degree of it varies considerably from country to country. This industrialization has been promoted by import substitution policies which favor domestic industry but which leave primary product exports to the mercy of world markets characterized by great fluctuation. Since the export of primary products still accounts for a very high percentage of each country's GNP, fluctuations in world markets can greatly hinder domestic developmental plans dependent on foreign exchange earnings. Furthermore, domestic industrialization is greatly hampered by the lack of purchasing power among the rural and urban masses; a situation not alleviated by export of industrial products that are unable to compete effectively in world markets. In general, import substitution policies have tended to create dependence of business on government, lack of foreign as well as domestic competition, and great inefficiency in domestic industrial production. This entire situation is further aggravated by constant inflation in many of the countries, a disinclination to invest in industry, foreign dominance of many of the economies, inability to proceed far in regional economic integration, and a host of other factors. As a final result there is a persistent widening of the gap between income in Latin America and income in the relatively quite economically developed countries of the world.

Like the rural aristocrat, the Latin American businessman is in a relatively affluent position, but affluence is not the only thing the two have in common. The businessman, no matter how modern his business may be, tends strongly to share many attitudes and values with the *hacendado*. Rather than being entirely or even mainly motivated by profit, the businessman tends to be heavily influenced by considerations of family, and is particularly concerned with personal and family prestige. These motivations can have a distinctly adverse impact on business efficiency (through the practice of nepotism) and business expansion (through the unwillingness to allow control of a firm to slip from family hands). A stock market cannot contribute to general economic growth when family firms persist and predominate.

Various studies show that businessmen, while not adamantly opposed to any and all socioeconomic change, are essentially very conservative. They tend to be economic nationalists, whether or not consciously motivated by private profit considerations. Government developmental programs, however, are seen as good only if they involve no drastic and immediate alteration in the social status quo. On the whole, businessmen tend to lay emphasis on government's duties in this area; they are not ideologically opposed to government's economic functions, but they tend to demand only programs that will be of obvious good to themselves. This "good" they naturally define in terms of their own values which do not emphasize profit at the risk of basic socioeconomic change.

Overall, businessmen appear quite capable of having their demands met by the political systems of the region. They have import substitution policies behind which to carry on their activities in a relatively leisurely, inefficient fashion. Governments are tending more and more toward regulation of foreign investment and related economic activities. Even the tax policies by which businessmen could be deprived of some affluence are not seriously enforced. In short, Latin American businessmen, judging from their positions of prestige and wealth, are quite powerful and successful in their political systems.

Third, urban workers have been placed in the context of prominent demographic features of Latin America. The region's population is today best described by the term "mushrooming" (to the extent that one estimate suggests a total population of 750 million thirty years from now). The same term is also quite useful in describing the urbanization that is occurring in the region, since this is proceeding at an even greater rate than population growth, due to migration from rural to urban areas. Both the population growth rate and the urbanization rate create and magnify many problems for socioeconomic development—basic problems such as sewage, lighting, and transportation. The great, underlying problem, however, is that the industrial process has not advanced at a rate nearly as great as population and urban growth, and furthermore has begun to enter a phase that makes large numbers of workers less and less necessary. Today automation has contributed to unemployment in the most industrialized countries of the world, and it is becoming more and more evident in Latin America, an area that already has a terrific labor surplus. As a consequence, there is great poverty among the urban masses, and slums are becoming a more and more prominent feature of urban areas. The migrant nature of much of the slum's population tends to provide it with a distinctly rural, traditionalistic character which fits very poorly into an increasingly complex industrial technology.

One might expect the urban masses to be a seething bed of revolutionary thought and turmoil, but this is not generally the case. Aspirations for betterment can be noted, even among the rural migrants (unless one assumes a lemming-like quality in the rural-to-urban migration, it is necessary to assume that those holding aspirations think they might be better pursued in the cities). But these aspirations seldom take the form of demands for major socioeconomic change. Organized workers, insofar as the formal demands of their leaders indicate, aspire toward and demand essentially middle-class, bread-and-butter rewards. Furthermore, the unions themselves strongly tend to be captives of their respective national governments, and regional organizations tend to be captives of foreign countries. As a result, even the bread-and-butter demands tend to be very modest, considering the worker's circumstances. Spontaneous organizations of slum dwellers also show certain aspirations in the form of demands, but again these tend to be quite minor, often reflecting the rural person's obsession with land.

On the whole, while the urban workers do have aspirations for betterment, they are quite similar to the peasants in that they remain essentially apolitical. They are outside the political system in that they do not really perceive its relevance to themselves. When political action does occur, it tends to reflect the traditional *patron-peon* relationship. For example, the government, in a paternalistic manner, grants to workers the high-sounding right to participate in national planning bodies, which the worker knows nothing about, and with which his leaders themselves are often incapable of coping.

In short, the worker for various reasons remains captive of other social and political groups; he is very vulnerable to sanctions; and he tends to accept his lot. He is given rewards in the form of high-sounding legislation dealing with the social and human rights of workers, but as with agrarian reform legislation, such rewards are essentially only symbolic outputs of the various political systems.

Fourth, university students have been discussed in the context of the campus. In general the composition of the Latin American student body is elitist, but despite this they tend to be fairly antiestablishment. This appears to be due in good part to their university-oriented concerns, such as university autonomy and co-government. These two principles have been prime student concerns for the last half-century in Latin America, and any infringement of them, real or imagined, creates student hostility. Thus, there is considerable campus unrest from time to time, due to the fact that the government, consciously or not, constantly tends to restrict the attainment of goals based on these principles. University autonomy is a particularly sore point, given the fact that the university budget is at the mercy of government willingness and/or ability to contribute funds for higher educational activities.

Therefore, much of the rhetoric and actual political activity of students can be regarded as outside the realm of socioeconomic change in their societies. Whether the university is autonomous and whether students participate in university government are questions not necessarily relevant to politics of change. However, the third major principle of the original University Reform Movement—that the university concern itself with social problems—is obviously quite relevant. Even concern for the other principles can spill over into this concern.

Society-oriented goals of students strongly tend to be idealistic. They tend to see themselves in, and are accorded by society, political roles motivated by purity and altruism. However, the evidence available suggests that most students are generally not politically active, and that when activism deepens it tends to be short-lived and as often as not is created by university-oriented rather than society-oriented concerns. They often react violently to major political events, such as to a military coup and/or suspension of constitutional rights, but this type of activity under the circumstances is met with even greater determination and violence, and as a result is also generally short-lived.

In addition to these obvious obstacles to student success in achieving goals related to socioeconomic change, there are two less obvious but major obstacles. The first of these is the lack of unity in student goals for change. They may share idealism, but idealism is not limited to any one economic or political philosophy or structure. It can range all the way from total anarchy to total fascism as solutions to social ills. Thus although they are discussed here as a social grouping or category, there is certainly no unanimous political and economic orientation among them, and the potential of their activism for change is therefore dissipated or diluted as one faction's political strength cancels out another's.

The second major hindrance to student political success in achieving goals of change is the simple fact of age. Whether one wishes to say that they are "coopted by the system" or that they "grow up and get a job," or whatever, the fact is that there is a very high turnover in both leadership and membership of student political organizations. There is no natural continuity in goals, strategies, and alliances, but there is continuity in further dissipation of political energies year after year as these goals, strategies, and alliances have to be constantly redetermined by new leaders and followers.

In sum, the university student in Latin America does not appear to be a major vehicle of socioeconomic change. After his schooling and his days of political idealism there is every indication that he falls into place in his society, adhering to its norms and standards. Given the relatively affluent background of most university students, the norms they reassume will be middle-class at the lowest, and as has been emphasized previously here, middle-class groups in Latin America are far from being oriented toward drastic socioeconomic change. The most that the university experience can seriously be expected to contribute to change through the middle-class student is, perhaps, some moderation in outlook.

Fifth, the clergy have been discussed in the context of their institution, the Roman Catholic Church. Once an extremely powerful political force, the Church in Latin America has been steadily declining in influence, reflecting the general secularization of the region. While socioeconomic changes in the last century have undermined the foundations of their tradition-bound institution, and as political power has diffused to economic and other secular elites, the Roman Catholic clergy have been unable to redefine their goals, and have proved incapable of using their ever-diminishing resources to promote popular goals and to recapture their prestige.

One of the fundamental political problems of the clergy today is that their institution can no longer expect to be automatically treated as a branch of government on policy matters, and when they attempt as individuals to enter politics, their ranks are racked by schisms. Further, the clergy have something quite in common with peasants and urban workers in that most are apolitical. That is, the majority of the clergy tend to have no conscious political motives and they rarely if ever participate actively in the politics of their country—a situation again favoring continuation of present conditions. On the other hand, the minority who do participate in politics in various ways have something in common with university students in that they are generally unable to agree upon the application of Church doctrine to current realities. The conservative clergy, who tend to dominate the upper levels of the Church hierarchy, project the general image of the Church as a traditional, noninnovating institution, while the progressives, generally in the lower levels of the organization, tend to push through, and even occasionally against, the system for socioeconomic changes.

Actually, the greatly publicized and often sensationalized demands of the progressive clergy tend to obscure the fact that the conservatives are the most politically influential faction within the Church in Latin America. They tend to demand little change, and they also tend to receive what they demand in terms of maintaining the status quo. Given the constant trend toward secularization of their societies, the conservative clergy benefit from government ineffectiveness in promoting socioeconomic change, while on the other hand the progressives are hindered from assuming a role in such change by the same secularization trend. In short, the Church, as an institution dominated by the conservatives who control it, has been placed in a weakened position by changes in its environment, but the politics of immobility allow it to continue resisting any changes which would further weaken its traditional base. The progressive clergy are unable to strengthen the position of the Church due to their inability to agree on goals, strategies, and alliances, and are themselves a good reflection of the fragmentation that characterizes their societies.

Sixth, military officers have been considered in the context of the military as an institution in developing countries in general and in Latin America in particular. It is quite clear that the military officers as a group constitute probably the most powerful and decisive element in the politics of most Latin American countries. The fragmentation of the societies, the premium placed on violence, the relatively modern aspect of the military, and its resources and manpower all make the military not only an interest group placing demands on government, but often make it either the government itself or an indispensable partner of government. Since formal political institutions are often quite ineffective, the military, which can monopolize and mobilize violence if necessary, fills the void left by the deadlock of civilian politics. However, such a role carries certain consequences, in that the military, especially when it actually runs a government, eventually comes to reflect the fragmentation and division of civilian government and of society in general. While its formal organization and power allow it to escape some of the more virulent effects of such fragmentation, its effectiveness is nevertheless always greatly lessened.

Considerable controversy exists over the question of whether the military in developing countries promotes or retards socioeconomic development overall. It is fairly easily seen that military officers seek to maintain and enlarge their institutional and personal interests, and the satisfaction of these often must be through the denial óf public funds to less privileged groups. In this sense, then, the military has a conservative effect on government's promotion of development. However, concerning broader questions of public policy, the picture is not so clear. In general, evidence suggests that, in the earlier stages of development, military officers are likely to demand policies which undermine traditional society. Industrialization, nationalism, urbanization, education, and growth of a middle class are all goals for which many military officers stand. However, it is during the intermediate stages of development that they are less likely to play a reformist role. As the middle sectors achieve some significant stake in the social status quo, and as the increasing unrest and participation of the lower sectors threatens this stake, the military appears quite inclined to step in to protect middle-sector vested interests. At this point, although still inclined to support industrialization and economic growth, officers are much less inclined to support reforms that might stimulate greater social and political uncertainty as a result of growing participation of new groups. In other words, while the military can and often does perform a progressive role in the process of socioeconomic development, its own attitudes and interests tend to prevent it from acting in this capacity to any great length along the developmental continuum.

Seventh, the bureaucrats have been examined in the contexts of public administration in general and public administration in developing societies in particular. Like military officers, bureaucrats both make demands on the political system and, as a formal institution of the system, meet or reject demands. Because of the relative weakness of other formal institutions, bureaucracy often tends to become the focus of the political system; bureaucrats decide which demands must and can be met, as well as those demands which can with relative safety be ignored. This considerable political role is not generally subject to effective external control from broadly based, highly organized groups of the lower sectors. However, permeated by and vulnerable to a number of outside influences, bureaucrats are quite sensitive to the demands of those who have a significant stake in society. Therefore they tend to be oriented toward the desires of relatively narrow elites rather than to the often unarticulated desires of those who have yet to achieve any important social position. Moreover, as middle sector members themselves in a fragmented society, bureaucrats tend to be very concerned with control and stability, and are little eager to create the uncertainties which unavoidably accompany rapid socioeconomic change. In short, bureaucrats are central to the processes of immobile politics and are much more likely to defend the status quo (and therefore their personal prerogatives) than they are to advocate and implement programs for the socioeconomic development of their countries.

It would be misleading and unfair to attribute this situation to a total lack of morality in Latin American bureaucrats. More accurate is the perspective that they must operate within a political system that is lacking fundamental consensus and that is fragmented into narrow groups. Although bureaucrats might be accused of failing to take brave measures to overcome the obstacles to goals of socioeconomic development and their failures as a modernizing group, the fact is that they collectively personify the malaise of Latin American politics in general. They are not and cannot be isolated from the setting in which they operate, and the politics of immobility becomes, by extension, bureaucracy of immobility.

This discussion of groups in Latin American politics has generally focused upon each as an individual if not united entity. However, the discussion would be incomplete if there were not some consideration given to them as interdependent elements within a single system, elements that sometimes ignore one another. Such consideration requires a return to some general concerns discussed in Chapter 1.

The number, size, and importance of socioeconomic groups have increased in Latin America, particularly in recent decades, under the impact of industrialization and similar factors. Today, in addition to the traditional oligarchy of military, church, and landowners, socioeconomic changes have prompted the emergence or heightened the importance of peasants, urban workers, businessmen, bureaucrats, and students. And with the varying participation of these groups in politics, new problems have arisen that often have not been alleviated or solved by the political systems of the region. The emergence of these new groups has been accompanied by various and greater expectations on their part, and these expectations have placed formal governmental institutions in an often extremely difficult position in that more is demanded of them than they can reasonably be expected to provide. There is thus a great discrepancy between demands placed on the political systems and system capabilities in meeting the demands, all of which tends to foster a stagnant or immobile political situation.

Put differently, all these groups want something from their government, while the government itself is part of a system that lacks substantial agreement among the groups about what exactly should be done. Without some consensus concerning such questions as what should be done about socioeconomic change and who is to benefit primarily from it, government institutions are crippled. They cannot act without the nearly unanimous consent of mutually antagonistic groups, and difficulties are further compounded when within a single group there is considerable disunity over what group interests are and what government should do to promote them. Without this consensus there are in-groups and out-groups, the former pursuing their own interests while more or less ignoring others, and the latter regarding the former as illegitimate captors of political resources, i.e., the formal institutions of government.[1] However, at least to some extent complete immobility can occasionally be avoided when circumstances and group interests coincide to produce agreement and action for change. Thus, for example, the Peruvian military has been able to promote limited agrarian reform because there is substantial agreement among most of the important political groups that this should be done. The large landowners of the coastal region were no longer able to resist the agreement among other groups that such reform was overdue, and they certainly were not able to resist the compulsory dictates of a military government. However, this linking of legitimacy and power tends to be the exception rather than the rule in most issues of Latin American politics.

Overall then, the fragmentation of power and lack of legitimacy in Latin American politics have debilitating effects on the political systems of the region. If, as was noted in Chapter 1, political systems use legitimate coercion in the process of making and implementing decisions for society, then it is obvious that the Latin American political systems are generally not very effective in those areas crucial to the promotion of change. Given the great disagreement over basic goals involved in change, and the consequent insistence of the out-groups on the illegitimacy of the power holders, no government can be really effective in acting as a vehicle for change. From this perspective, the primary reason for the inability of the political system to promote change is that short of social revolution, change-oriented government is permeated and weakened by conditions in the social environment that it is trying to reform. That is, the inability to establish legitimate, fairly autonomous institutions of government is closely linked to inability to insulate them sufficiently from narrow elites or from the general effects of fragmented societies. Governmental institutions cannot escape from their fragmented milieu, and while this does not mean that some change cannot and does not occur, it does mean that a government under these circumstances is a poor vehicle for carrying the burden of achieving the rapid socioeconomic change that is often demanded of it.

In Latin America, as perhaps elsewhere, institutional groups such as military officers and bureaucrats have a definite political advantage over relatively unorganized and loosely-knit groups such as peasants and urban

---

[1] Irving Louis Horowitz, "The Norm of Illegitimacy: Toward a General Theory of Latin American Political Development," in Arthur J. Field (ed.), *City and Country in the Third World* (Cambridge, Mass.: Schenkman Publishing Company, 1970), pp. 25–48.

workers. Their organized position within society enables these institutional groups to articulate their demands and to be more successful in receiving what they demand from the political system. And although such institutional groups are not without impressive problems, the other groups of Latin American politics are at a clear disadvantage. Indeed, as was emphasized earlier, such groups as peasants and workers often fail to make known any desires they may possess due to their inability to perceive the political system as relevant to themselves. Furthermore, on those rare occasions when small numbers of peasants or workers are organized for political action, their leaders are as often as not bought off in some fashion by elites or groups with opposing interests.

SYSTEM DEMANDS

While this overview will hopefully provide some understanding of the problems of demands placed on a political system and the system's capability in meeting them, recall that in Chapter 1 several types of demands were discussed as well as several aspects of system capabilities. Turning now to these more specific concerns in the context of the various groups, a very common demand is, of course, the demand for system allocation of goods and services. Military officers have been particularly successful in demanding and receiving large proportions of most government budgets in Latin America. Similarly, bureaucrats have been quite successful in making and receiving their demands both through their importance in system decision-making as well as through their ability to identify their desires with government needs. Both of these institutional groups are so located within government as to be fairly secure in their political importance, and from this position they are able to make quite specific requests for the allocation of government resources. On the other hand, groups such as peasants and workers are neither well-placed nor well-organized to make specific demands for specific benefits. Rather, groups such as these are prone to make incoherent or ambiguous demands. Similarly, although students are perhaps not as removed from the political process as peasants and workers, they share their incoherence and ambiguity of demands. Students tend to focus not on specific allocation of benefits but on broad and sweeping changes which they feel would alleviate conditions as they perceive them. The clergy, in the context of allocative demands, also tend toward ambiguity. Socio-economic changes have undercut the power of their institution. The granting of further demands of other groups for changes would further diminish the prestige of their institution. That is they do not so much request goods and services for themselves as they offer resistance to such demands by other groups that threaten the status quo. Businessmen, however, have demands in this area which are much more specific and of direct, material concern to themselves. What government does regarding such policies as import substitution and taxation not only affects economic development but the success or failure of business ventures. Overall, businessmen have been quite successful in voicing their demands and having them met, although much of their potential political power is not achieved due to the heterogeneity of businessmen as a group. Policies very beneficial to some might be equally detrimental to others, and the force of business demands can be lost through their frequent contradictions.

If one were to rate the various groups according to their relative success in having their allocative demands met by the political systems of the region, it would seem fairly safe to say on an overall basis that military officers, bureaucrats, businessmen, and large-landowners are in the top half of the scale, the clergy are in an intermediate position, and students, workers, and peasants are in the bottom half. Ranking within these subcategories varies from country to country. In most systems the military are fairly dominant because their ability to resort to violence, but in Costa Rica and Uruguay, and perhaps in Cuba and Mexico, the bureaucrats are probably most politically potent. One has only to look at the land tenure pattern discussed in Chapter 2 to realize that except in Cuba and Chile, the large landowner essentially maintains his prestigious position despite occasional set-backs. Businessmen are likewise important in all the systems except Cuba, but their political importance varies considerably from country to country due to the differing degrees of economic development achieved. Businessmen in Honduras and Nicaragua, for example, are not as important to and within their respective political system as are their counterparts in, for example, Mexico and Argentina. The clergy have been rated as intermediate in political importance due to their marginality concerning allocative demands for themselves and their tendency to act as a veto group toward various demands, generally from the less politically prestigious groups, which appear to threaten the status quo. That is, they are an occasional ally for the more conservative groups, but do not themselves stand out in this area. Of the least important groups, the peasants are almost certainly at the bottom of the scale. Unorganized, politically ignorant, kept in their place by the traditional rural social structure, they so seldom enter politics and are so marginal to the political system that it would not be a great distortion in most cases to leave them entirely off the political scale. Urban workers, with some noteworthy exceptions, resemble the peasants in that their demands are at best only poorly articulated, and their political prestige is generally quite low. Finally, it is difficult to place the students anywhere, in that they can be extremely vociferous in making demands for sweeping social changes. These changes do not occur, but the force of their demands may be fairly influential in obtaining the more narrow interests of their fairly elitist group. In any event, except for a few historical examples in Mexico, Venezuela, Chile and Cuba, they tend to be in the lower part of most countries' scale of politically important groups.

Another type of demand, which often but not necessarily complements demands for goods and services, is that the government regulate the economic, social, and political life of the country in such a way as to protect the interests of the group(s) making the demand. Regulatory demands may be very specific or very broad, but they generally take the form of demands by one group for regulation of another. For example, a government loan to businessmen in a certain industry may create the narrow demand that the businessmen concerned publicly account for expenditures of the sum involved. More broadly, workers may demand in various ways that the government regulate business, while businessmen demand that government regulate workers; or students may demand broad changes in an administration's foreign policy, while military officers demand tighter control over "leftist" students. And in the political systems of Latin America the demands by one group for regulation of another may become a battle for group survival. That is, if a group is able to secure a commitment from government to regulate the activities of another, the victory—even if it is more apparent than real—takes on the hue of an attempt not just to regulate but to eliminate the political power of the other group. Certainly, if government were more effective than it generally is in Latin America, demands for regulation would achieve just such a result in many cases. The demand by socialistic students and workers that government regulate businessmen could easily lead (*if* the demand was met and *if* government institutions operated effectively) to the elimination of businessmen as they are today. Similarly, demands are often voiced in no uncertain terms that the large estates be actually abolished, or that the military be eliminated, or that the clergy be totally circumscribed in their activities.

As the system actually works, however, demands for regulation of other groups are generally recognized only if they come from elites who want to maintain or impose order, and if meeting the demands would not change the basic rules of the game. That is, regulatory demands tend to be met in order to keep one group from gaining ascendancy over all or most others. Thus, for example, businessmen and the military can throw their weight against urban labor when it becomes too organized and vocal. Similarly, landowners have been known to support urban labor in order to harm businessmen with, for example, rapid wage increases. All or most major groups have occasionally worked together successfully in order to rid themselves of a military administration that has become too overbearing. In short, in the constantly shifting play of political forces, demands for regulation are used to continue the immobility of politics since a major change would threaten one or more of the major groups.

The demand for participation in the political system, the last major type of demand to be discussed here, is of particular relevance to Latin America, especially in the context of change. The demand for participation generally must precede demands that government promote socioeconomic change.

As in most areas of the world, participation in Latin American politics is highly uneven. Over the years, all the most important socioeconomic groups have earned the right to participate meaningfully to some extent. But the question in contemporary Latin America concerns the rate and extent to which demands for participation should be met. Earlier in this century, demands of the emerging middle sector for participation in the political affairs of their countries led to a broadened political arena, and bureaucrats, businessmen, students, and other middle sector groups were granted a larger political role. But, the emergence of new groups has not meant the elimination of the old, and today in those Latin American countries that have reached the intermediate stages of development, the middle sector groups share political power with the older elites. However, now that these groups have gained the privilege of political participation with attendant socioeconomic benefits, they are allied with the older elites in being reluctant to broaden the political participation of the lower sectors.

Although the lower sectors have generally been unable to effectively express demands to participate in politics (where they have such demands), some of the more organized of them have provoked considerable anxiety among the middle sectors and older elites with their demands for rapidly expanded participation accompanied by insistence on rapid and basic socioeconomic changes. Uncertain of their ability to maintain themselves in the face of such broadened participation, the middle sectors have encouraged military intervention in ousting popularly-favored administrations. Once in control themselves, they have clamped down on the participation of lower sector groups. In other words, the middle sector in Latin America is not going to act as some "vanguard of the proletariat" in demanding broader political participation for the masses.

Problems of participation have been reaching crisis proportion for some time now in several countries in Latin America. Demonstrations, riots, strikes, and other more or less violent activities are often calculated to force greater concessions from the elites in terms of political participation. As noted earlier, for example, university students often make demands for participation in national government. Sometimes aligned with urban workers and other politically marginal groups, the students have a militant and often violent record of attacking oligarchical and foreign interests and military governments. Although university students definitely express their interest in reallocating the benefits of government (perhaps after a revolution), their principal strategy seems to concern recognition of basic demands for broadening political participation. Joining in this demand to grant rapidly expanded participation to the lower sectors, the radical clergy, a few peasant and labor leaders, and some dissident elements of the middle sectors have sought to organize members of the lower sectors into a political force. However, the price of pressing too rapidly for mass participation often turns out to be repression, as the case of Brazil clearly suggests. Of course, submission to the more radical demands for mass participation in politics would substantially alter the present operation of the political system, and those now in control of it are and will be very reluctant to yield to demands that could, and often probably would, not only abort their personal careers but also destroy the interests of the groups that they represent.

In other words, until recently groups could be admitted to the political process without breaking the deadlock of politics in Latin America. As long as participation of the lower sector groups remains limited, major changes in which one or more other groups are eliminated seem unlikely. The threat of rapidly expanding participation is a challenge to the politics of immobility because it would undermine those groups that presently benefit most from stagnation and that are determined to avoid, for as long as possible, any adverse change in their situation. On the other hand, as the demands for greater participation by the lower sectors conflict with demands by the upper and middle sectors for their restricted participation, the strains on Latin American political systems become more acute. While there is the fairly remote possibility that formal government institutions will break down under the strain, it appears more likely that, barring some exceptional events, government will simply become less effective relative to the growing demands of the people. Unable to take decisive action to promote socio-economic changes, government will continue to balance quarreling interests by compromising goals of development and by adjusting conflicts over what is possible in a fragmented situation. In order to accomplish this, demands for participation will be resisted to the greatest extent possible so as to keep the arena of conflict smaller and more manageable.

SYSTEM CAPABILITIES

The idea of system capabilities was examined in Chapter 1; simply stated a capability refers to the way and extent to which a political system performs certain functions. When this concept is applied to Latin America it becomes obvious that the political systems of the region are less capable in some ways than are those of the more developed countries. That is, they perform at the levels expected of them in an immobile political context, but they do not perform effectively in certain areas necessary to foster socio-economic development.

One of the areas to which the idea of system capabilities refers is the regulation of society and its members, and system capability in this area varies greatly with the cooperation needed to enforce rules and regulations.

Of course, bureaucrats are formally charged with implementing system rules and regulations, but without the cooperation of important groups outside government institutions, implementation and enforcement become highly irregular, if not totally absent. For good or bad, this tends to be the norm rather than the exception in Latin America. Whatever the legal content of a regulation, its real content tends to be defined in the political struggle over its implementation. As previously noted, bureaucrats are under constant and strong pressures of various sorts to make individual exceptions to general rules. Those with money or social status, or those who have political pull for whatever reason, are at a definite advantage in buying favorable bureaucratic treatment. For example, agrarian reform legislation may be passed by a legislature but its intent and thrust can be, and apparently usually is, diluted and even thwarted by the influence landowners bring to bear on the bureaucracy. Similarly, constitutions and laws purporting to regulate politics are grossly misleading if taken at face value. Somehow, government institutions are unable to implement regulations without making very selective and often fatal exceptions to the spirit and letter of the law.

To avoid misunderstanding, however, the impression should not be gained that Latin American governments do not in any way perform the regulatory function. Due to the nature of politics which permeates government agencies charged with implementation of regulations, government regulates not according to formal and legal dictates but according to dictates of outside forces from which government cannot be insulated. On this basis, of course, those who have the most influence with the implementing agencies are those who are benefitting most from the current system and who desire regulation and reduction of change. Regulation thus becomes the province of those who favor order over change, serving the satisfied and controlling the dissatisfied.

Concerning the extractive capability of a political system, performance in this area very greatly affects performance of the regulative function, since government institutions cannot regulate if those with resources withhold them from use in government operations. The main way of extracting resources is through taxation, but Latin American governments are generally not very effective in this area. Business taxes are evaded, as are land taxes and the general income tax. Due to the generally very low income level of the majority of the people, government does not have a large tax base to begin with. Again, those who would most suffer from a government capable of taxing effectively are also those who oppose both tax reform and programs that might increase the independence of adequately-funded, reform-oriented government institutions. Thus, the most well-meaning administration becomes caught in a circular trap: it is not able to extract sufficient funds to support programs aimed at overcoming the low level of economic development, and at the same time it cannot increase its resources unless the level of economic development is raised.

Regulating only those without power to resist, and unable or unwilling to extract sufficient resources to promote programs of basic development, the political systems of Latin America also tend to rate very low in their distributive capability, a situation that perpetuates the circumstances of economic underdevelopment and political immobility. Under the best of conditions, financial, human, and other resources of government are severely limited and are unlikely to trickle down to those in the population who most need them. By ignoring land tenure patterns, or by failing to implement agrarian reform programs, the government sanctions great rural inequality and essentially ignores or rejects its distributive function in this area. By allocating relatively large sums for military expenditures, government has just that much less to spend on other programs. By distributing many of its funds to its own bureaucrats, government creates a larger and more cumbersome bureaucracy which constantly employs more but which does not do substantially more. Of course, all governments spend in such areas as education, welfare, and so forth, and the extent to which they do this favors some redistribution of wealth. However, those countries that show the greatest tendency to emphasize such programs are those that have already undergone social revolutions or that, for a number of reasons, have progressed relatively far along the developmental continuum. Even Mexico, for example, which has not only undergone a revolution but has also progressed economically, has major problems in this area. Although one-fifth to one-fourth of the federal budget goes to education, university, and even secondary education is still considered by many Mexicans to be the privilege of the few. For example, only 17 percent of all children between the ages of 13 and 18 and attending school.[2] Although education at the primary level is compulsory in most Latin American countries, the laws are generally not emphasized, schools are unable to serve most of the children, and whether because of desire or need, most children who attend soon leave to earn a marginal living.

Latin American governments in general are unable to make basic changes in distribution of the limited resources and services that they possess. Rather, resources are dispersed to various important groups in order to gain their support for a particular regime, and rarely do really significant expenditures go to politically marginal groups. In other words, Latin American governments do perform the distributive function, but they operate in a politically immobile environment, and under these conditions even the most well-meaning regime tends to be ineffective in performing this function to achieve goals of socioeconomic change.

Those who control the political systems of Latin America tend to be quite good at manipulating symbols to gain support and to assuage if not

[2] Ernest A. Duff and John F. McCamant, "Measuring Social and Political Requirements for System Stability in Latin America," in *American Political Science Review*, Vol. 62, No. 4, December 1968.

satisfy the demands of various groups. Although many Latin Americans do not identify their nation with those who run its government, government leaders generally seek to make this identity more credible and widespread. For example, the ability to link nationalist sentiments to a particular regime is regarded as a distinct political asset. However, the effort by most government leaders to gain support by symbol manipulation is really an indication of general government ineffectiveness in other functions. Furthermore, if symbols must constantly be used to secure emotional response for an administration and its policies, there is good reason to believe that the administration cannot rely on a consensus on goals. By itself, the use of symbols must eventually fail to mobilize support sufficiently broad to break through the immobility of politics. As with fragmented societies everywhere, the symbols of broad unity are weaker than are those that represent narrow allegiances.

Finally, concerning the responsvie capability of political systems, it should be obvious at this point that political institutions in Latin America are largely unresponsive to the lower sectors, even when, as occasionally occurs, segments of these become aroused. With the limited participation of the lower sectors, government is most concerned with adjusting the conflicts between fragmented elites, and it is in the common interest of the elites to restrict the responsiveness of government to the masses. When a government does begin to consider the demands of the latter, the chances are that its responsiveness to the elites will diminish. However, the politics of immobility plays into the hands of those groups that would rather have a generally unresponsive government. Such a government may not help one's own group, but neither will it greatly enhance the position of opponents. For those groups generally content with their current situation, an unresponsive and ineffective government has its distinct advantages.

On balance, then, a substantial burden of promoting rapid socioeconomic development has been placed on Latin American government, but for a number of reasons government is inadequate to the challenge. Its particular if not unique problem is that it cannot isolate itself from factors that immobilize innovation and effectiveness. Contradictory demands from the fragmented society outrun government capabilities to cope. This is related to, but more than, problems of inadequate resources—it is also a problem of basic disagreement over broad goals that government should pursue. Lacking legitimacy for its specific actions, government becomes trapped between the irreconcilable elites, and it jeopardizes its own survival if it attempts to break the deadlock. To elicit, much less to meet, the demands of the masses would be to risk, if not guarantee, political suicide. Thus government is caught in a trap, facing constant demands for change but unable to take decisive action either to reject the demands or to meet them.

All this does not mean that a potential for change does not exist in Latin America. Without a doubt comprehensive, although poorly understood, changes in the demographic, economic, social, and political life of the region have occurred and will continue to occur.[3] However, the important question involves the direction of change—whether development, immobility, or decay—and the form of change—whether personnel, policy, or revolution. It is much easier to judge the past from hindsight than it is to evaluate what current problems mean for future change in Latin America. The danger of comparing the present with the past, whatever development may have occurred, is to encourage a smug satisfaction with past achievements and to play down the massive problems facing the region today.

Perhaps the only important exception to the politics of immobility in Latin America is the atypical case of Chile. Within the rules of the game and based upon elected institutions, the socialist-inspired government of Salvador de Allende has pushed for policies of nationalism and social justice. Allende's government was hardly the choice of the majority of Chilian voters, though. With only 36 percent of the vote for Allende's coalition, the 1970 election was thrown into the Chilean legislature where the opposition supported his rise to the presidency on the condition that he not basically change the democratic rules of the game. As the first socialist ever to be elected president of a Latin American country, Allende promised that he would change the system through the system. His government nationalized foreign copper interests and other large multinational corporations such as ITT and refused to compensate the owners. With these moves against foreign interests, Chile's economic situation worsened. The government also looked inward to push for a more equal distribution of wealth. Legal and illegal seizure of land was promoted or tolerated, breaking up most of the large landowners' estates and threatening the smaller ones by not taking steps against land-hungry squatters. Sometimes the land was managed by government-run cooperatives; sometimes not. The uncertainty that resulted from all these changes cut into the growth and production of the economy.

The desires, demands, and system response of the Allende government have, up to this point, been quite impressive. But the cost has been heavy. Allende may not be able to do much more through the system. If Chile's relatively large middle class comes to feel imperiled, they could withdraw their crucial support. Allende has also unleashed many demands for change which, if not satisfied, could lead to trouble for the entire system. Castro in Cuba could push for rapid social change despite early economic problems but Allende, trying to work within the system, may not be so fortunate. If Allende goes outside the system, the Chilean military, which

3 Michael Micklin, "Demographic, Economic, and Social Change in Latin America: An Examination of Causes and Consequences," in *The Journal of Developing Areas,* Vol. 4, January 1970.

has avoided politics more than other military establishments, might intervene. So the immediate future in Chile is quite uncertain. The early victories for rapid change were the easiest because they were achieved through the system and with the qualified support of the opposition parties. If the government leaders stay within the system but push for even more drastic change, this unique experiment in Latin American politics may become, in the long run, just another failure of government to promote socioeconomic change. It is simply too early to be sure.

Put differently, the optimistic perspective that major changes of all kinds will lead Latin America to a comfortable future is not of much help in studying the perplexing failures of government to promote comprehensive socioeconomic change. But also to be avoided is the perspective which suggests that there is really no hope for rapid development, and instead we must expect economic stagnation and political immobility, or at best we must expect changes so gradual that they inevitably fall behind the rising needs of Latin Americans.[4] Admittedly, if one looks at the groups discussed here the general impression is that, taken together or individually, they are too divided, apathetic, and/or satisfied to be the bases for fundamental change. The peasants are apathetic; urban workers are largely apolitical, and the activists are divided; students are radical and active, but isolated; businessmen and landowners are conservative and generally protective of their privileged status; the clergy are mainly apolitical, the hierarchy is mainly conservative, and activists are lacking in common goals; bureaucrats tend to be a brake on, rather than an accelerator of, socioeconomic change; and the military, despite occasional ambivalence, is more concerned with protecting middle-sector gains than it is with promoting participation of the lower sectors. But the problem with looking at groups in this way is that a conservative perspective is created. The politics of immobility fosters ineffective government, unable to promote change, but the growing gap between rising demands and declining effectiveness of the system may foster a desperate and explosive potential for change. In other words, although one must maintain a healthy skepticism toward government as a promoter of rapid socioeconomic change in Latin America, there is the chance that the strains already present in the political systems will eventually stimulate some kind of change. If new problems and crises arise with which government cannot cope, then gradual or perhaps even rapid rearrangement of the system may occur. The revolutionary potential in Latin America may be largely dormant, but it is nevertheless there if for no other reason than that the process of economic and political development remains relatively incomplete. Traditional institutions and ways have at least been under-

---

[4] Albert O. Hirschman, *Bias for Hope* (New Haven, Conn.: Yale University Press, 1971), Chapters 14 and 15.

mined, and the current fragmented situation carries with it the possibility of change, whether radical or gradual, violent or peaceful, or toward development or decay.

To return very briefly to the question of why there is so much talk of change in Latin America but so little change presently occurring, the answer is quite simply that those socioeconomic groupings presently in control of the region's political systems do not want basic change and are successful in preventing it. It is an elitist culture and an elitist politics, and while elite groups may mutually despise one another, they have in common the desire not to risk their present substantial benefits for the sake of future nebulous gains. In short, demands on a political system for basic change are essentially directed toward groups that fear change and that will resist it for as long as possible, and political immobility furthers this end.

For bibliography, see those sources cited in earlier chapters, especially Chapter 1.

INDEX